TOWARD VATICAN III

TOWARD VATICAN III

The Work That Needs to Be Done

Edited by

David Tracy

with

Hans Küng and Johann B. Metz

CONCILIUM

The Seabury Press • New York

1978
The Seabury Press
815 Second Avenue
New York, N.Y. 10017

Printed in the United States of America

Library of Congress Cataloging in Publication Data

Main entry under title:
Toward Vatican III.
"A Crossroad book."
Papers originally presented at a colloquium at the University of Notre Dame, May 29-June 1, 1977.
1. Catholic Church in the United States—Congresses. 2. Church renewal—Catholic Church—Congresses. I. Tracy, David. II. Küng, Hans, 1928- III. Metz, Johannes Baptist, 1928- IV. Title: Vatican III.
BX1404.T68   262'.5'2   77-28606
ISBN 0-8164-0379-1
ISBN 0-8164-2173-0 pbk.

CONTENTS

Part 3
Church and Ecumenism

Part 4
Church and the Individual

Part 5
Church and Society

Preface: Historical Background of the Papers

ON May 29 to June 1, 1977, a colloquium was held at the University of Notre Dame entitled "Toward Vatican III: The Work That Needs to Be Done." Some seventy-one theologians and social scientists met to discuss central theological issues for the church. As the president of Notre Dame, Father Theodore Hesburgh, C.S.C., reminded the participants in his letter of invitation, the title "Vatican III" was not literal but symbolic. Indeed, the colloquium was not an official church meeting, but was genuinely symbolic of the concern and commitment of Catholic theologians and social scientists to the church in this critical moment of its history.

The occasion was made possible by the fact that the distinguished international theological journal *Concilium* decided to hold its editorial board meeting in the United States in order to celebrate the republication by The Seabury Press of the English-speaking issue of the journal, after a lapse of two years. Since *Concilium* was founded twelve years ago to continue the work of Vatican II, the symbolic and hopeful conciliar theme of the colloquium seemed entirely appropriate to the many participants.

At the instigation of Andrew M. Greeley, a member of the board of *Concilium,* and Msgr. John J. Egan of Notre Dame's Center for Pastoral and Social Ministry, the plans for the meeting were initiated in the summer of 1976. Hans Küng and Johann B. Metz, representing the board of *Concilium,* and David Tracy, as president of the Catholic Theological Society of America, joined Greeley and Egan in the extensive planning for the session.

After several discussions, the agenda described below emerged as the best focus for the meeting. Papers were solicited from three groups: theologians from the editorial board of *Concilium,* theologians from the Catholic Theological Society of America, and a representative group of

American social scientists. Hans Küng assumed the major responsibility for the papers of the *Concilium* group, David Tracy for the Catholic Theological Society, and Andrew Greeley for the social scientists. The meeting itself was officially sponsored by the University of Notre Dame under the leadership of Msgr. Egan of the Center for Pastoral and Social Ministry.

The agenda agreed upon by the three groups followed the format of the issues of *Concilium*. This format allows for a threefold general division: "Christian Faith," "Christian Ethics," and "Churchly Praxis." Under the first general rubric, "Christian Faith" (encompassing dogma, ecumenism and fundamental theology), the topics are "Church and Doctrine" (papers by Schillebeeckx, Peter and Murphy) and "Church and the Ecumenism" (papers by Küng, Dulles and Alberigo). Under the second rubric, "Christian Ethics" (encompassing moral theology, spirituality and sociology of religion), the topics are "Church and the Individual" (papers by Pohier, Geffré, Böckle, Burrell, Barry, Kotre, McCready and Sullivan) and "Church and Society" (papers by Metz, Curran, Coons, Manno and Cafferty). Under the third general rubric, "Churchly Praxis" (encompassing pastoral theology, liturgy and canon law), the topics are "Church and Reform" (papers by Müller, Bassett, Duquoc, Laurentin, Huizing, Shea and Durkin) and "Church and Worship" (papers by Maldonado and Bourke). The authors, all distinguished scholars in their own fields, were given the assignment *not* of producing new scholarly research but of providing new and substantive reflections from the viewpoint of her/his own discipline on a particular topic under the general rubric of "Towards Vatican III: The Work That Needs to Be Done."

Unfortunately, it proved unfeasible to reproduce here the reports of the general sessions and especially of the smaller discussion groups where the most intense and fruitful exchange occurred. Indeed, as in any meeting, the exchanges, conflicts, similarities and overall collaboration occurred best in the small groups. There the smaller number of participants and a longer amount of time united to allow extended and collaborative discussion of the topics addressed by the papers. Perhaps it is not too sanguine to hope that the present publication of the papers will free other small discussion groups to raise the issues anew in their own settings and from their own perspectives.

In the meantime, the editors hope that the publication of the papers will encourage a church-wide effort at fruitful collaboration on the issues which beset, intrigue, and engage us all.

Three final practical notes:

1. The introductory section includes (a) the text of the letter of Father Hesburgh to all participants, and the texts of the opening re-

marks of Anton van den Boogaard (President, *Concilium* Foundation),
J. B. Metz (Acting President, *Concilium* General Assembly), and David
Tracy (President, Catholic Theological Society of America); (b) the full
list of participants from the various groups.

2. Each author was invited to make any revisions of the original
paper which he/she desired. Most authors did some revisions but none
so substantial as to change the original text. Hence the reader does
have texts which present the substantive positions presented to the
colloquium for discussion. In four cases (Professors Bassett, Böckle,
Laurentin and Murphy) the position papers are considerably expanded
beyond the earlier summaries delivered at the colloquium itself. In
most cases, the position papers are revised either for style or to expand
and conflate the text in keeping with the editorial requests for conforming to the length desired.

3. Unlike the colloquium itself, the present volume divides the contributions into two basic categories: theological and social scientific.
This should allow the reader, who lacks the colloquium advantage of
immediate small group discussions, the possibility of relating for
herself/himself the theological and the social scientific (the latter as
explicitly or implicitly theological) papers of these two major groups at
the colloquium.

I hope that the publication of these diverse and valuable papers will
allow the reader the same kind of intellectual stimulation and theological reflection on major issues which the actual experience of the colloquium promised—and produced. My assigned task, however, is to
provide the necessary historical information rather than offer my own
(in fact, fully positive) interpretation and evaluation of the papers.
For that evaluation, each reader—and, one hopes, the church community as a whole—will have to decide. That decision should be all
the easier, I believe, given the fact that each paper clearly addresses
a vital issue with clarity and scholarly integrity.

Mr. Eric Holzwarth and Mr. Robert Jones played invaluable roles as
editorial assistants for this volume. To them and to all the contributors, especially Hans Küng and Johann B. Metz for their generous
editorial aid, my deep appreciation.

David Tracy

PART 1

Introduction

Letter of Invitation

OFFICE OF THE PRESIDENT
UNIVERSITY OF NOTRE DAME
NOTRE DAME, INDIANA 46556

April 21, 1977

DEAR ———:

On May 28–29, the editorial board of the international Catholic journal *Concilium* will hold its first meeting in the United States on the campus of the University of Notre Dame.

After the meeting, there will be a colloquium of international scholars sponsored jointly by Notre Dame, *Concilium* and the Catholic Theological Society of America, chaired jointly by Father David Tracy, the president of the CTSA, and Msgr. John J. Egan, Director of our Center for Pastoral and Social Ministry at Notre Dame. The colloquium will begin May 30 and conclude on June 1.

In this colloquium, theologians and social scientists will discuss the subject: "Vatican III: The Work That Needs to Be Done." The meeting is not designed to be a call for "Vatican III"—a title which is intended to be symbolic—but rather to block out the scholarly research in theology and in the social sciences which needs to be done before the Church can come to its next critical turning point. Rather than discuss the present and immediately past questions which face the Church today, the participants will be asked to articulate the new questions which should occupy our scholarly concerns in the years ahead.

Obviously such a meeting has no official status, can make no claim to be "representative" of anyone other than the invited participants in attendance, and will be able to discuss at most a small part of the "new agenda" for world Catholicism.

I wish to extend a cordial invitation to you to participate in the meeting.

The Center for Pastoral and Social Ministry will assume the expense of your room and board during the meeting at Notre Dame. Msgr. John J. Egan will be in touch with you on the details of the meeting.

Ever devotedly in Our Lord,

[signature] , ᴄꜱᴄ

(Rev.) Theodore M. Hesburgh, C.S.C.
President

Introductory Address by
Anton van den Boogaard

President, *Concilium* Foundation

Mr. President, ladies and gentlemen:

It is my pleasure to give you my special thanks on behalf of all the theologians of *Concilium* for inviting us to hold a colloquium together with the members of the Catholic Theological Society of America.

The president of this university, Father Theodore Hesburgh, wrote the following striking passage in his invitation: "In this colloquium, theologians and social scientists will discuss the subject: 'Vatican III: The Work That Needs to Be Done.' The meeting is not designed to be a call for 'Vatican III'—a title which is intended to be symbolic—but rather to block out the scholarly research in theology and in the social sciences which needs to be done before the Church can come to its next critical turning point. Rather than discuss the present and immediately past questions which face the Church today, the participants will be asked to articulate the new questions which should occupy our scholarly concerns in the years ahead."

That this meeting became possible, we owe likewise to the support and the hospitality of your famous University of Notre Dame.

May I include in my thanks to the president of Notre Dame, Father Theodore Hesburgh, to our chairman, Monsignor John Egan, and to all those charged with the no doubt considerable task of organizing this colloquium.

Our thanks also to Father James Burtchaell, the provost of this university, whose warm and spontaneous words emphasize once more the hospitality of the University of Notre Dame.

We are all particularly happy that the annual meeting of the editorial board of our international Catholic review *Concilium* should this time take place in the United States and that it should coincide with the reappearance of the English edition.

When founding the review we outlined the following purpose: the renovation of theology and the Church in the spirit of the Second Vatican Council. In other words: the review was to serve the dynamism of the Council. We had in mind a genuinely Catholic review, that is to say, a review which would be directed to the whole of the Catholic world and encompass theology as a whole. It was to be an organ which, in a scientifically justifiable way, would address itself to a fairly large audience all over the world, particularly to all those charged with pastoral work. *Concilium* was to act as a bridge between theory and practice, between theology and the Church. We are fully aware of the fact that even after years of hard work, we are still far removed from this purpose. For that reason, we intend to continue striving after this aim in the future.

At the present moment, our review appears in seven languages. We try to promote its international character by inviting authors from various parts of the world and from different cultures. In the past years we have mainly invited theologians of the younger generation, and have taken special care to promote contributions from the Third World. The number of our authors and regular contributors amounts to over 600 scholars and specialists in various fields of research and from all parts of the world.

What then—in all modesty—may we expect from our colloquium, and what were our motives for organizing it? I think I may safely say that we have acted from similar considerations as those which, in 1970, made us organize an international congress at Brussels: out of concern for the Church. The central focus of this congress was on the problem of the "Future of the Church." Seven years later, we may wonder how much of what theologians then imagined about the future of the Church has come true.

Aren't we faced with a situation where the enthusiasm of many for renewing the Church has been quenched, where many people are sitting down in sad resignation, where the overriding feeling is one of indifference and doubt, where people have started wondering if it is still worthwhile to strive for renewal in the Church, if it is not far better for a person inspired by Christian or, at least, religious motives, to commit himself totally to building a better world? Plurality of thought, even among Catholic theologians, has become so great that I, being a layman, sometimes wonder just how much theology, with the help of the humanities, still has to offer to us in terms of bringing a message of encouragement and orientation. At our Brussels congress, in 1970, I was still able to say that immediately after the Second Vatican Council we got the impression "that the old, venerable authority of the Holy See had been replaced by the authorities of many chairs of theology." At this moment, I have the impression that people have become indifferent even to this type of scientific theological authority, and seek their inspiration elsewhere. For some people, the source of inspiration is the charismatic movement, which, beyond the goals of scientific research, seeks immediate contact with the supernatural sources of integrated human life; for others the new motive for commitment lies in a political option for a better, more just world. It is particularly among young people that I observe this option for either one or the other of these directions, for it is the young who appear to react against the present middle generation, who fought for their own freedom by severely criticizing their Church and secular leaders.

Because of this struggle, the middle generation has learnt to live with uncertainties; they have even made a life full of risks, devoid of all certainty, into their own ideal. The coming generation—young people between 18 and 25—appear to long for certainty and a sense of security again.

Yet the current situation may be a sign of warning to us members of the older generation; it may prompt the question if, after the Second Vatican Council, we brought out, in full relief and in a way that sounded credible, all aspects of a genuinely religious and Christian faith. For, in our concern to re-establish forgotten truths, we may well ourselves have forgotten to mention other truths and values. The consequence of this might well be that the young have difficulties finding the right track, being faced, on the one hand, with the unnatural supranaturalism of the past and, on the other hand, with a secular strife for changing the world which tends towards a closed type of humanism. Yet it is these young people who, in a couple of years' time, will direct the future of the world and of the Church.

It seems that the feeling of unhappiness which one can often notice in the Church, when the participation of the youth in the life of Church is mentioned, is really to be found on both sides. In the same way as the Church feels pessimistic about the young, the young feel pessimistic about the Church. The average young person has become indifferent to the institutional Church of this moment. The Second Vatican Council promised to give new impulses to a renewed participation of the young in the life of the Church, but at this moment little is left of these new impulses. In the past ten years there was an all too obvious "exodus" of youth from the Church, in numbers which exceed the available figures by far (although even these figures keep going up). The current of this exodus is widely divergent, ranging from non-ecclesiastical neo-spiritualistic forms of religion (such as, for example, the Jesus people), through surrogates for religious satisfaction (such as, for example, narcotics) and consumption without any form of commitment, to secular political engagement (which in many cases is—at least indirectly—motivated by Christian patterns of thought about justice, etc.). One can hardly talk of "uneasy feelings with respect to the institution of the Church" with this large group of young people who left. Church problems have simply ceased to matter to them; there is no longer any point in discussing them.

The criticism of the Church of many young people or their indifference to the Church is often phrased in terms of a judgment passed on Church officials. They know them from statements in the press, or from radio or television. The judgments are often superficial and people hardly feel the need to differentiate. The criticism may be very hard!

Next, people object to a number of situations in the Church which they fail to understand. One might even say that a number of hot issues in the Church and in theology have totally ceased to matter to many young people. Many of them are no longer emotionally involved in Church matters in any way.

The young will not be willing to participate until a structural change has taken place, until the present closed structure has been transformed into an open structure. R. Sauter in his critical review of the discussion about youth held at a synod of the German Catholic Church, addressed the conference of bishops in the following way: "You do not know the praxis. Whoever talks about faith to young people, will soon become aware of the tremendous alienation of the Church among young people. No solemn theological statements are going to change anything about that." For the truth is that the Church is, in general, unable to 'give satisfactory answers to the questions of modern man. It is obvious that young people are quicker to become aware of this and experience it in a more pungent way than older people. The young have only one wish, namely, for the Church to become more credible.

Finally, I have to mention that the need for institutionalizing dialogue between the teaching office of the Church and theologians, which I already mentioned at our congress in Brussels, is equally hard felt at this moment. Unfortunately, this dialogue is still nonexistent. In my opinion, the absence of this dialogue is another factor which makes for a polarization within the Church and slows down the development of ecclesial life.

It is my hope that this colloquium will treat many problems which have the interest of our young people, and perhaps even provide an answer to some. This is the reason why I talked about them at such length. They are the ones who will make the Church of tomorrow!

Try to inspire our youth, and renew our confidence in God through prayer.

Finally, on account of the difficulties of the present polarization within the Christian community of faith, I hope that you theologians, in spite of your critical attitude towards the Church, will feel called upon to remain within the Church with all your hearts. For it was the Church who mediated in delivering to us the message of the Gospel, which all of us will have to pass on to future generations.

Introductory Address by
Johann B. Metz

Acting President, *Concilium* General Assembly

It is a good thing if you are the last in a long row of speakers, because you get the chance to demonstrate that "imminent expectation" of the end is not an illusion but is now going to take place: the end of all the speeches and the beginning of the actual dialogue.

The context of world-wide dialogue within the church and theology—to which *Concilium* is committed—has changed. It is no longer a European monologue, camouflaged as a dialogue; furthermore it is not even a dialogue between Europeans and the North Americans (that means a dialogue along the North axis of the church); but it is and should increasingly become a so-called "trialogue," that is, a dialogue between European, North American and Third World Christians.

In my opinion it is the first time that the main conflict in the world is settled within the heart of the one Catholic Church. I point to the so-called North-South conflict, which has replaced the "classic" East-West split. This great North-South conflict reflects itself within the church in the relationship between the churches of the North and the churches of the Southern parts of the world which traditionally are Catholic. *This is the hour of trial for the living unity of the one Catholic Church.*

In this I see a parallel to the fate of the American dream of equality, freedom and happiness for all—a dream which was (as you know) originally a European dream of America and led to an errand into the wilderness. This dream can only be realized if it is not limited to Europeans and North Americans, but is understood as a *human* dream, extending its promises to *all* people. The errand into the wilderness of a few should become an errand into the future for all. *This is the hour of trial for America:* if it is ready to extend the promises of its dream to all and by this—and not by the ideology of national security—is going to realize the dream for itself.

In our meeting we shall talk about the future of the church. The work to be done is guided by a vision. Defining this vision I may remind you of a statement of your President in his inaugural address; Jimmy Carter said: "Today I do not offer you a new dream, but rather I point to a strong belief in the old dream." Likewise we shall here not talk about a new vision of the church, but shall recall a dangerous and provocative memory of the old messianic vision, which shows the church as a community of love and justice, as a promise to all and for all who live in darkness and misery.

Let's do our best!

Introductory Address by David Tracy

President, Catholic Theological Society of America

On behalf of the Catholic Theological Society, I express our thanks to the University of Notre Dame, to Father Hesburgh, Father Burtchaell, Msgr. Egan, to the Board of *Concilium* and to the social scientists.

Our task at this brief meeting is a modest but a serious one: as Father Hesburgh's letter of invitation to us all makes clear, we do not claim to represent the church. We will try to reflect in the working sessions upon the future needs of serious scholarship for the church. As the several position papers already make clear, where criticism is needed, it is urgent that it be spoken clearly and forcefully; where tradition is genuine *traditio,* not mere *tradita,* and is in danger of disintegration, it is urgent that it be respoken, reaffirmed, and represented for those who will come after.

Each of us—within this context of real commitment to this time and space—shares this world of multiple meaning within which we try to communicate, and finds the need to see if we can work not merely singly but communally in a time comprising the reality of real crisis and the possibility of retrieval and development.

Each of us recognizes, I believe, that no one of us or no sum total of all us possesses the overwhelming word of truth that must be spoken. Yet, we also recognize and affirm by our presence here and by our commitment to serious and sustained conversation together that we need to hear one another and work, as professionals—theologians, philosophers and social scientists—to advance a collaborative effort which otherwise might go undone.

To affirm the genuine pluralism we find in our midst is not to affirm that pluralism which Herbert Marcuse accurately labels "repressive tolerance," wherein anyone can say anything because no one, finally, is taken seriously. To affirm the genuine pluralism of our scholarly disciplines, of our positions, of our different analyses of the situation is to affirm a fundamental enrichment of possible ways of envisioning our common past, present and the future we attempt to aid. For to affirm serious pluralism is to affirm a strenuous pluralism of scholarly professionals where each should be heard because each thinker, as theologian or social scientist, precisely as dedicated to his or her professional task, will advance reasons, evidence, warrants, backings, arguments for the analysis offered for our common study.

Theologians recognize that with their multiple responsibilities to the diverse and overlapping realities of church, academy, and our different social, political and cultural worlds we must learn how, in Bernard Lonergan's eloquent phrase, really to collaborate with one another clearly, consistently, professionally, systematically.

Our cultural contexts are diverse; our theological, philosophical and scientific methods are distinct; our analyses of the situation and of alternative solutions are multiple. And yet, by our commitment here to serious and sustained conversation initiated by the position papers and continued and enhanced by the three days of working sessions together, we do really affirm both communally and individually that amidst all this pluralism there is the desire and, as we all hope, the reality of genuine collaboration on the crucial scholarly issues for the future.

Theologians also recognize far more than in the past that their traditional partnership with their philosophical colleagues must be expanded to include a genuine collaboration with professional social scientists whose analyses of the actual social realities always informing and transforming, occasionally even determining both theological problems and our real possibilities for advancement must be carefully attended to and recognized.

This three-day meeting of scholars, therefore, should begin on a note of the genuinely strenuous mood: a communal determination to learn how to hear one another, how to collaborate on our common questions, proposed answers and commitments, how to aid disciplined reflection upon the reality of the issues for the church's life in the approaching future.

Such sustained conversation for so brief, if intense, a period cannot hope, much less pretend, to resolve all the complex and serious issues before us. Yet this working session can hope to initiate a collaboration of scholars who will perform their partial yet crucial tasks for the church as a whole: critical, disciplined, collaborative reflection upon the real problems and the genuine possibilities for ongoing reform and retrieval of Christianity in the modern global village. As the earliest model for conversation in our Western intellectual tradition, the Platonic dialogues remind us that only the deliberate attempt to allow the subject matter itself to determine the outcome of our inquiry can assure that inquiry's real contribution to the church. Neither theologians, nor philosophers, nor social scientists claim to have all the right questions, much less all the right answers. Yet precisely such professional dedication and realism is the partial but real contribution we can and must try to make communally to the church and the society.

The hope is, therefore, that these three groups—*Concilium,* the Catholic Theological Society of America, and our social scientific colleagues (each of which groups, let us recall, contains its own important, even crucial diversities)—can in these three days commit themselves to this process of sustained, strenuous, working collaboration. To recognize clearly that we are not in fact representative of either the whole church or even of our distinct disciplines as a whole is to recognize a truism worth recalling. For that recognition in its turn may free us to recognize more clearly that serious collaboration on common issues for the future must begin somewhere. The risk and the hope which each one's presence here evidences will demonstrate that genuine communal inquiry did really begin here.

LIST OF PARTICIPANTS

Concilium

Giuseppe Alberigo
University of Bologna

William W. Bassett
University of San Francisco

Gregory Baum
University of St. Michael's
    College

Franz Böckle
University of Bonn

Anton van den Boogaard
President of the *Concilium*
    Foundation

Paul Brand
Concilium Foundation

Christian Duquoc, O.P.
University of Lyons

August Wilhelm van Eiff
University of Bonn

Casiano Floristan
University of Salamanca

Claude Geffré, O.P.
Institut Catholique, Paris

Andrew M. Greeley
National Opinion Research
    Center
University of Chicago

Norbert Greinacher
University of Tübingen

Gustavo Gutiérrez-Merino
Catholic University of Lima

Peter Huizing, S.J.
University of Nijmegen

Bas van Iersel, S.M.M.
University of Nijmegen

Hans Küng
University of Tübingen

René Laurentin
Catholic University of Angers

Luis Maldonado
University of Salamanca

Johann B. Metz
University of Münster

14

Alois Müller
University of Freiburg

Roland Murphy, O. Carm.
Duke University

Jacques Pohier, O.P.
Saulchoir Faculties

Luigi Sartori
Seminario Vescovile (Padua)

Edward Schillebeeckx, O.P.
University of Nijmegen

David Tracy
University of Chicago

Anton Weiler
University of Nijmegen

Publishers

Dr. and Mrs. J. Laubach
Matthias Grünewald Verlag

Rosino Gibellini
Editrice Queriniana

Manuel San Miguel
Ediciones Cristiandad

Monique Cadic
Editions Beauchesne

Alfonso de la Fuente
Ediciones Cristiandad

Werner Mark Linz
The Seabury Press

Justus George Lawler
The Seabury Press

Frank Oveis
The Seabury Press

Catholic Theological Society of America

Myles M. Bourke
Fordham University

Edward Braxton
Harvard Divinity School

David Burrell, C.S.C.
University of Notre Dame

Anne Carr, B.V.M.
University of Chicago

John Coleman, S.J.
Jesuit School of Theology at
  Berkeley

John J. Connelly
St. John's Seminary, Brighton,
  Mass.

Agnes Cunningham, S.S.C.M.
St. Mary of the Lake Seminary

Charles Curran
Catholic University of America

Avery Dulles, S.J.
Catholic University of America

Mary Durkin
Chicago, Ill.

Michael Fahey, S.J.
Concordia University, Montreal

Francis Fiorenza
University of Notre Dame

John Hotchkin
U.S. Catholic Conference

Edward Konnerman, S.J.
St. Mary of the Lake Seminary

Matthew Lamb
Marquette University

Bernard Lonergan, S.J.
Boston College

Richard McCormick, S.J.
Georgetown University

Suzanne Noffke, O.P.
Dominican College, Racine, Wis.

Carl Peter
Catholic University of America

Luke Salm
Manhattan College

Michael Scanlon, O.S.A.
Augustinian College, Washington, D.C.

John Shea
St. Mary of the Lake Seminary

Social Scientists

James Barry
State University of New York at
    Buffalo

Pastora Cafferty
University of Chicago

John Coons
University of California at
    Berkeley

John Kotre
University of Michigan

William McCready
National Opinion Research
    Center
University of Chicago

Bruce Manno
University of Dayton

Teresa Sullivan
University of Chicago

Invited Guests

Virgil Elizondo
Mexican American Cultural
    Center in San Antonio

Langdon Gilkey
University of Chicago

George Higgins
U.S. Catholic Conference

Eugene Kennedy
Loyola University

William McManus
Bishop of Fort Wayne-South
   Bend

Richard Malone
National Conference of Catholic
   Bishops

Host

John J. Egan
Center for Pastoral and Social
   Ministry
University of Notre Dame

PART 2

Church and Doctrine

Roland E. Murphy

Vatican III—Problems and Opportunities of the Future: The Bible

I. PRELIMINARY CONSIDERATIONS

In view of the central role of the Bible in the life of the Church, there is need to update and to expand the official Church teaching relative to the Bible. This means going beyond the 1943 encyclical of *Divino afflante Spiritu,* and also the excellent 1964 statement of the Pontifical Biblical Commission on the historical truth of the Gospels, as well as the pertinent statements in the 1965 Constitution on Revelation *(Dei Verbum)* of Vatican II.

Many of the statements in the *Dei Verbum* constitution were, in the nature of the case, compromises, attempts to reflect a consensus. Perhaps the most outstanding example is the ambiguous relationship of Scripture and Tradition. At the time, this was a happy ambiguity, insofar as it amounted to a rejection of the theory of the "sources" of revelation. It may even be that more time is still needed before anything definitive can be said. But this issue, along with others, could easily be one of the points on a future agenda.

The Church's official understanding of the Bible in the modern period cannot be allowed to remain at this level of compromise and of inconsistent use of the Bible in its official documents. Here one is reminded of Oscar Cullmann's criticism of the faulty use of Scripture in the conciliar documents of Vatican II *(Dialogue on the Way* [Minneapolis: Augsburg, 1965], pp. 138–40), or of similar statements by George

Lindbeck (*Vatican II: An Interfaith Appraisal* [University of Notre Dame Press, 1966], p. 223).

II. PROPOSALS

1. An effective use of the Pontifical Biblical Commission in the theological life of the Church. This commission could be one of the most effective means in a rich theological life of the Church were it broadened and given some leadership. The need for this is all the more imperative in view of the recent question raised by Paul Minear, an outstanding biblical scholar and ecumenist ("Ecumenical Theology— Profession or Vocation?" *Theology Today* 33[1976/77]: 66–73). He questioned whether in the future academe rather than the Church might not claim the interests and energies of biblical scholars and theologians. The wide range of opinion in response to his article ("Symposium on Biblical Criticism," *Theology Today* 33[1976/77]: 354–66) indicates that his question is well taken. The pressures of university life become ever more demanding, and it is all too easy for Catholic scholars to yield to these concerns if the Church shows herself uninterested in, or even afraid of, the thrust of biblical scholarship, if the Church fails to make effective use of its own scholars. It is incumbent to tap the vast resources belonging to the Church in the persons of the dedicated Scripture scholars among her children.

a. It would be appropriate for the Pontifical Biblical Commission to work through several bodies already existing in the Church, such as the Catholic Biblical Association of America, the Pontifical Biblical Institute, the École Biblique, the corps of German scholars associated with *Biblische Zeitschrift,* and the Catholic biblical associations of various countries (Italy, Spain, South American countries, etc.). This would help to depoliticize and dehierarchize the Pontifical Biblical Commission, and make available the best biblical scholarship within the Church.

b. The decisions of the Pontifical Biblical Commission, along with its arguments or deliberations, should be made public. It is an open secret that the 1975 decision on the biblical evidence relative to the ordina tion of women was not supposed to be made public.

c. There should be official recognition of the ecumenical dimension of biblical study within the Church. Ultimately this should lead to non-Catholic scholars being consultors of the Pontifical Biblical Commission. The reasons for this are several, but especially the fruitfulness of cooperation between Catholic and non-Catholic biblical scholars, which has already been manifested in the many bilateral and multilateral ecumenical dialogues (for details regarding ministry, authority, etc., see N. Ehrenstrom and G. Gassmann, *Confessions in Dialogue* [World Council of Churches, 1975]. A particularly felicitous example of such cooperation is *Peter in the New Testament,* edited by R. E. Brown, K. P. Donfried and John Reumann [Minneapolis: Augsburg, 1973]).

d. A working relationship between the Pontifical Biblical Commission and the International Theological Commission should be established.

2. Specific biblical issues should be confronted by the Church:

a. The issues of biblical inspiration and inerrancy are not as urgent today as they once were. Nonetheless, the statements pertinent to these questions in the *Dei Verbum* (chap. 3, no. 11) of Vatican II could be improved. Should the Christian be weighed down by the need of a complex explaining away of the formulas used in this chapter? The exposition is not informed by the most incisive theological thinking (either of P. Benoit or of K. Rahner, who have divergent theories on inspiration). The exposition merely repeats phrases and sentences of previous councils or official statements, and probably that was all that was intended. But as an expression of where common Catholic understanding of inspiration and inerrancy really is, the statements in no. 11 are simplistic. The final phraseology of no. 11 was fortunate as regards inerrancy: "that truth which God wanted put into the sacred writings for the sake of our salvation." The addition of "causa salutis nostrae" at the end has enabled biblical theologians to give greater nuance to the claim of inerrancy. But the most consistent and correct exposition of the meaning of biblical inerrancy has been presented by Norbert Lohfink, S. J. ("Über die Irrtumslosigkeit und Einheit der Schrift," *Stimmen der Zeit* 84[1964]: 161–81). It is this kind of explication that should find expression in the teaching of the Church.

b. Accepting the role of the Bible as a critique of the Church and the multiplicity of traditions that have grown up. The words of Vatican II have to be taken seriously; the "teaching office of the Church is not above the word of God, but serves it" *(Verbum Dei, no. 10)*. Hence there should be a wedding between the achievements of biblical scholarship and Church teaching. There seems to be an unwillingness to face disturbing facts turned up in biblical research, e.g., differences between the gospels, uncertainties about the structure of the Church and ministry. What Raymond Brown has written about the American scene can be applied fairly widely across the Church community ("Difficulties in Using the New Testament in American Catholic Discussions," *Louvain Studies* 6[1976]: 144–58, esp. p. 157): "If dogmatic formulations are historically conditioned and sometimes need to be reformulated, as *Mysterium Ecclesiae* maintains, biblical criticism must make its contribution to the reformulation—a reformulation that has to be approved by Church authority, to be sure, but a reformulation in which exegetes should have a consultative role."

c. *Mysterium Ecclesiae,* issued from the Sacred Congregation for the Doctrine of the Faith, dated June 24, 1973 (cf. *The Pope Speaks* 18/2 [1973]: 145–57), suggests another point for consideration in a future council: the hermeneutical problem. The document speaks of the difficulties encountered by the Church in the transmission of divine revelation, and it mentions specifically the difficulties that arise "from the historical condition that affects the expression of Revelation," and observes "that the meaning of the pronouncements of faith depends partly upon the expressive power of the language used at a given time and under given circumstances. Moreover, it sometimes happens that some dogmatic truth is first expressed incompletely (but not falsely), and at a later date, when considered in a broader context of faith or human knowledge, is expressed more fully and perfectly." The statement goes on: "It must be stated that the dogmatic *formulas* of the Church's magisterium have suitably communicated revealed truth from the very beginning and that, remaining the same, these formulas will continue to communicate this truth forever to those who interpret them correctly. It does not follow, however, that every one of these formulas has been or will be suitable for this purpose to the same extent."

The issue here is directly that of the interpretation of the historical dogmas that have evolved in the history of the Church. Despite the fact that the terrain of hermeneutics is constantly shifting, the Church cannot afford to take a hands-off attitude. The understanding of the faith delivered to the fathers is at the heart of the Church's mission, and it cannot escape the difficulties inherent in the process of tradition. *Mysterium Ecclesiae* opens the door to ongoing interpretation, without espousing a particular theory (whether of Aquinas or Gadamer). The fact, and the propriety of reinterpretation has at least been recognized. But there is a severe time lag from a pastoral and also a theological point of view. Partisans of Vincent of Lérins will continue to quote, "Quod ubique, quod semper, quod ab omnibus creditum est" (*Commonitoria,* chap. 2). Hence a more comprehensive and yet incisive statement on hermeneutics would be desirable.

The hermeneutical problem is, of course, at the heart of the interpretation of the Bible itself. How is one to interpret ancient texts? What role do the "normative" texts play in the methodology of individual theologians, and in the theological articulation of Church documents? These are questions that are answered in various ways today, and there is little unanimity. The liberation theologians argue from a necessarily limited, but also justifiable, context; they fix on Exodus and liberation themes in the biblical sources. The Church's teachings are not always successfully articulated as growing out of biblical data: sometimes biblical quotations are supplied as a panache rather than being the starting points, or at least guiding points, of theological development. Despite the difficulties, there would be a gain if both the magisterium and the biblical theologians looked at their own hermeneutical approaches. It may well be that there is no one approach, but great gain would be forthcoming from such an investigation.

David Kelsey has recently analyzed the approaches of several theologians to the biblical text (*The Uses of Scripture in Recent Theology* [Philadelphia: Fortress, 1975]; see also K. Reinhardt, *Der dogmatische Schriftgebrauch* [Munich: Schoningh, 1970], for a survey of the use of Scripture in Christology). Kelsey has shown the importance of an initial *discrimen* in the theological enterprise. This is a prior act of the imagination, a theological vision which determines the patterns to be studied. The construal of the discrimen varies among theologians, and this accounts in part for their differences. My purpose is not to suggest that the Church canonize any one methodology, but rather that a plurality of methodologies be recognized, if this is indeed correct.

d. Christian understanding of the Old Testament. The treatment of the Old Testament in chapter 4 of *Dei Verbum* is inadequate because the Old Testament is viewed principally as preparation for the New. This is, of course, a perfectly valid Christian stance, based upon the New Testament, and it is a time-honored approach among the Fathers of the Church. However, the approach tends to go to the New Testament too quickly. The Old Testament is then seen as merely a collection of "types" fulfilled in the New Testament. But typology is not where Christians are at today. What is needed is a serious development of what is only adumbrated in these words of chapter 4: "These same books, then, give expression to a lively sense of God, contain a store of sublime teachings about God, sound wisdom about human life, and a wonderful treasury of prayers, and in them the mystery of our salvation is present in a hidden way." These words respect the literal historical meaning of the Hebrew Bible. This meaning should not be flattened out in favor of a "higher" or Christocentric meaning. Otherwise the inherent spiritual strength of the Word of God to Israel is glossed over.

Modern Christians need to resonate to the faith of the Old Testament emphasis on this life (as opposed to the next, of which Israel has no knowledge) as a necessary ballast to Christians who are tempted to over-eschatologize their understanding of life. Those who believe in the Resurrection will come to a better appreciation of it if they have appropriated what the psalmists have to say about Sheol and death. K. Skydsgaard has described the proper perspective for both Catholic and Protestant Christianity: "We must both learn to think more biblically, more in accordance with the Old Testament. For the primitive Church, Israel was a figure of the people of God *on the way*—'wandering.' Israel was the people of God that never found ultimate peace, and was never allowed a fixed and abiding resting-place, but always had to make a new start. . . . Even though the new people of God is radically different from the old, this dimension of 'new start' applies to the Christian Church as well'' (''What Still Separates Us from the Catholic Church? A Protestant Reply,'' in *Post-Ecumenical Christianity, Concilium* 54 [New York: Herder and Herder, 1970], pp. 41–42).

e. In modern times theologians have recourse to biblical foundations in attempting to solve the problems of racism, war, liberation of the socially oppressed, sexism, poverty, etc. The Church has not brought to bear the biblical basis (or lack thereof) for these urgent issues. They are not to be answered simply by a biblical text, but it is the mission of the Church to address herself to these issues in a biblical perspective. Doubtless this task would call for a collaborative process involving several theologians. The consistently international collaboration of the *Concilium* membership provides a kind of model of the way in which these questions might be taken up.

Edward Schillebeeckx

Questions on Christian Salvation of and for Man

IN the post-Vatican II era we have noticed a certain polarization within the Christian churches. In the name of the Christian idea of salvation, many Christians have come to regard our socio-political endeavors to establish peace and justice in our history now as a humanistic and even Pelagian enterprise which endangers "salvation by faith alone." Thus in almost all churches a wedge is driven between the so-called orthodox, contemplation-oriented "churches of salvation" and the so-called heterodox, action-oriented "churches of liberation."

That which in former times appeared to interest religious people only has now become a matter of interest to the human sciences, techniques and activities of all kinds: all are striving after the healing, whole-making or salvation of man in society. It cannot be denied that (apart from the distinction between faith and reason) the quest for an integral and livable humanity, as an issue in itself, more than ever has the attention of all mankind. The answer to this problem is becoming all the more urgent in our present time, as we notice, on the one hand, that people fall short, fail and are injured, while, on the other hand, we can already have fragmentary experiences of human healing, whole-making and self-liberation. For the question of how to reach a livable humanity arises from the context of the actual conditions of disintegration, alienation, and human wounds of various kinds. The quest for salvation, *the* theme of all religions, has now more then ever become the stimulating force of modern history, even in those cases where religion is explicitly disavowed. Religions are not the only explicit thematizations of this universally human theme of salvation. The quest for salvation is the main incentive of current history, not just in the religious and theological sense, but nowadays also as a theme in itself. Man becomes aware of the fact that human history is the place where salvation or whole-making is decided on; and the decision is an explicitly conscious one.

As a result of the world-wide expansion of our technical and scientific civilization, our actions bear consequences for all mankind. That is to say: the effects of the activities of modern man on the levels of science and technology are to be situated in the macro-cosmos of the common interests of all men. For the first time in human history, mankind as such finds itself faced with the task of accepting world-wide responsibility for the consequences of its activities. This need for a joint responsibility calls for an *ethic* of world-wide responsibility.

For the first time in human history, therefore, mankind is at the crossroads of a critical shift, a point where by his actions (both by what he does and by what he fails to do) man can decide on the future of the *world,* and therefore also on its *meaning.* Moreover, the situation calls for human action which no longer depends exclusively on individuals—rather what is required are arrangements on a socio-political basis. The present pressing demand could be formulated as a call for personalizing and democratic socialization.

However, what is meant by ''meaningful humanity,'' which ought to be the guiding principle for this joint responsibility? One might ask whether there exists a universally, intersubjectively binding, yet non-dogmatic vision in this respect, acceptable to all men. The critical question, therefore, is the following: Taking account of the level of problem-consciousness man has developed up to this present day, while longing for a better future, what do we mean by a true and good, happy and free human being in a righteous society? What is meant by a *livable humanity?*

We have become more modest today in our attempts to state in positive terms what it means to be human. E. Bloch wrote: ''Man does not yet know who he is, but, alienated as he may be from himself, he is able to know for certain who he is not, and, therefore, what it is in this situation of alienation that he does not want to remain, or, at least, ought not remain.'' The definition of human existence is not a pre-existent datum. For Christians it is not even just a coming reality, but an eschatological reality. Some would pretend to have a blueprint of what it means to be human. They have a completely outlined image of man, a concrete vision of future society, a complete theory of salvation—a dogmatic system that, paradoxically, appears to be more important than man, for whom it is meant. This totalitarian vision inevitably leads to totalitarian action, which is then only a matter of the application of technology and strategy. Moreover, as a matter of course, the ones who neither accept nor use *this* concept of true human existence are regarded as the enemies of true humanity.

Our times have become more modest in this matter. Nature, creative ordinances and Evolution (with a capital E) cannot provide us with criteria to judge what a livable, true, good and happy humanity means. Neither can they therefore tell us which are meaningful, ethically responsible actions that promote true humanity. Nor can a so-called universal human nature, which, being intrinsically pre-defined (such as is the case with plants and animals), would be directed towards an essentially pre-defined goal. For the same reason, neither can the modern version of this latter line of thought, the so-called law of nature. What is more, self-reflection, independent of time and space, cannot arrive at a crystallization of some kind of general "substratum" of reasonableness among all men.

Structuralists have discovered deep structural constants in human societies, but these do not tell us anything about the specific properties of any concrete society. These structures have no direct relation to concrete empirical reality, but only with the models which man has made of this reality. By doing so, structuralism has indeed discovered one aspect of human reality, namely that man is a model-developing being; but (being consistent) it abstains from the question of how these models relate to reality. Structuralism excludes precisely the human individual, the subject, and therefore cannot provide criteria for a society worthy of human beings.

Existentialism, in its turn, has indeed analysed "existentialia," i.e., basic dispositions of human experience: fear, despair, love, hope, suffering, death, happiness, finiteness and guilt. And these aspects are extremely important in human life; they are related to the *quest for* what is ultimately worthy of a human being, but as such they do not provide an answer to this question: What is a basis of hope for a livable humanity in the midst of finiteness, guilt and suffering? Clearly they only say what it is we must be liberated from and to what purpose: to reach happiness. But how? And what does true happiness for all and everybody mean?

Finally, neither can we accept the positivistic view of values and norms. In this case, through empirical analysis, one indeed arrives at statements establishing which norms and values are operative in a certain group of society. This sociological insight is indeed important and even extremely relevant, e.g., for positive legislation; in order to be viable a law must indeed be supported by a reasonable consensus of all the members of that society. But it is impossible to elevate "factuals," or actually operative norms which score the highest points in statistical research, to a universal norm of ethical and meaningful human behavior. Highly civilized cultures disappeared in the course of time precisely for that reason.

Therefore, the critical consciousness of man should put us on the right track. If reason is a specifically human faculty, then the human capacity of judging the ambiguous phenomena of human history on the basis of norms is the proper critical task of man. Man is a being caught up in history. In his very essence, man is a narrative, a historical event rather than a pre-determined fact. He reveals something of this essence nowhere but in the course of his historical passage: in the very history of humanity. Man is situated and thematic freedom, not a free initiative in a vacuum or in a void. Salvation and humanity being "whole," integrity in a truly human, free way is precisely the *theme* of the whole story of man. Neither an idealistic nor a materialistic reading of this history does justice to this story of man.

Critical consciousness is not just (a) an awareness of the fact that part of the concrete nature of man consists in his being caught up in an environment of phenomena which give us no direct revelation of the true and the good, but which at the same time render these unrecognizable and veil them in such a way that there is a need for a standard to judge by; it is also (b) an awareness of the fact that the critical capacity of human reason is co-dependent on the historical circumstances in which it is situated, so that even the relation between *reason* and the concrete *historical circumstances* must be reflected on; (c) finally, it is also a consciousness that the past as well as the present and the time in between can be misjudged because they themselves take part in the ambiguity of all that is historical. Human reason is critical, rather than being dogmatic or nihilistically skeptical, only to the extent that it takes into account the ambiguity of the phenomena which reveal and simultaneously veil the true and the good, i.e., to the extent that it takes into account the historical conditioning of human thinking and the ambiguity of meaning or plurality of meaning of every period in time—the past, the present *and* the time in between, which are all open to different interpretations. Therefore, human consciousness is critical only to the extent that it does not stop at passing a critical judgment on the given phenomena, but is also capable of self-criticism with regard to critical reason itself (a thing that seems to have been beyond the grasp of eighteenth-century Enlightenment).

Instead of a positivistic attitude, instead also of a philosophically pre-determined definition of "human nature" (e.g., in the Aristotelian-Thomistic or Spinozian and Wolffian sense), instead, finally, of a historically necessary product of history, which would come flowing from the rational depth-course of history (as in a Marxist definition of true and free humanity), the only thing we have at our disposal is *anthropological constants*. These indeed reveal human values to us. On the basis of these human *values* and in a historical, changing process, we must fill in the concrete *norms* in a creative way. In other words, these anthropological constants point in a general way toward lasting human impulses, orientations, and value spheres, but they do not directly provide us with concrete norms or ethical imperatives on the basis of which, here and now, a more human and livable humanity can be called into existence. They do present us, however, with constitutive conditions (from the analysis and interpretation of our own contemporary situation) which, over and over again, must be filled in and colored anew and which are presupposed in all human activity, if man, his culture and society are not to be desecrated, hurt and made unlivable. Taking into account the socio-historical shape of our concrete society, viewed in the light of the value spheres which are acknowledged to be constants within our current problem consciousness, man is indeed able to set up concrete standards (norms) for human activities on a medium-long or even long-term basis.

I propose to analyze seven of these anthropological constants. I view them as a kind of system of coordinates which focus on the human *person-identity* within *social culture*. We are then concerned with profiles of man and his culture, constitutive aspects which man must take into account while creatively developing concrete norms for ever-growing humanity, and therefore for the salvation of man.

I. THE SYSTEM OF COORDINATES OF MAN AND HIS SALVATION

1. Relation to Human Corporeity, Nature and Ecological Environment

The relation of the human person to his own corporeity—man *is* and *has* a body—and via his own corporeity to the greater nature and to his own ecological environment is a constitutive aspect of our humanity. It also relates to human salvation.

If, in our activities, we fail to take into account this aspect of our humanity, we will eventually control nature in such a one-sided way or condition man in such a way as to destroy the basic principles of our own natural environment, and in doing so we will preclude our own humanity be interfering with our natural management or ecological basis. In our relation to nature and to our own corporeity we are faced with boundaries which have to be respected if we wish to live in a human way and even, in extreme cases, to survive *tout court*. Technical possibilities are, therefore, not necessarily also ethical, humanly meaningful and responsible possibilities.

This also holds for the physical and psychical limitations of our human capacities. Even if we are (still) unable to define in an empirically scientific way the precise limits of human changeability, of human conditioning, of the burden man can take, in an extra-scientific way we are convinced that there inevitably must be such limits. This extra-scientific though cognitive certainty reveals itself in a spontaneous manner in individual and collective protests as soon as people experience that they are being overburdened. The elementary needs of man (e.g., food, sex), his passions (e.g. aggressivity) and his corporeity in general cannot be manipulated in an arbitrary way without man experiencing that his humanity is being affected in its soundness and wholeness, happiness and livability (a thing that will manifest itself in spontaneous resistance).

This first anthropological constant opens a vast field of human values that call for humane standards with respect to one's own corporeity and its natural environment. However, these are standards which we ourselves have to derive from the concrete situation in which we now live. This already opens a perspective on the relationship of man towards nature, which is indeed not exclusively dictated by the human value of mastering nature but also by the equally human value of esthetical appreciation and enjoyment of nature. The limits set by nature itself to its technical manipulation by man and for man reveal a dimension of our human existence which is not exhausted by the technical mastering of nature. On the other hand, this same constant warns us of the danger of an anti-technological or anti-industrial culture. Scientists who reflect on their own enterprise emphasize the anthropological relevance of instrumental reason. The philosophy of culture has analyzed man's incapacity to live in a purely natural environment. Man must create himself a human *Umwelt* in nature if he is to survive without the refined instinct and the strength of animals. For that reason, a rational change of nature is necessary. Thus a "meta-cosmos" (F. Dessauer) is created which delivers man from animal limitation and provides an opening towards new possibilities. In times when the "meta-cosmos" hardly differed from nature, only a small part of the population enjoyed the advantages of culture and the masses were forced to work as slaves in order to free the happy few from material care. (One may rightly wonder whether much has changed in our highly industrialized "meta-cosmos." This first, fundamental anthropological constant seems to be insufficient.) The "meta-cosmos" provides man with better housing and a better home than the natural cosmos. Therefore, technology in itself need not be dehumanizing. Rather it may be a help towards attaining a livable humanity; it is an expression of and at the same time a condition for the humanizing of man. After all, it is a historical fact that all reflection on the meaning of life has always presupposed the creation of a "meta-cosmos." Moreover, the humanization of nature is not completed, although looking at our advanced technology one could easily be led to think it is. Man can indeed influence his own ecological situation within nature, but he remains dependent on it, a situation which manifests itself particularly in those cases where he disturbs the conditions of life. The effort to emancipate man from nature on the one hand, without, on the other hand, disturbing his own ecological basis is an eminently human task which cannot be realized without "instrumental reason."

In addition, it appears that the creation of meaning and the development of certain views on the world and on man is co-mediated by the instrumental technical reason and is not only the result of the immanent development of ideas. Ideas concerning marriage, love and sexuality have shifted in our time (e.g., in comparison with biblical ideas) largely for the sole reason that science and technology could provide means which before were not available to man. As soon as technical possibilities become available, interference with nature looks like quite a different thing from times in which any form of interference with nature was experienced as a sly and therefore evil interference with divine creation ordinances. As soon as this happens, man starts running the risk of concluding he is both capable of and allowed to solve all his physical and psychical, social and general human-life problems in a purely technical way, based only on the factual availability of technical possibilities and capacities. But there is a difference between the technocratic interpretation of the ideal of a livable and humane life and the anthropological relevance of science and technology. The dehumanizing character that is often part of this interpretation does not proceed as such from technology but from the concomitant question of meaning which has already been solved in a positivistic sense. Therefore, it is neither science nor technology with their capacity of promoting humanity which are subject to criticism, but very often their implicit presuppositions and assumptions.

Thus, this first anthropological constant reveals a whole scale of sub-constants of all kinds—e.g., that man is not only reason but also heart, not only reason but also imagination, not only freedom but also instinct, not only reason but also love.

If Christian salvation is indeed salvation *of and for man*, it must have an essential relation with this first anthropological constant. To recall one aspect of what was said before: Christian salvation also has relations with ecology, with the conditioning of man and with the burdens which are being imposed on him in his concrete life here and now. Those who call all this alien to Christian salvation might be dreaming of salvation for angels, but not for men.

2. Human Existence Is Human Co-existence

Human person-identity entails our co-existence with fellow men. This is also an anthropological constant, which reveals a field of human values in which man must search for standards to promote salvation here and now. Togetherness, fellowship, by which we give ourselves to others and in which we are confirmed in our existence and in our person-identity by others, is part of the building-up of person-identity itself: being allowed to be, the confirmation by others and by the community that we exist, that I am allowed to "be there," with my own name, my own identity, as a personal and responsible self. This person-identity is only possible if others allow me to be myself in my own inalienability but also in my essential limitations (*divisum ab alio*, ancient philosophy said). In this limited individuality, a person has an essential relation to the others, the fellow men. Our very faces (nobody ever sees his own face!) indicate that man is oriented towards and is meant for the other and not for himself. The human face is an image of oneself *for others*. Thus, by this concrete appearance, man is predestined for the encounter with fellow men in this world. This entails the assignment to accept the others in inter-subjectivity as they are, in their differences and in their freedom. It is precisely in this reciprocal relation with others that man will overcome the limitations of his own individuality in a free and loving acceptance of the other, and that he acquires person-identity. The fellowship in which we accept one another as persons, i.e., as goals and ends and not as means to an end, is an anthropological constant which requires norms without which, here and now, sound and livable humanity is impossible. This also implies that well-being and being-whole, salvation and sound humanity must be *universal*, must concern all and every man, not just some privileged persons, even if from the preceding it appears that being-whole entails more than interhumanity on a *personal* level. Nobody can enter into a relation of a real encounter with all people. After all, there is not only an "I-you" relation: the presence of a *third* person, of a "he," is the basis of society which cannot be reduced to an "I-you" or "we" relation. It is especially E. Lévinas who observed this very well. This leads us to a third essentially human dimension.

3. Relation to Social and Institutional Structures

Thirdly, there is the relation of the human person to social and institutional structures. In the course of history we, human beings, indeed call into being these structures. But they become independent and grow into an objective form of society, in which we live and which in turn influences our interiority, our person. The social dimension is not something that is added to our person-identity, it is a dimension of this very identity. As independent entities, the structures and institutions create the impression of being unchangeable laws, though we ourselves can change them, thus destroying their claims of being natural laws. These much-vaunted sociological and economic laws do not exist independently of what men do or independently of human reason and human will to preserve them. They essentially exist under the historical hypothesis of the objectively present social and economic polity; they are contingent, and changeable, and therefore can be changed by man (although underneath all kinds of social changes, even radical ones, sociologists and cultural anthropologists may perhaps detect a deeper, almost unchangeable stratum, and consequently a structural constant). In treating them as laws of nature or metaphysical issues, the empirical sciences, which rightly point out these sociological or sociopsychological laws, nevertheless fail sometimes to recognize their essential subordination to the hypothesis of our current (changeable) objective form of society.

This constant also reveals to us a field of values, namely the value of the institutional and structural elements for a really humane life: another field of values that requires concrete norms. On the one hand, there is no lasting human life without a certain degree of institutionalizing; person-identity calls for social consensus, to be carried by structures and institutions which enable human freedom and the realization of values. On the other hand, factual, historically developed structures and institutions have no general validity. They are changeable. From this the concrete demand arises to change them where, as a result of changed circumstances, they have come to enslave and disfigure man instead of liberating and protecting him.

4. *The Space-Time Structure of Person and Culture*

Time and space, the historical and geographical location of persons and cultures, is an anthropological constant from which no man can escape.

Here we are first of all confronted with a dialectic tension between nature and history, which coincide in concrete human culture and which cannot be removed, not even by optimal social structures. It is a dialectic which belongs to the components of our finite human existence and of which death only is the ultimate exponent, a limit situation. This means that, apart from all kinds of suffering which to a great extent can be remedied by man, there are sufferings and threats to life which no technical or social intervention can remedy. The historicity of man, his finiteness from which he cannot escape in order explicitly to place himself on a level above time, makes for the fact that human existence is also experienced as a *hermeneutical* enterprise, i.e., as a task to *understand* one's own situation and to *critically unmask* the nonsense in history brought about by man. In this attempt towards self-understanding, in which the question of truth and untruth is also asked, man can receive help from all kinds of empirically analytical and theological sciences, but in spite of this man experiences truth as being at the same time both a thing *remembered* and a thing *to be realized*. If understanding is the specifically human way of experiencing, then understanding is as universal as history itself. It follows that the pretension to take a stand outside the historical action and thought of man is a threat to real humanity.

Many other problems are connected with this constant. I will point out only a few. There may be historically and geographically co-defined acquisitions which, at this point, can no longer be regarded as free or arbitrary, although they did come up in history at a fairly late date and at certain places and therefore cannot be called *a priori* necessary or *a priori* universal presuppositions. Certain values may have developed which call for standards applying, i.e., in the highly industrialized and highly cultural conditions in which Western man lives, but not necessarily applying in other cultures.

A few examples may suffice. Owing to the high level of his welfare Western man is called to international solidarity, especially with regard to poor countries (apart from the historical question of how far the West itself is responsible for bringing about the poverty of these countries). To the extent that this same constant reveals the historical and geographical limitations of each culture, it follows that, in view of the limited potential of people's imagination in a certain culture, the critical memory of the great traditions of mankind, and also of its great religious traditions, will act as a necessary stimulus in the search for norms for actions that, here and now, promote a sound and livable humanity. This critical memory plays an important role in man's hermeneutical enterprise to seek for light for future actions.

Finally, this fourth anthropological constant reminds us of the fact that the explicit discovery of precisely these constitutive constants is itself part of a historical process; our becoming conscious of it results from human hermeneutical praxis.

5. The Relation between Theory and Praxis

The essential relation between theory and praxis is also an anthropological constant. It is a constant precisely insofar as through this relation human culture, as a hermeneutical enterprise or a grasping of meaning and as an effort to affect a change of meaning and improve the world, attains durability. On the level of the sub-human (e.g., animal) world, durability and the possibility of survival of the species and of the individual are assured by natural instincts, by adaptability to the changed or changing environment, and finally by the evolutionary law of the strongest in the struggle for life. If man wants to avoid making his own history into a kind of spiritual Darwinism, i.e., a history in which it is the will and the thinking of the stronger ones and the victors who pre-dictate what is good and true for our humanity, then on the human level the dialectics of theory and praxis will be the only humanly responsible guarantee for a lasting and ever more humane culture.

Where dealing with the problem of orthodoxy and orthopraxy, theologians often appear to mix up two levels of thought. On the one hand, there is the level of the *fides qua*. This expression means that faith is only authentic to the extent that it leads to action. Believing but failing to act accordingly reveals that one evidently does not really believe. This is what makes a person's faith "incredible" for others. However, this matter has nothing to do with the problem of theory versus praxis. The latter should rather be situated on the level of the *fides quae* (or of the content of faith): a statement of faith does not become true because it is put into practice or untrue because it is not put into practice. Consistent praxis does not determine the truth value of a theory. The eleventh Feuerbach thesis of Marx about the so-called primacy of praxis over theory can cause confusion in this respect. Marx himself offers an interpretative theory of the world, but he offers a theory which should be read as a criticism of certain groups and which is therefore apt to be used for a particular, determined (society-changing) praxis. Even in this case, theory comes before praxis, but it happens to be a theory with a practical critical intention. Theologians often mix up these two levels and then refer to the primacy of the praxis over faith (see e.g., Th. Schneider, "Orthodoxie und Orthopraxie: Überlegungen zur Struktur des christlichen Glaubens," *TThZ* 81 [1972]: 151). What it really comes down to is the primacy of *faith* (a kind of theory or affirmation of truth), which as such, commits itself to action; *theological* reflection can only follow afterwards, as a "second step," providing a control and criticism of all those forms of action that pass as Christian. Thus, theory *not only* has a post-practical function. It also (consciously or implicitly) precedes the praxis. The praxis as such does not provide a basis for the truth value of a theory (e.g., it is possible to hold a Nazi theory and very consistently to act accordingly, but this loyal consistency has no bearing on the truth value of the theory!).

6. *The Religious and "Para-religious" Consciousness of Man*

It seems to me that the "utopian" moment of human consciousness is also an anthropological constant, even a fundamental one.

Here it is the future of man which is at stake. What future does he want? By utopian moment I mean all kinds of (conservative or progressive) totality constructs which enable man to give some meaning to or conquer the contingency or finiteness, the precariousness, including the problem of suffering, failure and death. In other words, I mean the way in which a certain society puts the hermeneutical enterprise into concrete forms in everyday life (see the fourth constant) or, protesting against a pre-given meaning, opts for a different social policy and a different future. Totality visions teach us how to live human life, now and in future, as a humanly meaningful, good and happy totality—a vision and praxis which will give meaning and coherence to human existence in this world (even if only in a distant future).

Here we must mention totality visions of a *religious* nature (the religions) as well as of *non-religious* character—visions on life, on society, world-views and general theories of life in which man expresses what finally inspires him, what kind of human existence he finally chooses, what the ultimate goal he lives for is and why he finds life worth living. All these can be called cognitive models of reality which interpret the whole of nature and history in theory and praxis and, now or later, let them be experienced as (to-be-realized) meaningful existence.

In most—but not all—of these "utopias" people can see themselves as the subject of actions that promote the good and the building-up of a good humane world, without being individually and at the same time personally responsible for the reality of history and its final outcome. Some will call this dominating principle destiny or fate, others evolution, still others "mankind," the species Man as a universal subject of the whole of history, or, in more vague terms, "Nature." For religious people this is the living God, the Lord of history. But, in whatever form, such a totality vision is always a *kind of faith,* except when one adheres to nihilism and therefore professes the absurdity of human life, a kind of faith in the sense of being a utopia that is not subject to scientific tests, and can never be fully rationalized. *Without faith nobody fares well.* In that sense faith, the basis of hope, is an anthropological constant of the whole of human history, a constant without which humane and livable human life and action become impossible; man loses his identity and ends up in neurotic conditions, or has irrational recourse to horoscopes and all kinds of *mirabilia.* Moreover, faith and hope are confirmed as necessary human constants by the nihilistic pretension which calls livable humanity an absurdity, and therefore is without faith and hope. This implies that faith and hope (whatever we take them to mean) are essential to the health and soundness, the livability and wholeness of our being human and humane. For those who believe in God this implies that religion is an anthropological constant without which salvation for man, redemption and real liberation which passes by a *religious* redemption is a bisected liberation and, . moreover, to the extent that it is presented as a *total* liberation of man, smashes to pieces a real dimension of being human, thus eventually dislocating man instead of liberating him.

7. Irreducible Synthesis of These Six Dimensions

To the extent that these six anthropological constants can be brought together in a synthesis, human culture is indeed an irreducible *autonomous reality,* to be reduced neither in an idealistic nor in a materialistic sense. The synthesis constitutes the man-healing reality which brings salvation. (The synthesis itself must therefore be called an anthropological constant.) The six constants gear into each other and condition each other. They design the basic form of human existence and keep each other in balance. To speak about the priority of "spiritual values" may sound nice, even just, but in fact it may destroy the material conditions and implications of the spiritual values precisely at the expense of these. Undervaluation of one of these deeply human constants dislocates the whole, including the spiritual. It wrongs man and his society and throws out of balance the whole of human culture. In doing so one consciously or unconsciously makes an attack on true and good, happy and free human existence.

On the one hand, it may be clear from the preceding remarks that the anthropological constants which open a perspective on fundamental value areas of human existence in no way provide us with *norms* which, here and now, have to operate on our objective social structures and given culture in order to arrive at more humane behavior. These constants design, so to say, only the system of coordinates in which concrete norms will have to be found in mutual consultation. These concrete norms can only be found after the analysis and interpretation of the concrete social structures and the position man, the person, occupies in them. Starting from the level of our problem consciousness reached up to this point as a minimal vantage point (perhaps this is also an important factor in our reflection on what is human), we can then, on the basis of negative experiences or contrastive experiences, as well as on the basis of already lived meaning experiences, and in the light of what we believe to be a valid "utopia," make an analysis of the gap between the ideal and factuality. The gap analysis will reveal the direction to be taken (allowing for alternative directions, however—cf. *infra*)—a direction which we will have to determine in mutuality and fill in with the concrete norms required at this present moment.

I said that we must allow for all kinds of alternative directions, for there may be huge differences in the way people view the utopian moment of our human consciousness as well as their analysis and especially their interpretation of the analytical results (for the very method of analysis already reveals a certain oriented utopian consciousness). The result will be pluralism, even if we apply a scientific analysis (which takes place within a conscious or unconscious interpretive frame)—pluralism also in the presentation of concrete norms—even if people recognize the same fundamental values to which the "anthropological constants" have drawn our attention. The norms to which each individual subscribes must be made the subject of discussion in dialogue and on the basis of intrinsic arguments if we wish to challenge other people with them. Even when their fundamental inspiration arises from a religious belief in God, *ethical* norms (i.e., norms which promote humanity) must be rationally justified in an intersubjectively valid discussion, i.e., a discussion open to all reasonable people. None of the partners in the discussion can hide himself behind a doubtful "I see what you do not see," while at the same time forcing others to accept his own norm. As in many discussions, the beginning situation can indeed be such that one of the partners in the discussion can see something that others cannot see. But in that case this "something" ought to be clarified for others in a free and rational communication process. Nobody can claim a storm-free zone (even though other partners in the discussion do not necessarily have to agree on the basis of the arguments presented). The fact that one has to learn to live with different views of the concrete norms required to attain livable humanity, here and now, belongs to the very predicament of creating modern, livable humanity. Sadness about this pluralism is itself part of our (especially modern) human predicament which we have to come to terms with. This cannot be done by a dictatorial rejection of other views. The art of living also belongs to the true, good and happy human existence within the boundaries of our historicity and finiteness, at least if we wish to avoid turning into "megalomaniacs" who pretend to be able to pass by their human finiteness. On the other hand, people's readiness to bring about salvation must not proceed from so-called political realism, i.e., from a view of politics as the art of the possible, the attainable, that which is within reach. Politics is the rather more difficult art of enabling that which is necessary for human salvation.

II. CHRISTIAN SALVATION

Christian salvation, liberation, or definitive and eschatological redemption from God in Jesus deals with the whole system of coordinates in which man can really be himself. This salvation or whole-being cannot be found exclusively in one or another of these constants, e.g., exclusively in ecological slogans, exclusively in "being nice to one another," exclusively in overthrowing an economic system (whether capitalist or Marxist), or exclusively in mystical experiences: "Halleluia, He is risen." Moreover, the true synthesis of all this will be a clear "already" *and* "not yet," both mysticism and political liberation.

Christian salvation, in order to be salvational, must be *universal* and *total*. Consequently salvation, in the sense of that which makes whole, should entail as a minimum requirement that no one group be whole at the expense of another one. This does not imply that Christian salvation can be reduced to the making of a universally human just society. It does imply, however, that the making of such a society is a minimum ingredient of Christian salvation.

This implies that whole-making, salvation of and for man, is also an *experiential* concept. The Christian concept of salvation would lose its rational meaning (i.e., rationally speaking it would not be a concept of salvation) if there were no *positive* relationship between the "justification by faith alone" and the construction of a more just, integrated world. Salvation must be at least a partial and fragmentary reflection of that which is experienced by man as whole-making. Salvation that is merely "promised" loses all reasonableness. Therefore, Christian salvation must satisfy minimum requirements if we wish to prevent this term "salvation," and, with it, *Christian* salvation, from dying the death of a thousand qualifications. By introducing salvation as an experiential concept, we are able, on the one hand, to safeguard God's freedom "to be God," i.e., a reality which cannot be pinned down to our human concepts of salvation, while, on the other hand, man receives the freedom "to be human," i.e., a living creature with his own say in the matter whether a certain type of salvation will or will not take place.

The central issue for the faithful is, then, whether they are actually doing the same thing as non-believers about building a new world of justice. In this case, the faithful world gives just another *interpretation* to this common praxis, which, being just an interpretation, would have no consequences of its own for the praxis. Religion has no contribution of its own to make to a praxis which would remain indifferent to a religious or non-religious interpretation. Consequently, the claim of religion to render an irreducible service to the world becomes problematic and distressingly ambiguous to the degree to which this service is understood as proceeding from extra-religious aims. Conversely, the claim of any religion to present its own specific interpretation of man and of the world is equally problematic and ambiguous to the degree that this interpretation lacks relevance for the praxis. Religion is neither an interpretation of the world which can be divorced from the praxis, nor is it a praxis devoid of all relation to a particular interpretation of man and of the world. It is therefore the task of theology to clarify how religion (or Christendom) serves the world in a way which is both *specifically religious* (or Christian, ultimately founded on prayer) and *practically, even politically active* in the world. For when we speak of religious and Christian consciousness (with its own critical and productive, i.e. action-guiding, force), we are really speaking of a certain pattern of human consciousness. The question, then, becomes: What is specifically religious about this consciousness, i.e., which knowledge and which reality determine our awareness in such a way that it can be called "religious" or Christian? At the same time, this means: How is the reality of man and the world to be judged in the light of this religious consciousness?

On the one hand, a non-dualistic definition of God as pure positivity, origin, basis and source of the promotion of all good things and opponent of all evil has a critically productive force of its own. On the other hand, the mystical praxis of Christianity is linked with its social and political praxis through the non-theorizable mediation of the history of human suffering. Salvation is then realized within the conditions of suffering finiteness.

Human suffering has its own critical and productive *epistemic* power. This should not be reduced to the purposive, emancipatory type of knowledge characteristic of the sciences and technology, nor to the various types of contemplative, esthetic and playful, so-called "aimless" knowledge, which keeps turning around its object. The specific epistemic value of the contrastive experience of suffering based on injustice assumes a *critical* attitude *both* towards the contemplative type of knowledge *and* towards the scientific or technological type. It provides the purely contemplative total perception, which already has some experience of universal reconciliation in its contemplation or liturgy, with a critical element. But at the same time it is critical of the dominating knowledge of the sciences and technology which presupposes that man is merely a ruling subject (thus neglecting the question of priority).

The productive epistemic value of suffering is not just critical of both positive types of human knowledge; it can also become the dialectic link between both, i.e., the contemplative epistemic force of the human psyche and its active dominating epistemic force. In fact, much can be said in favor of the thesis that the contrastive experience of suffering (with its implicit ethical demand) is the only experience capable of linking these two intrinsically, since it is the only experience which unites characteristics of both types of knowledge. For just like contemplative or esthetic experiences, experiences of suffering *overcome* a person, albeit that the latter are of a contrastive nature whereas the former are positive. On the other hand, to the extent that the experience of suffering is a contrastive experience, it opens perspectives for a praxis which aims at removing both the suffering itself and its causes. It is on the basis of this inner relationship, a relationship of critical negativity, both with the contemplative type of knowledge and with the type of knowledge which seeks to master nature, that the specific "pathetic" *(pati)* epistemic force of suffering is *practically* critical, i.e., it is a critical epistemic force which promotes a new praxis anticipating a better future and actively committed to realizing it. All this entails that, in our given human predicament and within the context of our concrete social culture, contemplation and action—paradoxically but nevertheless truly—can be brought together intrinsically only by the criticism of the accumulated history of human suffering and the ethical consciousness developed in the course of this history of suffering.

For the experience of suffering as a contrastive experience can only exist on the basis of an explicit longing for happiness, and, to the extent that this is an experience of unjust suffering, it presupposes at least some vague form of awareness of the positive meaning of human integrity. As a contrastive experience it indirectly implies an awareness of the positive vocation of and to the *Humanum*. In this sense, all action which seeks to conquer suffering presupposes at least an implicit and vague anticipation of a possible, future universal meaning. As opposed to the purposeful knowledge of the sciences and technology and to the purposeless knowledge of contemplation, the specific epistemic value of the contrastive experiences of suffering is that of a knowledge which begs for a future and even opens one. Thus, next to "purpose" and "purposeless," "future" (not evolution but eschatological future) becomes a valid concept. For on the basis of its ambivalent characteristics (having properties in common both with contemplation and with action) and of its ethical character of protest, the specific epistemic value of suffering is that of a knowledge which does not ask for purposefulness or aimlessness, but for a future: for more humanity and for the coming suppression of the causes of injustice. For in the negativity of its experience, or even because of this negativity, it possesses a form of ethical protest against "letting it be," it has a critical epistemic force which appeals for a praxis of opening the future, a praxis, moreover, which refuses to submit to the self-evident absolute reign of purposive technocracy (for this is one of the causes of suffering). Therefore, the contrastive experience of suffering is the negatively and dialectically awakening consciousness of a longing and a quest for future meaning and future real freedom and happiness. It is also a longing for the conciliatory, "aimless" contemplation, as an anticipation of universal meaning to be linked, because of the contrastive nature of the experience, with a new future-creating praxis which is to conquer evil and its sufferings.

Carl J. Peter

Doctrine and the Future: Some Suggestions

"HAVE confidence in faith, this great friend of intelligence." These words appear in one of the closing messages issued by the Second Vatican Council.[1] They reflect a conviction; religious faith is more than a casual acquaintance of the human quest of meaning and truth. On closer inspection it is clear that these words were intended to describe an actual situation. Their authors really thought that religious faith is *in fact* a friend of human intelligence.

This may seem to some to amount to a case of wishful thinking on the part of the participants in Vatican II. At the very least it is not self-evident that *friendship* is the best (or even an accurate) category with which to describe the relation in question. One has only to think of that expression of religious faith which has come to be known as doctrine. In so doing one need not imply (and I surely do not intend to imply) that doctrine is the most important aspect of religious faith or the only one worth taking into account. But it is a fairly obvious candidate for consideration when one speaks of faith as a friend of intelligence.

It is one thing to ask whether and/or how doctrine has been such in the past. That is not my primary question here. What I am more concerned with is whether doctrine can be such in the future more than it is at present and still retain its identity. I think an affirmative answer is warranted. Indeed in my opinion one of the most important things those responsible for formulating doctrine in the future could seek to accomplish would be this. They could keep in mind the words of Vatican II with which this paper began and try to make those words ring true for more hearers than is the case today. In short they could try to make religious faith (and especially the church's expression of that faith) something the human spirit, with its insatiable desire to know, could regard unhesitatingly as a friend and colleague. For that situation to come about, Christian doctrine would almost inevitably have to be widely regarded as an effort of the church to render service to the whole of humanity. In what follows I should like to suggest a number of ways in which doctrine might come to be seen as helpful in humanity's collective efforts to achieve a better self-understanding. But before making such an attempt, a clarification of terminology is in order.

In the first two volumes of his projected series, Jaroslav Pelikan described Christian doctrine as that which the church believes, teaches, and confesses on the basis of the word of God.[2] That is how doctrine will be understood in this paper. It refers to far more than churchly creeds and professions of faith but does not have as wide an extension as theology. It springs from, calls for, and seeks to strengthen conviction, trust, and confidence. But it is not independent of that inquiry regarding meaning and truth which is characteristic of theologizing. Understood in this sense, doctrine has, I should like to suggest, the potential for becoming a more effective way in which the church can exercise its mission to serve humanity.

DOCTRINE AS CONVICTION CHERISHING FREEDOM

Before, however, doctrine is likely to be widely recognized as any kind of desirable service rendered by the church, it will have to lose some of the threatening and ominous connotations it still has for not a few people. Too often it has stood in the popular mind for the tenets a church member was expected to profess (or at least not to deny openly) or else pay certain consequences. Rightly or wrongly it still has something of an image problem in terms of the spontaneous reaction it elicits. For how many is this the case? I do not know but I have a suspicion it is true of more than any church has a right to pass over lightly, especially in a consideration of how doctrine might be faithfully and yet more effectively formulated in the future.

Believing, teaching, and confessing may be carried out on the basis of the word of God in such a way that both Christians and others are set to thinking about the meaning of life because they want to do so. Let us suppose that churches of the various communions, and in particular the Roman Catholic Church, were in the future to come up with ways of expressing their distinctive convictions that would more frequently and more spontaneously invite serious thought and reflection. This accomplishment would have brought those churches a long way toward rehabilitating doctrine as a healthy, normal, and necessary function in their life and mission. Each success might put another nail in the coffin of the charges that doctrine stifles thought and restricts freedom. But how to avoid such charges or at least hòw to avoid giving grounds for the same?

I am not sure but would like to propose this for consideration. Doctrine is one way the churches try to concretize the Gospel and keep the Good News from sounding like vague generalities and pious platitudes. The churches might take under advisement a short-term policy of not speaking out officially on the wide variety of issues they have addressed themselves to in the recent past. I am not suggesting a moratorium on doctrinal statements. I am not saying that the churches in general or my own church in particular have failed to make people *want* to think about concrete religious meaning and truth or to consider commitment to concrete religious values. I am also aware of the fact that in some countries the churches may have to continue to speak out frequently, especially where basic human rights are in jeopardy and the possibility of criticism is effectively denied to other groups. But of this much I am sure. If the churches or their official spokespersons speak out too frequently on too many issues, even the most conscientious may be unable to find the time or summon the energy required to think about and make decisions regarding all the matters treated. Their freedom may be all but paralyzed if they are or feel overwhelmed by challenges to understand, judge, and choose concretely on the basis of the word of God. This is something those responsible for formulating doctrine should keep in mind. Increased concern to avoid overwhelming and disorienting its hearers is likely to be a real service to the word of God. It might help more people give that word a fair hearing. For a while teaching less frequently and on fewer but genuinely crucial issues might amount to teaching more effectively.

DOCTRINE AS CONVICTION APPRECIATIVE OF HOW HARD IT IS TO BELIEVE

It is not likely that doctrine will ever appear to be a much-needed service to humanity or a close friend of intelligence unless it shows in its very formulation a sensitivity and an appreciation of how hard it is to believe as a Christian—at least for so many today. Whether one does or does not accept Jesus Christ as Lord, an empty stomach pains; subhuman standards of living are degrading; cancer can kill just as surely; and discouragement is at times deep and paralyzing. This obstacle to belief in the God Jesus taught His followers to call Father has been around a long time; that fact does not make it any less formidable.

Even if it does so humbly, Christian doctrine often speaks with confidence and assurance about matters where so many find assurance doubtfully meaningful and likely unwarranted. Most churches try time and again to find ways that will propose the ultimate power underlying the universe as one that is not hostile but rather loving like a parent. The doctrine of providence attempts to bring this out. In so doing it speaks of the undetectable as graciously influencing the observable. But as soon as the Christian begins to answer questions as to what this means and why one might think it to be the case, he or she begins to qualify and adjust the description of the provident God to accord with empirical facts which include cruel natural disasters and a senseless disproportion between human suffering and values derived therefrom. When Christians say providence involves the excess that was the cross of Jesus, others wonder whether this combination of doctrines does not lead as easily to a word game as to thoughts giving important insights into life and its meaning. Doctrine would not be doctrine if it gave up its persuasion and assurance. Can it retain its identity while still conveying the impression that its formulators took into account the serious nature of the challenges to disbelief? I think this is possible and desirable.

So far I have spoken of obstacles confronting doctrine as an expression of the Good News in a world where there seems to be at times so little of the latter. I have also tried to show that reflection on the referents of religious language makes it harder rather than easier for many to accept Christian doctrine as either meaningful or true. Last but not least one should consider the impact that history and the empirical sciences cannot but have when they deal with subject matter about which church doctrine has its own understanding and convictions. The result is that there are, given the information explosion we are living through, far more questions than adequate or ready-made answers. When the church speaks with conviction and assurance in such areas where very intelligent men and women wonder what the answers to their questions are, when the church in its doctrine seems to propose answers to those questions before all the data have been faced up to directly and satisfactorily, many wonder how and why the church proceeds as it does. All the questions regarding the implications of the word of God will never be answered so fully that they will never need to be raised again. If the church were to wait to teach until any and all rightful impact exercised by philosophy, history, and the empirical sciences on faith had been taken into account, doctrine would surely have no future. Such a suspension is not at all indicated. Conviction can be real and true before the last word has been spoken in answers to questions having a bearing on that conviction. The church should not hesitate to live and teach simply because the meaning and truth it confesses are subjected to a questioning for which no fully intellectually satisfying answers have yet been found. But it should not express its faith in believing, teaching, and confessing without making it clear that the seriousness of those questions is appreciated.

DOCTRINE AS CONVICTION CULTIVATING HOPE

The purpose of Christian eschatology has been described as that of bringing disciplined thought into believing hope and hope into worldly thinking.[3] Doctrine ought to share in a significant way the second part of that objective.

What is considered possible often sets limits that planners respect (and rightly so) in their efforts to find solutions to human problems. But that outer limit of possibility is frequently a line drawn on the basis of an assumption of how much individuals and groups will do or put up with in efforts to satisfy the needs of others. Doctrine is the church's expression of a faith that responds to a word of promise making the greatest of exceptions to human expectations (the Resurrection) the basis for a struggle to enlarge horizons of understanding, judgment, choice, and planning. Because of the hope it proclaims it has a potential for making one raise his or her sights and aim higher. Sometimes the practitioners of the natural and/or behavioral sciences point to problems that are theoretically solvable but that remain practically unresolved because of the sacrifice of ease and preference that the solution would demand of large numbers of people. Motivation is the crux. Many work to improve the lot of others to the extent, for example, that the law requires them to do so. They need a challenge to hope for a new heaven and earth if they are to rise above their relative satisfaction with their own *status quo* and exert efforts for others by going more than halfway in the exercise of a generosity exceeding justice.

Doctrine ought to engage in a give-and-take with the world of secular thought, which rightly judges and criticizes its shortcomings and oversights. But doctrine will be of precious little service if it simply reacts and takes seriously this type of experience. It must seek to foster hope and thus enhance experience by challenging human beings to the heroism which can make what was otherwise impossible a realizable project. But this it will do if it conveys hope capable of influencing thought and choice.[4]

DOCTRINE AS CONVICTION IN A DAY OF PLURALISM

In *An Essay in Aid of a Grammar of Assent,* Newman turned his attention at one point to the fact that Roman Catholics are asked to accept doctrinal propositions so various and notional that but few can know what they are and fewer yet understand what they mean.[5] Such for him is the state of mind of multitudes of good Catholics, perhaps the majority, that having but little intellectual training they have never had the temptation to doubt and never the opportunity to be certain.[6] He did not think there were two rules of faith, one for the educated and another for the theologically uninitiated. He thought both groups shared a common faith as Catholics in the real assent both made to the church as teacher, indeed as infallible teacher. In that assent both accepted the individual teachings of that church, though some did so only implicitly, without knowing what those teachings were or without understanding what they meant. In that real assent to what is elementary, one takes upon himself or herself from the first "the whole truth of revelation, progressing from one apprehension of it to another according to his opportunities of doing so."[7]

Now it is clear that doctrine faces a very different difficulty today than that envisioned by Newman in this context. He asked how Catholics could assent to what they did not even know or understand as calling for their assent. I suspect that if he were around today, he would still find such Catholics; even the educated have at times a very definite blind spot or lacuna in their background—they are hard pressed to say accurately what their church's official doctrine really is on many issues. But the situation facing those who formulate doctrine is vastly different in this sense. There are very many Catholics who cannot and do not accept one or another church teaching while knowing well enough that it exists and what it means. It may be *Humanae Vitae* and may also be *Mater et Magistra*. Newman was talking about Catholics who did not assent explicitly because they did not know that assent was called for or understand the meaning of the teaching to which they were asked to assent. We are dealing with Catholics who know and understand both only to find they cannot assent. His problem is not the same as ours. But is it close enough that his solution may be a help to us today in asking how the church may believe, teach and confess on the basis of God's word in an age of pluralism and dissent? I think it may be.

Acceptance of the church, an acceptance accompanied by lack of assent to *some* of its teachings, is one thing. Acceptance of the church, an acceptance accompanied by dissent from *some* of its teachings, is another. This second condition describes, I think, many Christians in very different traditions. I am concentrating in this section of my paper on Roman Catholics but in no way intend thereby to imply that this phenomenon in my own church has no parallels elsewhere.

There are definite indications that Roman Catholics in this country at present are in considerable numbers not of a mind either to accept all the doctrines presented officially by their church or to dissent from them all. Indeed they want to accept and be accepted by their church despite their rejection of some of its doctrines. Would they wish the same acceptance were they to feel compelled to reject all its doctrines? I very much doubt it and think the burden of proof rests with anyone who replies in the affirmative. Let me try to be a bit more concrete.

Attitudes toward their church's traditional doctrine regarding sexuality seem to have changed notably for many American Catholics. That doctrine wins less acceptance, one learns, than the idea that it is important to provide the opportunity for a Catholic education in Catholic schools even if considerable sacrifice is involved.[8] How long this attitude toward Catholic schools will last I cannot say. But if it is there (and I confess to hoping that it is) then I think one question is very much in order. Could this willingness to regard Catholic education and indeed Catholic schools as an important value tell us something? Could it, interpreted theologically, mean these Catholics still have something of a real assent of faith that allows them to or even inclines them to want Catholic education and its institutionalization in schools despite their inability to accept some other Catholic doctrines? I think the answer may be yes. By stretching (not, I hope, to the point of breaking) what Newman held about those who did not assent to some doctrinal propositions for want of instruction or comprehension to those who withhold assent or choose to dissent despite both, I am really trying to make a case for something. I am convinced that the Catholics who withhold assent or who dissent in our day with regard to some of their church's official teachings while embracing others must not automatically be assumed to want to have their cake and eat it too. Perhaps that is the case with some but I urge care and caution before one reaches even this conclusion. Even if that were to prove to be a fact, have we any reason to think it is typical? I would have to be convinced that we do; too many signs point to the contrary.

It does not follow that dissent of any and every type from whatever teaching one may choose is compatible with living Christian faith. The same would hold, *pari passu,* for Catholics and dissent from distinctive teachings of their church. If Catholic bishops and the pope point this out, they render a service. Still can one, by genuinely wanting to be a Catholic, have the real assent of Catholic, Christian faith while finding himself or herself able to give assent to some but not all of the propositions proposed officially as doctrine by the Catholic Church? What the case would be at Vatican IV I cannot say. If Vatican III were to be held in the near future, I would urge those formulating its constitutions and decrees at least to consider a yes as a response. This is not to suggest simply a possible sprinkling of conciliar and papal holy water by way of accommodation. What I would envision would involve previous and simultaneous efforts (building on those of the present) to bring about a greater consensus as to what being a Roman Catholic Christian genuinely commits one to in terms of meaning, truth, and values. Such efforts would be called for to achieve something I regard as very important: a greater unity on the level of doctrine. They would also be a safeguard against the danger of giving the impression that an adult may be a Roman Catholic Christian without being committed to anything distinctive in terms of belief and confession.

All or nothing in terms of acceptance of traditional formulations of Catholic convictions might be one attitude those responsible for formulating doctrine in a hypothetical Vatican III might adopt. They might, on another view of the matter, not have the problem of dissent to the extent that we do today. In other words, they might not have to take a stand as to all or nothing. Yet again they might even ignore dissent as much as possible even if it were still a pressing concern and let the church with God's grace tough it out. But I should like to suggest another course of action, one that may deserve some consideration.

Participants in such a council might try to formulate doctrine in a way calculated to be faithful to our Catholic tradition and its previous formulations of doctrine. But they might do so with ecumenical sensitivity and at the same time with the conviction that fidelity would not mean their teaching would literally repeat or be reducible to past formulations on a one for one basis. Their intention might be to seek greater consensus on the level of doctrine while presuming that dissent among Catholics, as a result of such a turbulent period as ours, is not a sign of rejection of Catholic and Christian faith unless the opposite is proved. If they were to proceed in such a manner, they would not insist on all or nothing. At the same time they would be far from conveying an attitude of take-your-pick by assenting to just any of the distinctively Catholic convictions. But to bring off what I am suggesting they would have to be able to state better than we can at present what our central and essential convictions are. That points to the need for a great deal of prayer and research now whether or not there is ever to be a Vatican III. Perhaps I am mistaken in this ever-so-cautious proposal; perhaps I am urging that something be considered which is not compatible with the nature of faith and the obligations of the church's pastoral office. I think that neither is the case. My hope is that I am proposing something worthy of consideration in an effort to make church doctrine appear more readily and widely as a service to humanity and a friend of intelligence.

DOCTRINE AND ITS CONTENT

It may appear strange that I have written a paper about doctrine and paid so little attention to its content. I have referred repeatedly to believing, teaching, and confessing but not very often to *what* is believed, taught, and confessed. This may seem doubly curious in one who has urged repeatedly that a better case can and should be made than is actually being made for the distinctive meaning, truths, and values transmitted in the Roman Catholic tradition. I have indeed concentrated on method and proposed considerations that might be kept in mind by those who formulate doctrine. I hold, however, to a distinction between method and content and have not the slightest intention of ignoring the latter, though at this point I can offer at best a sketch of what I think might help. I shall refer to three areas where doctrine might express Christian meaning and truth more effectively.

The first is doctrine about God. Divine sensitivity to, appreciation of, and solidarity with human distress and suffering mightily need better expression in our teaching. Any number of theologians have sensed this need and are reacting to it. Their efforts are a genuine service to many. When doctrine about God is formulated by the church in the future, I hope this will be kept in mind. In the past our formulations have done a better job of expressing divine lordship and transcendence than the consoling divine presence in our suffering. The latter too is part of our tradition and springs from biblical symbols of great importance for us today. As one who accepts Vatican I's doctrine about God, I would hope a future council might consider speaking more directly to the grounds of protest-atheism.

As to doctrine about Christ, I suspect most would agree that the concerns expressed in what has been called nonexclusivist Christology will be with us a good while. As one who confesses to having some serious problems with a number of expressions of this Christology, I think we must in our doctrine about Jesus the Christ express His unique importance and unsurpassable dignity while at the same time not doing so at the expense of others' religious insights, aspirations, and attainments.

Were it not for a paper that will be given on ecumenism, I would mention the same concern with regard to ecclesiology, the importance of Roman Catholicism, and the Christian witness of other churches. Instead I shall conclude by saying that Vatican I had a doctrine about doctrine. Vatican III, if there is one, might do so as well. It might say many things about believing, teaching, and confessing on the basis of the word of God. But if it considered some of the qualities of doctrine that have been presented in this paper, it might reject or modify them.

But I do think it would, for having done so, be in a better position to make doctrine and the faith it attempts to express look like a friend of intelligence.

Notes

1. "Ayez confiance dans la foi, cette grande amie de l'intelligence." Cf. *Nuntii quibusdam hominum ordinibus dati,* in *Sacrosanctum Concilium Vaticanum: Constitutiones, Decreta, Declarationes,* first ed., vol. 2, p. 972. Cf. also *AAS* 58(1966): p. 12.

2. Cf. *The Christian Tradition: A History of the Development of Doctrine,* vol. 1 (Chicago: University of Chicago Press, 1971), p. 1, and vol. 2 (Chicago: University of Chicago Press, 1974), p. 5.

3. Jürgen Moltmann, *Theology of Hope* (New York: Harper & Row, 1967), p. 33.

4. "The Church—Can It Help Man Move Forward?" in *The Church and Human Society,* The Villanova University Symposium, vol. 6 (Villanova, 1975), pp. 133–57.

5. *An Essay in Aid of a Grammar of Assent* (London: Longmans, Green, 1888), p. 146.

6. Ibid., p. 211.

7. Ibid., p. 153.

8. This is at least what I have been able to draw from Andrew Greeley's *The American Catholic: A Social Portrait* (New York: Basic Books, 1977), p. 272.

PART 3

Church and Ecumenism

Giuseppe Alberigo

For a Christian Ecumenical Council

I. AN ECUMENICAL COUNCIL, NOT A NEW GENERAL CATHOLIC COUNCIL

After the first seven ecumenical councils, the successive general councils have marked, from the global Christian point of view, a sanctioning of the progressive reduction of Christianity to one of its constitutive traditions, first the Western (Constantinople IV, Lateran V), then Western-Roman, from Trent on. With Vatican I this tendency becomes so radicalized that some come to conclude that the very possibility of celebrating a council is, for Catholicism, a thing of the past.

Vatican II expresses, relative to this development, an embryonic inversion of this tendency. Indeed, although still being a general council of the Roman Catholic Church, by posing the issue of the Christian witness expressed in terms relevant to modern man, and posing the question of unity (also with the decree *Unitatis redintegratio* and with the presence of observers), the Council explicitly opens up problems that transcend the area and the strengths of individual confessional traditions and which invest the totality of contemporary Christianity.[1]

The concrete development of the work of Vatican II was only timidly consistent with this orientation, especially to the extent that the Council concentrated its attention on the ecclesiological issue, with "ecclesiocentric" deformations (cf. chap. 3 of *Lumen Gentium*), as perhaps was inevitable, given its exclusively Catholic composition.

Were the Catholic Church to celebrate a new general council, one can legitimately fear that it would constitute an occasion of regression rather than of development, to the extent that it would almost inevitably stress those aspects specific to Catholicism, with the result of widening the distance and increasing the misunderstandings relative to the other traditions. Not even the possibility of dealing with the reform of the church would reduce the risk of this negative outcome, because it would always be an internal Catholic issue, and, almost certainly, a dominantly ecclesiastical approach. Thus it is predictable that a new "Roman Catholic" council (a Vatican-III type) would not be able to develop further the profound intuitions set by John XXIII at the basis of the convocation of Vatican II. Such prophetic tendencies, in fact, were and are destined for all the Christian churches, and only in a common effort can they find sufficient development and realization.

II. RENEWAL OF THE CHRISTIAN MESSAGE AND WITNESS

The urgency of confronting the problems relative to the Christian announcement and witness among men directly involves, and in an ever more urgent manner, both Christians and churches. It is becoming ever more widely recognized that almost all the churches live more oriented toward the past than the future. Often tradition is humiliated by traditionalism, and the salvation message is reduced to repetition, characterized by a notable consistency, but without impact on the human condition. A significant symptom of this is the marginal state of eschatology in theology as well as in Christian life. Consequently, one frequently notes the overwhelming of a Christianity-in-search by the "established" form of Christianity; the certitude of faith tends to undergo a cultural and psychological process by which it is transformed into historical and social certitude, and theological reality (the definitiveness of the Father's love in Christ) shifts into human possession. Thus it becomes ever more difficult to separate the historical trimmings from the nucleus of faith, which is one of the major problems not only of the more ancient churches but also of the younger. In this respect the various Christian traditions, including the more ancient and authoritative, are finding it difficult to make significant progress alone, each enclosed in its respective autarchy, which is often lived as self-sufficiency and thus as possession to safeguard rather than as a gift to invest (cf. Matt. 25:14–30).

In this situation, the opportunity presents itself of discovering the fecundity of Christian division, which can express itself in the possibility of realizing a common search, starting from the recognition that each tradition has its own limits and, above all, every other has its limits. The various churches can help each other fraternally (being "sister" churches) to identify that which is decadent or of secondary importance, and thus also to grasp, and more fully than would be possible by any church alone, that which is essential for the faith and which should be stressed by all, so that nothing be lost of that which in every great Christian experience has been manifested of the greatness of God (cf. Acts 2:7–11).

III. FOR A GREATER CHRISTIAN UNITY IN THE COMMON FAITH

Another dimension of the Christian situation of our time is the stalled state of Christian unity, caused by the difficulty of involving common Christians in issues that go beyond ecclesiastic structures, and thus the ecumenical movement does not have significant impact on Christian witness. Thus it is urgent to consider whether such an impasse does not suggest the revising of the strategy for unity, reorientating itself directly toward the issue of the Christian message and witness to mankind, rather than that of the inter-Christian dialogue, seeking to recover or to rediscover a unity of confessed faith that can also live in imperfect and thus various and incomplete ecclesial situations (whereas a complete ecclesial unity with an insipid faith would only have a sociological and ideological significance).

Thus it would be a matter of considering the central issues of the Christian message and witness to our brethren in the context of the problems, the cultures, the sensibilities of today, and, only in a second and subordinate moment, of probing the functional problems more relevant to the Christian communities and of the church. Among these, those relative to the possession and use of economic resources by the Christian communities, and their relation to the various expressions of power in all its oppressive forms, would seem to merit a priority attention, and finally, those issues concerning ecclesial order and ecclesiological doctrine.

The hegemony that the problems relative to ministry have established would merit a rigorous analysis, which might reveal a certain dominancy of this aspect to the detriment of an "economic" prospective to Christianity, and with a limited reference to the *sensus fidei* of the church.

IV. CONCILIARITY AND ECUMENICAL COUNCIL

Traditionally and semantically, the council is a moment of unity, even if the councils of union (Lyons II, Florence, Trent) did not realize their goal; the only exception was the Council of Constance which, however, dealt with a schism internal to the West and in a moment of vacuum of the papal power. In any case, all Christians are in agreement in evaluating in an extremely positive light the services rendered to the profession of the faith by the great ecumenical councils of antiquity, and especially by the first four councils.

In recent years the World Council of Churches (Faith and Order) has developed an important reflection regarding "conciliarity" as a permanent ecclesial modality, that is, as a direct institutional expression of the dynamics of communion (*koinonia* and *sobornost*).[2] In this perspective the council, and especially the ecumenical council appears as an instance of coordination and, at the same time, of transcendence and of verification of the experiences of faith of the local communities, and not only as an ecclesiastical instance which is exceptional and, often, remote from the daily life of the churches. One cannot conclude from this, however, that the ecumenical council can be a physiological moment of assembly ratification. It has always been an occasion of verification of the faithfulness of the churches to the Gospel and, consequently, cannot cease to be a moment of tension, of more urgent searching for reform. To connect the council to a method of ordinary conciliarity in the life of the churches is certainly fruitful, but it doesn't at all imply its "normalization" or its insertion in mere ecclesiastical routine.

V. THE COUNCIL AS EPIPHANY OF THE SPIRIT

In their more fruitful moments the councils became the expression of the urgings of the Spirit to the churches so that, overcoming their own particularisms and concerns with consolidation and security, they might accept the challenge of reundertaking with faith and hope in the Lord the search for a greater evangelical fidelity to a commitment to a more intense reciprocal charity. Thus the council, instead of merely providing the occasion for the self-affirmation of one church and its historical identity (the council as "representation" of the church), should strive to be an occasion for the deepening of the relation to the Gospel in the context of the history of mankind, and thus a tension toward the purification and integration of the reality of the churches through a greater disposition for "transfiguration" (the council as "image" of the church).

In this perspective, preparation and reception of the council constitute two moments that are neither bureaucratic nor automatic, but rather two phases of the conciliar event, destined to guarantee its contact with the community (the horizontal relation), just as the actual council constitutes the moment of direct evangelical confrontation (the vertical relation), and has, moreover, an unsuppressible liturgical dimension.

The principal subject of the council can be none other than the Holy Spirit, whose invocation should constitute the center of the promotion and of the preparation of the council itself, just as the deepening of pneumatology should represent the corresponding theological endeavor.

VI. PREPARATION AND LIBERTY OF THE COUNCIL

The decision to celebrate a council unfolds by way of untypical paths, that is, by developments that cannot be thought out rationally beforehand (historically: by the initiative of the emperor, of the pope, the pressure of a heresy, of a schism, or the disposition and consensus of the church to realize the council event). In any case, the request and the preparation of a council are factors of great importance, because they manifest a desire and indicate a theme regarding which there is a convergence of the *sensus fidelium,* but they do not constitute in themselves the cause of the definitive commitment for the celebration of the council. These observations wish to underline the necessity of jealously safeguarding an effective margin of unforeseeableness regarding the council's celebration, and to guarantee the liberty of the assembly regarding its work.[3] Contrary to the past, when the threats to the council came principally from political powers, or at least from external conditionings, it seems that in our time the council's liberty might be threatened above all by the programming of the bureaucratic-ecclesiastical apparatuses, as was the threat during Vatican II.

VII. RELATION BETWEEN THE ANCIENT AND THE YOUNG CHURCHES

The constant cultural shifting of the modern world, and even more of Christianity, from a situation of Europe-centeredness and Western-centeredness to more intercontinental dimensions, with a specific development of the African and Latin American influence, constitutes the significant context for the shape and the significance of a future ecumenical council. The experience itself of political internationalism has shown that the limits of the international structures lie in their tendency to become anonymous because of the balance of opposed powers, or to become in fact transformed into an occasion of dominance by clever and unscrupulous powers. All this suggests the need of a particular attention to guarantee an effective access of the "new" churches to the preparations of the future council and, then, to the council itself. It would be short-sighted to safeguard only the representation of the various confessions, without privileging instead that of the local churches, because it is becoming ever more clear that the confessional differences are often of very reduced significance, whereas the more fecund differences and charisms are encountered rather in the variety of civilizations.[4]

VIII. TOWARD THE OVERCOMING OF CHURCH-CENTEREDNESS

Today, to assume a position favorable to a Christian ecumenical council means to commit oneself to the maturing of a new Christian season in which the Spirit asks of all the churches an exceptional openness to conversion, especially regarding the capacity to rediscover with conviction (spiritual and operative) the center of the faith in Jesus of Nazareth and in his Gospel of salvation, and to profess this to mankind in a clear witness. A witness, thus, which knows how to overcome church-centeredness in all its forms, that of the individual churches and that of the great church, that triumphalistic form (which has led many to hold that the "light of the nations" phrase which introduces the Constitution of Vatican II refers to the church and not to Christ!), as well as to that more cautious form of the *ecclesia semper reformanda*. A witness, moreover, that is centered in Jesus and in the brethren. In this perspective, the council should be an occasion and an instrument of the submission of the churches to their Lord and of service to mankind. The question must be raised whether the doctrinal contrasts which still divide Christians (the eucharist, ministry, etc.) cannot be fruitfully re-examined in the light of that which is truly non-evangelical about them in the context of a rediscovered communion in the very nucleus of the faith.

IX. FUNDAMENTAL CHARACTERISTICS OF THE COUNCIL

The promotion of an ecumenical council implies a convergence regarding some fundamental characteristics of the council itself:

1. The council is a historical structure of service and, at the same time, a sign of *koinonia,* and thus of the ordinary conciliarity of the church. The analysis of the assembly (or assemblies) of Jerusalem offers precious indications as does that of the conciliar tradition.[5]

2. Such indications, however, are not decisive, because every council is conditioned by its own historical context, and thus each assembly tended to assume its own specific shape. The (Roman Catholic) tendency to fix into a type the conciliar structure is a recent development, and has received limited consensus, even within the area of Catholic theology itself, to the extent that such a tendency is a consequence of the thesis regarding the "source" character of papal authority relative to every other authority. As is well known, Vatican II disregarded this tendency.

3. As representative but also as prophetic image of the communion of churches laboriously in search of fidelity in unity, the council should not be a projection in reduced scale of the actual state of the churches. That is, it is desirable that a council not only express the present ecclesial consciousness but also anticipate—through the impulse of the Spirit—the near future. This requires that these two aspects of the soul of the church be both present to the council.

4. The area involved in the promotion of the council should be the widest possible, avoiding, however, a counterproductive syncretism. This could be achieved by establishing a preliminary consensus regarding the venerable Nicene-Constantinople creed as objective basis of admission to the council.

5. The choice of the members of the council constitutes obviously a crucial moment. It will be important to move beyond a "parlimentarization" of the choice, that is, a proportional designation by the organs of the various churches. That would give to the council an excessively geometric character and would generate a tendency toward relationships of a predominantly diplomatic nature. The alternative would be based on the application of the sacramental criterion, particularly cherished by Catholics and Orthodox. It is clear that this approach enjoys a solid basis in the traditions of the ancient councils, synthesized in the formula *Concilium episcoporum est.* However, it is known that even within these churches, the exclusive admission of bishops to the councils has been repeatedly disregarded, and in any case is the object of studies and debates, particularly in the light of the prevalence of the communitarian element over that of the hierarchical within the churches themselves, and the stress upon the universal priesthood of the faithful. On the other hand, the particular character of each church must be respected, and it will be necessary to guarantee the possibility of the participation of each within the council with those members freely designated by each on the basis of publicly motivated criteria. At the same time, it would be important for the assembly thus composed to integrate itself through the addition of a certain number of members (about a third of the plenum?) chosen by the assembly itself, according to integrative criteria (also the drawing of lots—cf. Acts 1:26), and thus transcending the proportional balance of the confessional representations.

6. The method of procedure also (determining the arguments and order of agenda, structuring the commissions and their composition) merits careful attention, especially regarding the determination of the final will of the council. The decisions should be unanimous, according to the more accredited conciliar tradition.

It might be asked if the vote should be expressed individually or rather by groups. The more obvious solution might be to vote by denomination, but that would almost certainly have a paralyzing or at least a minimizing effect. Thus it might be more advantageous for the council to express itself according to continental (or sub-continental) groupings, in obedience to the territorial nature of the churches. In such a case the decisions would be adopted in two phases: above all, within the continental group, with individual vote (by person), and, finally, in the plenary assembly with vote by (continental) groups. In this final phase the rule would be that of unanimity.

7. The source of the authority of the council can only be Christ himself, and not delegations or ecclesial recognitions or even a self-investiture.

X. VALUE OF THE CONCILIAR DECISIONS

A problem which deserves particular attention is that of the formal value of the decisions of the council. The conciliar traditions in this regard seem univocal, indicating that the ecumenical councils have always considered their decisions binding, both for the churches present in the assembly and for those absent. In this regard the practice of the World Council of Churches to approve only recommendations to the churches must be set aside; otherwise the function itself of the council could be substantially deformed. This does not contradict the awareness that even the most solemn conciliar decisions underwent a process of assimilation that was always decisive and which led to the acceptance or rejection, in whole or in part, of the decisions themselves.[6]

XI. A COUNCIL WITHOUT HEAD?

The relationship between the pope and an eventual ecumenical council constitutes a fundamental issue, and not only for the Roman Catholic Church. It is a widespread conviction that if it were desired to clear up first this relationship in all its aspects, this would lead, today, to a paralysis of the entire initiative. It would thus be desirable that the problem be faced in substantial rather than formal terms, and that solutions be sought applying certain guaranteeing elements, in the confidence that the Spirit will yet again guide the church in finding a balanced and fecund ordering of this tension. It would be essential in this regard to assure a sufficient participation of the church of Rome and of its bishop at the council, as, indeed, also of the other great traditional patriarchs of Constantinople (Moscow), Antioch, Alexandria and

Jerusalem. It would also be important that the faith uninterruptedly professed by these churches constitute an obliged point of reference for the council and for any of its decisions. Beyond this, there should be a loyal recognition that the problem of a visible head of the council and of the church is left open and unprejudiced, in a spirit of research, of fidelity and of penance. The "headless" character should be lived as expectation and search of fullness, not as renouncement or indifference.[7]

XII. THE PREPARATION

The preparation of the council, in any case, will constitute the most immediate phase of the whole initiative, that destined to examine every problem in order to present at its conclusion a comprehensive proposal. Such a preparation should be guided by the general lines enunciated in a summary manner above (see IX). In particular, it should develop through the contribution of multi-confessional work groups, in which not only specialists but also pastors, not only ecclesiastics but also the common faithful should play their part. It might be fruitful to study the same problems by continental (and also sub-continental) groups, and also by culture groups (the Anglo-Saxon, the Latin, the Greek, the Russian-Slav, the Arab, etc.)

XIII. THE PRE-CONCILIAR ASSEMBLY

The concluding moment of the preparatory phase could be constituted by the reunion of a pre-conciliar assembly destined to examine the possibility of convoking a true ecumenical council, assuming eventually the initiative and determining the modalities of convocation.[8] The hypotheses formulated above regarding the ecumenical council could be applied also to the pre-council, regarding which the reservations which many sources might formulate regarding a true ecumenical council would not apply.

Notes

1. As a consequence of the historical role of Vatican II, the World Council of Churches has also intensified its reflection regarding councils in the last ten years; cf. *Councils and Ecumenical Movement* (Geneva, 1968).

2. The World Assembly of Uppsala (1968) formulated the conciliar perspective of the WCC, launching the idea of "conciliarity." Successively the theme was deepened in the Assembly of Louvain (1971) of Faith and Order in a resolution of the Fourth Committee: "Conciliarity and Future of the Ecumeni-

cal Movement (*Unità della chiesa e unità del genere umano* [Bologna, 1972], pp. 459–64). Consult also the comment on the resolution by K. Raiser, "Konziliarität: Die Disziplin der Gemeinschaft," *Zeitschrift für evangelische Ethik* 16 (1972): 371–76, as well as the studies of L. Vischer, "Die Kirche als konziliare Bewegung," in *Um Einheit und Heil der Menschheit*, ed. R. Nelson and W. Pannenberg (Frankfurt, 1973), pp. 235–48, and "Drawn and Held Together by the Reconciling Power of Christ," *The Ecumenical Review* 26 (1974): 166–90. The theme was reproposed in the dialogue of Salamanca (1973) (*What Kind of Unity?* [Geneva, 1974]), and finally an important contribution of J. Deschner was presented at the Assembly of Nairobi (1975): "L'unità visibile, comunità conciliare" (*Il Regno documenti* 21 [1976]: 76–79), the substance of which is repeated in section II: "Le esigenze dell'unità" (ibid., pp. 152–56).

3. Regarding the eventuality of an ecumenical council soon, see L. Vischer, "Christian Councils: Instruments of Ecclesial Communion," *The Ecumenical Review* 24 (1972): 72–78, and ". . . ein wirklich universales Konzil," in *Ökumenische Skizzen* (Frankfurt, 1972), pp. 234–44; and successively the study promoted by Faith and Order, "Councils, Conciliarity and a Genuinely Universal Council," *Study Encounter* 10 (1974), 24 pp., and the study of H. Mühlen, *Morgen wird Einheit sein. Das kommende Konzil aller Christen: Ziel der getrennten Kirchen* (Paderborn 1974).

4. On this point cf. Mühlen, *Morgen*, who, regarding the orientation of the WCC, is of a different opinion and proposes only confessional representation, and in general proposes as reference point the model of the Council of Union of Florence, without taking into consideration the fact that today Christian churches and cultures are not co-extensive, as in the fifteenth century.

5. One of the most recent contributions to the theology of the council is that of Pierre L'Huiller, "Le concile oecuménique comme autorité suprême de l'église," *Analekta* 24 (1975): 78–102.

6. Regarding reception, one can consult the studies of A. Grillmeier, "Konzil und Rezeption," *Theologie und Philosophie* 45 (1970): 321–52, and of Y. Congar, "La 'reception' comme réalité ecclésiologique," *Revue des sciences philosophiques et theologiques* 56 (1972): 369–403 (English translation: "Reception as an Ecclesiological Reality," in *Election and Consensus in the Church, Concilium* 77, ed. Alberigo/Weiler, pp. 43–68), and the article of W. Hryniewicz, "Die ecclesiale Rezeption in der Sicht der orthodoxen Theologie," *Theologie und Glaube* 65 (1975): 242–66.

7. This problem is bound up with the issue of the next pontificates and of their relative programs; cf. regarding this G. Alberigo, "Rinnovamento ecclesiale e servizio papale alla fine del XX secolo," *Concilium* 8 (1975), ed. G. Alberigo and W. Kasper.

8. J.-J. von Allmen ("Ministère papal—ministère d'unité," *Concilium* 8 [1975]: 131–38) has advanced the hope that the next pope will undertake the initiative of an ecumenical pre-council. Also, the churches of Eastern Orthodoxy have held in 1976 a panorthodox pre-conciliar conference (Geneva, November 21–28; cf. *Episkepsis*, 1976, pp. 158–69) in preparation for the panorthodox Council; regarding which cf. "Saint et Grande Concile de l'Eglise: Propositions de la Commission préparatoire," *Contacts*, 1972 80 bis.

Hans Küng

Vatican III: Problems and Opportunities for the Future

PREFACE: THE SITUATION

From Vatican II the ecumenical movement received a strong impulse. Across the board, Catholic theology began to tackle the important ecumenical issues. Catholic authorities entered into wide and various contacts with other churches and ecumenical organizations, and the newly founded Roman Secretariate for Church Unity developed under Cardinal Bea into a powerful source of ecumenical expectations. Catholics got to know the Christians of other denominations and learned to appreciate their heritages.

In recent years, however, powerful counter-forces have brought the ecumenical movement both within and without the Catholic Church to a *standstill.* The sources of this situation are to be found, in diverse measure, in the inflexibility of many church leaderships, especially that of Rome, in tensions within the World Council of Churches, and in a strong reactionary polarization of the grass roots of many churches and nations. All this has led to intense disappointments. Most Christians today no longer understand the confessional differences between the Orthodox churches, the Catholic Church and the churches of the Ref-

This discussion paper is based on theoretical and practical insights, experiences and convictions, which have emerged in the course of long years of work and discussion in the Institute for Ecumenical Research of the University of Tübingen. In particular I wish to extend my thanks to Akad. Rat Dr. Hermann Häring for his assistance in preparing this systematic statement. As a complement to this statement, I should like to recommend the paper "A Declaration against Resignation in the Church," which we prepared in Tübingen some time ago.—H.K.

ormation; they find the practices cementing the separation (the obstacles hindering mixed marriage, intercommunion, unwillingness to act in cooperation with each other) absurd. The danger of an ecclesiastical homelessness becomes acute. Many Christians are saying: "Jesus, yes; the church, no!"

At the same time the progress of ecumenical discussion has reached a *critical stage*. Many issues, in particular the decisive classical controversial points of church teaching and discipline, are viewed by numerous theologians and laymen as having been resolved. The Faith and Order Commission, in any case, has come to the end of its list of traditional controversial points requiring discussion. Steadily increasing is the pressure on church authorities to take the decisions necessary in order that the present phase of ecumenical conversation and loose contact may come to its natural term in a phase of reciprocal recognition and unification. At this point the demand for intensified study appears as a mere palliative; the diplomatic exchanges seem like meaningless acceleration while idling; the multiplication of commissions at all levels like a smoke screen to cover up the results already achieved; the evocation of conservative forces within the church and the allergic reactions of the grass roots sound to many like a subterfuge to avoid doing what now has to be done.

In this matter, the *situation* of the Catholic Church is not fundamentally different from that of the other churches. There, too, one feels oneself blocked by the unrest in one's own ranks. Many a bearer of highest authority in the church has moulted from a promoter of ecumenism into a defender of confessional territory. All this, it must be noted, is the obverse of the intensive efforts of the Faith and Order Commission in recent years to push forward, under the label of "conciliarity," from the phase of theological clarification into that of binding decisions.

Geneva, however, can only succeed when Rome cooperates. Rome, however, will only act when the pressure of ecumenical awareness in the universal church remains intense and massive expectations are continually brought to bear on her. In order that the situation of those responsible, however, not deteriorate further, it is necessary to develop a comprehensive strategy.

Two questions must be posed: (I) What successes have ecumenical theology and practice already achieved? (II) Which tasks can be expected to be achieved in the coming years?

I. THE BALANCE OF ECUMENICAL SUCCESSES

The Catholic public today is in danger of forgetting the theological and practical successes of the past decade. These must be brought back into public awareness. In this way, those responsible for decision making in the church can be confronted once again with the state of theological research and of ecumenical practice.

1. Classical Points of Controversy

a. Scripture and Tradition: In the definition of the relationship between Scripture and Tradition, no irreconcilable differences of opinion exist today. The primacy of Scripture over all later Tradition is, in principle, recognized today even within the Catholic Church. On the other hand, the other churches recognize today that de facto their own traditions also possess considerable force in guiding the thinking and research of their members. The fact that in the Catholic sphere the binding character and concrete functioning of particularly significant traditions—conciliar decisions, for example—has not yet been fully discussed offers the other churches an opportunity to put their questions to us with all desirable clarity. For the Catholic Church, however, this is an opportunity to correct one-sided accents.

b. Grace and Justification: The relationship between faith and works stood for centuries as the central and decisive controversial topic between the Catholic Church and the churches of the Reformation. Today consensus among the churches on this point is the furthest advanced of all. Contemporary discussions of this topic are almost everywhere conducted interconfessionally. The major historical contributors to this topic (Paul, Augustine, Thomas Aquinas, Luther, Calvin, Karl Barth) and the impulses coming from contemporary theology can no longer be reckoned as the exclusive property of this or that confession. This is the clearest indication that world-wide theological reflection on this point has entered into a post-ecumenical phase.

c. Church and Sacraments: No unbridgeable opposition exists today in issues such as the church's fundamental form, its origin, its various dimensions and tasks, its eschatological character and its vocation to continual renewal. Scripture is acknowledged generally to be the normative basis for ecclesiology. The ecumenical consensus reaches in fact well into the complex issues of church office.

In the area of sacramental theology, the basic differences have been settled, namely, the relationship between Word and Sacrament and the origin, number and effect of the sacraments. This holds, at least in principle, also for the issue of the Eucharist, to which we shall return shortly.

Many theologians and churches see the decisive difficulties in the way of ecumenical consensus no longer in the issues concerning the nature of church office and of the Eucharist, but rather alone in the questions of who possesses the true office and who is able to celebrate a valid Eucharist. This shows how much the neuralgic point of ecumenism has shifted from the theoretical questions of theology to the practical attitudes of church authorities. The divisive differences have been resolved and the remaining differences are no longer divisive. Ecumenism is now primarily a question of the practical consequences, and it poses itself in particular as an enquiry into those churches that claim alone to possess the true church office.

2. Consensus Documents, Official and Unofficial

A whole series of important papers and documents worked out in bilateral or multilateral discussion deserve to be analyzed, underlined and brought into public awareness within the Catholic Church. These papers reveal an astonishingly high measure of agreement or at least convergence among the participating churches. Particularly significant are the documents concerning the questions of Eucharist and church office and the various plans for church union.

a. Consensus papers dealing with the Eucharist: There is space only to mention the most important documents. A *first group* of documents present themselves as *comprehensive consensus declarations* and illuminate the Eucharist from various points of view. They succeed in finding a new, biblically oriented language, which is no longer stamped by the controversial issues of the Reformation. Among these are:

1. The *Louvain* paper of 1971 issued by the Commission on Faith and Order: "The Eucharist in Ecumenical Thought."
2. The *Dombes* report on Office and Eucharist, 1973, issued by representatives of the Lutheran, Reformed and Roman Catholic churches in France.
3. The paper "Für ein gemeinsames eucharistisches Zeugnis der Kirchen" issued in 1973 by the Protestant/Roman Catholic study commission in *Switzerland* (nos. 41–55).
4. The corresponding sections of the *COCU* Union Plan for the U.S.A.
5. The relevant sections of the report on the Eucharist prepared by the joint study group of the Australian Council of Churches and the Catholic Episcopal Conference in *Australia*.
6. The declaration of the Orthodox/Roman Catholic Theological Commission in the *U.S.A.* concerning the Eucharist.

The first three documents are closely related in structure and content. In them, it would appear, a new ecumenical way of speaking is taking form under the inspiration of the Louvain declaration.

A *second group* of documents is primarily concerned with *individual points of controversy*. The convergences achieved here reveal deep agreement in the objective intention; the remaining differences are matters of accentuation or concern secondary though serious issues, which of themselves would no longer justify division. To this group belong:

7. The common declaration on the teaching concerning the Eucharist issued in 1971 by the Anglican/Roman Catholic International Commission *(Windsor Declaration)*.
8. The paper of the *Swiss* discussion group (cf. document 3, nos. 56–71).
9. The report of the conversations authorized by the *Lambeth* Conference and the *Lutheran* World Federation, 1970–72.
10. "The Eucharist," declaration of the joint study committee of the National Council of Churches and the Roman Catholic Church in *New Zealand*.
11. The final report of the Catholic/Lutheran Conversation in the *U.S.A.:* "The Eucharist," 1967.
12. The 1970 position paper of the Anglican/Roman Catholic Commission in the *U.S.A.* regarding the doctrine of eucharistic sacrifice and the role of the priesthood in the Eucharist.
13. The corresponding passages in the final report of the international Catholic/Lutheran Study Commission "The Gospel and the Church" (*Malta* Report, 1972).
14. The pertinent explanations of the *Leuenberger Konkordie*.

A *third group* of numerous documents deals with the *concrete regulations and possibilities* of intercommunion and eucharistic hospitality. Among these the following deserve particular mention:

15. The 1971 study "Intercommunion or Community?" of the Faith and Order Commission.
16. The 1972 directives for the faithful of the diocese of Strasbourg regarding eucharistic hospitality in mixed marriages.
17. The 1973 position paper of the Institute of the Lutheran World Federation for Ecumenical Research, Strasbourg, on the question of Lutheran-Catholic communion in the Lord's Supper.

The sum of these documents offers impressive testimony to the degree to which confessional differences in the teaching and practice of the Eucharist no longer constitute church-dividing obstacles. In particular, they make clear that the churches today can no longer evade the issue of eucharistic hospitality or intercommunion.

b. Consensus documents regarding Church Office: In view of the well-known difficulties here, joint documents dealing with the question of church office are less numerous than others. Nevertheless the matter has been dealt with in the following documents:

18. The paper worked out by the Faith and Order Commission in *Marseilles,* 1972, "The Ordained Office in Ecumenical Perspective."
19. The *Dombes* report on Office and Eucharist (cf. document 2).
20. The paper of the *Swiss* discussion group (cf. document 3).
21. The *Malta* report (cf. document 13).
22. The final report of the Catholic/Lutheran Discussion in the *U.S.A.* "Eucharist and Office," 1970.
23. "Reform und Anerkennung kirchlicher Ämter," the Memorandum of the joint study group of university ecumenical institutes in *Germany,* 1973.

Difficult as the conversations between the Catholic Church and the other churches in this matter may be, a *clear convergence* of position in these documents becomes apparent: no fundamental difficulties appear to stand in the way today of a common understanding of church office. The point of departure is the general agreement (1) that the officeholder as a rule is called to his office by ordination; (2) that he receives a special function in the apostolic succession of the church; (3) that the office of proclaiming the Word of God is the primary power entrusted him; (4) that the presidency of the eucharistic celebration belongs to the powers entrusted him. In this connection, one notes in all the documents the tendency to disengage as far as possible the question of the Eucharist from that of church office and to revalue the role of the whole people of God in the liturgical celebration.

New *developments* have brought the problematic on the Catholic side into motion again. We have begun to take seriously the exegetical and historical data regarding the origin and development of the church's offices (U.S.A., Malta, German Memorandum) and to give due regard to the charismatic dimension of the church. One is prepared to admit that at least in cases of necessity the presbyteral and episcopal succession can be bypassed (Malta, Memorandum). These positions go hand in hand with a relativizing of the traditional Catholic theory of apostolic succession (Malta, U.S.A., Memorandum). That the authorities in the Catholic Church put up massive resistance to this trend is also well known.

The further development of ecumenism is thus stalled on the issue of *mutual recognition* of church office. The Malta report pleads "that the Roman Catholic Church seriously weigh the matter of recognition of the Lutheran ministry." Dombes proposes a concrete strategy for the achievement of mutual recognition. In the U.S.A., the demand has been raised to recognize the Lutheran ministry. The Memorandum holds mutual recognition to be required for theological reasons. The church's leadership is thus presented by the theologians with a serious responsibility to which it must respond.

c. Plans of union: Astonishingly frequent are the negotiations dealing with church-union in the classical sense of the term, which until now have been conducted exclusively at the regional or national level. At present, there are approximately forty such negotiations going on in the world as a whole; roughly ten each in Africa, Asia and Europe, six in North America and the rest in Latin America. In only a few cases is the goal a mere federation. Roughly ten negotiations involve parties of the same confessional tradition; six or so are confined to the general Protestant spectrum; and in more than twenty cases the Anglicans are also involved.

It is objectively difficult and here not to the point to give an up-to-date survey of the present state of these negotiations. The Faith and Order Commission undertakes this task in its biannual reports. Two plans in particular however deserve special mention:

24. The "Plan of Union of the Church of Christ Uniting" remitted for study to the ten participating denominations in 1970.
25. The plan of union of the Church of North India.

Despite spectacular failures, at the moment more than two-thirds of these negotiations must be judged positively. Even the COCU, after a depressing phase of dampened enthusiasm, seems to be awakening to new life. Precisely the COCU example makes clear that the real obstacles to union lie not on the level of theological differences and not necessarily on the highest levels of church leadership, but rather in the middle levels of decision making ("middle judicatory structures"). There the rival characteristics of denominational identity are most strongly developed and present the most difficult obstacles to be overcome. It is significant that the Catholic Church has not participated in any of these negotiations with a direct commitment to the declared goal of union. Though this hands-off attitude is explicable in terms of traditional Catholic ecclesiology, it places the Catholic Church in a position of grave responsibility.

3. Topics Ripe for Discussion

The more the problems of the Eucharist (intercommunion) and of church office generally (and of the episcopal office in particular) are cleared away, so much the more do the issues come to concentrate on the *particular form of office* and the concrete practice of *ecclesiastical authority* in the Catholic Church. Especially coming into focus are the issues of the exercise of ecclesiastical authority, the Petrine ministry and the infallibility question.

a. Authority and the Church: This question has long been bracketed out of ecumenical discussions, because, by reason of its formal character, it is involved in all aspects of church doctrine and discipline. Now, however, the time has come to attack this matter directly. Last year the Faith and Order Commission took the initiative in this direction. In the same year, the joint Anglican/Roman Catholic discussion groups prepared its report on "Authority in the Church," in which both parties were able to achieve essential agreement extending even to the matter of a universal papal primacy.

b. The Petrine Office: Although the Anglican side was in principle prepared to accept a universal primacy under well-defined conditions, numerous general details of such a primacy naturally remain yet to be dealt with. Anyone familiar with the abundant discussion of recent years can see that other churches as well would be prepared to discuss seriously a papacy conceived in the true sense of a primacy in service and exercising in the church universal the pastoral role of Peter. Where reservations appear, it is inevitably in connection with the concrete (juridical) form assumed by the papacy over the centuries.

c. Infallibility: The papal claim to infallibility still remains the central and most difficult obstacle to all union-efforts with the Roman Catholic Church. In varying degrees, this holds as well for the infallibility claimed for the councils, especially those of the Middle Ages and the modern period. This whole complex must now be dealt with. It is necessary to test new solutions as the Anglican/Catholic Commission has done with its proposal to take the indefectibility of the church in the truth of the Gospel as the starting point for a solution.

4. Reforms in the Catholic Church

Just as important as these theological successes are the practical matters of church reform. Since Vatican II, the Catholic Church has made its own, important intentions of the Reformation. Among these are the following:

a. A new emphasis on the Scriptures: One of the most decisive achievements of Vatican II is the new emphasis on Scripture in theology, in the liturgy and in church life. The Latin Vulgate has been replaced by modern translations from the original text. A new three-year readings cycle for the Sunday liturgy has opened up the Scripture for the ordinary Catholic. Across the board, notable efforts are being made to reshape teaching and preaching in the spirit of Scripture, and to re-evaluate the wealth of Catholic tradition in its light. Biblical perspectives provide the coordinates of the new theology taking form today.

b. Genuine popular liturgy: The liturgy is almost everywhere celebrated in the vernacular so that all attending can take active part in it. The new rites for the sacraments have gained immensely in simplicity and intelligibility. The character of the Eucharist as a community meal has come once again to the fore, and traditional controversial issues, such as the vernacular, the chalice for the laity and concelebration, have been settled at least in principle.

c. Revaluation of the laity: Already the popularization of the liturgy meant a major step in this direction. Further elements of this development are the growing self-awareness of the laity, and the increasing interest in active participation in the most diverse areas of church life. Consultatory and, in some measure, even decision-making representative organs on the local and regional level have come into being.

d. National adaptation of the church: Growing awareness of the particular churches (parish, diocese, nation) within the universal church presses for realization. National episcopal conferences are in a position to carry forward the urgently needed practical decentralization of the church.

e. Reform of popular piety: Reform of the fasting regulations, of indulgences and devotions, a paring back of the rank growths in Marian piety are but a few examples. A new attraction to the Bible, meditation and the original forms of Christian devotion, together with a growing awareness of human and social needs, are the hallmarks of contemporary piety.

5. Effects on the Life of the Congregation

In all four areas, however, the balance of success remains problematical. For the day-to-day life of the church is determined neither by theoretical programs nor by official reform regulations. What has been the real effect of all these developments on the life of the congregations within the Catholic Church?

a. The ambivalent situation: The experience of the past years shows a mixed balance in respect to the reform of church life and the realization of ecumenical convergence. The new theology and the new liturgy, the new concentration on Scripture and the new emphasis on ecumenical cooperation have evoked powerful negative as well as positive reactions. And even those who welcome the changes have experienced mixed results, both for themselves and for their congregations.

Many congregation members approve or disapprove of ecumenical activities without understanding or appreciation of the objective reasoning underlying them. A sober discussion of the issues is virtually impossible to achieve. Instinctively, the participants in such discussion take their positions *pro* or *contra;* reasoned argument becomes mired down in a morass of emotion. Often it becomes apparent that no effort has ever been made to communicate the reasons behind the reforms to the ordinary members of the congregation. Thus all too many Catholics have responded half heartedly to the reforms, unable or unwilling to identify themselves with either the old or the new order. This ambivalence raises a question for the leadership of the Catholic Church. It is the leaders of the church who, in the first place, have reacted ambivalently. They were not prepared to accept the compromise character of so many conciliar documents or to admit the intentional unclarity of many an overly cautious or diplomatically formulated passage in them. They sought to evade giving clear answers to the well-founded demands of the other churches—an attitude which unfortunately is also to be found in the leadership of the other churches, when they are confronted with the well-founded concerns of the Catholic side.

b. The polarization of congregations: In many lands, in the Catholic as well as in the other churches, a growing division between "conservative" and "progressive" factions is apparent. This is not the place to analyze the complex motives behind this phenomenon. In any case, the lack of convincing leadership on the part of the papacy and the episcopate has been a major contributing factor. The emotional loss of confidence that many Catholics experienced in the wake of the recent reforms has been accentuated by the ecumenical experience of alternative forms of Christian teaching and piety. In this way the ecumene has served as a catalyzing factor in the polarization process, and it is understandable that many bishops and pastors, confusing the external catalyst with the active agents within the Catholic Church itself, have sought to obstruct ecumenical influences. Nevertheless, this is a shortsighted reaction, which overlooks the real sources of the malaise. Polarization is only a symptom of the spiritual vacuum into which the official church has slid in the course of gradual stagnation during the past years. In this way, the blame for the deteriorating situation is not placed where it belongs, but instead is pushed off onto ecumenism.

c. Ecumenical specialization: Under the circumstances, the ecumenical movement has lost its attraction for many Catholic Christians. One group is afraid of compromising dogmatic orthodoxy and so opposes ecumenism as a threat to faith; others, frustrated by the absence of concrete progress, either abandon ecumenism to pursue other interests, or else take the resolution of the most pressing personal problems (mixed marriage, religious upbringing, ethics) into their own hands. The church's leadership, meanwhile, keeps postponing decisive action with the excuse that so many complex problems of detail have yet to be worked out. In this way, the ecumenical movement is losing the dynamism which only grass-roots interest can insure, and it shrivels down to a mere job for specialized theological puzzle-solvers, whose abstruse arguments have little or nothing to say to the ordinary Christian. The danger of such an ecumenical specialization can hardly be ignored.

d. The new ecumenical practice: In congregations in many lands, a new ecumenical practice has tacitly come into being, a practice which has little or no relation to the prevailing official norms. Understandably this development is difficult to analyze. Its forms are manifold; numbers and facts are difficult to come by. Such a practice can only develop in areas outside official recognition; this, however, is the reason why it is so often ignored or condemned. Many Christians no longer see the division of the churches exclusively as a scandal. From repeated positive experiences, they have learned to see that, together with the other Christians, all worship one and the same God and acknowledge one and the same Savior Jesus Christ; in consequence, they see themselves and the others as all belonging to one community of the baptized, in which all share the same Spirit, the same faith, the same action and the same Eucharist. This new grass-roots ecumenism is a source of great hope; at the same time, however, the dangers latent therein are manifest. If the authorities of the church do not succeed in integrating these ecumenical impulses into the church's official life, they stand in danger, and not only of simply losing the initiative. The longer this situation persists, the more difficult it becomes to integrate such attitudes at the grass-roots level into a union of churches on the institutional level.

6. *The Consequences*

a. The ecumenical movement is now ripe for *concrete action:* in terms both of the unity of the church and of the truth of the faith, it would be irresponsible further to evade the results of so much theological effort and to ignore the reasonable expectations of so many Christians.

b. The *Catholic Church* in particular must acknowledge that it bears a special responsibility for clearing away the sources of ecumenical conflict. It is the specific positions of the Catholic Church which in a qualitative way have done so much to deepen the divisions of the churches. The problems of ecclesiastical teaching and disciplinary authority, of an absolute jurisdictional primacy and infallibility of the pope constitute first-order obstacles to further ecumenical progress.

Every effort, therefore, must be made to bring the results of exegetical and historical-theological research to bear on the prevailing dogmatic positions. Where corrections are in order, these must be undertaken. At the very least, a cooperative relationship to the other churches must become a heuristic principle of Catholic theology and ecclesiastical practice.

c. The leadership of *all the churches* can inspire little confidence so long as it does not show itself ready and able to put into practice the results of ecumenical theological labor. Among the matters calling for such realization are the mutual recognition of ministries, the extension of eucharistic hospitality, and the establishment ultimately of full eucharistic communion. The recognition of a universal ministerial primacy would be much easier to achieve were the Catholic Church prepared to reform both the concrete forms and the theoretical foundations of the papacy in the directions already indicated by various constructive proposals now existing. Further reforms of the Catholic Church would more quickly achieve their goal, if they could be worked out in cooperation with the other churches and then consistently carried out on the congregational level. Not the perfection of the particular forms of a single denomination but rather the search for a common form for a truly ecumenical church must be the guiding intention of such efforts.

d. With a convincing *spiritual leadership,* the church authorities would be in a better position to blunt the forces of polarization in our churches and so to remove one of the most serious obstacles to the future of ecumenism. Nevertheless, it must not be forgotten that the Spirit also moves down at the grass roots. If the new practical ecumenism on this level is officially repressed or driven out of the churches, the spiritual damages for a long time to come will be irreparable.

II. THE BALANCE OF ECUMENICAL NEEDS

All successes of the ecumene notwithstanding, we have still not achieved a truly ecumenical organization for ecumenical work. Our labors are far more centered on working over our divided confessional past than in working out the future of the coming united church! We are more concerned with preserving continuity with our past traditions— obviously something not to be neglected—than with discovering the new implications of our present ecumenical experience! Thus ecumenical theology stands in danger of falling back into an idyllic, confessionally specialized provincial theology, out of touch with contemporary reality. Against this trend we must consciously take our stand. How can we do this?

There are: (1) inner-Catholic problems, which must be settled by the Catholic Church on its own; (2) interconfessional tasks, which can only be fulfilled by the concerted action of the churches working together; (3) common goals, in realization of which all the churches must grow together namely the problems of the world at large and of contemporary men and women with all their questions, difficulties and expectations. To understand and to respond to such problems the churches must learn to think and act and live as the one Church of Christ.

1. Inner-Catholic Tasks

a. Theoretical and practical coming-to-grips with the past

Theoretical: For centuries, the Catholic Church has shown itself in principle opposed to the ecumene. With an attitude of sovereignty and superiority ecclesiastical authorities determined matters of teaching and discipline without any serious efforts to hear the views of those affected. The Catholic Church acted on the supposition that it alone was the true Church of Christ, that it enjoyed full possession of the truth and full competence for sovereign decision making. Having defined itself solely in terms of the divine authority entrusted it, rather than in terms of the community of believers, and having absolutized the position of the hierarchy and the papacy, the Catholic Church was incapable of recognizing dissident individuals and churches as serious discussion partners in matters of fundamental importance.

The consequences: The Catholic Church cannot become ecumenical simply by loud proclamations of good intentions. It can become ecumenical only to the extent that it learns to adopt new attitudes in its dealings with those both within and without the church. It must find place for public opinion within its ranks; it must develop a feeling for dialogue and for vigorous, passionate discussion; it must learn to take seriously both Catholics and non-Catholics, individuals as well as churches as partners in dialogue. To this end, we need intensified theological and sociological study, not only of the existing communication structures of the Catholic Church but also of possible alternatives. The time has come to replace the structures of command and prohibition by those of consensus, structures of power-monopoly and official secrecy by those of community and frankness.

Practical: For centuries, the Catholic Church has been guilty of dealing badly with the other churches. Looking back on the events of the past, the Catholic Church itself has had to admit that the style in which its representatives acted was often shameful.

The consequences: It is time to withdraw all the excommunications issued against the Reformers and other Christians, who, in opposition to the hierarchy, sought to call attention to important neglected aspects of the Gospel. It is time as well to draw at last the practical consequences from the withdrawal of the excommunications against the Orthodox churches.

The Catholic Church must undertake self-criticism of the anti-ecumenical attitudes it assumed as a reaction to past criticism. Thus the development of the absolutistic concept of the papacy in the West is, in part at least, a reaction to the critique exercised by the patriarchal churches of the East. The often one-sided and premature decisions of Trent were the reaction to the critique of the churches of the Reformation. The solemn declarations of the doctrines of papal primacy and infallibility, as well as of Mary's immaculate conception and bodily assumption, were the conscious reaction to the convictions of the other churches and of extensive inner-Catholic opposition.

Naturally we cannot simply turn back the clock. What we can do, however, is to admit that certain developments were exaggerated and that they were governed by motives which were not always of Christian inspiration. In particular, we must learn to distinguish between the evangelical intention—what John XXIII called the substance of faith—and its often dubious modes of expression and initial interpretation.

Above all it is important that we analyze the manner in which the church has habitually dealt with dissidents and so-called heretics. We must learn to recognize the unworthy traditions of inquisition, defamation and ban which thus established themselves in the Catholic Church. Such studies could help us attain the needed critical distance from our past and so free us to seek pardon for the injustice we have done others in the course of our history. The abolition of the inquisitorial practices still operating in secret both in Rome and in many a diocese, where theologians, pastors and laymen are involved, would be a major step in the direction of a better future.

b. The reform of our own organizational structures

The past fifteen years have shown that the Catholic Church is unable to come to grips, within her present organizational structures, not only with the broader challenges of our times but also with the diverse needs of the church on the local, regional and universal levels. On the one hand, the church is called upon to preserve her unity and to strengthen the universal ministry of the pope and the regional ministry of the bishops; on the other hand, it must find place for the diversity of the various nations, cultures, political and social situations. The church must find structures which will render it more flexible and better able to make decisions, and which will better fit it to respond to the demands of particular places and times. In recent years, the following demands have been repeatedly raised:

—the consistent, uniform enforcement of a retirement age for pope
and bishops;

—periodic re-election, at least of the bishops;

—election of all important decision-making officials by electoral col-
leges of men and women truly representative of the affected congregations, regions (dioceses) or universal church;

—strengthening of the synodal principle on all levels, the establishment of national synods, meeting regularly, which would bear full
responsibility for determining their own agenda and enjoy full
power for decision;

—the establishment of a representative synod of bishops, not simply
as a mere facultative body for consultation but as an institution
resting on the episcopal power of order and thus capable of taking
initiative, of deciding in concert with the pope, and of exercising a
fraternal control on the exercise of papal power;

—re-organization of the parish and congregational structures in order
to make room for unreserved lay collaboration in all the activities
of the local church;

—declericalization of the apostolate, abolition of compulsory celibacy, and equal rights for women in church life and office.

These demands are all adequately founded in the relevant theological
literature. Should they appear revolutionary to anyone, let him recall
that corresponding demands have long since found realization in other
areas of public life, and that, for most other churches, they represent
self-evident postulates long overdue in their realization. Above all, let
him take notice that these demands in no way whatsoever compromise
the true catholicity and unity of the church; on the contrary, they are
the necessary means for rendering these attributes more visible and
effective.

  c. An ecumenical concept

  Since the Second Vatican Council, the Catholic Church has not only
entered in relations with the World Council of Churches, but also has
opened up bilateral contacts with many individual churches and confessional federations. Nevertheless the documented results of such
contacts reveal the absence of a consistent policy in this regard. Evidently the Catholic Church has yet to formulate a *single unified concept*
of its ecumenical future.

  On the world level, the Catholic Church must—generally
speaking—seek a place between the churches of the Reformation and
the churches of the East. Hers is the opportunity to serve as the
mediatory bond between these so divergent traditions. At the moment,
however, she stands in danger of raising new barriers between these
traditions, without being aware of the full implications of her attitudes.

In this connection, the Catholic Church must clearly think out her tactical position: she can seek ecumenical union according to the historical order of the divisions; she can pursue individual unions by way of simultaneous, bilateral conversations with as many churches as possible; she can concentrate her efforts on the World Council of Churches. Each of these tactics has its specific advantages and disadvantages. Presumably the best course is a *combination of several ways* at once. A union with the Anglican Church, for example, could be pursued most intensively, and simultaneously every effort be made to make use of the opportunities for Catholic/Orthodox dialogue. At the same time, however, we have the obligation to enter into binding negotiation with the Protestant churches and to coordinate the efforts of all such conversations with each other.

Furthermore the Catholic Church must attempt to coordinate the ecumenical conversations and negotiations on all the levels involved, universal, regional and local, taking account of the unofficial initiatives as well as of the official, institutional contacts. This will only be possible when the higher levels are prepared to incorporate the impulses coming from the lower levels and to proceed in accordance with the principle of solidarity in the course of theological and organizational negotiation. All available experience with church union indicates clearly that only those proposals have a real future, which find root in the lower levels of the church. Obviously this by no means excludes the role of a genuine spiritual leadership, prepared to give responsible reasons for its decisions and concerned to achieve unanimity by consensus rather than uniformity by outward conformity. Neither does it exclude upper-level discussions designed to solve the outstanding issues.

Included in this concept is the idea of a model framework for an eventual church union: such a *model of conciliar union* is not only the object of intensive World Council efforts since the foundation of this body; it is also a model incorporating genuine Catholic tradition. It is time to seize the opportunity. We are the ones who are indebted to the other churches; we have an obligation to make clear to them, at long last, how we expect our relationships to them to take shape in the future. Only then will they be in a position to speak to the point with us, to enter into serious negotiations and to formulate a plan of union.

2. Interconfessional Tasks

The ecumenical experiences of the last years have shown that all the churches are confronted with similar difficulties when they undertake serious attempts at reform. Evidently all are subject to the same dynamic laws which slow progress and obstruct the achievement of the common goal. Now is the time to become aware of these resistance factors and to develop strategies for overcoming them.

a. Tradition and confession-building

The churches are not only marked by the confessions and traditions which have found official, normative recognition within them, and which, as a rule at least, are subjected to a continual process of critical review and development. In practice, unconscious traditions, manners of speaking and thinking, and the day-to-day forms of piety play a decisive role in forming the life of a church. They stamp the life of the individual members and of the congregations and can serve as a severe obstacle to the union of separated churches. It is therefore absolutely essential to begin as early as possible to reduce such unconscious, emotionally charged factors working against union on the middle and lowest levels of the church; this is a task for official action of the church.

The churches should begin now to establish common study projects aimed at dealing with the cultural, sociological and psychological factors which have given rise to such traditions and which have so stamped the identity of the different churches in different lands. Possibilities must be found to bring into the open the operation of such tradition-building and divergence, to confront them critically with the original message of the faith, and so either to overcome them or to put them into the service of an ecumenical future. It hardly needs to be said here that such study projects need to be adapted to regional and national diversities.

b. Church communication and decision making

All the churches are compelled today to reconsider the processes of internal communication, the quality of their internal opinion making, and the paths of decision making. From this critical reconsideration arises the need for correctives and in many cases fundamental reforms. In such a revision, sociological and religious-sociological factors are not the only aspects to be considered. Scripture and the genuine Christian tradition offer criteria which must be respected: variety within all due unity; the priesthood of all the faithful alongside the special office of ministry; the indispensible role of the local church alongside the structures of the universal church; the right of the charismatic and the prophet to be heard alongside the official minister; above all, the obligation of all to listen to each other and to the Word of God.

Because the ecclesiastical authorities are often helpless, too ill-informed, too anxious and overloaded with other tasks, we need special interconfessional study groups to deal with these matters. Theirs is the task of analyzing and comparing the communication processes of the churches, of providing for the exchange of information and of developing models for an undistorted communication, a free public opinion and a balanced process of decision making. We need models for resolving conflicts and for obtaining consensus, models which can support the congregational, interdenominational and ecumenical exchange on all levels and prevent these from being lamed or broken off. It is imperative to find answers in keeping with the modern sense of justice and inspired by the principles of humanity and the Christian message—answers to the specific problems of our times (factions in the church, lobbying for particular projects and points of view, procedures in doctrinal conflicts, cooperation with governmental and social institutions, the use of the media and communications technology, organizational and administrative technology).

c. Trans-confessional currents

Among the most astonishing experiences of recent years is the phenomenon of trans-confessional currents, either running parallel in all the churches or running through all the churches without regard for denominational boundaries. Examples of such currents in Europe and North America are:

—the strong polarization between "conservatives" and "progressives"; the conservatism, spiritlessness and over-agedness of so many church leaders;

—the institutional exhaustion of many Christians and the problem of restricted identification with their churches;

—the new trend toward inwardness and spirituality;

—the charismatic movement.

These phenomena can only be dealt with by a common effort. They represent a challenge to the churches: they must be recognized in their ecumenical potential and put to service for the common goal.

d. Ecumenicity at the grass roots

Of special significance is the unofficial ecumenicity that has established itself among zealous Christians and pastors of all churches on the congregational level. In many places in the world, an anticipatory practice of the signs of the not-yet-officially-achieved unity has become the rule:

—the practice of intercommunion and of common eucharistic celebration in groups and in private homes;

—the unreserved participation in the services and the Eucharist of other churches extending an open welcome to those of other churches;

—the rising number of pastors, who despite strictest prohibition, extend eucharistic hospitality or practice ecumenical religious instructions, and who have in theory and practice set themselves apart from the officially prevailing interpretation of church office in their own denominations;

—the witness and influence of base communities in places and situations, in which the normal apostolate of the denominations plays little or no role and in which the denominational differences have become irrelevant (student parishes, the worker-apostolate, pastoral work among social outcasts and in regions of extreme social underprivilege).

If the ecclesiastical authorities for the time being feel themselves unable to extend official recognition to such practices, then at the very least they must honestly and intelligently acknowledge their existence, analyze them in their significance, and draw the needed consequences for the future. The better course, naturally, would be to recognize in such volatile expressions of unofficial ecumenicity the working of the Spirit and thus avoid driving them out of the official churches into a no-man's land between the confessions.

e. Antidotes to ecumenical self-satisfaction

One often hears the objection that official ecumenism is simply a new form of self-adulation, that it has fallen irretrievably into ecclesiastical complacency, that it exhausts itself in polite words and gestures, that its commissions are composed only of harmless, for the most part second-class personalities, and that, all in all, it only serves to strengthen the traditional preponderance of the institutions within the major churches. Regrettably these charges are not without foundation. To avoid such dangers, the churches need to develop a joint tactic of resistance. Otherwise they will simply continue to reproduce the same problems the ecumenical commissions believed they had resolved. The following considerations are important.

The practice of official dialogue: Those called to membership in the theological commissions must be competent theologians of stature within their respective denominations. Their nomination should be a matter of common decision and not be left to the arbitrary will of particular ecclesiastical authorities. The members of ecumenical dialogue and negotiating commissions must represent the whole theological, cultural and social spectrum of their denominations—yes, even when this is unpalatable to the official authorities and when, at first at least, it represents a hindrance to rapid progress. We must see to it that the ecumenical dialogue not devolve into an esoteric occupation for a limited group of ecumenical specialists: it is a task which must be borne by men and women who have a contribution to make at all the various levels within the churches.

The claims of official ecumenism: Official ecumenism is not only called upon to make clear its intentions; it must also make clear its limitations. In respect to the middle and lower levels of the church it must see its task as a subsidiary one; it is not entrusted with the responsibility for total church reform. The congregations have their own right and obligation to get to know the members and the congregations of other churches, to achieve ecumenicity in their own locality, and to contribute to the establishment of a normative practice.

The significance of the smaller denominations: Until now, the significance of the smaller denominations and the churches without official ministry has largely been overlooked in the ecumenical perspective. The major denominations negotiate with each other and discuss the topics which they see as important. In the eyes of many of the smaller churches, ecumenism has become a conservative pastime for the influential and affluent. In this connection the smaller denominations have a double contribution to make. In the first place they can communicate experiences which are rare in the major denominations: experiences of friendship, celebration and fraternity, experiences of conviction and decisiveness where matters of confession and essentials are involved. In the second place, the churches without official ministries are in a position to show us that the offices of the church must not be disfigured by ideology, that their nature is that of ministry, and that by the measure of their service are they to be measured. They can show us that the nearness of the Lord is not realized primarily in official representation but rather in the community of believers and in the service of the poor. Finally they can show us that the individual local congregation is the primary and original expression of the church in its fullness. Thus it would be a grave mistake to make the recognition of other churches depend primarily upon the existence of specific offices.

f. The development of united forms of action

We need more than simply a comprehensive vision and strategy for ecumenical union. Parallel to our efforts in the direction of conciliar union, we must undertake those measures without which no plan of union can come to life. We must begin to institutionalize the ecumenical church through such instruments as joint theological and catechetical education, joint construction of churches and parish centers, and structural linkage or amalgamation of social and charitable organizations. Theologians, pastors and catechists of all confessions must become experienced in the diverse styles of speaking, thinking and devotion prevailing in the different churches. They must become adept in the techniques of translation and of dealing with the emotional values inherent in the other confessions.

3. The Church in the Service of the World

When the churches forget the persons to whom they were sent, they lose their reason for being. All ecumenical activity is thus meaningless, when it loses sight of the concerns of the world and exhausts itself within its own provincial problem sphere. The overcoming of the ecclesiastical past must be oriented to the future of mankind. A number of common goals spring from this consideration:

a. The joint re-formulation of the original faith: The Christian faith must be testified to in such a way that the world can learn to understand it anew. We must acquire the ability to criticize our traditions, be they old and venerated or newly formulated, be they normative in character or merely factual. We must learn to measure them on the questions and needs of the world as a whole and to push forward to new expressions which can shine forth in the world with unifying and convincing power.

b. The joint testimony of a fraternal community: As believing Christians, we join together in community, not in order to separate ourselves from the world but rather to find solidarity with all mankind. For this reason we dare not attempt to fix the church in one particular form. So long as we are unable to determine the future shape of mankind, we are only relatively in a position to decide questions such as whether the church of the future will be large or small, more institutional or more charismatical, more uniformly or more manifoldly organized, whether its expressions will take the form more of a pastoral service organization or more that of a tightly-knit base community—indeed whether such possibilities are even real alternatives for the future church.

III. THE CONSEQUENCES FOR THE CATHOLIC CHURCH

A comparison of the successes achieved (I) and the demands yet to be fulfilled (II) with the present reality of the Catholic Church forces us to soberness.

1. Consequences on the Universal Level

a. The Catholic Church must strive together with the World Council of Churches to achieve a *conciliar model* of union. All the churches must enjoy full recognition as churches in such a "council." Under the necessary limitations, such a "council" must be capable of making binding decisions. Its task will be to pave the way for the further manifold processes of union on all levels and in all respects (institutional, spiritual, liturgical and ministerial). Such processes cannot be commanded from above; they must be given time and support to grow organically.

b. At the same time, the Catholic Church—on the basis of existing theological consensus efforts—is called upon to extend *full recognition to the offices* of the other churches inasmuch as these exercise comparable functions. Moreover the churches without official ministries are not to be denied their ecclesial character.

c. Likewise the Catholic Church is called upon to clear up as quickly as possible the differences which separate it from such churches to which it is most closely related in teaching and organization, namely with the *Anglican* and the *Orthodox* churches. A particular union with these churches under a universal, pastoral Petrine ministry is not to be excluded.

d. The doctrinal discussions with the *Reformation* churches must be pursued with all possible commitment, in order that significant agreements can be reached in the near future and so proclaimed as officially binding. In the meantime practical steps in the direction of ecumenical union must also be taken.

2. Consequences on the Local (Regional) Level

a. Official efforts at union on the universal level have a *subsidiary* role. Efforts on the national level must prepare for and complement them. Ecumenical experiences on the local level, however, are the starting point and the goal of all efforts, for it is on this level that the ecumenical problematic first takes on ecumenical life.

b. It is the right and duty of the local ecumene—naturally in loyal solidarity with the regional and the universal church—to awaken ecumenical initiative and to transform the theoretical results of discussion and negotiation into *a manifold of practical forms of action*. Ecumenicity doesn't first become legitimate when it finds official authorization; on the contrary, it is the restrictions and prohibitions from above which must prove their legitimacy. In this light, the attempt to ban the unofficial forms of ecumenicity into the sphere of illegitimacy until they are authorized from above appears as a serious mistake.

c. The local ecumene sees clearly that the unity of Christians is less encumbered by explicit doctrinal differences than by factors such as diverse forms of devotion, emotional attachments and anxiety about retaining self-identity. The local ecumene must attempt to combat such difficulties by finding *new common experiences of the faith* through common prayer, celebration, witness and action.

3. The Prerequisites

In order to fulfill these demands on all levels, the Catholic Church must fulfill certain prior conditions.

a. The union of churches can only be effective for the Catholic Church when it consistently *carries forward the reforms* inaugurated by Vatican II. She can do this, however, only when she begins now to clarify her reform expectations in common study with the other churches and when she orients her efforts toward the ecumenical forms of the future.

b. The Catholic Church can only hope for a union when it is prepared to *divest itself of certain historical prerogatives* which today are generally acknowledged to constitute an insuperable obstacle to ecumenical progress and which in theological perspective are no longer justifiable. Among these are: the exclusive Catholic notion of *apostolic succession* in the episcopacy of the Catholic and Orthodox churches (as opposed to the recognition of the ecclesial and sacramental office of the churches of the Reformation); the autocratic jurisdictional primacy of the popes in its medieval and modern form (as opposed to a pastoral primacy); the *verbal infallibility* of the popes and the councils (as opposed to the notion of the church's being supported in the truth of the Gospel despite individual errors).

4. The Practical Problem

Until now at least, the present leadership of the Catholic Church has shown no inclination to draw the practical consequences from the results of theological research or to fulfill the prerequisites listed above. In this situation, ecumenical efforts within the Catholic Church are confronted with the following problem.

a. The Catholic Church is still juridically organized in centralistic and autocratic fashion. Without the approval, indeed without the *initiative of the pope* or of a council, none of the above mentioned conditions can be fulfilled in such a way that they might be legitimate according to canon law or binding for the church as a whole. Leaving aside the possibility of a formal breach of church law, there is no other way to deprive the pope of his prerogatives or to officially recognize the ministry of the other churches or to sanction the general practice of intercommunion and eucharistic hospitality. Two questions arise at this point.

b. The first question: How can the pope be moved to act? In this connection, the demands for a binding retirement age, election by representative bodies and a powerful Synod of Bishops gain special significance. Likewise the call for a *new council* gains in urgency.

c. The second question: How can the existing juridical structures be brought into motion from below—without a "revolution"? How, without revolution, can we obtain fulfillment of these overdue ecumenical demands? To this question, no general answer can be given. Nevertheless, even the Catholic Christian is obliged *to obey God* before all respect for men.

d. *Various possibilities for acting are conceivable:*

i. An *open protest* coupled with the broadest possible public appeal to the pope and the bishops—the problem of the Catholic Church is in no small measure a problem of civic courage on the part of the bishops, the theologians, the pastors and all those who are in position to exercise public pressure on the Church.

ii. A *public sign:* By this is meant, no appeal for uncoordinated actions anticipating an ecumene not yet attainable. Such signs are continually being erected. What is needed is that all those who are concerned to take such actions responsibly proceed to act in concert and in the open at a prearranged point of time.

iii. *Unflagging argumentation:* When the pope and the bishops no longer adequately fulfill their leadership function, the key role devolves upon the pastors and theologians of the Catholic Church. With unflagging argumentation they must take a stand for the needed changes, they must courageously draw attention to the losses caused by church division, and they must work for reconciliation with all the forces in their power. They must see to it that hopes are not extinguished and that those engaged in ecumenism do not lose heart. They have the duty to protect those on the front lines of ecumenism from defamation and eventual sanctions, when, in obedience to their own consciences and to their faith in the one Jesus Christ, these front-line fighters push into new ecumenical territory beyond the lines of official policy.

iv. *Spiritual intensification:* Ecumenical efforts are not beyond the danger of degenerating into discussion technology and organizational management. Indeed in our present situation it is especially important to call attention to this danger. In the face of official opposition on the part of ecclesiastical authorities, the grass-roots ecumenical efforts can only hope to succeed when they are supported by a deep and confident faith and when they succeed in articulating both the unifying force of the Christian message and the common concerns for all mankind.

In all the churches, we have come to the point of ecumenical no-return! We can refuse to go forward; we can drift aimlessly and ultimately dry up; but to go back is impossible. Well then?

Avery Dulles

Ecumenism: Problems and Opportunities for the Future

VATICAN Council II was fortunate in having at its disposal a corps of experts who had thought long and hard about ecumenism. As a result the conciliar decree *Unitatis redintegratio* is not simply a respectable document. It is light years ahead of any previous Roman pronouncement on ecumenism and also, it may be observed, theologically more advanced than anything issued from Rome on the subject since the Council.

This last remark has implications for our present theme: What would be on the ecumenical agenda of Vatican III, if such a council were soon to be convened? The first item of business, I submit, should be to protect the clear teachings of Vatican II against the obfuscation and retrenchment by which they are threatened. A new council, or even a future meeting of the International Synod of Bishops, would do well to reaffirm with emphasis the leading principles of *Unitatis redintegratio,* so that they can no longer be ignored or interpreted out of existence. Among these principles I would single out the following for special emphasis:

1. The Church of Jesus Christ is not exclusively identical with the Roman Catholic Church. It does indeed subsist in Roman Catholicism, but it is also present in varying modes and degrees in other Christian communities to the extent that they too are faithful to what God initiated in Jesus and are obedient to the inspirations of Christ's Spirit.

2. As a result of their common sharing in the reality of the one Church, the several Christian communities already have with one another a real but imperfect communion. The relations among the

churches, therefore, are not simply "foreign relations," such as might exist among separate sovereign states, but "domestic relations" analogous to those obtaining among groups within a single political society. In some respects the relationship is even more intimate, for all Christians are incorporated into the one body of Christ, animated by his Spirit. The divinely given intimacy among all Christian groups makes the restoration of full communion among them all the more imperative.

3. The real though partial communion that obtains among the churches demands appropriate expression. According to Vatican II, this means common witness, common worship, and common service. Together the churches can give testimony to their faith in the triune God and in the incarnate Son, Jesus Christ. In unison they can turn to God in grateful adoration and devoutly invoke the aid of the Holy Spirit. And they can coordinate their efforts to serve the larger human family, thus setting in clearer relief the features of Christ the Servant (cf. *UR* 12).

4. In view of the serious differences by which they are still separated, Christians cannot fully unite in their witness, worship, and service. Each group must be careful to maintain its integrity, in conformity with its actual convictions, and not treat important differences as if they were of small account. To act as if there were more unity than truly exists would be to posit a false sign. These reservations are particularly pertinent where there is question of regular eucharistic sharing across confessional lines.

5. The goal of the ecumenical movement is not the reabsorption of all into the Roman Catholic Church, as the latter presently exists. Rather, there is need for mutual giving and mutual receptivity, preparing the way, it may be hoped, for full ecclesial communion. The Roman Catholic Church has no intention of dissolving itself or abandoning its essential structures, but it is prepared to reconsider, in thoughtful dialogue, what is or is not really essential. It is important that all parties to the ecumenical dialogue be prepared to recognize their own present shortcomings and take care not to obstruct the future leading of the Holy Spirit (cf. *UR* 24).

6. In order to find ways of overcoming the present barriers among the churches, serious dialogue should be pursued. Dialogue means something more than common study of the same problems and exchange of information about one another's beliefs and practices. More fundamentally it means mutual openness in speaking and listening, with a view to eventually transcending barriers that at present seem insurmountable. Such dialogue, to be fruitful, must at every stage be accompanied by prayer so that all may be open to the Holy Spirit.

These six points, I believe, accurately summarize important aspects of the teaching of Vatican II, but they are not widely understood or accepted by the Catholic clergy and faithful. They therefore need to be reaffirmed so as to make it unmistakably clear that the Catholic Church is firmly and publicly committed to these principles.

Principles, however, are by definition only beginnings *(principia)*. The Church cannot make practical progress by simply mouthing principles. In the years to come there is need for a clearer articulation of goals and strategies for what may be called the ecumenical apostolate. The Catholic Church does not seem to be adequately equipped with organs formally charged with the elaboration of ecclesiastical policy. In theory, the pope himself is expected to set policy in matters that concern the universal Church, but he is too preoccupied with other responsibilities to be able to devote his attention to all the necessary policy questions. He consequently delegates many important decisions to curia officials who act in his name and by his authority. This arrangement is not satisfactory because the curia is by nature a staff and is not exempt from the diseases to which all bureaucracies are subject.

The world episcopate, through the International Synod of Bishops, would seem to be the organ best equipped to formulate and review ecclesiastical policy for the universal Church in the ecumenical area, as in other areas. The Synod could set up a division for policy planning and, as necessary, utilize for staff work the services of Vatican bureaus such as the Secretariat for the Promotion of Christian Unity. A future general council could, of course, have much to say about ecumenical strategy, but it would seem that there are sufficient resources at hand for establishing policies without waiting for another council. The principles laid down by Vatican II offer a sufficient basis for the formulation of ecumenical policy. In order to facilitate policy decisions, however, there must be a much clearer vision of the goals of ecumenism than presently exists. To this important issue the following reflections will be devoted.

What is the aim or purpose of ecumenism? Is ecumenism the same thing as the apostolate of Christian unity, and, if so, what does unity mean in this context? A number of conceivable goals could be envisaged. Without discussing all the legitimate goals, it may be sufficient here to characterize three sets of objectives, each giving rise to a distinct style of ecumenism.

1. Ecumenism might begin with the vision of the universal Church as a society with a single system of government and of doctrine. The goal

would then be seen as the establishment of a single organized church, similar to our present denominations except that it would hope to include all Christians. In government, all would acknowledge a single body of pastors; in their profession of faith, all the members would be held to the same essential doctrines; and in their worship all would make use of the same sacraments. This is substantially the goal of classical ecumenism as it has existed since the Edinburgh World Missionary Conference of 1910 and as it was interpreted at the Third Assembly of the World Council of Churches meeting at New Delhi in 1961. Although this goal seems exceedingly remote and perhaps unrealistic, it has inspired persevering and concerted efforts over the past sixty years and more.

Down to the middle of the twentieth century this model of ecumenism was accepted in Catholic circles, as exemplified, for example, by the apostolate of Father Paul Wattson (1863–1940) of the Atonement Friars. But Catholicism had its own distinctive vision of the kind of unity that would eventuate—namely the acceptance by all Christians of the pope and of the entire Catholic system of dogma and sacraments. In this perspective ecumenism meant the effort to bring other churches and communities back into the Roman obedience. This goal was clearly articulated in many papal statements down to, and including, Pius XI's encyclical *Mortalium animos* (1928).

Vatican II, however, distanced itself in two major respects from the kind of Catholic ecumenism just described. In the first place it linked the concept of reunion with that of reform. Scrupulously avoiding the language of "return to the fold of Peter," the Council acknowledged that Catholicism, in its present form, suffers from deficiencies in conduct, in ecclesiastical discipline, and even in the formulation of doctrine, and consequently that the Catholic Church, insofar as it is a human and earthly institution, stands in need of continual reformation (cf. *UR* 6). Second, Vatican II acknowledged that the life and truth of Christ are at work in other communities, and consequently that they need not think of abandoning anything that the grace of the Holy Spirit has wrought in their midst (cf. *UR* 4). In view of these two principles the Council may be taken as implicitly teaching that the united church of the future would not arise through a capitulation of the other churches and their absorption by Roman Catholicism. The desired *una sancta* could be a joint creation, simultaneously fulfilling and transforming all the churches that enter into it. The Catholic Church, while it would in no way be dissolved, would be modified by entering into this more comprehensive unity.

The Council, however, did not look upon the united future church as a new construction. It assumed that the dogmas and essential structures of the Catholic Church, including the papacy as an embodiment of the Petrine ministry, would survive in the one church that is to be (cf. *UR* 3). Thus the Vatican II position on the goals of ecumenism stands in a certain continuity with the prior Catholic pronouncements. For this reason the Catholic conception of the "one true Church," even with the qualifications introduced by Vatican II, still remains too specific to have wide appeal to other Christians.

If the realization of a single unified ecclesiastical organization, understood in the sense just explained, were the only goal of Catholic ecumenism, ecumenism itself would be a subject of interconfessional controversy rather than a unifying force. Fortunately, however, this tightly structured type of unity is only one of several ecumenical goals that are operative in Catholic ecumenism. We turn, therefore, to our other two models.

2. Our first model began "from above," taking its departure from the essential doctrinal and governmental structures of the universal Church, and seeking to devise methods of integrating all Christians into the same organizational framework.

Another model begins, so to speak, "from below." It views the local church, under its bishop, as an essentially complete realization of Christianity. Christian unity is seen as a communion among local churches which acknowledge one another's doctrines, pastors, and sacraments. The universal Church is understood as a communion of all the local churches, including those groups of churches which, by sharing a common heritage, constitute units within the total communion, as do the ancient patriarchates of the East.

Applying this model to the ecumenical problem, one may look upon groupings such as the Roman Catholics, the Anglicans, and the Orthodox as clusters of local churches. The ecumenical problem, on this view, is to extend the communion already present within these clusters so that there may also be communion among the clusters. Full mutual reconciliation may require protracted negotiations and concessions, until each group is satisfied that the others deserve to be received into full communion.

This model of ecumenism can find much support in the language of Vatican II, which used "communion" as a key category. It seems to enjoy the favor of Pope Paul VI, who has spoken of Anglicanism as a "sister church."[1] In several important addresses Cardinal Jan Willebrands, the President of the Secretariat for the Promotion of Christian Unity, built into this theory the concept of *typoi*.[2] A group of local churches within a single region or tradition, he suggested, might constitute a *typos* or characteristic expression of the universal Church. The total Catholic Church could then be regarded as consisting of several distinct *typoi,* one of which would presumably be Roman Catholicism. The Anglican churches, Cardinal Willebrands implied, might eventually become a *typos* within an enlarged Catholic communion of churches. His suggestion undoubtedly evoked favorable echoes in many Anglican circles, but it is too early to say whether it has been equally well received in all segments of the Anglican communion.

The communion model of ecumenism, promising though it is, cannot yet be said to have been worked out in sufficient detail so that one may judge its adequacy to the total ecumenical situation. There are problems with regard to the way in which both the point of departure and the point of arrival are envisaged in this theory.

With regard to the point of departure, the theory seems to rest upon a sacramental and hierarchical vision of the Church which is more easily shared by "catholic" than by "protestant" constituencies.[3] The unity of the Church is seen as a sharing *(communio, koinonia)* of holy things—those handed down as a sacred patrimony from the beginning. Among these "holy things" the hierarchical ministry and the Eucharist are viewed as central. A local church is seen as a eucharistic community gathered under the presidency of its bishop. This model applies very well to the ancient churches of the East, including the Orthodox, somewhat less well to the Anglicans, rather doubtfully to the Lutherans, and with great difficulty to Protestants of a more "free church" tradition. More reflection is needed to specify how the concepts of local church and ecclesial communion are verified in these less traditional communities.

With regard to the point of arrival, clarifications are still needed to show what the Roman Catholic Church would require as conditions for full communion. Does this really differ from the kind of doctrinal and disciplinary subjection to Rome described under our first model? If so, the second model would not seem to offer a really distinct option. The ultimate goal of the *communio* theory would be the coalescence of all the churches into a doctrinally and juridically unified church having a variety of rites. The present Orthodox and Anglican communions would be reduced to "rites" similar to the so-called "uniate churches" of the East.

Some exponents of the *communio* theory, such as Emmanuel Lanne, are critical of the uniate model on the ground that it separates liturgical rite from doctrine. They would hold that the notion of *typos* includes a certain degree of doctrinal autonomy.[4]

Vatican II provided some basis for this opinion. It spoke of a "hierarchy" of truths, differing in their relationship to the fundamental Christian faith (*UR* 11), thus implying that some doctrines, although defined, could be treated as secondary and therefore perhaps not essential to ecclesial communion. In its discussion of the Eastern churches, moreover, the Council asserted that many of the theological formulations in their traditions might be seen as "complementary rather than conflicting" in comparison with the teachings of the Western churches (*UR* 17). In view of the references to the Council of Florence in the following paragraph (*UR* 18), the Council may have intended to suggest that in a future union between East and West, the Christians of the East would not be required to accept the theology that undergirds the addition of the *Filioque* to the Western creed. Following the same line of reasoning one may speculate that a certain measure of doctrinal autonomy might be accorded to Protestants coming into union with Rome. Could certain Protestant formulations, such as *sola fide* and *sola Scriptura,* be regarded as "complementary but not conflicting"?

These questions, to be sure, are at the present stage very embryonic and conjectural, but the very fact that the Decree on Ecumenism does not exclude them makes it mandatory for ecumenists not to leave them unexplored. If the Catholic Church can envisage the possibility that non-Roman churches within the Catholic communion might have a system of doctrine and a church order not identical with that of Rome, this would be immensely significant.[5]

Even if full communion implied that non-Roman churches could not enjoy more autonomy than the present "uniates"—surely a very pessimistic hypothesis—this does not remove all significance from our second model of ecumenism. For the partial communion that presently exists among separated churches can be increased to the advantage of all. By a mutual sharing of the treasures handed down in their respective traditions, and of the new insights gained from prayerful reflection on current developments, the churches could enrich one another and thus draw into closer communion, still imperfect but nevertheless approaching the full communion of the desired *una sancta*. This rapprochement would itself be a goal worth pursuing for its own sake.

3. The two models just considered rest on the presupposition that union or communion is more perfect to the extent that differences (except for relatively minor adaptations) are eliminated. If one thinks of the Church as endowed by Christ with certain inalienable gifts, and as having to live forever off the patrimony committed to the apostles, it stands to reason that Christian unity must be achieved through a common acceptance of what has been faithfully handed down.

Perhaps, however, this ecclesiology is itself limited in value. If one thinks of the Church more in terms of response and process, and less in terms of substance and conservation, greater scope can be found for diversity and innovation. Just as Christian art, music, and poetry can creatively explore the unlimited potentialities latent in the Christian idea, so the churches, one might contend, can provide an indefinite variety of authentic realizations of the Christian life, all of which seek to refract, in their own times and cultures, something of the immeasurable riches contained in God's deed in Christ.

If this dynamic vision of the Church has any validity, it points the way to a third style of ecumenism. It is not essential—according to this view—for the churches to cling perpetually to some supposed apostolic patrimony or to subscribe to any universally binding set of normative doctrines, ministries, or sacramental rites, for all such forms may be changed as the Spirit may inspire. Christian unity does not mean uniformity. Ecumenism requires the churches to avoid mutual hostility and apathy. It impels them to edify and stimulate one another, whether by mutual approval or by mutual criticism, as circumstances seem to indicate. On this theory the unity of the total Church would consist in a dynamic interaction of diverse and autonomous denominations. Juridical or organic unity, important for both of our previous models, would be of doubtful value in the third.

Although one should beware of imagining that all Christian communities are equally faithful to Christ, it is quite true, in my opinion, that every major Christian tradition has something to teach the others, and something to learn from them. The interaction model of ecumenism is therefore valuable, at least as a supplement to the first two. This model, moreover, has the advantage of easy applicability to the kind of religious situation that presently obtains in a country such as the United States. The pluralism is so great that positive relations among the churches cannot suitably be predicated upon common doctrines and usages or upon the prospects of formal juridical union. If ecumenism is not to become the concern of a particular clique of churches, it is important for each church to cultivate cordial and fruitful relationships with others markedly different from itself.

An analogy from daily life comes to mind. There is something special about the family—a unity of persons who live in the same house, sharing many material and intangible things in common. But our life would be greatly impoverished if we had no contacts except with members of our own family. We need the stimulus of encounter with people whose past experience, ideas, and customs are radically different from our own. They enrich our lives and help us to gain a sense of our own identity. We frequently form deep friendships with persons quite unlike ourselves—persons who perhaps vehemently disagree with some of our most cherished convictions. Just as our best friends may be persons with whom we have little in common, so too, it may be thought, a community of friendship could exist among churches dissimilar in doctrine and ecclesiastical order. The very disparity with which such

churches reflect the mystery of Christ may be a source of mutual stimulation and respect. They may develop warm ecumenical relationships
based on their ability to challenge and listen profitably to one another.

A possible third style of ecumenism, then, is the promotion of a
heterogeneous community of mutual witness and dialogue. By this I do
not mean a casual agreement to disagree, but an earnest and committed
mutual questioning and accounting.

Reflecting on the three models of ecumenism here proposed, I see no
necessity to choose among them. All three seem to be legitimate and in
some cases appropriate. Perhaps also, none of them is a completely
adequate model. The Roman Catholic Church, in the modern world,
stands in ecumenical relationships with Christian communities of all
three types: those which may feel prepared to contemplate acceptance
of catholicism in its Roman expression; those which, notwithstanding
certain deeply rooted differences of faith and order, can be treated as
bound to Rome by certain family resemblances; and those which, because of sharper divergences, are more realistically viewed as friends
belonging to a different ecclesial family.

There is a temptation to rank these three types of relationship so that
the first is considered most satisfactory and the third the most deficient.
In that case the third model of ecumenism would be a mere stepping
stone to the second and the second to the first. On more mature consideration, however, this appears to be an oversimplification. In daily life
friendship is not necessarily inferior to family relationship nor is it a
mere means to establishing family ties, even though friends sometimes
become members of the same family in the course of time. We cherish
our friends, at times, because they bring an independence of judgment
and a freshness of experience we could not expect from members of our
family living under the same roof. In like manner Catholics might value
the Baptist churches and the Society of Friends for their capacity to
bring insights and provide examples for which one would look in vain
to churches of a more traditional and sacramental type. Does not the
Baptists' emphasis on "believer's baptism" and the Quakers' insis-
tence on spontanteous prayer have much to contribute to Catholicism
as it seeks to renew itself? Some of the Protestant free churches, precisely because of their greater distance from Catholic Christianity, may
have more to say to Catholicism than other groups whose thought and
practices have long been familiar. And perhaps, also, Catholicism has
more to offer them by way of challenge and stimulus.

Vatican II made very solid advances in Catholic ecumenism. Where
its recommendations have been followed, as in the bilateral conversations, great progress has been achieved. But the program of Vatican II

is still imperiled by the lack of ecumenical understanding and commitment on the part of Catholics, both pastors and faithful. It is urgent that the ecumenical movement be revitalized by full Catholic participation.

The division of Christianity into a multitude of competing and antithetical churches continues to weaken the Christian witness in the modern world. It prevents secular society, riddled by painful divisions of its own, from looking to the churches as a healing force. The ecumenical movement has dreamed of a restoration of an *una sancta* in which the many churches become one church.

Commitment to this ideal has evoked noble efforts, but the dream has lost some of its appeal. The good name of ecumenism, in various quarters, has been tarnished by a compulsive desire to level all differences and to seek agreement even at the cost of compromise. Reacting against such excesses, some have felt justified in returning to a rigid and complacent sectarian stance. The most promising developments, avoiding both of these extremes, seek to show how the gifts of the various traditions can be harmoniously put to work for the benefit of all. The effort to form a community of witnessing dialogue, without premature agreement or self-liquidation on the part of any church, would seem to be the most realistic program for the present. Such dialogue might or might not lead in time to full consensus about faith and order. But even if it does not lead to full organizational and doctrinal unity, this style of ecumenism cannot fail to benefit all the churches that engage in it. To set the goals and strategies for such an ecumenism is the highest priority for the policy makers in this domain.

Notes

1. Pope Paul VI, "Remarks at the Canonization of the Forty Martyrs," October 25, 1970; text in *Documents on Anglican/Roman Catholic Relations* 1 (Washington, D.C.: United States Catholic Conference, 1972), pp. 42–43.

2. See Cardinal Willebrands' address of January 18, 1970 in *Documents on Anglican/Roman Catholic Relations* 1, pp. 32–41. Here Willebrands defines a *typos* as follows: "Where there is a long and coherent tradition, commanding men's love and loyalty, creating and sustaining a harmonious and organic whole of complementary elements, each of which supports and strengthens the others, you have the reality of a *typos*." For further indications see Cardinal Willebrands' address, "Prospects for Anglican–Roman Catholic Relations," *Documents on Anglican/Roman Catholic Relations* 2 (Washington, D.C.: USCC, 1973), pp. 61–73.

3. The terms "protestant" and "catholic" are here used with lower-case initials in conformity with the terminology popularized by the Amsterdam As-

sembly of the World Council of Churches in 1948. See Lukas Vischer, ed., *A Documentary History of the Faith and Order Movement, 1927–1963* (St. Louis: Bethany Press, 1963), pp. 76–77.

4. E. Lanne, "Pluralism and Unity: The Possibility of a Variety of 'Typologies' Within the Same Ecclesial Allegiance," *One in Christ* 6 (1970): 430–51, especially pp. 443–48.

5. I have set forth some reflections on this possibility in several articles; see *The Survival of Dogma* (Garden City: Doubleday, Image Books, 1973), chap. 10, "Dogma as an Ecumenical Problem."

PART 4

Church and the Individual

Jacques-Marie Pohier and Claude Geffré

Church Reform and Individual Life

"RATHER than discuss the present and immediately past questions which face the Church today, the participants will be asked to articulate the new questions which should occupy our scholarly concerns (in theology and in the social sciences) in the years ahead." This sentence from the letter of invitation of the president of Notre Dame, Father Hesburgh, explains which themes we have chosen to open the discussion in the field of moral theology.

I

A first series of questions which seem to us important can be grouped under the following theme: Is it possible—is it even necessary—that the moral rule in a given field be the same at the same time for all the individuals and all the cultural and ethnic groups throughout the *catholicitas* of the Church?

In fact all the historical, anthropological, social, psychological, etc., disciplines show that the meaning of a given behavior in a particular area of human action changes greatly from one culture to another, from one society to another (diversity in synchrony), and even from one period to another of an individual's or a group's development (diversity in diachrony). For example, sexual activity does not have the same meaning for a fifteen-year-old, a thirty-year-old or a sixty-year-old. But neither does it have the same meaning for people living in Chicago in 1977, for peasants in India in 1977, for the aristocrats of Florence during the *Quattrocento,* for the Christians of Corinth of the first century, and for the semi-nomadic tribes of the time of Abraham.

Even if we retain the idea of an optimal "norm," or the more debatable idea of moral progress as a more or less continual development, we cannot dismiss this conviction common to all human sciences: that it is impossible and useless to say that the meaning of sexuality for a seventy-year-old is inferior or superior to its meaning for a thirty-year-old or a fifteen-year-old, or to say that the signification of sexuality for a peasant of India is superior or inferior to its signification for an inhabitant of Chicago or Corinth or Florence. These individuals and these societies are in different situations. They have different objectives and different problems to solve, and the meaning of sexuality for them is largely determined by their specific objectives and problems.

It would therefore be absurd to impose upon the peasant of India the American idea of sexuality, or to impose on an adolescent or an old person the thirty-year-old's idea. Something analogous to this could be observed at Vatican II, when a desire was expressed to propose to the whole "Catholic" Church a conception of marriage which was due mainly to Western bishops and theologians. The Asians, Africans and South Americans refused, saying that in their cultures marriage had a different meaning.

This poses a particularly important challenge to the Roman Catholic Church. This challenge, of course, has already been important for the theology of natural law that has prevailed for centuries. Yet this is not the most important problem, for this theology of natural law and its use by the magisterium are recent things, and belong more to the *per accidens* of Christian faith rather than the *per se*. The challenge is more important for the way the Church conceives its catholicity: i.e., the catholicity of its juridical discipline. Does this catholicity consist in reducing all the singulars to one, unique universal, or in articulating legitimately different realities within an organic whole? This question is beginning to be asked in ecclesiology, in liturgy and even in dogmatics (e.g. in ecumenism). It has not yet been asked in moral theology. How can we articulate within a "catholic" ensemble the legitimate diversity of meaning (and therefore also of praxis) of sexuality in the different cultures and societies, on the one hand (synchrony), and throughout the different stages of development of an individual or a group on the other hand (diachrony)?

This problem pertains also to theology in general. What meaning can any one, non-differentiated theological discourse have, whether it is the discourse of Roman circles, or whether it is the unique and identical discourse that *Concilium* distributes in nine languages, according to the theory that it is identically valid and significant for a Christian of Brazil, Holland, Italy, Poland or Japan?

This problem applies also to the so-called "plan of God." Does this divine plan imply that sexuality must have the same meaning for everyone at a given moment of history? Or does it imply that all cultures and all individuals must gradually work towards the same conception of sexuality? We could ask an analogous question about forms of government. During all of the nineteenth century and later in Europe, the popes, bishops, pastors and theologians condemned and combatted democracy. Today their successors tend to consider it the only form of government that is truly in conformity with Christian values and with the "divine plan." Here again, is there a single model towards which all societies should tend?

II

Another group of questions can be formulated under the theme: "Changes which transform a sector of human activity from the public or social to the personal or private, or inversely, from the personal and private to the public and social."

Here again, sexuality is a good example. Pre-modern societies of the Christian era in the West exercised strict control over the sexual life of individuals. I think it was less for reasons of individual morality than for social and collective reasons. Control of sexual activity was necessary because it fulfilled objectives that were supremely important for society: the survival of the ethnic or national group by procreation, and by procreation the productivity of manual labor and support for the family and the fatherland (the child is a future breadwinner, a future cane for the aged, a future soldier), etc. For example, the organization of marriage had decisive effects on the transmission of goods, on the organization and division of work, on means of production and the channels of distribution, etc.

Today, in Western societies at any rate, the sexual life of individuals has practically no influence on all these realities, which have become completely independent and linked to other causes. We could therefore formulate the hypothesis—to be verified!—that society will no longer attend to the sexual life of people, except in extreme cases where sexual life still has an effect on the major objectives of society: e.g., on the individual level (pathology and sexual delinquency, dangerous to the common good), or on the collective level (negative birth rate menacing a social group, as in the Federal Republic of Germany, or extremely high birth rate, as in India). Outside these cases, society will lose interest in the sexual and even affective life of its members, since it will no longer have any serious effects on society. There will only be an interest in those few individuals mentioned who pose a problem, and this only to the extent that a threat to society must be removed. For example, the United States or the Soviet Union can tolerate a fairly high rate of divorces, for, in spite of the disadvantages, this divorce rate has only little influence on the realities which these societies hold as most important. We thus see an important sector of morality go from the social and public sector to the private and personal.

We must therefore ask ourselves whether or not the enormous importance given to marriage and sexual morality by the Catholic tradition was simply a transposition into Christianity of the importance that pre-modern societies attached to the structure of marriage and to control over sexual life. If Christianity had been born in a society where it was less necessary to control sexuality and marriage, what then would Christian morality have been? And what should Christian morality be in the case of a society where technical and cultural evolution (which is not in itself either moral or immoral, pro-Christian nor anti-Christian) has changed the social, political, economical, biological, etc., reasons for having to control carefully the sexual life of the people?

But taking another look at things, we can also observe the opposite trend: realities which seemed to belong to the sphere of the individual or of relations between a few individuals left to their own initiative, now become social realities. And society, which could formerly allow individuals to act without interference, now finds itself taking charge of and controlling either formerly private sectors of life or entirely new sectors. This is clear in the case of business and work. Previously the buyer and the seller, the employer and the employee could be left to deal among themselves, and society intervened only in extreme cases (just as now perhaps, the man and the woman could be left to regulate between themselves—except in extreme cases—their marriage and their fertility). The principle of free enterprise and of free employment gives the partners the task of structuring their own relationship.

But society now observes that this *laisser-aller* ends up in monstrous situations, such as the supra-national and supra-political power of multi-national companies, or the absence of true labor legislation, or the massive nonobservance of such legislation even where it exists (jurists say that this is the most abused of all juridical corpora). Many other examples of this passage from the private to the public could be given: the use of energy, the exploitation of the under-earth, the sea bed and space, organization of health care, the problem of the free circulation of individuals, ideas, etc.

For moral theology, there is a double task in the future. On the one hand, sharing in the diagnosis of this drifting of the "continents" of morality (just as the earth's continents are moving) with those who are reflecting on these problems. Just as the figure of this world, so too the figure of morality passes. Not because there is now more immorality or more morality, but because the tasks which realize the human condition undergo modifications.

On the other hand—and this is more specific—we must study those things which traditional Catholic morality has linked to former configurations of the human condition and its tasks, configurations which have become "obsolete." We must study how faith in the God of Jesus Christ can be articulated through these new configurations of the human condition. What can Christian morality be in a society where the function of a "judgment of the world" or of "salvation in Jesus Christ" would be perhaps more in terms of organization of work or the circulation of capital, persons, ideas, knowledge, information, and the organization of health services, rather than in terms of controlling marriage and sexuality, for example. Moreover this is true not only because these are the things society is more dependent on, but because the *life of individuals* depends more on the organization of work, the disposition of raw matter, the circulation of ideas and information than on the control of marriage and sexuality.

These are a few of the questions which seem to merit the discussion and work of theologians in morality in future years. Faced with these questions we are divided between two contradictory attitudes. On the one hand, we feel somewhat wearied by the banality of these questions, and this reaction is shared by all those who are familiar with the social, anthropological, historical and psychological sciences. Indeed at this level it *is* a question of banalities. But on the other hand, we feel a little tired of the extremely difficult task of making these "banalities" be seen as banal by the Roman Catholic Church. If one places oneself within this Church (and we do!), within its magisterium, its pastoral activity, its theology, its juridical organization, etc., then one can no longer say that these are banalities. How can these banalities effectively become banalities within the Catholic Church? That is, how can the Catholic Church structure its life, its magisterium, its thought, its pastoral activity, its organization, its praxis around what we're calling banalities? The very fact that we formulate the problem in this way makes it clear that there is an enormous task to be done. This in itself should stir up optimism, courage and decision. But it would also perhaps be tendentious to convoke Vatican III before an important part of this work is already finished.

Franz Böckle

Faith and Deeds

"A turning wheel that causes no motion elsewhere does not belong to a machine." Referring to this statement of Wittgenstein, Robert Spaemann[1] asks the question whether or not religion in our industrialized society is comparable to such a wheel that actually sets nothing else in motion while turning. It would seem that religion remains more and more without consequences for human behavior. Why indeed is that so? Are there any specific causes for it? Spaemann points out two different reasons.

One reason follows from the observation that wherever religion associates itself with certain behavioral patterns, it becomes, without fail, a foreign body in society. As examples Spaemann points to the woman's position in Islamic religion, the holy cows in India or the prohibition of birth control by the Catholic Church. The industrial society pushes a religion that identifies with such singular norms further and further aside. It is sectarian, or as Spaemann phrases it, "a religion with statutory ethics becomes a sect," and is tolerated with a smile wherever it has been established already.

Another way of depriving religion of its function is its total adaptation to the needs and requirements of society. In this case the wheel of religion is turning along without religion ever affecting the machinery of society. The machine would run the same way if religion did not turn with it. This happens wherever we seek to define religion in terms of ethical function. Religion has "the peculiarity that it can only fulfill its ethical function as long as it is not defined by it."[2] Obviously the turning of the wheel has another function. For our personal as well as social behavior, faith and the insights gained through faith must be neither a foreign body nor a mere satellite. What then is the required

110

and necessarily appropriate function of faith in the realm of behavior? What role does theology play in ethics? Does a specifically Christian ethos exist at all? Are the moral demands different for a Christian than for anybody else by virtue of his faith?

For some years theologians have been ardently discussing these questions. At the same time, they are by no means purely academic questions. We are dealing with the specific aspect of the importance of the Christian message for the public. The second Vatican Council provided additional stimulus by proclaiming the joint responsibility of Christians in the social realm. Accordingly, in theology too a shift of emphasis was made. Within the program of a "theology of the world," a "political theology" or a "theology of liberation," one is opposed to an individual narrowing of the Christian message. The Christian password in life must not only be "save your soul," but "you too, especially as a Christian, contribute your share to the salvation, pacifica- cation and humanization of the world." However, passwords are usually so general that there can be no objections to them. The con- cretization of such general statements only causes difficulties, for which it will just not be sufficient to make individual, concrete social de- mands. Without any doubt the abolishment of racial discrimination, the struggle against mass poverty and the protection of the right to live of the born as well as the unborn are fundamental requirements for which Christians, above all, have to strive. The task of moral theology or of theological ethics, however, is far more comprehensive. Quite often fundamental requirements are competing with each other or can only be realized step by step. Any minister or bishop in the southern parts of Africa who struggles with determination for more justice for the black population knows that this cannot be done in one day. Priorities have to be recognized and concrete plans of action have to be developed. Often this can only be done by taking into consideration the reasons for and against, and by determining finally the action in practice through an evaluation of the best alternatives. As a normative theory moral theol- ogy is a practical science. Therefore, it cannot be satisfied with general postulates, rather it has to express concretely which norms and what forms of order result from the Christian message and what is their relation to moral reason. In the past and still today this relationship between the Christian faith and its practical realization in life has been the core of the question of the essence or distinctiveness of Christian ethics—a question which is basically as old as the history of Christian mission. In order to find a practical solution to this question, one must avoid two extremes according to Spaemann's previously cited warning.

On the one hand, the Christian faith should not be analyzed in terms of ethics. Wherever one tries to define religion by its ethical function, it

loses its function as religion. It can no longer be the salt of the earth or
the leaven of the world. This statement is undoubtedly of fundamental
importance. And one should always keep it in mind. But it will not do
to suspect, generally, the efforts of the so-called political theology or
theology of liberation of ignoring this insight in principle. By the same
token, moral theologians or theological ethicists cannot be so re-
proached. As far as I can judge from a general view, they all proceed
from the mutual conviction that Christian faith is the basis for a specific
existence in faith. Catholic theologians speak more freely in this context of a religious existence because for them faith, hope and love are
basic religious acts of human beings. It seems to me, however, that the
difference observable here between the confessions is rather a difference in terminology. Considering essentials, we are all equally convinced of the meaning of faithful or religious existence: it is that which,
in the New Testament, Paul calls the "life from the spirit" or the "life
in Christ." It is a question of a life based upon a decision in favor of
God. For the faithful human being who decides for God and is bound
by that decision, God becomes a living reality. Faith grasps the truth of
life and dares to trust it. And at the climax of the biblical unfolding of
revelation, we are told in the New Testament "that *a human being is*
this truth, namely Jesus of Nazareth. It would be more correct to say
that this truth was brought to light and revealed through him, through
the way he lived in fulfilling his existence."[3] And in this context it is not
so much a question of enlightenment about God but rather of the truth
about man. Jesus is and lives this truth. "Therefore it is well to say: for
Christians the specifically Christian mode of being is to find the way to
Jesus' manner of existence. Not really to God and not really to Jesus
but to his way of existence. 'Following him' is meant in this sense.
More pointedly expressed, it is not a question of confession to him, but
of being and staying in and with him. Those are not necessarily mutually exclusive."[4] It is important to recognize in Jesus' manner of existence the ultimate reality that determines human life and how to relate
to that. Jesus calls this ultimate reality that determines his life "Abba,
father." It is from this personal, trusting attachment that he gains his
life. This basic decision in favor of God, in the spirit of Christ, requiring
a life of faith, hope and love, forms the core of the Christian ethos. As
long as this decision is based on a reflected relation to the message and
deeds of Christ this can be seen as an exclusively Christian attitude.

Only with this conviction in mind, which is shared by all moral
theologians, do the controversial questions of this discussion become
apparent. For now, on the other hand, the second extreme must be
avoided, and that means the Christian message to the world must not
be narrowed down in a sectarian way. Christianity, on the contrary,

claims to be a universal message for all people. And it is the universality of the message which constitutes the real interest of the so-called discussion of propriety, i.e., the question regarding the truly Christian element of Christian morals. It would certainly be justified in this context to ask whether there are commandments and prohibitions for interpersonal behavior that are only for Christians, based on their faith, recognizable and thus obligatory; but this is rather an academic question and distracts from the real goal of the discussion. We are not so much interested to know whether the moral norms that Christianity has given for the coexistence of mankind are original or even exclusively Christian; ultimately and above all we are interested to know whether they can be communicated. We want to know whether they can at least be made plausible and comprehensible to everyone who is willing to study them with us. And we believe that in fact it should be possible to teach all people the consequences for interpersonal behavior that follow from our faith in God and in the power of his redeeming love. Therefore, the decisive question is not which and how many ethical truths Christianity has received from the history of human thought, rather, it is essential to show that in Christ God gave his complete affirmation of the human being. In the initially cited article of Robert Spaemann, he writes: "With respect to the modern universality of technical civilizations Christianity therefore does not have the same problems of adaptation as other religions have. It can discover in it a spirit of its own, . . . the commandment of charity is not tied to a particular conception of human self-stylization. . . . Christianity, however, seems to tear down differentiations as it tore down initially the differences between Jews and pagans. Its only intolerance seems to be directed against intolerance. And looked at from this aspect, Christianity's only demand ought to be to abolish all those residues which hinder the establishment of an order of universal consent."[5] This universal order is the topic of moral theologians in their discussion of the essence of Christian ethics. However, communication and the establishment of consent are only possible if that which is ethically required can be understood. To act morally means to act responsibly. And this requires acting out of insight. This demand for insight does not mean that the acting person has to understand in every case the reasons for a certain act in order to be able to act responsibly at all. It can be sufficient for him to be guided by a competent authority who possesses this insight. If a matter, however, is positively not comprehensible at all, or if someone has no insights at all about what he is to do, then he cannot assume responsibility for it. His moral decision would be reduced to a mere act of formal obedience. Certainly, the deed executed out of such obedience could be morally justified indirectly as an act of obedience; formally, however, it could not be regarded as a genuine moral act. In the same way, also, the norms that are to regulate our responsible attitude towards human beings and the world must in principle be open to reasonable human insight. This does not negate the fact that individual values that determine a norm receive a special foundation and security through faith in revelation. The value, however, that determines the act must be clearly recognizable to human understanding.

This fundamental statement is in no way meant to deny the influence of the Christian faith on behavior. We are only striving to realize correctly the connection. Faith in Jesus and his words led to a basic attitude in the early church as well as to a certain behavior on the part of individuals and communities that allow one to speak rightly of a Christian communal ethos. But this does not at all mean that it is to be understood in an exclusive and sectarian sense. It is precisely this ethos of faith that, in its anthropological dimension, is most deeply human and able to be communicated.

FAITH IN GOD CONSTITUTES THE TRUE MORAL AUTONOMY OF MANKIND

Modern thinking is imprinted to an almost unparalleled degree by the call for autonomy. The term itself is not new. From its Greek origin, the term has signified, since the middle of the fifth century B.C., the goal of city-states to be able to determine their own inner affairs without interference from another power. In the period of the religious wars it meant, furthermore, the claim to self-determination in matters of religious confession. Kant then introduced the term into philosophy and, thereby, raised it beyond the realm of institutional autonomy to the status of a fundamental human claim. Autonomy now implies the possibility and duty of man, as a reasonable being, to determine his own fate and also to be in harmony with a law given to man by man. The common denominator in this modern claim of autonomy is the rejection of any kind of outside determination or heteronomy. From which direction heteronomy must be feared is a question that has received different, even opposing answers. Is it the variety of desirable objects that affects the human being and threatens the autonomy of his pure reasonable will? Does heteronomy therefore mean to be dependent and determined by natural needs and society? Or, is it not rather the escape into subjectivity and abstraction that leads to the social self-estrangement of human beings? Therefore, should not the freedom from any kind of heteronomy be sought precisely by proceeding from human and social needs? Does mankind gain its freedom as free self-determination from the transcendence of these needs or from their extensive expression and satisfaction? These are the controversial questions raised by the claim of autonomy. Regardless of how the questions will be solved, all participants in the discussion unanimously agree upon the meaning of autonomy as a morality grounded in the human being and to be understood only through him. Therefore, it becomes a problem to employ the term autonomy for theological ethics, and yet call a purely humanistic autonomy "autonomistic." In theological ethics it is simply self-understood to see the ultimate basis of man's moral obligation as a radical claim on the human being by God. But everything depends on the way this divine claim is understood. And it is understood correctly only if looked upon as the universal horizon and the ultimate basis of human freedom. Dependence on God and human autonomy are not mutually exclusive. On the contrary, the dualism of autonomy and heteronomy can be truly overcome only where heteronomy itself allows autonomy, where the spirit of God makes a claim on man and yet allows him freedom: in a theonomous autonomy of the human being.

Yet it would be unfair not to admit that it is difficult to harmonize the many forms in which the moral teaching of the church is grounded and mediated with the thesis of autonomy. The main type of preaching is one of heteronomous moral commandment. Laws or prohibitions, which are established either by nature or by biblical revelation, are seen as an ever-valid and incontestable expression of divinely willed decrees. They are norms of the divine justice, guaranteed by God himself. On the contrary, however, it must be pointed out that this is not necessarily the case, that it is, in fact, not the classic type of Catholic moral theology at all. Based on faith in creation, the fundamental ethical obligation of mankind is rather to be seen in moral self-determination. Certainly a human being is not free if these norms are imposed on him from without. He himself has to set these norms, however, not from arbitrariness, but from freedom. It is precisely his freedom which proves to be his obligation. However, this is only the case if freedom is his charge and he himself is his own obligation. Moral duty does not arise from a conglomeration of necessity and chance. The moral laws, as a creation of reason, are ultimately based on the particular existence of human, i.e., finite reason which is confronted with the task of realization of freedom in this world. We have to respect philosophy's statement that law is a fact of reason, and its belief that no more can be said. The question, however, follows whether on that basis the fundamental moral norm can be made to transcend individual subjectivity and be conclusively comprehensible to every human being. Does the self-reconstruction of reason not necessitate the assumption of something absolute that is the ultimate basis upon which this reconstruction is postulated in advance and that is capable of convincingly establishing the recognition of a moral fundamental norm? Is it merely the "remnant of a metaphysical dogmatism" if Fichte—in attempting to accomplish a self-reconstruction of reason through the fact of the 'I'—arrives at that absolute 'I' of God which, as an absolute, is the significant and yet hidden basis of the human self? It is not our task to give a philosophical answer to that. We can only try to show that our faith in God does not absolve us from the duty to realize our freedom in this world, but rather confirms this being-as-an-obligation-to-oneself as characterizing reasoning creation. We do not need God in order to give us sanctions or prohibitions, but we are convinced that only the recognition of creation and the knowledge of our own creaturely existence constitute the obligation to a reasoned fulfillment of freedom. We are afraid that without this—which is ultimately without God—everything would be immaterial and indifferent in face of the autonomous will. And that would mean that autonomy itself would be endangered from within.

Theology looks upon the human being as a created being and, in the light of biblical faith in creation, can understand him only in the unique relation of God to the human being. God has put a claim on man that at the center of his personal being he is a creature. In understanding faith in creation one sees that the moral laws as facts of reason are nothing else but the dependence of a human being—whose personal freedom is totally claimed—on being at his own disposal. An existence based on the claim of obligation theologically proves to be the necessary condition of man who is indebted not to himself, but knows himself, rather, to be constituted as a created being. He himself may be aware of this origin only in its anonymous form as duty, or as the dictates of conscience. His autonomy as a moral being is gained to the degree that he submits himself to this basic claim. The acknowledgment of his creaturely existence constitutes the autonomy appropriate to mankind. Theological thinking, in its explanation of the human being as a created being, has incorporated the philosophical understanding of his finiteness. It affirms the anthropological assumption that neither as an individual nor as a collective being may man view himself as an absolute being. Man must realize the fulfillment of his freedom within the frame of this experience of contingency.

What has been said here is not a modernistic discovery of the twentieth century but coincides with the ingenious beginning of the doctrine of the natural law of morals by Thomas Aquinas. It deals with the relation between divine sovereignty and human autonomy, with the relation between causa prima and causa secunda, where the creaturely effects are not produced partly by God and partly by the created being, but are entirely embraced by the causa prima, and at the same time are caused by, and entirely in the order of, the created being. As a result of reason human beings are destined to find their way about in the world by thinking and acting. Therefore the establishing and forming of moral laws is their most innate mission. Of course, that does not mean that every individual ought to make his own laws. "Human being" in this context means "humanity." In the cultural historical process of mankind fundamental norms were developed and applied to concrete situations. This task will never end; it belongs to the ongoing task of human beings. The autonomous character of this mission is not invalidated by the fact that during this process man must not ignore his own natural conditions—for instance the data of natural historical evolution—or the fact that he has to take into consideration fundamental, common human values. Of course, one must not underestimate the fact that, in the course of cultural history, religious faith always proved itself to be an important factor in the discovery of meaningful human values. This will be the subject of the second thesis.

FAITH DEEPENS AND SECURES VALUE INSIGHTS WHICH ARE OF IMPORTANCE FOR CONCRETE ACTS

For this thesis and the following a methodologically important differentiation between value insights and moral judgments is indispensable. Only a human act can be morally judged. Only human acts are morally good or evil, morally right or wrong. For instance, one may ask whether it was morally right for the Israelis to facilitate the access to the airport of Entebbe with a lie. Was it morally permissible in this case to lie? An answer is only possible by an evaluation of benefits. This is the meaning of our saying that there are always certain ideals and values underlying will and deed. However, these ideals and values themselves do not yet constitute concrete rules of acting. By the term "values" we understand for instance freedom, life, physical integrity, but also marriage, family, community, property and sexual fulfillment. In the philosophy of law one speaks of recognized legal rights. They are the realities of experience, which are presupposed for any reasonable order of human coexistence. They demand recognition and in that respect are obligatory. Beyond that there are value concepts which refer as a kind of stereotype to an act that realizes certain values. Thus the value of fidelity is an expression of being willing to keep a promise. In this case we are dealing with an act-related value, and thus an already moral value, which remains not only obligatory for human coexistence but not to be relinquished. However, even these basic values do not yet constitute a concrete moral judgment or a concrete rule for acting. First there need to be examined such cases where, for instance, without a break of faith a promise should not be kept. This is precisely the main problem of today's discussion of basic values. A normative theory has to deal according to logical priorities with the knowledge and establishment of the ideals and values which are to determine our acts. A normative theory cannot do this autonomously. Indispensable help can be found within the various branches of the humanities. Neither does this task begin in a vacuum. Rather, the development and foundation of morally relevant insights are accomplished during a long cultural historical process, in which the different factors of experience, discovery and understanding work together. The importance of these factors for gaining insight into values is being analyzed today by different groups. The primary and basic provisions are already present in the natural history of mankind. Discoveries about evolution point to a phylogenic connection between man and other organisms. Insofar as one can recognize in human beings analogous fundamentals of structure (for instance, in competition and devotion to unsociable sociability), they certainly do not yet form a moral norm; but it is justifiable to speak of a disposition. It is well known that man, due to his highly differentiated cerebrum, has extensive possibilities to shape his instinctive behavior according to his imagination. Nevertheless, he cannot handle his natural disposition indiscriminately; it is something like a structural time schedule. Particular importance is given to human experience. Everybody likes to refer to his experience when making moral decisions. Ethical reflection requires critical argumentation of this source of morally important insights. It is obvious that only experienced conviction and not just the actual deed can become important for a normative theory. Constancy and scope alone are not sufficient. Values cannot be guaranteed by majority decisions. Experienced conviction has rather to confront with argumentation the insights coming from different realms of experience. It will become necessary to describe the different experiences in their respective form in order to relate them critically to one another.

Particularly divergent interpretations of meaning have to be critically related to one another. Those aspects that prove true in the critical analysis of this relation demand consideration and possibly integration within existing insights, and require new priorities (for instance the integration of different or newly experienced values in the existing interpretation of sexuality). Methodologically it is the question of plausibly connecting research into meaning with research into facts: the facts have to be established and consequently examined as to possibly implied ideal values. The methods of hermeneutics offer themselves for such research. Hermeneutics gains its persuasiveness by re-establishing its preconditions and by proceeding candidly through the materials of interpretation. After all, it is critical reason that establishes priorities on the basis of experiential knowledge. However, it cannot do without a certain conception of man, without a horizon of understanding. In the process of reasoning an important function is placed on the insight of faith. In the case of an ethical theory that is based on Christian faith, it is important to point out the knowledge gained from theological insights in their shared human aspect. Thus, for example, our faith that God loves all mankind and appoints all for salvation in Christ deepens our insight into the dignity of human beings. From the knowledge that men are called upon, it follows that every human being has his own personal value which belongs to him, no matter of which possible social system he is a part. This value cannot be denied to him by any social system. This understanding is humanly comprehensible and is—at least today—a knowledge that is not shared by Christians alone. This insight, however, does not at all seem to be compelling—as is proven by the discussion on the problems about the beginning and the end of human life. For Christian ethics this insight is essential. The struggle for its basic recognition must become a political issue, that is, Christians cannot refrain from attesting the same human dignity and right to live for the mentally retarded and the unborn—no matter what opportunistic considerations may demand, or what opinion the democratic majority has. What is indispensable for Christians is, in its true intrinsic value, comprehensible also in philosophical terms, even though it may not be of equal cogency. Consequently, a morality without consideration of these insights into value is not possible among Christians. But that does not turn it into an exclusive and sectarian morality; rather it should prove itself a fermentation of comprehensive humanization. This, however, is only possible if we recognize the limits that our own faith puts upon us. This leads to the third thesis.

FAITH PROHIBITS AN ABSOLUTIZING OF CREATED GOODS AND IDEAL VALUES

Every theologian who is convinced that God alone conforms to the idea of the good knows that within the world he will encounter the good only in the reflection of ideal values. Therefore, a human moral deed means in principle a search for the good among ideal values. Man can choose only among ideal values. The most important basis for the moral judgment of acts is the insight into the values prescribed for our acts. The acknowledgment that a specific value is given to us and is of obligatory character can, in the most general form, easily be changed to a moral judgment. "Given with obligation" implies in principle already "to respect in acting and behavior." If man is bestowed with dignity due to his being human, then we have to respect this dignity. If life and physical integrity are valued highly, we have to honor them. Apodictic phrases, as known to us from the decalogue, show this clearly. They have the same function as the list of basic rights in our bill of rights. They contain a doctrine of values. You shall honor your father and mother! You shall not kill! You shall not commit adultery! This ritualized, regular repetition of important demands was meant to remind Israel of the fundamental values of their coexistence. One might interpret these demands as follows: "Israel, remember, your parents deserve respect. Life is sacred. Property must be protected." In this very general form these sentences can be reduced to analytical judgments. You shall not kill means actually: to kill unjustly is unjust! Such analytical judgments are, of course, always and without exception valid. As soon as we ask, however, how actually is human dignity to be respected, or what does it mean to kill unjustly, these judgments become synthetic and thereby conditional. Thus, for instance, is capital punishment immoral? Tradition allows capital punishment if the execution of the law breaker represents the only and adequate means to protect law and order. This shows, in the last analysis, even the prohibition to kill is not absolutely valid, i.e., without reservations and exceptions. In fact, we even have to state in principle: moral norms can be valid unconditionally and without exception only if they demand the realization of an ideal goal that by proven fact can never compete with another more important, and therefore more desirable ideal value. The logic of this thesis can hardly be refuted, and it is equally easy to understand that such an ideal value cannot be reduced to a contingent value. Therefore, all ethical norms concerning interrelated human behavior are ultimately based on a judgment of preference. We are dealing here in fact—even though not always in a verbal formulation—with hypothetical imperatives. They demand and prohibit certain behavior not for its own sake but because this behavior, according to a general reasoned evaluation of ideal values, realizes the preferred value among the generally recognizable conditions.

With these statements we have reached the core of the discussion on the establishment of norms in modern Catholic moral theology. Traditional moral theology claims absolute authority for certain moral judgments. Thus, for instance, as is well known, we are taught that lying is never permitted even if it may save the life of a person unjustly persecuted. A false statement or similarly a sexual act other than for the purpose of procreation are, as such, to be rejected absolutely. It is further taught that there could be no reason and no circumstances possible that would ever justify such behavior. Today there are many moral theologians who object to such absolute authority in the judgment of human behavior for every single case, no matter what the consequences may be. However, they do not object to the fact that the objectively moral quality of a deed depends on the ideal value to be realized. The principle that a moral deed is judged by its object and by its goal is maintained; it is believed, however, that a conditional, a contingent ideal value cannot absolutely determine a certain action. To be sure, man has an absolute obligation to morals of absolute value; yet as a contingent being in a contingent world, he can realize the good which lays claim to him absolutely only for and through purposes that, as contingent purposes and values, are nothing but relative values, and as such never prove, a priori, to be the highest value that is above competition with any higher value. With respect to values we have only one possibility to ask always which is the preferred value, which means each concrete categorical decision must be based ultimately on a choice of preference in order not to commit the mistake of making absolute something that is contingent. Saying this we neither doubt the relevance of obligatory values nor do we contest generally binding norms. To set generally binding rules does not, in itself, mean to set rules for all times in the same way (universally), nor does it mean to set such rules, requiring or prohibiting a certain behavior, independently of any possible condition, and, therefore, without exception (absolutely). For instance, the conviction persisted until very recently that law and order can in fact be secured only if law breakers can count on the possibility of being sentenced to death; therefore, the generalizing judgment was correct: capital punishment (in general) is permitted. Today it might be difficult to make a plausible case for the execution of law breakers as the only and adequate means to save a constitutional state. Consequently we have to state in a general way: capital punishment (in general) is not permitted. Both these apparently contradicting judgments are correct, depending on the relative presupposed conditions. They express a moral norm which is valid "ut in pluribus." If further analyzed the expression "general validity" of morals means to be valid in general, i.e., these norms are valid as far as they express the general situation and as far as they consider comprehensively and adequately the necessary conditions. Norms of this kind are not just well-meant advice that can be dealt with as one pleases. They express obligatory values that no one who wants to act responsibly can ignore. They help the individual in his painful search for morally correct behavior, but they do not release him from examining whether and in what way the general rules apply to his specific case. Only by considering all values and circumstances involved can he recognize how to act in the best moral sense.

CHRISTIAN FAITH DEMANDS A RADICAL DIVORCE FROM EVIL

Man has never stopped asking about the source, roots and implications of evil in the world. Books analyzing this question, from those dealing with so-called evil, including social evils, to those dealing with so-called good or the anatomy of human aggression, have a big market. They indicate an unusual interest. It is also believed that a decisive first step toward an explanation of evil has been accomplished through the analysis of interhuman aggression. But whoever judges soberly will also detect a lot of good. Our young generation is quite sensitive concerning questions of justice. We can find a great deal of selfless willingness to help and joyous eagerness. A growing sense of solidarity and joint responsibility toward solving difficult questions of pollution and sociopolitics has become quite obvious. On the whole, good and evil keep the balance so to speak. Or in other words: we live with the balance of powers.

We can suppose that this situation was not essentially different at the time of Jesus. It is closely linked to the historical existence of man. This situation has to be taken into consideration in order to interpret correctly the prophecies and demands in Jesus' Sermon on the Mount. In the so-called antitheses as transmitted by Matthew, Jesus deals explicitly with the question of overcoming evil. It seems that evil is characterized by an inner dynamic toward escalation. Whoever gets hit, hits back, and not always in the same measure. Where there is *one* village destroyed by terrorists, the counterattack leads to the destruction of *two* villages. Where there is *one* hostage taken, in the act of revenge *two* hostages will be taken. The law of the Old Testament tried to stop such an escalation by prohibiting any extension of revenge. There was a strict law: for an eye only one eye, for a servant—we can say, for a hostage—only one hostage, etc. Jesus, in opposition to that law, wants to show with his antithesis that such limitation of revenge indeed prevents an escalation, but that, on the other hand, evil will never be overcome. The law tames and domesticates evil but is hardly apt to overcome it. Therefore, Jesus tells his disciples: if you, in your faith in the coming kingdom of God, want to help not only to limit evil but gradually to overcome it, you must be willing in any given situation to offer your left cheek if someone hits you on the right. Only by doing this will you not merely interpret the world but, by your deeds in faith, will you change the world. In the same way, you are to renounce a system of religious guarantees, as represented by the oath. You shall not abuse God as a guarantee against your mendacity. The knowledge that you are all brothers should suffice to approach each other with full trust: "let your yes be yes and your no be no." The same applies to marital strife. Troubled people cannot find help by conforming to the common practice of divorce, nor by a quantitative increase or decrease of possibilities for divorce; real help can be found only through a change of mind, a qualitative change in the attitudes and desires of man himself. Jesus does not thereby condemn a legal settlement of conflicts or even in principle the effort toward law reforms. But this dimension is not the primary concern in his message. He strikes at the roots of evil which ultimately has its origin in man's thought and desire. "His radicalism affects the essence of man, who must see himself in a new light before God and among his fellow human beings." The antitheses of the Sermon on the Mount indicate and stress values which demand particular attention from those who have devoted their life to God's rule and kingdom. A specific Christian ethos should express in its system of norms such antithetical structures. In this way it could clarify its continuing character. A linear progress of morality is probably possible only through a radicalism which, initially, cannot be precisely reasoned. Here we can perceive an element through which the faithful transcends himself—without relinquishing a grounding in reality—in an act of courage that cannot be further analyzed by reason.

Translated by Michaela Kurz

Notes

1. R. Spaemann, "Christliche Religion und Ethik," *Philosophiches Jahrbuch* 80 (1973): 282–91.
2. Ibid., p. 286.
3. M. Seckler, "Kommt der christliche Glaube ohne Gott aus?" in *Wer ist das eigentlich Gott?*, ed. H. H. Schulz (Munich, 1969), pp. 189f.
4. Ibid., p. 190.
5. Loc. cit., p. 286.

David B. Burrell

The Church and Individual Life

THE church we have come to know, and which we hope will be advanced by these discussions, serves as a shaping context for our lives. As a way of reminding us how linguistic a metaphor "context" presents, I shall treat the church as a community of discourse. More specifically, in coming to know the church as we have, we can recognize how she offers an ensemble of symbolic expressions and performances which exercise us in addressing what it is to be and to become a human being. We learn how to use the expressions as we participate in the activities; and to allow the expressions to guide us in finding our way is to let them shape our lives.

The expressions, as well as the performances which show us how to use them, are inherently symbolic. The set of statements gathered into a summary rule of belief for Catholic Christians, and proclaimed communally in the course of weekly worship, can be used as a creed because it collects the *symbola fidei*. That is, the statements it contains are framed in a language appropriate to expressing the inexpressible: the relations between divinity and humankind, and hence the parameters of human destiny.

To express what we know we cannot properly speak about, we need to employ ordinary expressions in an analogous fashion. That simply means that we must have recourse to a set of expressions whose usual employment shows they transcend their current application (normative notions generally), or put descriptive terms to a highly metaphorical use. In either case, we need to be instructed how to employ expressions so volatile: how to control the metaphors, and how to apply the evaluative notions.

The creeds themselves show us how to use the expressions they contain: initially, from the situations in which we are taught to recite them, and then by the way the statements present themselves as succinct summaries of biblical narratives. We are normally directed to proclaim our faith in a sacramental setting, where the one whom we are all addressing is the one whom we are worshipping: the Holy One, blessed be He! The context is communal even if each voice is individual; the words embody a tradition as they announce a revelation.

The point of it all is to proclaim my willingness to respond to Him and to his invitation, as the people responded to his law given them by Moses. The invitation emanates from the Lord and the response is mine, yet the language in which both are framed belongs to a community: the church. I respond to that invitation by announcing my belief in expressions embodying a tradition, yet I make my response to the Holy One—not to a church official. For I am invited to participate in a proclamation of faith, not summoned to an inquisition.

By reminding ourselves that the normal setting for proclaiming one's faith is that of worship, we can effectively safeguard the inherently analogous character of the expressions employed. We will also ready ourselves to see how such expressions can continue to play a role in shaping a person's becoming what he or she is called to become—expressions like "sinner," "witness," "disciple."

The other way in which credal language receives direction is by returning us to those biblical narratives which each statement purports to summarize. We know of the God of Abraham, Isaac and Jacob through the stories of his interacting with those individuals and their descendents—his people. We believe that He presents Himself in Jesus through the accounts of that man's life, death and resurrection. God's revelation assumes a predominantly narrative form.

The point seems obvious enough: we are offered the stories of these lives as patterns for understanding and shaping our own. The understanding which biblical revelation affords is self-involving. If we overlook the obvious point served by its narrative form, and look to biblical revelation for knowledge of another sort, we will surely miss the point entirely. And that would truly be tragic, for the point is precisely liberation from death to life: "that believing this you may have life through his name" (John 20:31).

By offering such a language—both expressions and practices—the church provides a context for becoming an individual. It is explicitly one of relatedness, set in a communal response to the Holy One. So it stands explicitly at odds with a myth of autonomy. Yet it can incorporate its own Promethean figures, led by one whose name is also mythical: Lucifer. To comprehend the story of Lucifer—more elaborated in subsequent tradition than in the Scriptures themselves—is to learn to use a key expression in the church's repertoire: "sinner."

The Gospels invite us to begin our journey to the kingdom by taking on the name of *sinner*. On the threshold of each eucharistic liturgy, we are given the opportunity to acknowledge ourselves to be sinners. I propose to begin here—with the public and personal fact that you and I are sinners—to detail one way in which church can function as the context for becoming a human being. The way I shall focus on is the passage to adulthood, showing how the Catholic tradition addresses that issue. I will take as a guide the Carmelite poet and theologian John of the Cross (1542–1591), drawing as well on the set of basic images and metaphors elaborated in the scriptures and in two Christian classics: Augustine's *Confessions* and Dante's *Divine Comedy*.

PASSAGE TO ADULTHOOD

To be able to look back on one's life and see patterns of distortion in every single thing—each endeavor, relationship or accomplishment— that's what it is to be sinner! When I turned forty-four the other day, I found myself rejoicing in that fact—that I was a sinner. What made that affirmation possible, I suspect, were the multiple ways in which I have had to suffer rather than do, undergo rather than undertake. So I rejoiced in this fact as well. In speaking of adulthood, I want to focus on this suffering which marks the transition to what Jung calls the "second half of life."[1] Suffering of this sort is not necessarily connected with pain—unless it be the painful state of not being in charge. But *that* suffering cannot be anything but salutary—for the world as well as for me. For even if I could take charge of my life, I wouldn't; my demons would. Appreciating that simple fact—the bugbear of autonomy— "made" my forty-fourth birthday: appreciating the fact that I was a sinner, and learning *how* I was.

I want to show how the Catholic tradition can help us to negotiate the passage to adulthood (as the "second half of life") by presenting that passage as a progressive discovery of fresh senses for key terms like "sinner." In this way, we can see how a community helps one to carry the burden of individuation. Augustine's *Confessions* and Dante's *Divine Comedy* each offer accounts of man's journey, the second shaped by the figure of a woman, Beatrice, whose love animated Dante's journey as it was guided by Virgil. And each proves to be at once a journey into the unknown and a journey home.

Beyond the metaphor of a journey, and the attendant images, the community which generated these classics offers a set of exercises which practice us in using that metaphor and in working with those images. These exercises are imbedded in liturgical rhythms—in the weekly round of worship, and the seasonal pattern of penitential periods and feasts. And these rhythms connect with our daily lives through the round of expected practices detailed in Matthew 25: feeding the hungry, welcoming the stranger, clothing the naked, caring for the sick, and visiting prisoners. (It is instructive to note how ethical Christianity has conspired to omit mention of the last!)

This pilgrimage model of adulthood contrasts nicely with what William Bouwsma identifies as *manhood:* a classical picture of the "finished man" reinforced with the bourgeois ideal of "having made it."[2] Jung's quite useful distinction of human life into a first and a second half will generally fail to take hold unless one can move beyond the picture of the "finished man." For Jung wants to be able to locate a shift in goals, in the way in which a person relates to his or her projects. On this scheme, the first half of a person's life will be taken up with building oneself, with establishing a place, with doing or managing the process of becoming. The second half, by contrast, will consist more in discovering how one is in fact more than oneself, by undergoing the consequences of decisions taken, and participating in the process of maturing.

One can easily see that this division of life into two halves is not merely a descriptive generalization, but offers a normative pattern as well. In fact, it stands in opposition to the standard rhetoric of our society, which knows little of compensatory movements, and so continues to urge us to go on trying to "make it." My argument will be that Jung's observations are normative, and that we can profitably identify the second half of life with adulthood. Thus the passage to adulthood becomes identical with that shift in horizons which spells a move out of the first and into the second half of life.

It follows from that hypothesis that we need an appropriate language to enable us to carry out the passage, a set of images which will allow this transition to take place in us by licensing it, as it were. The language which I shall propose comprises a set of images rooted in Augustine and Dante, and elaborated into a finely tuned set of rules for their use by the sixteenth-century spiritual master, John of the Cross. I propose this language as one especially well suited to facilitate the transition from first to second half of life, the passage to adulthood. Broadly speaking, the transition is one from doing to suffering, attained, in John's words, by exercises in detachment. Yet the effect of the exercises in detachment is not abasement, but liberation.

If I can make this case plausibly, I shall have warranted the way in which I have taken Jung's observations as normative. I would prefer not to argue directly for the identifications which I have set forth as a starting point: the second half of life with adulthood, and both with a transition from doing to undergoing. I intend rather to show that these linkages offer us a way of using human notions like growth and fidelity. Moreover, without these distinctions and identifications, notions like fidelity have little bearing on the way an individual conceives his or her development. Yet to be unable to use the language of fidelity leaves us in a wasteland, as Anthony Burgess has spelled out so trenchantly in *Clockwork Orange*. Allow me to characterize the transition more accurately, opening with Augustine and Dante, to show how one classical language for the inner life—that of John of the Cross—can succeed in spelling out its dynamics.

The crucial intellectual turning point in Augustine's life came when he was able to locate his fascination with the Manichean explanatory scheme, and identify the fascination as excessive. Although his disillusion with Faustus occasioned it, the recognition went beyond the inadequacy of Faustus' accounts to seeing how the project of pretending to explain everything—evil included—was a misguided one. As a result, he could come to appreciate how a specific strength of Christianity lay in its not presenting itself as a total explanatory scheme.

Dante's epic opens "midway this way of life," when the pilgrim's direct assault on the mountains is cut off first by a roving leopard, then by a fierce lion, and finally by a gaunt wolf. So he is compelled, if he would attain his goal, to go by another more circuitous route. Both stories are reminiscent of Jesus' words to Peter in the epilogue of John's Gospel: ". . . when you were young you put on your own belt and walked where you liked; but when you grow old you will stretch out your hands, and someone else will put a belt around you and take you where you would rather not go" (John 21:18). The writer glosses this verse heavily: "In these words he indicated the kind of death by which Peter would give glory to God," and the Jerusalem Bible footnote nails that down with "martyrdom." Yet the description could apply equally well to parenting, of course, or any other form of responsible caring, which is always a kind of death. To identify the transition from first to second half of life as a kind of death carries us to the heart of the writings of John of the Cross.

It is crucial to note that the transition is never deliberate. In fact, it cannot be, for the momentum generated by forging one's own life is too strong. It happens only as we encounter the beasts. That is, the shift in horizons turns less on conviction than on fear. Yet everything depends on what we fear. As Kierkegaard has Anti-Climacus put it: "What the child shudders at, the man regards as nothing. The child does not know what the dreadful is; this the man knows, and he shudders at it."[3] If children fear the dark, adults learn what really to fear. We all readily understand this, and we can grasp it more clearly once we appreciate the paradox of autonomy: if I *could* take charge of my own life, *I* wouldn't; my demons would. It is this inevitable fact which dogs the ideal of the finished man; so much that to appreciate it is to stand on the threshold of adulthood, ready to pass into the second half of one's life.

To pass on is to lean heavily on the language of John of the Cross. For once we have identified those alien powers which we have permitted to dominate our hearts, we can begin to sense how fettered we actually are. Then we will gain some little courage to smoke out the ways in which our cumulative rationalizations have become incorporated into an acceptable picture of ourselves. The very process of making myself—in fact, all of the strategies associated with the first half of life—have in effect delivered me up to a near-perfect bondage. To recognize this *cul-de-sac* for what it is leaves me at least ready to hear—if not quite prepared to undertake—a program of detachment. As John of the Cross puts it: "Freedom cannot abide in a heart dominated by the appetites—in a slave's heart; it dwells in a liberated heart—in a son's heart."[4] Ernest Becker's analysis of character armor comes in handy here: the very tactics which tend to bring us success in the project of fashioning ourselves contribute by that very fact to keeping us deceived about our real situation. For such tactics succeed in the measure that they ward off terrors we know to be lurking there yet dare not allow to impede us.[5]

The disciplines of detachment which John of the Cross develops are designed to deliver a person up to the transforming action of God, or better, to the purifying and saving power of God in the Spirit of Jesus. And John's powerful faith in the inward activity of that Spirit clearly animated the journey he maps so painstakingly, as every new step can be linked systematically with a new "posture" of prayer.[6] Few of us may possess a like faith, or similar experience in prayer, so we may find ourselves unable to adopt his language. Yet we cannot fail to appreciate its grammar, and the way that grammar contributes to understanding the shape of the transition we have located. As Dante puts it:

Like one who loves the gains he has amassed
And meets the hour when he must lose his loot,
Distracted in his mind and all aghast . . .

Even so was I, faced with that restless brute
Which little by little edged and thrust me back,
Back to that place wherein the sun is mute.[7]

"Midway this way of life," the skills we developed so assiduously to serve us in "making it" cease to show us the way.

After proffering his initial counsel "to have a habitual desire to imitate Christ in all your deeds by bringing your life into conformity with his," John enjoins us to find satisfaction and joy in nothing except what is for the service and glory of God. This operative counsel is spelled out in the famous maxims:

> Endeavor to be inclined always:
>   not to the easiest, but to the most difficult;
>   not to the most delightful, but to the harshest;
>   not to the most gratifying, but to the less pleasant;
>   not to what means rest for you, but to hard work;
>   not to the consoling, but to the unconsoling;
>   not to the most, but to the least;
>
>   not to the highest and most precious, but the lowest and most
>   despised;
>   not to wanting something, but to wanting nothing;
>   do not go about looking for the best of temporal things, but for the
>   worst;
>   and desire to enter into complete nudity, emptiness, and poverty in
>   everything in the world.[8]

A formidable program this, calculated to discourage anyone. Yet the message is clear: desire wearies and possession cloys. If only we could find a way to possess without possessing! This demand shapes his program.

John goes on to spell out ways of implementing these maxims in specific disciplines of detachment—all with an eye to preparing one for God's own Spirit to take the initiative and introduce us into a freedom we can only glimpse from afar. Yet there are parallel disciplines of detachment for most of us, built into assuming the responsibilities which accrue to us, as we own the tasks which come along with parenting or with "advancement." There is an inescapable logic here: one seeks a position, driven often enough by ambition or whatever, only to find that it involves an immense amount of work! Parenting works the same way, granted a degree of freedom whether to have children or not. Indeed, it is nearly impossible to spell out reasons—if there be any—for having children, but once undertaken the venture entails a passel of responsibilities. One can even discern an analogous pattern in friendship, although we seldom regard friendship as a task since it is so close to the inward "task" of becoming oneself. Yet it begins in a kind of attraction, and leads on inescapably through gratification to sacrifice.

What seems to be going on here is a gradual yet definite passing over from shaping one's own life to allowing the work to shape it. That description can be misleading, of course, since one must discern among works. To allow some works to shape our lives would not be appreciably different—outwardly at least—from shaping them ourselves. As Augustine put it, "Men call the games they play business."[9] So the disciplines of detachment must include strategies of discernment as well.

This is the point where a community can offer direction to our lives, when that community is one which transcends the worlds of work and professional associations. Ideally, such a community will provide rituals rich enough to shape our lives by giving us the language and the sustenance to find a way through the fears which emerge once we see that it is pointless to try to ward them off. These rituals will show their power precisely by contrast with those rituals which serve to reinforce a brittle character armor by systematically repressing those same fears. They will do this by offering us a language analogous enough to continue to illuminate us, and nourishment enough to sustain us when no illumination is forthcoming. Guided by such a language and strengthened by such nourishment, we will be freed to recognize work that is pointless for what it is. To learn how to use an expression like "sinner" again and again, and to continue to find it liberating, is to understand what I can only gesture to here.

The paradigm I am working from, of course, is a liturgical community: one in which people can and do worship God. The pattern is the ancient one of the *berakah:* hearing the word and responding to it by giving thanks. My contention is that the disciplines and rhythms of such a worshipping community will allow genuine fears to emerge and to replace those *ersatz* anxieties attendant upon our systemic efforts to ward off the real fears.

How can we characterize these disciplines of detachment? What is it to be faithful to a work in a discerning way? Two features stand out: first, to respect the material with which one is asked to work, and second, to develop patterns of collaboration with those with whom we are asked to work, learning how to confront as well as to encourage. The aim is gradually to yield one's own project to the work which develops, in the measure that we can discern how the work detaches us from the myopia of "my own" perspectives, and the isolation of my self-project. The logic of this process is two-fold: it is at once a death to my timetable and projects, as well as an enlargement of my *self*— inwardly, through suffering.

Perhaps laying out the dynamics in this way will not prove effective, unless one explicitly attends to the voice of the Spirit inviting us, calling us to "go forth," as John of the Cross insists in the *Spiritual Canticle*.[10] For trying to present the dynamics of detachment without reference to that power risks abstracting our considerations from the very context which animates them, and also leaves the entire discussion open to be mistaken as offering one more meditation exercise for living in our world of complexities. Furthermore, all that is negative and destructive seems to have been glossed over. Doubtless the scenario of the transfiguration of Jesus on Tabor should explicitly preface any account of the disciplines of detachment beholden to John of the Cross. Recall that that numinous episode occurred as the four of them—Jesus with Peter, James and John—"went up the mountain to pray" (Luke 9:28).

What I have tried to do is to show how significant a shift in horizons is involved in moving into what Carl Jung has called the "second half of life." I have argued that this shift is no less significant than the process of inward liberation from "appetites" detailed by John of the Cross' analytic description of the way through death to life revealed in Jesus. I have further suggested that it is illuminating to identify that shift in horizon with authentic adulthood, by contrast to the ideal of *manhood:* the finished, autonomous man. What marks that difference is the paradox of autonomy: if I *could* take charge (of this work, of my life), *I* wouldn't; my demons (neuroses) would. Once we begin to show how the "take-charge" ideal of the first half of life must work to suppress one's fears, we are emboldened to allow those very fears to emerge. Finally, questing for the language and sustenance to brave these fears and to continue on the way which begins to show itself *is* the adventure of adulthood.[11] That this journey entails more suffering than doing suggests that the process will in fact lead one to a truth beyond oneself.

ROLE OF CHURCH

The foregoing exercise has shown how some of the resources of the Christian tradition can be brought to bear on a perennial issue, that of human growth. In discussing how that tradition might serve humankind into the future, we will want to elaborate other ways in which the church can become the sort of community guiding and sustaining us through similar passages. The most pressing ones carry us into social and political issues. For example, how can church practice assist in developing alternative contexts for living and producing, along lines suggested by E. F. Schumacher's *Small is Beautiful?*[12]

Schumacher himself relies heavily on the Catholic tradition. How might the effort to provide a context for measured human development call forth dimensions of that tradition hitherto untapped? Does the journey beyond Vatican II invite Catholics to explore a new form of sectarian community? Has *aggiornamento* too easily played into our Constantinian tendencies? These are a few of the questions which suggest themselves to one who looks to the church as offering from her tradition a living context for those passages which we cannot escape as well as the timely alternatives which beckon us to decision.

Notes

1. On the "second half of life," cf. inter alia C. G. Jung's "Stages of Life," in *Collected Works*, vol. 8 (New York, 1960).

2. William J. Bouwsma, "Christian Adulthood," *Daedelus* 102 (1976): 77–92.

3. Søren Kierkegaard, *Sickness unto Death* (Princeton, 1954), p. 145.

4. *Ascent of Mount Carmel* 4.6, in K. Kananaugh and O. Rodriguez, ed., *The Collected Works of St. John of the Cross* (New York, 1964; reprinted Washington, 1975), p. 80.

5. Ernest Becker, *The Denial of Death* (New York, 1973), esp. chap. 4; also Herbert Fingarette, *Self-Deception* (London, 1969).

6. This assertion represents an interpretative hypothesis suggested by John C. Gerber, C.S.C., as we offered a seminar in John of the Cross. It deserves to be tested throughout his writings.

7. *The Comedy of Dante Alighieri: Hell,* trans. Dorothy Sayers (Harmondsworth, 1949), Canto 1.55–60, pp. 72–73.

8. *Ascent* 13.3–6 (in *Collected Works,* pp. 102–3).

9. Augustine, *Confessions* 1.9, trans. R. S. Pine-Coffin (Harmondsworth, 1961), p. 30.

10. *Spiritual Canticle,* Stanza 36 (in *Collected Works,* p. 547).

11. A remarkable study of this passage, using the *Divine Comedy* as an epic vehicle, is Helen Luke's *From Dark Wood to White Rose* (Pecos, N. M.: Dove Publications, 1975).

12. E. F. Schumacher, *Small Is Beautiful: Economics as if People Mattered* (New York, 1973).

PART 5

Church and Society

Johann B. Metz

For a Renewed Church Before a New Council: A Concept in Four Theses

The basic thesis: I should like to draw your attention to a necessary change in the life of the church that cannot result from a new council but at the least must be presupposed if a future council is not simply to reproduce or confirm the present misery of the church. This change has to take place first in the direction of the church's stronger concentration on the North-South axis (thesis 1) and, in connection with this, in the direction of a mystical-political radicalization of the church's life through discipleship and apocalyptic (theses 2–4).

Thesis 1: From a church of the West to a Church of the North-South axis; or, the church in changing from a citizen's church to a church of class conflict.

1.1. An epochal new situation has resulted from a change in the societal problems of the world, and a challenge of the first order has arisen for the universal church. Today our world's great societal problems cannot be simply defined by the so-called East-West conflict. This East-West conflict has in the meanwhile been superseded by the so-called North-South conflict, that is, by the opposition between the rich industrial countries of the North and the world's poverty areas in the South. These southern regions traditionally have a population that is largely Catholic. They therefore belong to the one Catholic Church. This North-South conflict, therefore, comes to the fore within the universal church as the relation of the central European and North American church to the church of the Latin American subcontinent.

How does the church come to terms with this situation? How does the one church come to terms with the obvious class conflicts between the countries of the North and the South if it encompasses both in itself? How are these class conflicts compatible with the lived unity of the church? How can they be harmonized with the church as the one Eucharistic community, with the church as the erected sign of eschatological unity? How does the church deal with the fact that in it many persons, indeed whole nations, live in collective darkness as if they were "no man's son"? Can the rich churches of the North facing the poor churches of the South equalize with almsgiving what in the meanwhile has become recognized as structural injustice?

1.2. These are questions directed today to the whole church and not only, not even primarily, to the poor churches of the South itself, but especially to the rich churches of the North. This question involves a central ecclesial problem since the church's lived unity and credibility are at stake. The answer to this problem will decide whether our Catholic Church is de facto a universal church or whether it is just a "europocentric church" with "dependencies" in the poor areas of the world.

1.3. A theology that recognizes in this situation a challenge of the first order to the church takes as its basis the mystical-political double structure and double obligations of the faith and of the church of which I will speak in more detail in the second thesis. Such a political theology does not thereby raise the Kingdom of God to a goal of politics and economics. But it insists that even the Kingdom of God is not indifferent to international trade prices (as the Document of the German Synod "Our Hope" states). Such a political theology does not confuse God with a (political) utopia, to which, as is well known, no one prays. But it insists that nothing incriminates our *one* church more than the attempt to preserve its political innocence by withholding its vote in the face of the suffering and conflicts of this world. If the church has already become political just by proclaiming the dignity of the person and the existence of all humans as *subjects* before God, then it has to stand up for this dignity in the face of the utmost dangers. It must not only fight that humans *remain* subjects under the pressure of collective forces, but also that people *become* subjects by transcending misery and suppression. The credibility of its orthodoxy demands this.

*Thesis 2: From an over-adapted church
to a church of discipleship: or, the
church in transition from a popular
"church for the people" to a radical
"church of the people."*

2.1. The "church" (I realize that this is just as unsatisfactory as it is an unavoidable generalization without any subject) cannot solve the crisis of its historical identity and its societal legitimation (cf. below 2.4.iii.b.) in a purely interpretative or hermeneneutical manner, but only by practical identification. The problem of its identity is fundamentally a theory-praxis problem. That praxis whose intelligible and identity-securing power cannot be replaced by an interpretation is called discipleship. The church's crisis is due to a deficit in discipleship and to difficulties in adapting to Jesus. The "church of discipleship" which is demanded does not amount to a special church of the few that easily distances itself from every form of a "people's" church. But rather it introduces the transition from a traditional "church for the people" to a living "church of the people."

2.2. This discipleship permanently exhibits a total double structure. It has a mystical and a situational practical-political component. Both grow in their radicality not in reverse, but in converse proportionality.

2.2.i. The discipleship of Jesus has in the end a mystical-political structure not because it is "a" way to individual moral perfection, but because it is "his" way to the Father. It is essentially "excess." It should not be relaxed by any middle of the road ideology or any ideology of balance (neither by an "as well as" nor by a "neither/nor") and robbed of its options. This mysticism of discipleship takes place neither outside nor above the political situation with its societal contradictions and sufferings.

2.2.ii. Whenever the mystical-political double structure of discipleship is neglected, then an understanding of discipleship finally gains acceptance that results in a praxis of a "truncated" discipleship: namely, discipleship as an act of pure inwardness, on the one hand, and as an exclusively regulative idea, as a purely humanistic-political concept, on the other hand. What results is either a reduction of discipleship to a purely social-political dimension of action or a reduction to a private-religious spirituality. The discipleship that continues Jesus' engagement for the honor of God within the individual and societal contradictions of our life remains excluded. This truncated discipleship has its theological pendant in the danger of a modern monophysitism that seeks only to legitimate itself through Christ but does not factually follow him, and undergoes the danger of a Jesuology without transcendence that understands discipleship as a copy of political patterns that are anyway in vogue.

2.3. Discipleship has not only applicative, but also strict systematic significance.

2.3.i. Discipleship is the central topic of Christology if the logos of this Christology is not to be simply confused with the (purely contemplative) logos of the Greeks. Christ must always be so conceived that he is never only thought of. In this sense Christology essentially expresses a practical knowledge. It stands under the primacy of praxis. Only in following him do we know to whom we have committed ourselves. The christological knowledge is primarily formed and handed down not conceptually but in stories of discipleship. Therefore, it also has an indispensably *narrative-practical* component.

2.3.ii. The praxis of discipleship should therefore not remain limited to individual moral praxis, for individual moral action is in no way societally neutral or politically innocent. Any Christology of discipleship therefore must inquire into the societal and political context of such a discipleship. In this sense, it is—necessarily—*political Christology*.

2.4. For example: the church of discipleship *as the church of poverty*—in view of thesis 1.

Poverty as the praxis of discipleship has a mystical-political double structure. Let me attempt to define poverty: "Poverty as a virtue is the protest against the dictatorship of having, of possessing, and of pure self-aggrandizement. It pushes toward practical solidarity with those poor for whom poverty is precisely not a virtue, but a life situation and a societal imposition." This poverty of discipleship cannot be strictly interiorized into a "poverty of spirit" that is indifferent toward the rich and poor and which finally degenerates into an illusion (strained and without consequence) that one possesses as if one did not possess. This poverty does not have any more spiritual meaning than its concrete literal expression. This literal, socially manifest conception of poverty has an eminent spiritual meaning and exactly thereby has significance for church and society.

2.4.i. Thesis 1 has already sketched the primary and indeed decisive challenge for the church. In the face of the challenge described there can anyone put down the topic of poverty as "socially romantic?"

2.4.ii. In a society whose public interest is almost totally determined by the goal of possession and therefore considers everything to be negligible that has no market value, the church has either a radical or a miserable existence. Of its very constitution, the church is specified by a praxis that has no immediate market value, e.g., friendship, gratitude, love, anamnestic solidarity with the dead, mourning, etc. The church must therefore increasingly become in itself a sign of protest against the dominance of a mere market society in which nothing exists that cannot be marketed, where no ideal of justice is publicly admitted other than the justice of the market and no ideal of humanity is admitted other than that oriented toward specific purposes. The Christian posture of protest, which is demanded here, is the socially manifest will to be poor.

2.4.iii. The socially manifest discipleship of poverty does not substitute for mysticism and spirituality. But it specifically designates the locale of mysticism and prayer and it demands that we not only pray for the poor, but also with them, that we are not only pious for the burdened and oppressed, but also with them. In this lies the radicality of the Gospel for the church of today.

2.4.iii.a. Only in this way can the church change from a populist-traditionalist "church for the people" to a church of solidarity, a "church of the people." In any case, for such a church to emerge it is necessary that the people increasingly learn and experience how much they themselves in their own history of suffering are included in the prayer language of the church. Obviously we do not have an ecclesial mysticism and spirituality in which the poor and exploited, the weak and browbeaten can see themselves as subjects of this language and promises. Obviously the liturgical and prayer language can and should not be the same for all without any reference to specific situations and persons. Obviously Jesus' promises for the lowly and oppressed should not be proclaimed without consequences and should not be applied to all in every possible situation if we do not want to commit a semantic deception in regard to his Gospel.

If the church can successfully accomplish this change, then it can more credibly witness that even the damaged and oppressed life has an invincible hope and promise that cannot be explained away as projection and opium for the people. Only such a transformation of the church can verify that the engagement for the honor of God and the struggle for more justice for all belong together as the two sides of a coin.

2.4.iii.b. If the church succeeds in changing, then it can overcome its crisis of identity and legitimation: the growing schism between church and people; the doubts from below that comparatively weigh the heaviest; the suspicion of "stale mysteries"; the disappearance of interiorized and highly burdenable convictions among the people; the growing inability to allow oneself to be consoled; the suspicion that the later church has already long lost its identity with Jesus and his intentions.

Thesis 3: From an ecclesial authority based on juridical-administrative competency to an ecclesial authority based on religious competency; or, the leadership of the church in transition from a leadership that "has" authority to a leadership that "is" authority.

3.1. Since authorities are no longer accepted without question but are exposed to the critical spontaneity of reason, something like a permanent crisis of ecclesial authority, specifically a crisis of its societal legitimation, exists. In a society no longer defined as religious, ecclesial authority can only avoid the impression of being an irrational, arbitrary domination if it legitimizes itself as an authority based on competency. It does not, however, suffice for ecclesial authority to have cognitive competency, that is, the competency to argue its point. For an authority that has only as much validity as its arguments is at the most an intellectual, but not a religious authority. It can be tendentiously dissolved into knowledge. Juridic-administrative authority, however, also does not suffice, and in my opinion it stands too much in the foreground. In this instance legal acts of sovereignty (possibly between the church here and the state there) and administrative and organizational superlegitimation cover up and hide the diminishing basis of consent for ecclesial authority. It is decisive today more than ever that a legitimation of ecclesial authority based on religious competency be added to the legitimation based on theological or legal-administrative competency. By religious competency is meant the form of a charismatic authority that not only "has" authority in a societal context and wears its signs of sovereignty, but also "is" authority in its total existence and praxis, an authority of witness with a radiant power to permeate ecclesial and societal life.

3.2. The criterion for such a religious competency of ecclesial authority is not open for disposition. It is determined. It is called discipleship. Religious competency results from radical discipleship.

3.3. Such an understanding of authority could finally effect that transformation of "domination" that is necessitated by our world-society if we are to survive humanly. What is domination under the conditions of a growing standardization and manipulation of humans? Obviously our societal systems have not at all yet learned to control "domination" in such a way that they do not again and again produce exploitation and oppression and do not stabilize a hopeless (promiseless) imperialism of people over people against which Jesus has proclaimed his message of the Kingdom of God.

Thesis 4: From a church of an evolutionistically softened eschatology to a church of the imminent expectation; or, the church in the field of tension between apocalyptic and politics.

This thesis points out the apocalyptic symbols as corrective factors in regard to church and society. They touch the heart of our belief system as well as the basic symbols ("evolution") of our life systems.

4.1. The church increasingly becomes for our society a *quantité négligeable* because no longer is anything expected of it. And finally nothing is expected of it because it makes the impression of being the secret accomplice of that resignation and hopelessness that permeates our modern, evolutionistically attuned consciousness, which we cover up with such predicates as "sober," "rational" or "pragmatic."

In the meanwhile Christianity's potentials of hope have become too interiorized, detemporalized, and individualized (referred to the situation of the individual's death). The absence of a temporally understood imminent expectation has in the end weakened and degenerated discipleship. For radical discipleship is de facto not livable "if the time is not shortened" and the "Lord does not soon return." Discipleship and imminent expectation belong inseparably together. Do not Christians present to the world the embarrassing spectacle of a people who speak of hope but do not actually hope for anything anymore? Do they still expect an end at all—not only for themselves but for the world and its time? Is the church still apocalyptic in this sense?

4.2. Crisis: Is a limitation and an end of time still conceivable? Or has the expectation of an end of time long been shoved off into the realm of mythology because time itself has become a homogeneous continuum that contains no surprises, the "poor infinity" of an empty, evolutionarily extended and corrupted "eternity," in which everything can happen but this one thing: that a second becomes "the door through which the Messiah enters history," and in which it is therefore time for the time. The symbols for the understanding of time have long been changed. The apocalyptic symbol of the breakdown and end of time has been exchanged for the pseudo-religious symbol of evolution which in its impenetrableness so much permeates us all that we scarcely perceive any longer its irrational quasi-religious domination over us.

Nevertheless, the reinterpretation of the "imminent expectation" into a "constant expectation" remains a semantic deception of the basic temporal structure of Christian hope. It indirectly confirms how much we Christians have succumbed to the anonymous pressures of an evolutionary consciousness of time.

4.3. Apocalyptic deficiency in theology and church.

4.3.i. If I judge correctly then all types of contemporary eschatology—the "realized" as well as the futuristic—are already adapted to an evolutionary understanding of time that forces them to privatize extremely all imminent expectations and compels them to conceive of God's future either strictly atemporally (in the paradox of time and eternity) or forcedly to project it on an evolutionary scheme. Has not such a consciousness of time permeated theology for so long that theology can understand itself as a type of permanent reflection not irritated by any imminent expectation or interrupted by any experience of "meaninglessness" and therefore not under the pressure of time or the pressure for action?

4.3.ii. Does not the church function as an anti-apocalyptic institution that absorbs expectations that can be disappointed (and these are the authentic expectations) and instead stabilizes timeless individual hopes? Does not the church function as an anti-apocalyptic institution that in the name of propriety and balance long ago removed all the eccentricities of Christianity, resigned itself to the course of events, and adapted to the way of the world without having to expect the imminent return of its Lord?

4.4. The passionate expectation of the "day of the Lord" does not lead to an apocalyptic dream-dancing that forgets all practical demands of discipleship. It is rather the time-symbol of evolution that lames discipleship. Imminent expectation, on the contrary, provides the hope that has been appeased and seduced by evolution with a perspective of expectation and hope. Only it brings the pressure of time and of action to discipleship; that is, it does not paralyze political responsibility but establishes its foundation.

4.5. Apocalyptic imminent expectation is and must remain the mystical correlative to an experienced political reality. A glance at the history of religions and especially at the New Testament teaches us the nature of this political reality. It is the time of crisis, the time of suffered persecution, of overwhelming injustice and inhumanity. Perhaps our contemporary age does not produce apocalypticists and allows apocalyptic language to appear so displaced because our age distributes (together with its crises, catastrophes, injustices and inhumanities) the sweet poison of an evolutionary progress and—despite everything—the illusion of an incessant growth which makes us all lethargic and insensitive to the extent of horror and misery. Does the church act and react at least here with apocalyptic sensibility and phantasy? Or does it also remain in apathy and mollification?

Charles E. Curran

Social Ethics: Agenda for the Future

THIS study will discuss the future agenda for the church in the area of social ethics and the relationship of church and society. The perspective will be that of Catholic social ethics with a realization that a truly Catholic social ethics is ecumenical both in terms of its relation to other Christian thought and action and in relation to all people of good will. This essay will consider the question against a broad general background but give special importance to the perspective of Catholic social ethics in the United States.

A first consideration logically should focus on the issues involved. What are the particular problems and questions facing the world and the church in the area of social ethics?

One point is certain. There will be no lack of issues. The future agenda can and must learn from what Christians and others have been doing in the past as well as from a true discernment of the problems of the present and the future. The Second Vatican Council grouped the issues of church and society under five headings—marriage and the family, culture, socio-economic life, life of the political community, and the fostering of peace.[1] The World Conference on Church and Society sponsored by the World Council of Churches in Geneva in 1966 divided its material into four sections—economic development, nature and function of the state, structure of international cooperation, and man and community in changing societies.[2] Recently the "Call to Action" conference under the auspices of the American bishops treated the following areas: church, ethnicity and race, family, humankind, nationhood, neighborhood, personhood, work.[3]

Theology as such has no exclusive insight into discerning the social problems facing the world and the church today. Theology, like all other individuals and groups within society and the church, must try to learn from all possible sources what are the primary issues facing the world and society today. Any true discernment process, recognizing the importance given to participation by Pope Paul VI in *Octogesima Adveniens*,[4] must call for the participation of all in discerning these problems—especially minorities and those who are oppressed and suffering. Newer problems have emerged in the last few years, but questions concerning the poor and discrimination because of race or sex will continue to be very significant questions.

From the theological perspective the more significant questions concern method—how theology should approach such social questions and how the church should carry out its social mission. These are the two main tasks to be pursued in this paper. However, these more methodological questions might best be raised in the context of a particular substantive issue. Social economic issues will be chosen to focus the methodological questions.

In the midst of the myriad social issues facing society, it is difficult to select one issue as primary, but the social economic issue would have to be considered very important if not primary. The papal encyclicals starting with Leo XIII concentrated on social economic issues. In the United States there was a strong emphasis on social justice in the literature, but in the last few decades this aspect has unfortunately waned. Social economic justice in the encyclicals and in American Catholic literature centered on the economic questions of safeguarding the rights of workers—a living wage, the right to join unions, provision against illness and sudden catastrophe, the right to own property.

The changed economic circumstances in the United States obviously influenced the decreased interest in social economic questions. The war economy of World War II artificially solved the problems of the depression. Catholics who used to be the poor of the land moved into the middle class after that war. The new poor (especially the blacks) were not Roman Catholic, and it was somewhat easy for the church to forget about them. Even the Spanish-speaking who are Roman Catholic were easily overlooked. American Catholics struggling to prove they could be loyal Americans tended not to be critical of America, the land of opportunity. The post-World War II struggle in which Roman Catholicism and the United States were the two bulwarks of the free world against the Communist menace only served to heighten the identification of American and Catholic and made Catholics less critical of their own society.[5]

However, the social economic problem still remains. In the United States such questions as tax reform and welfare reform, although they are not radical questions, show the importance of the socio-economic

sphere. Even more fundamental are the problems of poverty still existing in the United States. The most significant development highlights
the world-wide nature of the question.[6] The developing nations of the
world feel the inequities of the present economic order. Liberation
theology coming from the South American experience calls for a radical change in the economic structures of society. North Americans
must look beyond their narrow boundaries to see the problem in its
total world-wide scale. Issues such as peace, human rights, and sexual
equality are always important questions, but the proper distribution of
the goods of creation remains very significant. John Coleman Bennett
has recently called attention to the importance of economic ethics.[7]
Thus social economic questions can well serve as illustrations of how
both theology and the Church should approach social ethics and social
action.

THEOLOGICAL APPROACHES

Various questions of theological methodology and approaches will be
raised, but first some assumptions coming from recent developments in
social ethics will be mentioned. First, Catholic social ethics can no
longer work out of the model of the nature-supernature, kingdom-world
dichotomy which too often characterized Roman Catholic thought in
the past. The gospel and the kingdom must be positively related to the
world and the social problems facing human existence. The second
assumption concerns the need for a historically conscious approach
which will be much more inductive.

Both these assumptions are comparatively recent in Catholic social
ethics. The Pastoral Constitution on the Church in the Modern World is
the first document of the hierarchical magisterium to incorporate such
approaches. Note the emphasis on overcoming the dichotomy between
faith and the world, the gospel and our daily life, and also the methodology which begins the discussion of particular social questions by an
inductive reading of the signs of the times. These two approaches are
even more evident in the Medellín documents issued by the South
American bishops in 1968. Although these characteristics did not appear in official Catholic Church documents before 1963, now they can
correctly be assumed as necessary aspects of any Christian social
ethics.

A third assumption recognizes the need for critical reason and an
emphasis on praxis. Moral theology in general and social ethics in
particular obviously are more disposed to accept such an emphasis.
Again there will be differences in the amount of emphasis given to
critical reason and praxis, but still one must underscore the importance
of such aspects in social ethics today.

Mediation

Roman Catholic theology has traditionally been characterized by an acceptance of mediation. Catholic theologies of the church and of natural law illustrate this fact. God and God's presence to us is mediated in and through the church. God's plan for human action is not primarily known directly and immediately from God but rather in and through our understanding of the human. The divine plan in no way short-circuits the human reasoning process, but precisely in and through human reason reflecting on our existence we arrive at what God wants us to do.

Contemporary emphasis on the gospel and on the kingdom calls for some kind of mediation. The hermeneutic problem in understanding the scriptures recognizes the need for a mediating principle going from the gospel to contemporary existence. How does one go from the gospel or the concept of the kingdom to the particulars of the social, economic and political world in which we live?

Contemporary liberation theologians such as Gutierrez also recognize the need for a mediating principle. Gutierrez acknowledges three distinct levels of liberation which affect each other but are not the same—political liberation, the liberation of man through history and liberation from sin.[8] Gutierrez calls for a mediation through utopias and eschews a politico-religious messianism which does not sufficiently respect the autonomy of the political arena. Faith and political action will not enter into a correct and fruitful relationship except through utopia. Utopia is characterized by three elements—its relationship to historical reality, the verification in praxis, and its rational nature.[9] Hugo Assmann calls for a mediation through a sociological analysis based on Marxism.[10] Assmann thus seems to argue for a very specific mediation.

Perhaps the American scene can offer another mediating principle—distributive justice. The Catholic tradition in the United States has emphasized distributive justice, as seen in the significant book of that title by John A. Ryan. Ryan used distributive justice as the canon for the proper distribution of the products of industry among the producers of the product.[11] In contemporary philosophical writing much more importance has been paid lately to questions of justice and distributive justice.[12] The concept of distributive justice thus enables Catholic ethics to enter into dialogue with many other philosophers and people of good will.

The particular questions that are being raised in the American context today emphasize problems that readily fit under the category of distributive justice—making medical care available for all; income maintenance programs guaranteeing a minimum income for all; an equitable tax system doing away with regressive taxes such as sales taxes or the existing social security tax.[13] The rubric of distributive justice addresses the very significant question of the proper distribution of the goods of this world. Questions of the international economic order can readily be approached in and through this understanding.

Distributive justice as a mediating concept properly emphasizes the biblical concept that the goods of creation exist for all human beings.[14] Too often, especially in the context of the United States, a rugged individualism and a poor concept of freedom have characterized the understanding of the ownership of goods. Distributive justice avoids the pitfalls of a narrowly individualistic concept of justice and rightly emphasizes the Christian belief that the God of creation destined the goods of creation for all human beings.[15] The concept of distributive justice remains quite generic, and there can be and will be disagreements about particular ramifications. However, it seems to me that it serves quite well as a mediating concept between the gospel demands and the realities of the present situation.

Mediation and Specificity

The acceptance of mediation recognizes the relative autonomy of the human, human reason and scientific data and their interpretation. Theological and ethical judgments cannot short-circuit these other aspects. Political, social and economic data and their interpretation must be respected by theological ethics in coming to its conclusions. Theological ethics can and should offer guidance for our choices in these matters, but such choices are heavily dependent on scientific data and their interpretation. Theology often cannot say which psychological theory or which sociological interpretation is more adequate for interpreting the reality in question.

Some so stress the autonomy of the human, human reason and human sciences that they contend that theological ethics is incompetent to draw any such specific conclusions about what should be done in practice.[16] I deny this assertion. Human judgments are not merely economic, social or political judgments. They are truly human and moral judgments even though they involve a great deal of complex scientific data and interpretation. It is precisely because of being mediated through such specifics of human sciences that such human, moral and Christian judgments cannot claim to be the only possible Christian interpretation. Sometimes it is rather easy to identify the concrete solution with the Christian approach, as in the condemnation of torture or the blatant violation of human rights. But in many cases the Christian solution cannot be so readily identified with any one approach, primarily because of the fact that the final judgment relies quite heavily on scientific data and their interpretation. In practice it will often be impossible to claim that there is only one possible Christian solution and no other. Take, for example, proposals made for nuclear disarmament or different ways of providing basic medical care for all.

Eschatology

Eschatological considerations have exerted a strong influence on contemporary theology. In the light of eschatology and of the fullness of the kingdom, the present social, political and economic conditions are shown to be imperfect and in need of change. The status quo can never be totally accepted by one who has an eschatological vision. The call to improve the structures of our world must always beckon the Christian.

At the very minimum an eschatological vision provides a negative critique of existing structures. However, ultimately such a critique should also call for a positive response which works to bring about change. The eschatological vision and the understanding of the kingdom can furnish positive aspects in terms of the values, goals, ideals and attitudes that must be present in all Christian approaches. These positive aspects alone do not arrive at concrete solutions. As mentioned above, such values must be mediated through the scientific data and their interpretation in coming to grips with concrete problems.

An eschatological vision calls for a continual effort to change the social, political and economic structures in which we live. However, the fullness of the eschatological vision will never be totally achieved. The Christian recognizes the power of sin in the world and the need to struggle continually against the forces of sin. The kingdom will never be perfectly present in this world; its fullness lies beyond our grasp. Imperfection and lack of completeness will characterize our structures. Likewise, one must reject the naive optimism of Protestant liberalism, which identified any change as necessarily good.

Too often in the immediate past some people readily accepted the need for social action and social change, but they quickly became disillusioned when such change did not occur. If the experience of the last decade teaches us anything, it is the need for a long-term commitment to bring about the kinds of social changes which are necessary. Romantic visionaries might be willing to give a bit of their time or a certain amount of effort in trying to bring about change, but they too readily become discouraged in the light of the long-haul situation. Consequently, the virtue of hope strengthens the individual to continue commitment to the struggle even when success seems all too absent. Relatively oppressive and unjust structures will not be changed readily, quickly or overnight.

Since the fullness of the eschaton serves as a negative critique on all existing structures, the Christian recognizes that the kingdom cannot be totally identified with any one specific approach. The Christian must always be willing to criticize all things—including one's own vision and tactics in the light of the eschaton. Too often Christians have too readily identified the gospel or the kingdom with their own cause, country or philosophy. Specifically in the United States, the older Protestants too readily identified the kingdom of God with the United States.[17] The immigrant Catholics at times strained too mightily to prove there was no incompatibility between being American and Catholic.[18]

Such a critical eschatological perspective calls for continual vigilance and self-criticism. The danger, however, always remains that people will use this as an excuse to do nothing and thus accept the status quo. The eschatological vision should never be employed as an excuse for non-involvement. Christian theology must be willing to criticize all ideologies and their approaches, but there are still some approaches which are more adequate than others and must be adopted in practice. The Christian and eschatological vision must be willing to become incarnate in concrete historical, cultural and political circumstances even though one recognizes the risks involved. In this context I prefer to use the term strategies to refer to the particular approaches that Christians can use in changing social structures. These strategies can and should be very specific, but they can never be absolutized and removed from critical reflection. In this way one avoids the dogmatization of many forms of ideological theories.

An eschatological understanding together with a recognition of mediation also tends to argue against the acceptance of any overly simplistic solutions to social problems. My own innate theological "prejudice" also argues for such complexity. It is too simplistic to reduce all ethical problems to any one type of opposition. Social problems cannot be simplistically reduced to just any one factor, be it that of class, sex, race or country. However, it can be that one of these aspects is more significant in a particular situation and thus furnishes the strategy that must be employed in that situation in order to overcome the oppression and injustice.

Although eschatological considerations are most important, I do not think eschatology alone (especially apocalyptic eschatology) can serve as an adequate basis for the development of moral theology or social ethics. I have proposed that the stance or logical first step in moral theology embraces the fivefold Christian mysteries of creation, sin, incarnation, redemption and resurrection destiny. The failure to incorporate all of these aspects stands as a negative critique of such past approaches as Catholic natural law, Lutheran two-realm theory, liberal Protestantism and Neo-Orthodoxy. More positively, such a stance provides the basic horizon or perspective within which moral theology and Christian social ethics should be developed.

Personal and/or Structural Change

Catholic social thought in general and especially since the nineteenth century has emphasized the need and importance of structural change. It is not enough merely to call for personal change and a change of heart. Catholic ethics has traditionally recognized structures and institutions as necessary aspects of human existence, even calling them natural organizations in the sense that human beings are social by nature and thus called to form groups, institutions and structures to creatively accomplish what human beings alone are incapable of doing. Liberal Catholic social thought in the United States has often been associated with the call to reform the social, political, and economic structures of society.[19] At times some elements of radical Catholic social reform have so stressed the personal element they have not given enough importance to the need for a change of structures.[20]

From my perspective both changes of heart and changes of structure are necessary in social ethics. Unfortunately these two aspects too often are separated and the need for both is not stressed. The ''Call to Action'' conference sponsored by the American bishops in Detroit in the fall of 1976 rightfully called for structural changes but said little or nothing about the need for change of heart and all the educational and motivational aspects that can help bring about such a change.

The present nature of the economic change required in the world is of such a nature that it cannot be accomplished without a somewhat radical change of attitude on the part of individual persons and especially individual persons existing within the more wealthy nations of the world. When change itself is not too radical, then there is no need for great personal change of heart and attitudes. This has been the assumption and the premise of liberal social reformers in the United States. The myth of ever greater growth insisted that change means that more people share more equitably in the ever growing progress—especially material progress. Progress implied more for everyone with no need for anyone to give up what one already enjoys.[21]

Already there are signs even in the United States that such an approach cannot deal with the extent of the problems that are being faced today. The energy crisis might call for a great change in life-styles and attitudes of many Americans. Ecological problems have made us very suspect of the older notion of progress and the fact that the future will be bigger and better than the present or the past. Especially in the context of the international economic order the rich nations of the world are called to a more radical type of change which cannot be accomplished without a change of heart of individuals and all that is entailed with such a change. Americans must be willing to give up some of their high material standard of living in order that other people on the earth might have an equitable share of the goods of creation. Recent proposals to the effect that small is beautiful remind us of the profound kinds of changes that are necessary. Thus, good theological ethical theory combined with the understanding of the magnitude of the problems that we are facing, especially in the areas of socio-economic ethics, remind us of the need for both personal change of heart and structural change. Any theological ethics which fails to recognize both will tend to be inadequate.

Harmony and Conflict

Catholic social thought, with its traditional emphasis on the natural law as an ordering of reason, has tended to see the world and society in general in terms of order and harmony rather than in terms of conflict and opposition. Catholic theory has seen no true opposition but rather concord between law and freedom. Good law does not restrict our freedom but rather tells human beings to do that which by nature they are called to do. Hierarchical ordering dominated our understanding of human nature as well as our understanding of human society and of the Church, with the lower aspects serving the higher. All the individual parts work together in proper coordination and subordination for the good of the whole. When applied to the economic order this called for the cooperation of all the individual elements and units in the economic order—capital, labor and management working together for the common good. The corporate society proposed by many Catholic theorists and espoused by Pope Pius XI in *Quadragesimo Anno* inculcates such an emphasis on hierarchical ordering and working together for the common good.[22] At times in practice there was an innate realism which recognized the existence of problems and the need for some conflict in such questions as war, strikes and disagreements; but the heavy emphasis in Catholic theory was on order and harmony.

The harmony-conflict question surfaces above all in views of society and the relationship among the classes existing in society. In the economic order, Marxism talks about a class struggle between the poor and the rich. How should Catholic ethics look at such conflictual understandings of human existence? In general, Catholic social thought in my judgment must give more importance to conflict with a somewhat decreased emphasis on order and harmony. A recognition of the presence of sin as well as a more historically conscious methodology will put less influence on order and harmony than in an older Catholic approach. However, a greater recognition of the role of conflict does not mean that all social relationships should be seen in terms of conflict or that conflict is the ultimate and most fundamental way of viewing the human scene.

Christianity ultimately calls for love and reconciliation. Love of enemies has been a hallmark of Christian teaching and preaching—if not, unfortunately, of Christian action. Christian social ethics can never forget the appeal to the human person as person to change one's own heart and to work for a change of social structures. Conflict for the Christian cannot be the ultimate nor can it be accepted for its own sake. However, on this side of the fullness of the eschaton, at times conflict can and will be an acceptable strategy in Christian social ethics. As a strategy, it can never become an ideology or an ultimate explanation of reality. However, there will be more conflictual situations than Catholic social ethics was willing to admit in the past. Thus, for example, conflict among classes might be a necessary strategy in bringing about social change, but conflict can never be the first or the ultimate or the most important reality.

Somewhat connected with conflict is the question of violence, which must be faced in our contemporary world. Here the Catholic tradition in its just-war tradition worked out an understanding that accepted violence in a just cause but at the same time insisted on limiting the violence. There are some today who call for a total pacifism, but I cannot accept such an absolute approach.

Detached and Participant Perspectives

What is the better perspective for arriving at good ethical judgments—that of a participant or that of a detached observer? Emphasis on critical reason and praxis shows the importance of active participation in the ongoing work itself. However, the need for critical reflection on praxis also calls for some type of self-criticism and detachment.

In my judgment there are advantages and disadvantages to both perspectives. History shows that the detached observer does not realize the extent of the problems faced by certain people or societies. White middle-class male theologians and ethicists have not been as aware of the injustices existing for other races, the poor and women as they should have been. If one is not involved in the oppression and injustice, there is a tendency not to realize its existence.

On the other hand, the participant can be so involved in a particular struggle that one fails to see other important aspects. I, for example, can never reduce social conflict totally to a struggle of the rich against the poor. I believe that this at times can be very true, but I also believe that there are other social problems, such as the evils of sexism and racism. Those who in the past fought the cold war against communism failed to recognize the divergent aspects among different communist countries and also were unwilling to criticize the free world. Advocates of feminine rights correctly recognize the wrongs done to women in society, but at times some tend to overlook the rights of the fetus. The ultimate advantages and disadvantages of both models call for the need for both perspectives in any theological or ethical enterprise.

Social Ethics as a Reflexive, Systematic Discipline

Theological social ethics by its very nature constitutes a reflexive, systematic discipline. Its discourse can be described as second-order discourse as distinguished from first-order discourse (e.g., preaching). Any second-order discourse will not have as immediate an effect upon action and change as first-order discourse. I affirm that social ethics should have some effect on social change, but I recognize there are other realities that have an even greater effect on social change.

ROLE OF THE CHURCH

Having treated some questions of theological methodology in the area of social ethics especially in the light of economic questions, this paper will now consider some ecclesial aspects centering on the social mission of the church.

Importance of the Social Mission of the Church

One cannot stress enough the importance of the social mission of the church. *Justice in the World,* the document released by the Synod of Bishops in 1971, strongly states: "Action on behalf of justice and participation in the transformation of the world fully appear to us as a constitutive dimension of the preaching of the Gospel, or, in other words, of the church's mission for the redemption of the human race and its liberation from every oppressive situation."[23]

The social mission of the church has thus been recognized as a constitutive dimension of the church. The challenge remains to make this a living reality on the pastoral level in the life of the church. Pastoral creativity and imagination must put flesh and blood on the bare bones of this statement. The force of the statement should not be lost—without a social mission the church is not truly church, for it is missing a constitutive aspect. This is true of the church on all levels of its existence but especially on the level of the local church. The parish community must not only be a worshiping community but also a serving community. How to bring this about in practice is perhaps the primary pastoral problem facing the church at the present time.

Peculiar circumstances on the American Catholic scene make this pastoral ministry more difficult but even more imperative. The mainstream of American Catholicism tried to prove there was no basic incompatibility between being American and being Catholic. The older distinction between natural and supernatural was used to point out the different spheres. The great contribution of the American church at the Second Vatican Council was in the advocacy of religious freedom and the separation of church and state. The subtle danger was to separate American and Catholic on the one hand and state and church on the other into two separate spheres. In such a way there was no incompatibility between them, but also the church or the gospel readily lost any influence on the state or the secular. Catholics had a different faith from other Americans but this did not affect their participation in the national life and questions facing society. There was a fear of admitting anything distinctively Christian or Catholic that one could bring to bear on the social and political orders. The Catholic ethos in the United States tended to eliminate faith, the gospel and the supernatural from political, social and economic theory and life. There is all the more need in the United States for a creative pastoral ministry making the social mission of the church a constitutive part of the church.

There have been some creative developments in the last few years in social ministry. The church and groups in the church can act as catalysts for various forms of community organizations. These community organizations can then work effectively for social change. Here the role of the church is neither patronizing nor paternalistic but rather enabling. Also, church groups can and should act as advocates for the poor and disadvantaged.[24]

Limits on the Social Mission of the Church

The proper understanding of the social mission of the church as well as the call for creative ministerial initiatives to make the social mission of the church a constitutive part of the church call for a recognition of the limitations involved in both comprehending and structuring the social mission of the church. First, the social mission is only a part of the total mission of the church. There are many other aspects of the mission of the Church, involving especially the preaching of the gospel and the liturgical celebration of the presence of the risen Lord in our midst with the concomitant hope that he will come again. The social mission should not be seen as opposed to these other aspects, for these other aspects by their very nature call for a social mission dimension. But the church cannot be reduced only to the social mission.

Second, there are many other individuals and groups other than the church who are working for the betterment of society. Catholics and Christians must avoid the narrow triumphalism of claiming to be the only ones working for social justice and struggling against the forces of oppression. Such a proposed understanding is unfair to all the other individuals and groups who have dedicated themselves to working against injustice.

Third, individual Roman Catholics are not only members of the church community; but they belong to many other groups, communities and societies which are also working for the betterment of society. One cannot and should not go back to a Catholic ghetto concept according to which the Catholic does not become involved in ecumenical, secular and other groups working for social change. Any structuring of the social mission of the Church must recognize that the social mission of individual Catholics must not be totally or perhaps even primarily in terms of Christian groups or organizations as such. Fourth, there has been much discussion in moral theology in the last decade about the existence of a specifically Christian ethic. My contention is that from the viewpoint of specific ethical content as well as that of proximate goals, attitudes and dispositions (such as self-sacrificing love, care for the poor and struggling against oppression) there is no distinctively Christian social ethical content. Obviously this is a disputed point, but at the very minimum one must be willing to recognize that Christians have no monopoly on social ethical wisdom or insight.

Pluralism

Different aspects of pluralism have been mentioned already in the discussion of theological methodology. First, there can be a legitimate pluralism on the level of theological methodology itself. Many would not agree with the methodology I proposed. Some, for example, would call for a more radical approach that would advocate a Christian witness to peace and voluntary poverty.

Second, there will be a pluralism because of the different possible scientific theories and interpretations of the data involved in complex social ethical questions. Third, on these specific issues the very complexity of the issues argues against the possibility of claiming with absolute certitude that there is only one possible Christian approach or solution.

The history of American Catholic social ethics reminds us of a pluralism of approaches that have existed even among those who did not accept the status quo. John A. Ryan put heavy emphasis on the role of the state to bring about reform. German-American Catholics distrusted the state and called for a very thoroughgoing reform on the model of the corporate society. The Catholic Worker movement espoused a radical personalism that distrusted all organization and even gloried in the name of anarchism. History thus indicates the pluralism which has existed in social ethics.[25]

It is interesting that Catholic social theory has traditionally recognized a legitimate diversity or pluralism on concrete questions facing society.[26] Recently I have argued with many other moral theologians that dissent (or, more positively, pluralism) will be increasingly present on some questions of more personal and individual ethics, such as contraception, sterilization, divorce and even abortion and euthanasia. The basic reason stems from the complexity of these specific questions, because of which one cannot claim that a particular solution is so certain that it excludes the possibility of error. One cannot speak about *the* Christian solution to specific concrete problems as if there were no other possible Christian alternative. For example, I will defend the position that truly human life exists before the presence of brain waves in the fetus and that capital punishment is wrong, but I cannot exclude from the church of Jesus Christ those who hold contrary opinions. In an era where pluralism is being recognized even in the area of personal morality, one cannot logically deny its existence in social ethics. In both areas, theology must continue to discuss the important question of the limits of pluralism.

Ecclesiological Consequences

My understanding of mediation, eschatology and pluralism concluded that often Christians and the church can agree in pointing out what are the problems and difficulties existing in society (a negative critique). In season and out of season the whole church should preach and respond to the basic gospel message of conversion which calls for Christians to struggle against the presence of sin not only in our hearts but also in the social structures of society. On the level of the general there should be more agreement among Christians and within the churches on the values, goals and ideals to be present in society, but as one descends to particular plans and strategies the very complexity of these issues will often mean that it is increasingly difficult to speak about *the* Christian solution.

In this area above all one sees the importance and need for smaller groups within the church. Groups of Christians can and should join together to work for a common purpose and employ a common strategy. In many ways the liberation theology of South America has grown up in the context of such small groups of committed Christians banded together to work for overcoming oppression. In the United States the Catholic Worker movement and other such apostolates illustrate the same basic reality. The peace movement in the United States in a more informal way sponsored the existence of such groups.

Although there have been some such groups existing in the United States in the past, it seems that they were not as numerous as in other countries. Perhaps this is because the Catholic Action approach with its emphasis on cell units was not as commonly existing in this country as elsewhere. However, I believe it is very important and essential for the good of the church to have a variety of such groups existing within the church.

In the last few years in the United States a number of such groups working for social justice and change have come into existence. Think, for example, of the justice and peace organizations which have sprung up in dioceses and in religious communities. Network, a group of women religious lobbying for social change, has attracted attention and support. There are many different types of groups which can and should exist. At times one might find various church groups on different sides of the same issue as has happened on the Equal Rights Amendment. At times even the bishops can function as such a group within the church.

In this view one sees the church as a larger community in which serious dialogue takes place about what the gospel calls us to do in terms of changing societies. Individual and smaller groups within the church would be able to do what larger groups and the entire church itself might not be able to do. I would hope that in this way many individual Christians would feel a vocation to join such particular groups in their witness to poverty, peace, social justice, etc.

There still at times is a role for the total church and its leadership both in terms of teaching and of acting on specific social problems. A whole church body either on a local or national or even world-wide basis at times can and should address specific moral questions. However, in so doing there are some cautions that must be taken into account. First of all, since such questions involve technical data and expertise, those who are addressing such problems must make sure that they have competently mastered all the details which are involved. Second, it will be impossible to speak out or act on all the issues facing society because of a lack of expertise, but the more significant questions can and should be chosen. Third, they should recognize that other Christians might disagree with the particular position that is being taken. In this way the position is proposed in the name of the church but with the recognition that even individual members of the church might disagree with a particular aspect of it. Here the moral credibility of the teaching is most significant.

In looking to the question of the future agenda of the church in the area of social ethics, this paper has purposely avoided a substantive consideration of the various issues. Instead, an attempt has been made to consider the theological methodology that should be involved in such discussions and also the ecclesiological implications of the social mission of the church.

Notes

1. Pastoral Constitution on the Church in the Modern World, nos. 46–93. For a reliable English translation, see *The Documents of Vatican II*, ed. Walter M. Abbot (New York: Guild Press, 1966).

2. *World Conference on Church and Society: Official Report* (Geneva: World Council of Churches, 1967).

3. The final recommendations of this conference were printed in *Origins: N.C. Documentary Service*, vol. 6, no. 20 (Nov. 4, 1976) and no. 21 (Nov. 11, 1976), pp. 309–40.

4. Pope Paul VI, *Octogesima Adveniens*, no. 22. This and other important documents on social justice can be found in *The Gospel of Peace and Justice: Catholic Social Teaching Since Pope John*, ed. Joseph Gremillion (Maryknoll, New York: Orbis Books, 1976).

5. David J. O'Brien, *The Renewal of American Catholicism* (New York: Oxford University Press, 1972), pp. 138–62.

6. Pope Paul VI, *Populorum Progressio*, no. 3, Gremillion, p. 388.

7. John C. Bennett, *The Radical Imperative* (Philadelphia: Westminster Press, 1975), pp. 142–64.

8. Gustavo Gutierrez, *A Theology of Liberation* (Maryknoll, New York: Orbis Books, 1973), pp. 36–37, 176.

9. Gutierrez, pp. 232–39.

10. Hugo Assmann, *Theology for a Nomad Church* (Maryknoll, New York: Orbis Books, 1976), pp. 116, 138 ff.

11. John A. Ryan, *Distributive Justice* (New York: Macmillan, 1916). See also John A. Coleman, "Vision and Praxis in American Theology," *Theological Studies* 37 (1976): 3–40.

12. John Rawls, *A Theory of Justice* (Cambridge, Mass.: Belknap Press of Harvard University, 1971); Robert A. Nozick, *Anarchy, State and Utopia* (New York: Basic Books, 1974).

13. Bennett, pp. 152–54.

14. E.g., Ryan, p. 358.

15. Recent documents of the hierarchical magisterium have stressed this universal destiny of goods of creation. See, Pastoral Constitution on the Church in the Modern World, no. 69, Gremillion, pp. 305–6; *Populorum Progressio*, nos. 22–24, Gremillion, pp. 393–94.

16. Such an understanding is proposed by Paul Ramsey in his critique of the World Conference on Church and Society held in Geneva in 1967. See, Paul Ramsey, *Who Speaks for the Church?* (Nashville: Abingdon Press, 1967), p. 53.

17. Martin E. Marty, *Righteous Empire: The Protestant Experience in America* (New York: The Dial Press, 1970).

18. O'Brien, *The Renewal of American Catholicism*.

19. Aaron I. Abell, *American Catholicism and Social Action: A Search for Social Justice* (Notre Dame, Indiana: University of Notre Dame Press, 1963).

20. E.g., Paul Hanly Furfey, *Fire on the Earth* (New York: Macmillan, 1936); see also William D. Miller, *A Harsh and Dreadful Love: Dorothy Day and the Catholic Worker Movement* (Garden City, New York: Image Books, 1974).

21. Such an assumption in my judgment lies behind many aspects of the social reform ideas of John A. Ryan, especially his theory of underconsumption. See George C. Higgins, "The Underconsumption Theory in the Writings of Monsignor John A. Ryan" (M.A. Dissertation, Catholic University of America, 1942).

22. Harold F. Trehey, *Foundations of a Modern Guild System* (Washington: Catholic University of America Press, 1940).

23. *Justice in the World*, no. 6, Gremillion, p. 154.

24. For the importance of Church organizations as advocates for the poor, see *Towards a Renewed Catholic Charities Movement* (Washington: National Conference of Catholic Charities, 1971).

25. David J. O'Brien, *American Catholics and Social Reform* (New York: Oxford University Press, 1968).

26. Frans H. Mueller, "The Church and the Social Question," in *The Challenge of Mater et Magistra*, ed. Joseph N. Moody and Justus George Lawler (New York: Herder and Herder, 1963), pp. 13–33. For confirmation of this in recent documents of the hierarchical magisterium, see *Octogesima Adveniens*, nos. 59–61, Gremillion, pp. 510–11; *Justice in the World*, no. 37, Gremillion, p. 521.

PART 6

Church and Reform

Christian Duquoc and Casiano Floristan

The Lethargy of Christian Spirituality in Developed Countries: Reasons and Perspectives

I propose, in the first place, to develop the interrogative character of Christianity regarding common ideas about God (the reason for Christianity's contemporary lethargy), without, however, underestimating its historical ambiguity. And, in the second place, I will present several affirmations leading to transformation drawn from a critical analysis of the dominant Western Christian position.

I. The present lethargy in Christianity is situated inside the following dialectic: equivocal and subversive.
  —Interrogation or subversion: forty years ago, Merleau-Ponty stressed that the newness of Christianity is tied to a double symbol, the death of God which challenges all conceptions of the Infinite and the assumption of man.
  —Equivocal or ambiguity: characterized by the autonomy and distance regarding the historical aspect of Christianity. This movement increased with the Aufklärung (Enlightenment) philosophy which opposes a rational form of God—the basis of freedom and tolerance—to the God of Jesus, oppressor.
I shall develop this under three aspects: the crisis, the double aspect of Christianity and the praxis of Jesus.
  a. *The crisis*. The reasons for this lethargy are many. They are organized according to a threefold perspective.

—The transformation of the technical, scientific infrastructure with its economic and political consequences—the phenomenon of industrialization and political democracy.

—The ideological consequences of this transformation: autonomy regarding exterior norms sustained by positive religions; the discovery of shared knowledge and power; the power to take the future into our hands; the archaic situation of the Church defending an order that is no longer at the level of our knowledge, technology and present social relationships.

—The Aufklärung assembles into one single ideology of freedom and tolerance a sentiment of progress and freedom as opposed to religious obscurantism.

b. *The double aspect of Christianity.* In virtue of its history and origin, Christianity is marked by a double character: equivocal and subversive.

—Equivocal: the Aufklärung has strongly denounced the historical monopoly of Christianity under the pretext of the absolute revelation in Christ. Thus, contingent and particular notions have become universal norms. The original history of Christianity, by its passage to the universal through an institution, unites the contingent or accidental character of its origin and the Absolute, recognized as the Divine. In other words, it does not affect God by its history but gives its historical positivity—both Jewish and Greek—an absolute character, thus founding a system of truth and of action in which man no longer has a creative part, only an executive function. In order to recognize the movement of history, its relativity, its creative fervor, Aufklärung opposed an absolute God (Deism) to the absolute positivity of the God of Jesus, leaving to history its human relativity and responsibility. One recognizes here the question asked by Lessing: "How can we affirm that a singular fact, Jesus' history, can take a universal and normative value?"

—Subversive: Hegel and Bloch stressed this aspect.

• Hegel does not absolutize a particular history: on the contrary, God is affected by history. From that point on, Christianity is opposed not only to the absolutization of its own history, of its particularity, but to the objectivization of God, taken out of all history. Hegel breaks with the God of Christianity and the God of Aufklärung.

• Having the way opened by Hegel, Bloch continues in a different perspective (cf. his work *Atheismus im Christentum*).

• Bloch, in setting up the revolutionary and messianic value of Christianity regarding a closed society, tries to show the inherent contradiction in institutional Christianity: on the one hand, to confess an objective God who stops all dynamism and hope; on the other hand, to place in history the messianism which has transforming energy.

• In taking for himself the name of the Son of man, Jesus dethrones the objective God of his prerogatives and symbolically announces his death as the condition of history oriented towards a utopian future. The lethargy in Christianity is created by Christianity itself in its ecclesiastical form, burying in itself the dynamic factor of the future and accentuating what is archaic.

c. *The praxis of Jesus.* Can the action of Jesus be inscribed in the above problematic? Or do we have to deal with an ideological interpretation of Christianity which has few resources for solving the present crisis? The action of Jesus attaches the recognition of God to a praxis of liberation. Consequently, it does not justify the absolutization of a particular history in Christianity. Thus, the critical analysis of Aufklärung was, in a way, true. However, it is not to be found in the way opened by Bloch who breaks all ties between the recognition of God and liberation.

It seems to me:

—that the death of God theologians stopped too short in their criticism: the objective God is not the God addressed by Jesus even if often this is the God worshiped by Christians;

—that the reconciliation between the Christian's knowledge of God and the movement of autonomy opened by the Aufklärung is not a theoretical question but a practical one;

—that the so-called liberation theologians open an original way, permitting one to think that the present lack of spiritual vigor in Christianity is not definitive, but that it belongs to the sociohistorical origins of the Western world. This perspective will be developed in the points below.

II. Propositions which seek to lead us out of the present spiritual lethargy:

1. First, colonization, followed by industrialization, made developed countries into dominating ones upon which depend underdeveloped and emerging countries.

    a. Underdevelopment, understood as an economic, social and political delay in African, Asiatic and Latin American countries in contrast to the progressive nations of the North Atlantic countries, is a global problem that concerns all humanity because it is the consequence of the development of the wealthy nations.

b. The misery of the underdeveloped countries and regions is not corrected by the help of the capitalistic countries, but by the making of new forms of production and fellowship in the underdeveloped countries which would put an end to "dependence" and which will foster liberation.

c. The occidental world with its Greco-Roman and Judeo-Christian roots has universalized—by colonization and domination—not only science, technology, philosophy and forms of society, but also the "Roman" way to live Christianity and the European way of elaborating theology.

d. The underdeveloped countries, in questioning the way of organizing and disorganizing the world in the Northern countries, equally questions those Churches which collaborate with the dominating nations.

e. The Marxist criticism of religion, which is a criticism of historical Christianity and of the ancient sacralized regime, is a structural criticism of Western society, insofar as it is bourgeois, oppressive and capitalistic.

f. The North Atlantic churches, to the extent that they have lived an oppressive regime, have acquired a taste for profit and power which is not gospel-like but typical of oligarchical and multinational groups.

2. The theological interpretation of Christianity (in spite of the fact that Christianity has been a reality in the "oppressed" countries) is done in an academic way within the dominant social groups (a clergy), having as a consequence an ideological process.

a. The theological and ecclesial crisis of the traditional Christian people (Christian countries) is understood consciously or unconsciously as a catastrophic fall of medieval Christianity, the first historic realization and the first important deviation of the original evangelical Christianity.

b. In the individual unconscious and/or collective unconscious of many pastors and lay people of the Church, there is a secret and unconfessed nostalgia for an ancient Christianity and for a society in which the religious factor is seen as decisive.

c. The Church has lived as an antisociety in the face of modern organized societies (following the democratic, parliamentary and bourgeois mode). She continues to act to a large degree in the same way against the actual Marxist tendencies which are concerned with the implantations of new socialisms.

d. North Atlantic theology, being elaborated within the Western geopolitical center, cannot understand the misery of the periphery and plays the game of the capitalistic bourgeoisie.

e. European theology being occupied by the double criticism of the Aufklärung—of Kant (freedom from all dogmatism) on the one hand, and of Marx (freedom from all idealism) on the other—focuses its attention on the rediscovery of meaning which henceforth faith refuses, when it should first pay attention to oppression in order to bring about transformation and find there the meaning of faith.

3. The essential pastoral act of the Church (evangelization) was realized by the Churches of the developed countries with the complicity of power and with exterior powerful means such as integration of the religious process into the process of domination.

a. To come to a renewal of the Church in the developed countries it is necessary that the Church recognize its historical and universal guilt, that she may be converted to the "third-world" of the poor and the oppressed and may give real proof of her conversion.

b. The transcending of the "Logos" of modern times (critical spirit of Aufklärung, world autonomy and technological and scientific development) is not obtained by an anthropological or political reversal, but by a conversion to the evangelical, historical, sapiential, symbolic and practical Logos of the modest agricultural and industrial social classes who live, in fact, as minorities or as marginalized majority groups.

c. The life of the believer in developed countries should be prophetic—both a critical and a practical witnessing for justice and freedom in the face of all economic exploitation and all dominating powers in order to defend the oppressed and the poor and in solidarity with them.

d. The distinction between civilization (Aufklärung, elitist and official culture) and "barbary" (popular culture, of the masses and the illiterate) has resulted in a contempt or an insufficient appreciation of the popular culture or popular religiosity of a Catholicism dominated by the powerful classes.

However abrupt, the above propositions are intended primarily to provoke discussion.

René Laurentin

Vatican III—Elsewhere or Something Else?

At the time of the pre-preparatory consultation for Vatican II, more than 400 bishops (about 1 in 5) proposed a new dogmatic definition on the Virgin Mary: Mediatrix (300), spiritual Motherhood (150), Coredemptrix (150) and Queenship (120). They were reacting out of habit. In the exceptional cases when Rome consulted the bishops, during the last centuries, it was always to define a new "marian dogma"; the Immaculate Conception in 1854, the Assumption in 1950. These proposals revealed a stereotype, and the pious thought that a definition in honor of Our Lady was a panacea for every problem.

Vatican II was oriented differently, towards taking into account certain realities: those of the Church and those of the world. It raised hope, mobilized Christians, and acquired (until some recent backsliding) a considerable credibility. In light of this, to think that the solution to the problems of the Church today is Vatican Council III is not the only way to go.

One must consider one's position. This paper is intended to pose some preliminary questions:

I. THE VATICAN OR ELSEWHERE?

If it were to be truly a council which would be relevant today, should it be held at the Vatican? That is questionable. From a Catholic viewpoint, Vatican II called for the *internationalization,* but not the *decentralization* of the curia. One is tempted to think that a new council ought to be decentralizing and decentralized. From the ecumenical perspective, can one any longer think of a council other than as ecumenical?

One is less able to since Paul VI, confirming the objections made a while back by Grummel and Congar, has deliberately qualified the Second Council of Lyon, at the time of its seventh centenary, as the *Sixth General Synod of the West,* and not as an *ecumenical council* (Letter of October 5, 1974). Assuming this position is all the more remarkable since Lyon II is, with Florence, one of the two medieval councils where the Orthodox were present and where a declaration of unity was signed. The city of Rome, center of Catholic authority, would be a difficult site for a council reuniting all Christians.

Where Then?

Existing conditions and methods rule out numerous places: such as those where a council would be in danger of not being truly free, or those not having the necessary resources. The countries of the East and the Western dictatorships are thereby excluded. Other sites would risk giving a particularist or political meaning, which brings into question the United States, Jerusalem, or even France—why risk it? Finally, Rome does not seem ready to accept a council outside of Rome itself. To propose another place would be utopian. But hypothetically a future council would in every way be utopian so one cannot conjure away the extra-theological question: What city would be best to host an ecumenical council from the material, functional, cultural and symbolic point of view: New Delhi? Nairobi? Brussels or Louvain? Geneva? Yet, the globe changes so quickly that it would be fruitless to propose these names or others as but fleeting suggestions.

II. A COUNCIL OR SOMETHING ELSE?

Is a council what the Church needs today? The question should be examined in the light of what the functions of the councils were in history. The principal types were:

—to condemn heresies;

—to reform the Church by returning it to its twofold source: the Scriptures and the Holy Spirit, who enables it to understand the demands of unity;

—to heal schisms: such were the Councils of Lyon and Florence which marked the union of East and West and that of Constance, which succeeded in settling the plurality of popes;

—to launch great undertakings: the Crusades are the most obvious but not the most edifying of this type, one might consider today a council for justice and peace, according to the dictates of the Gospel;

—to realize the place of conscience and the real function of local churches on a provincial, national or continental scale: the Council of Latin America at Rome from May 29 to July 9, 1899, the Councils of Baltimore in 1852, 1866 and 1884, the Council of Shanghai (1924).

Do Today's Problems Overwhelm the Functions of a Council?

Moreover, in what measure is the function vested in councils not realized by periodic assemblies of episcopal conferences and synods at Rome? If these bodies are convened for the same purpose as that of councils yet do not achieve this objective, to what is this to be attributed? To the limits of their juridic structures or to their functional defects?

III. WHAT ARE THE NEEDS OF THE CHURCH?

We must draw back a bit to ask a basic question: What does the Church need? Let us begin by indicating, rather than restricting, areas:

—a renewal of the vitality of faith;
—a remedy for the Christian identity crisis; a confirmation of the Church in a reaffirmation of faith, one which professes witness of God in the heart of the believer;
—the restoration of the Tradition which was dominant before the Council and neglected since the Council;
—a renewal of the mystical or political order or a better articulation of the "mystical" and the "political" whose disassociation created a kind of breakdown in the Church;
—a clearing away of the prejudices which cause a crisis of credibility: notably, prejudices involving the role of women in the Church and in society, and sexuality in marriage;
—a renewal in "formation," in communications, in community life, in an openness to cultural plurality (in the sense of the other and the God wholly other);
—a revision of power and authority in the Church in line with Vatican II: bishops today do not want to be reduced to administrative and financial tasks, to dependence on the consideration of the supreme authority and to the regard of their colleagues to provide the level of prophesying and of creativity which the Church needs today;
—a renewal of ministries;
—a reaffirmation of freedom of conscience: not only "religious liberty" (in the judicial sense according to the narrow perspectives of

Vatican II) but Christian freedom according to the Spirit, the source of authentic liberty at all levels;
—a reorientation of the theology which, since the Middle Ages, has become, according to a manner of believing, the affair of clerics or academicians enclosed in a technocratic intellectualism too often foreign to the needs of people.

Thus would it be desirable that the Notre Dame colloquium be attentive to the work which can be called: the new American pastoral theology; that which manifests itself in contact with human and pastoral realities in some very diverse sectors, while interpreting that which is really encountered by the people of God, that which is unfolding there, without neglecting the theology of *Healing* (Guérisons), which responds to a profound human need according to the precepts of the Gospel, where Christ began by healing and sent his apostles forth to the same mission. I have been struck by the awakening which has occurred in this sense in the United States: Healing was the central theme of Nixon's resignation speech and of the inaugural address of his successor. To establish a process of healing is also the central theme of certain 1976–1977 best sellers, among which are the books of Ruth Carter Stapleton—sister of President Carter—in her role at once religious (as a Baptist minister) and academic (University of North Carolina). We are then at the antithesis of official European theology. But can this theology heal itself so that it becomes sensitive to its opposite?

It is also necessary that theology resolve the problem of scientific precision in a threefold manner: first, the seriousness in the practice of each discipline concerned; then, the articulation of diverse disciplines that the "interdisciplinary" (so often cited) juxtaposes more often today; that would require an overstepping of the spirit of the system which prevails today to the detriment of the scientific spirit. Finally, to understand that theology *as such* (as the knowledge of God) is not a science in the strict sense, because its object is hidden (received by the outward testimony of the Church and the interior testimony of the Holy Spirit); certain, in this sense, of the interior assurance which God gives but according to a certitude not verifiable by the standard of scientific procedures.

Lastly, it is necessary that theology recover some of the dimensions lost during the centuries: esthetic, poetic, practical and confessional dimensions without forgetting the dimension of praise and thanksgiving—a return to the Holy Spirit, a resurgence of hope, not in words but in reality. It is that which motivated John XXIII. It is that which can achieve the impossible, if it is a council.

Translated by Robert V. Lott

Alois Müller

Church and Reform

I. PRELIMINARY REMARKS

1. All the statements of this section deal with Church reform in different fields; this one is closely related to the statement on canon law reform. But we have to treat here more fundamental aspects of church reform, and especially the question of how the Church should behave when reform happens.

2. In Church history "reform" means either lifting of grievances (e.g., simony, idleness of the clergy) or simply evolution to a more adequate behavior of the Church in a changed situation. The Church always needs reform either in the one sense or in the other.

3. Adaptation of the Church to changed conditions cannot be realized at once by legislation, but it is a permanent process with several "points of condensation."

II. TENDENCIES AND FATE OF THE REFORMS OF VATICAN II

1. Seen as a whole, Vatican II has brought a reform in the sense of evolution and adaptation in three main directions of advance: making up for the lack of enlightenment, opening towards the Protestant churches, and opening to the democratic, pluralistic, postindustrial world of the sixties. "Enlightenment" means here admitting of critical rational thinking to all problems which are accessible to this means, as it appears in the critical methods of biblical exegesis, the more historical approach of dogma evolution, the psychological criticism of religious phenomena, and the applying of sociological criteria to Church life. Such "enlightened" theological thinking has allowed theologians and the whole Church to take over modern standards (such as freedom

of conscience and religion, pluralism) and facilitated the dialogue with the Protestant churches, where the enlightenment process had started much sooner.

2. Vatican II brought decisive reforms in the directions mentioned above. However, it had to push them through against powerful resistance and therefore it often had to clothe them in compromise formulas, e.g., about episcopal collegiality, the Jews, the non-Catholic churches, marriage, etc. The great performances of the Council were breakthroughs, but most of the traditional positions are also to be found in the wording of the documents, generally with no convincing syntheses.

3. Soon after the Council, counter-trends established themselves in the Roman curia, in certain episcopal conferences, but also at the very base, among the people. As a first step they interpreted the Council following its most traditional passages instead of its deepest intentions, and then they tried to counter the Council by the subsequent legislation.

4. By such retrogressive movements the curial and hierarchical instances rapidly lost the confidence of those who had set their hearts on reform. This was also one of the essential reasons for the setting in of wild, uncontrolled, individual reform initiatives. They again had a feedback, so that more and more retreat was called for even by bishops who were formerly bent on reform. Also, the Pope's audience speeches preferred warning against "progressism" to defending reforms. In the Lefebvre movement culminates paradoxically that effort to "save the Church" by annuling the Council.

III. THE PROBLEMS IN THE POST-CONCILIAR AGE

1. After Vatican Council II had started to remedy the lack of enlightenment with its tendency to rationalism, a growing emphasis on nonrational feelings about the faith became manifest in the so-called charismatic groups. So the demand for rationality was competed with at the very moment that theology became able to satisfy it. It is not yet clear whether this enthusiasm was merely a reaction or would have come anyway. Enlightenment always runs the risk of taking the nonrational as nonexisting and of applying its own method to fields where it is not adequate, and thus provokes antirational reactions.

2. While the Council began the "opening of the Church towards the world" in the early sixties, at a time of great optimism regarding the achievements of our civilization, the society of the seventies is becoming more and more disillusioned to the point of cultural pessimism in view of—among other things—the "re-barbarization" of Western

civilization. That is why the Council's showpiece, *Gaudium et Spes,* today is sometimes considered naive and outdated.

3. In the countries in which the Christian religion is of long standing, the reforms of Vatican II did not bring about the expected fresh élan in the Church. Rather—partly in chronological sequence, partly in causal consequence—these reforms were followed by a breakdown of the sociological solidity of the Church community. Hence the present-day awareness of the Church is an awareness of the crisis. That sociological weakness is due partly to the greater doctrinal elbow room, the relativization of Church authority and the changed place of worship in the Christian life.

4. The conciliar "turning towards the world" has led to a new starting point in the post-conciliar Church, as expressed in the "theology of liberation" as well as—at least partly—in the movement "Christians for Socialism," this being an interpretation of the Gospel as inspiring the political emancipation of oppressed nations or classes.

IV. THESES FOR A CHURCH REFORM OF TOMORROW

1. Universality is only possible through a *pluralistic development.* This is why the principle of the "specific way" of each local church must be respected by the Church authorities as far as possible. Uniform development and ruling does not lead to universality, but to predominance of one tendency over the others. If one is afraid that a particular way will "infect" the other regions by imitation, it would only show that conditions for that way exist also elsewhere.

2. The reform must turn away from a pendulum movement between the poles to become an *integrative method.* The pendulum movement means that, for instance, a more rationalistic tendency is simply pushed away by a more mystical one and vice versa. But such polar tendencies must be related to one another in a dialectic manner. That is what I mean by integrative method: the critical currents must integrate, e.g., the mystical insights of former stages, and mystical renewals must integrate rational acquisitions.

3. Among the reform movements of all sorts, the strategy of the *coup d'état* must be *given up* which means that no movement can operate any longer with the intention to declare its own aims as doctrine for the whole Church. There is a temptation of progressives, conservatives, and other currents in the Church to present their ways, which are just a *possibility* for some, as if they were the only legitimate *rule* for the whole Church. But this contradicts the proper bases of ecclesial thinking and leads to mutual defamation and contempt. Nobody has to snatch the rudder. This is valid also for Roman decisions insofar as they are changeable by their very nature.

4. The relationship between Rome and the episcopal conferences—be they national or regional—must clearly be organized along the lines of the *principle of subsidiarity*. It is not required by the nature of St. Peter's office that Rome intervene in all Church affairs. Everybody knows the disadvantages of such a method: lack of familiarity with local problems and mentalities, unilateral and partial information through the objectionable methods of the nuncios. Subsidiarity gives "Rome" the possibility to intervene against actual local abuses. But all ecclesial processes must become more transparent and communicative and must stop oscillating between secrecy and irrevocability.

5. It is an urgent task to go on developing the practice and the structures of *shared responsibility* of the people of God. The Church is never a democracy in the sense that basic religious authority comes from the people. It comes from Christ. But that does not mean that consequently it can be handled exclusively by the hierarchy. On the contrary, Vatican II's doctrine about the people of God must be given practical consequences concerning decision making on all levels.

6. The *bishops' synod* must obtain more freedom of action and possibly different statutes. The issue is clear and I am not able to give concrete advice. But the present situation of the synod, where it is merely a consultative body whose power is severely limited by the pope and the Roman curia, compromises its meaningfulness.

7. On the level of the individual church community, the principle of the territorial parish should be supplemented by the development of *base communities (communautés de base)*. The territorial parish as a framework for Church membership must be maintained. But basic communities offer an increase of freedom for special concerns. They must keep contact with the local Church structures (at least at the diocesan level) and vice versa.

8. The subject of *ecclesiastical offices* must be rethought. Here the key ideas are: diversification of Church ministry on the one hand, conditions for ordination on the other. The fear of a new clericalization must be overcome by an actual abolition of psycho-sociological differences between the clergy and the laity.

9. The idea of mission must consist in the Church of every country being *missionary in character*. Historically speaking, it is no longer necessary that one people be evangelized by another. However, a certain subsidiarity between churches still exists. There is everywhere an indigenous church that has to be missionary, from Germany to Papualand. However, this must mean also a culturally, structurally and eventually financially independent and autochthonous church.

10. It is necessary to establish a *dialectic unity* between the Church's own life and the Church's activity towards the outer world. The discovering of the Church's worldly commitment often has led to a certain

taboo of the Church's interior life, while the traditionalistic wing over-emphasizes the latter against the political commitment. But here too both aspects must be balanced as in a sound psychic personal life.

11. The Church's *diaconal commitment* to society must become self-evident: the Church is servant. The commitment to the weak and the oppressed belongs to the Church's mission in the name of the Gospel. Mostly it implies a political engagement that includes the risk of mistakes. That risk should not be feared.

12. Ecclesiastic office-holders must learn to speak in a *different tone of voice* when they address the Church or the general public. Church leaders are no longer leaders in society. Nevertheless they often are obliged to speak publicly. Then they shall remember they are not, vis-à-vis the society, doctors of the faith, but simply members of a public society, and their authority does not derive from their Catholic faith.

13. The Church must operate as an *integrative force* between religion and secular society. This can be illustrated by the issue of religionless Christianity which Bonhoeffer made famous. Now it is certainly true that faith is involved with the world, but it would be a strange paradox to give faith an influence on all fields of human existence to the exclusion of the religious sphere. On the contrary, the Church has to offer a common base of interpretation and inspiration for both the secular and the religious dimension of human life.

Mary G. Durkin

Pluralism and Church Reform: Pastoral Theology Looks to the Future

THE success of any attempt at Church reform in the future will depend on the ability of those who initiate the reform to accept the pluralistic nature of the Catholic Church and to understand the necessity of considering the experiences of the various groups which comprise the Church on matters of reform. For those who have been in the position of imposing reform from above, as well as for those who have grown accustomed to expecting this imposition, the full implications of pluralism seem to lead to a lack of unity and possibly even to anarchy.

Within the limits of this paper we will try to deal with this concern by addressing ourselves to the positive aspects of pluralism and by demonstrating an approach to pastoral theology which would be an initial step toward determining what factors should be considered in the theological discussion of Church reform. In the process of demonstrating the relationship between the *science* and the *art* of pastoral theology we will address several (but by no means all) of the issues which need attention if reform of the Church is to be effective in addressing the experiences of the Church membership. These issues include sexual polarization, the role of women in the Church, the role of the local Church, the types of ministry needed in a local Church and the manner in which symbols and symbolization are related to religious experience. In addition, this paper and the companion paper on Church reform ("Doing Ministerial Theology: A Skills Approach" by John Shea) will consider the relationship between the professional theologian and the pastoral minister, a relationship which has profound implications for Church reform.

PLURALISTIC CHARACTER OF THE CATHOLIC CHURCH

From the start we must affirm the need for a central religious and theological identity for the Church. Gregory Baum has demonstrated the value of the tension which exists between the local Church and the universal Church in the Catholic tradition.[1] This tension, when correctly understood, is a powerful deterrent to the extremes of sectarianism and of Roman authoritarianism. The need for a central religious and theological identity does not negate the reality of the pluralistic character of the Church.

Pluralism, correctly understood, calls for a unity in the midst of diversity. This is a unity which occurs when different units of a social organization are able to discover elements which they share in common despite their individual identities. Pluralism is a positive factor when groups, without sacrificing the richness of their individual group experience, are able to forge a common, individual, group-transcending identity. For this common identity to be meaningful it must be reflective of experiences which are shared by the diverse groups.

In the past the common religious and theological identity of Roman Catholicism was determined by Church leaders and theologians who had little familiarity with or understanding of the experiences of the diverse groups which constitute the membership of the Church. In an age of unquestioning loyalty to Church authority most members of the Church accepted this common identity with little thought of its lack of relevance for their lives.

However, in an age where an increasing number of the Church membership, if not its leadership, is aware of the contradictions between many statements which attempt to articulate a common identity and the actual experiences of their lives, we are faced with the need to develop a new means of forging a common religious and theological identity. Obviously such an identity will be much less extensive in scope than previous attempts which sought to include prescriptions for every aspect of individual and group life.

Those of us engaged in the task of theology can attest to the contribution which the acceptance of pluralism in theology has made to the enterprise of theological reflection. At the same time we are quite cognizant of the pitfalls of an "anything and/or everything goes" attitude which ignores the need for a common theological identity. We recognize the need to establish criteria which will help us judge the validity of the Christian claim of various theological positions. We must apply the same demand for critical standard to various calls for Church reform. In addition to recognizing in what instances Church reform should be left to the individual needs of various forms of local Church—parish, diocese, national synod, etc.—we must establish criteria which will help determine if these particular Church reforms are in keeping with the common identity of the Church. The determination of this common religious and theological identity will be possible only when there is a consensus among particular churches concerning such an identity, always being open to the critique of the Christian Scriptures and Tradition.

For a future council or synod to successfully address the formulation of a common identity and determine the implications this would have for Church reform it will first be necessary for those who participate in the council or synod to be aware of the religious identity of those they represent. These representatives also must be aware of the elements of the identity which transcend the experiences of the particular group and speak to the broader identity of the entire Church. Questions which must be considered include: Just what does the religious identity of a Church in a highly technological Western society hold in common with those of churches in third-world nations, oriental cultures and eastern-rite countries? How is it possible to forge a common Catholic identity from these various identities? How do we reform the universal Church and the local Church so this common identity is open to development and responsive to the changing needs of various human societies?

THE PRINCIPLE OF SUBSIDIARITY AND PASTORAL THEOLOGY: WOMEN'S ROLE AS AN EXAMPLE

As a beginning step in the process of forging a common religious and theological identity it seems imperative that some theologians attempt to analyze those factors which determine the religious identities of various groups of people while others establish criteria for determining the validity of the Christian claim of the religious identity of any group. A pastoral theology, aware of the importance of the principle of subsidiarity in human societies, should be responsible for focusing theological attention on the importance of this approach for Church reform.

Pastoral theology, which began in response to the need for systematic doctrine and practical up-to-date guidelines for the exercise of pastoral ministry and evolved into a practical theology which deals with all that constitutes, conditions and makes possible the day-to-day actions of the Church, should also be responsible for helping a group articulate its religious identity. In addition pastoral theology should seek to determine the key issues which must be addressed in Church reform if it is to foster a healthy, positive pluralism which will allow diversity in the midst of unity.

This view of pastoral theology requires increased cooperation between the professional theologian, who is concerned with the scientific discipline of pastoral theology, and the pastor, who is engaged in the practice of the art of pastoral theology—or who, as John Shea indicates, is doing ministerial theology. The minister who hopes to be successful in doing ministerial theology must be familiar with the endeavors of the professional theologian. In turn, the professional theologian must be open to the questions which the minister asks as a result of doing ministerial theology. Without the questions raised by the minister doing theology with the lower levels of Church organizations it will be difficult for the professional theologian to be in touch with the concrete, particular experiences of Christian life in its various manifestations. Without the critiquing review of the professional theologian the pastor risks the danger of particularism and ultimately sectarianism.

One example of the danger of this particularism can be found in the response of various groups to the problem of women's role in our modern society. Despite widespread attempts to gain equal rights for women there is some indication that sexual polarization is on the increase as a reaction to the demands of certain women's groups. In the United States alone we find the development of two quite contrary views of women's role and the relationship between the sexes. Some representatives of both the Total Woman approach, which advocates submission of women to men, and feminism, which in its more radical forms calls for complete withdrawal from patriarchal society, claim a Christian basis for some of their critique of contemporary culture. Both also have implications for the direction of Church reform vis-à-vis women's role. If we were to investigate the experience of women in other cultures we would undoubtedly find still other interpretations of a Christian view of women.

It is necessary for those engaged in the practice of ministerial theology to seek to articulate a Christian perspective regarding the experience of the women they work with rather than simply accepting the conventional wisdom of the day on the subject. In turn the professional theologian must apply the scientific principles of pastoral theology to the various experiences articulated by ministerial theologians and search for a common response to the situation of women, recognizing the need for individual groups to retain those elements of their particular views which are not contrary to the Christian tradition (as *traditio*). A Christian view of women's role in human society must allow for diversity in the midst of unity.

A PASTORAL THEOLOGY FOR SUBURBAN WOMEN: AN APPROACH TO
A PASTORAL THEOLOGY FOR WOMEN

At the present time much of the attention on Church reform and the role of women is focused on the issue of ordination of women to the priesthood. Though this is an important concern for theological discussion, it is a concern which is receiving adequate attention from various sources. A much more crucial question, which has been somewhat overlooked in theological discussion, deals with the pressing issue of the development of a Christian view of women's role in the social order and their relationship to the males of the society. Since Church reform does not take place in a vacuum, but in social situations which involve men and women, Church reform in the future must be cognizant of the views and experiences of women. As theologians attempt to articulate a common religious and theological vision for the Catholic Church they must be aware of how the relationship between the sexes influences the religious identity of particular groups.

As a result of having spent many years of my adult life in a quasi-ministerial position with groups of women, I elected to attempt to develop a pastoral theology for the group with which I was associated, upper-middle-class suburban women.[2] Though the group is limited the method used in this exercise is an example of an approach to pastoral theology which might contribute valuable insights into the religious experiences of diverse sectors of the Church membership. This would be an important first step toward forging a common religious and theological identity.

To briefly summarize my work, using a method of correlation I attempted to identify the paradigmatic experience of a group of women who had been educated in the late forties, the fifties and the early sixties. Through participation in their experience and listening to the questions of meaning which they were asking, as well as to those which they were unable to articulate, I came to realize that they were caught in a dilemma. Through historical and sociological analysis of the situation of these and similar women I identified the paradigmatic experience of these women as that of having opportunities for freedom which their previous cultural education had not anticipated. They were searching for a new model of appropriate behavior which would fit their present situation.

The second step in the process involved a search for an appropriate symbol from the Christian tradition which might clarify or illuminate the situation, which might give it a sense of directivity. Since most of these women were or had at one time been members of a local parish Church I developed a theological vision of a parish Church as a *Spirit-*

filled community which knows of God's plan of salvation through Jesus Christ and proclaims this knowledge in celebration and fellowship.

This stage of the process involved theological reflection on the meanings present in human experience as well as the meanings present in the Christian tradition. The social-science analysis of the contemporary situation revealed the importance of community in the development of personhood. The particular experience of the women indicated a need for a community support system to challenge and encourage them as they sought to redefine their role as married women. The tradition of the local Church in its early manifestations in the biblical period and in its more recent manifestation in the immigrant communities of the United States provided insights into the manner in which a modern local Church community might be responsive to the needs of the contemporary situation while maintaining a continuity with the Christian tradition.

When the paradigmatic experience of opportunities for freedom is critiqued by the Christian tradition of the local Church it becomes possible to suggest changes in life-style, which is what occurs in the third step of this approach to pastoral theology.

Since membership in the Church community would call for a *response* to the challenge of Christ,[3] the image of the Christian woman as a *Responsible Woman* took shape. In addition, the local Church would need to be restructured in such a way that it could assist the women as they sought to determine the implications of being responsible women.

Since there was diversity, even among these women, I could do no more than establish guidelines which might assist them as they attempt to design a life-style in keeping with the image of Responsible Woman. It is not clear that the image of Responsible Woman would be fitting for all women in the United States, let alone in other parts of the world. It is certainly obvious that the life-style changes which would flow from the image would vary from culture to culture. The image itself is a response to the articulation of the experience of a particular group of women. Its validity for other groups depends on its ability to symbolize the experiences of these groups.

The restructuring of the local Church recommended in my study also has validity in so far as it applies to the situation of a particular society. For this situation it was recommended that new approaches to Church community be considered, that there be a revitalization of the spirit of the immigrant parish Church which had united people in a faith community, and that alternative approaches to parish Church be initiated when a parish is unable to provide a community spirit.

In addition, local churches should respond to the needs of women by promoting opportunities for women to use their abilities within the Church community and by encouraging them to contribute their talents in the world beyond the local community. The local Church also should initiate means for reducing the tension between the sexes occurring because of women's new freedom. Women should be encouraged to share their ideas on how to lead multi-dimensional lives, while men should be allowed to explore the problems that changing sex roles have caused in their lives.

John Cobb calls for the establishment of small groups where people can articulate their deepest aspirations and work out means of achieving them.[4] John Gilbert challenges religious education to help people symbolize their religious experiences and find ways of verifying the validity of these experiences.[5] Local churches follow these directives could provide an opportunity for developing a Christian response to a serious cultural problem.

This example of the process of developing a pastoral theology for a specific group is used merely to demonstrate a suggested approach to broadening the scope and methodology of pastoral theology for a pluralistic Church. The image of the Responsible Woman is tentative and calls for further study which would symbolize the religious experiences of other women. Only then will we be able to attempt to find shared themes which might help us articulate a theological position on women in contemporary society which reflects the pluralistic character of our world.

Just as the image is tentative the methodology is provisional and needs refinement. My own rather unique position of coming to the task of professional theology after many years in a quasi-ministerial role allowed me, in this instance, to combine some tasks which might under other circumstances need to be separated. I would not be able to engage in the participating and listening aspects of this approach for other groups, but would need to rely on the work of ministerial theology. Clearly, we need new forms of ministry (a topic which has, most recently, been examined in great depth by Bernard Cooke[6]) if we are to have a method of pastoral theology which adheres to the principle of subsidiarity. The professional theologian will need to consider the work of the ministerial theologian as well as the work of his or her colleagues in other academic disciplines when formulating theological statements and recommendations for Church reform.

IMPLICATIONS FOR CHURCH REFORM: POINTS FOR DISCUSSION

This approach to pastoral theology raises several points for discussion as we seek to identify the direction in which our scholarly endeavors should proceed. These suggestions are not exhaustive, but intended as a preliminary basis for our discussion.

1. The primary motive underlying all attempts at Church reform should be to create an environment which will encourage diverse groups to articulate their individual religious identities while also searching for shared aspects of these identities which will form a common religious identity.

2. The task of pastoral theology will be to encourage the articulation of diverse religious experiences, to critique these experiences through the use of the symbols of the Christian tradition, and to attempt to articulate a common religious and theological identity.

3. The critical questions of human existence which often are asked in non-religious language should be identified and, whenever possible, clarified through reference to the symbols of the Christian tradition.

4. Pastoral theology should be cognizant of the principle of subsidiarity when proposing theological statements and recommending Church reform.

5. The professional pastoral theologian should encourage the practice of ministerial theology which will seek to help individual groups symbolize their religious experiences and articulate their religious identities.

6. The professional pastoral theologian must be aware of the reinterpreted post-modern consciousness, both from the point of view of the questions it asks and the answers it gives to the questions.

7. The understanding of human organizations developed in the social sciences should be applied to Church reorganization at all levels. The purpose of Church reorganization should be to create structures which will allow individuals and groups to gain a better understanding of their religious identities while maintaining a consciousness of a common central religious identity.

8. Local Church communities should be restructured in such a way that they allow members an opportunity to verbalize their deepest aspirations and work out ways of achieving these in a manner congruent with their religious experiences.

9. Both professional theologians and ministerial theologians must understand the process of symbolization and its implications for an understanding of questions of meaning.

10. New ministries should be initiated which will serve the articulated needs of a restructured local, national and universal Church.

The ability of the Catholic Christian tradition to contribute directivity to the lives of its members and to the quest for meaning of the wider culture depends on the manner in which the Church of the future is able to respond to the human experience in its various manifestations. Reforming the Church to meet this challenge requires openness to that experience on the part of scholars and Church leaders. Pastoral theology must continually articulate the challenge as well as propose possible responses.

Notes

1. Gregory Baum, *The Credibility of the Church Today* (New York: Herder and Herder, 1968), chap. 4.

2. For a more detailed account of this example see Mary G. Durkin, *The Suburban Woman: Her Changing Role in the Church* (New York: Seabury Press, 1976).

3. For a more detailed study of the Christian as responder see H. Richard Niebuhr, *The Responsible Self: An Essay in Christian Moral Philosophy* (New York: Harper & Row, 1963).

4. John B. Cobb, Jr., *Theology and Pastoral Care* (Philadelphia: Fortress, 1977).

5. John P. Gilbert, "Theological Pluralism and Religious Education" in *Religious Education*, Nov.–Dec. 1975.

6. Bernard Cooke, *Ministry to Word and Sacraments: History and Theology* (Philadelphia: Fortress, 1976).

John Shea

Doing Ministerial Theology:
A Skills Approach

WHATEVER else the word "Church" refers to, it designates a collectivity of people with similar yet divergent convictions, values and behaviors. When this collectivity undergoes a fundamental reevaluation of its identity and purpose, it is natural to "look around" and see what needs to be done. In May of 1977 this can be an overwhelming experience. For, quite simply, everything needs to be done. Every dimension of Church life has been shaken by the tremors of the last fifteen years. Within both the geographic and psychic territories of the Church there is a need for healing and rethinking, for new approaches and imaginative programs, for genuine cooperation and explicitly shared convictions and values.

In this situation of universal change the temptation is to talk universally. The tendency is to handle the multi-dimensional church as a single entity and diagnose it as a single organism. But to approach the problems of the Church globally is, in a way, not to approach them at all. What is needed is to delineate areas, analyze them in terms of their theological, psychological and sociological assumptions and develop strategies of improvement. Constructive change focuses on what is achievable within defined perimeters and moves in systematic stages with both the obstacles and reinforcements to change sharply delineated and the tasks clearly assigned. Both to avoid narrowness and share insights each focused area must be in dialogue with the concerns of other areas. Yet the initial movement in "meeting needs" is to select out an area and pursue its problems and possibilities.

This paper is concerned with the grass-roots community. In one ecclesiology this area of Church is the bottom, the last link in the hierarchial chain that moves from God through the pope and bishops on down. In another ecclesiology it is the "top," not the farthest point from God but the actual locale of divine activity which must be symbolized and celebrated. But whatever the placement, the local church comprises at least 95 percent of Catholic Christians and is the continuing source of revenue for the Church at large. The Church must be judged—in the light of the Gospels—by the official documents it produces and the stances it takes on personal and social issues. But a complementary path of evaluation is to ask the question of the quality of the life of its members. What is the formative power of the local Church on the attitude and behavior of the individual? Does the local community encourage religious depth and social responsibility? Are faith convictions the operative guidelines for the activity of the community and the individual? Are the diverse needs of the community's members being ministered to? Although there are many important issues in the other strata of the Church, the quality of life on the foundational stratum is critical.

Within the highly variegated life of the local Church this paper focuses on its theological activity. On the pastoral scene people ask questions about what is creative and destructive in their interpersonal lives (marriage, family, friendship) and the systems in which they live (Church, school, job, government, hospital, etc.), formulate perspectives, and allow those perspectives to guide their behavior. In a Christian setting these perspectives are the product of the relating of concrete human situations to the inherited Christian symbols and their theological interpretations. This relating creates a certain consciousness which suggests corresponding attitudes and behaviors. It becomes the permeating context which provides direction and energy for the human person. This interpretive activity is engaged in order to relate authentically to the basic givens of human existence (birth, death, aging, sexuality, etc.) and to concrete interpersonal and social situations. Its truth lies largely in its ability to facilitate the health of the individual and the community. In order to do this it must adequately reflect the many impulses in a given situation, but this adequation is subordinate to the effect it produces. This theological activity, although often unacknowledged, goes on whenever groups or individuals are involved in decision-making processes.

One task of Christian ministry is to analyze, facilitate and encourage this process in the light of Christian perspectives and values. This task is one of doing ministerial theology and demands a discernible and trainable set of skills. Within the constellation of pastoral ministerial tasks doing ministerial theology is central. This activity energizes and gives meaning and direction to the total ministerial operation of any Church group. It celebrates and thematizes the deepest peril and possibility of person and situation and so provides motivation and vision. *De jure,* this task belongs to the priest whose role designation is to unravel the meanings and behaviors which our relationship to sacrality suggests. *De facto,* this task falls to whoever is capable of doing it.

Although the skill of ministerial theology belongs to a specific person, it can never be exercised in isolation. The pastoral minister does theology in concrete interaction with people and systems. In other words ministry is always understood and exercised in relation to Church. As such the minister becomes facilitator, catalyst and resource for the theological activity of an individual or group. This means a triple stance for the minister in relation to the people. (It is extremely important for the minister to know at any given time which stance he/she is adopting.) He/she initiates the type of question or perception which will lead to a faith appropriation of the situation. He/she helps the people hear and clearly articulate the religious, theological and ecclesiological dimension of their situation and programs. He/she becomes a theological resource, relating the contemporary situation to Christian perspectives and values.

The skill of doing ministerial theology borrows insights and procedures from counselling, community organizing and academic theology, but is not reducible to any of these endeavors. Because ministerial theology is engaged with individuals and groups, the principles and skills of effective interrelating are necessary. Because ministerial theology occurs in the context of institutional responses to human needs, the principles and skill of effective programming are necessary. Because ministerial theology relates both people and programs to faith convictions and perceptions, the insights of academic theology are necessary. Although ministerial theology is an eclectic skill, it has a distinctive place in grass-roots Church communities.

Perhaps the most needed area of clarification is the relationship between ministerial and academic theology. The roles of the ministerial and academic theologian complement each other in a total view of ecclesial life. As such, dialogue between them is necessary. But this dialogue will be mutually fruitful only when doing ministerial theology is established as a definite discipline and recognized task, not of the university, but of the pastoral scene. Until ministerial theology is sharply delineated and has clear criteria of excellence, dialogue with the long-standing practice of academic theology will be uneven. Ministerial theology is not a less rigorous form of academic theology, nor is it an application of a theology which was fully worked out in a university environment. It is a creative enterprise in its own right.

Academic theology is an indispensable resource for this enterprise but not a model for it. In turn, ministerial theology cannot be a model for academic theology. Through ministerial theology the academic enterprise could come in contact with the larger Church constituency. Also, the input from ministerial theology could suggest the direction and energies of academic research. The two disciplines are distinctive yet interlocking, and their interaction is necessary for an enriched Church life.

Therefore the area where work needs to be done is the training of people for the specific task of doing ministerial theology in the grass-roots Church. The purpose of this ministerial activity is to allow faith perceptions to influence personal and social life. Since the environment of local Church life is people and systems, doing ministerial theology entails three distinguishable yet inseparable abilities: helping abilities, change agent abilities and theological abilities. In concrete pastoral situations these three abilities interrelate and constitute the single skill of ministerial theology. The helping and change agent abilities are the process components of the skill: the theological ability is the content component. These three abilities will be only generally described. The purpose is to show their complementarity for the task of ministerial theology rather than to thoroughly explore their procedures and training techniques.

HELPING ABILITIES

The first locus of ministerial theology is the interaction of the minister and people. One characteristic of the minister qua minister is helping. Therefore the minister needs a clear model of how he/she is relating so that he/she might systematically be an effective helper.

Before outlining a developmental model of helping it might be useful to mention a body of knowledge that forms an illuminating backdrop to the skill of helping. In the last twenty-five years psychologists have distinguished various stages of life and the crises and tasks associated with each stage. The foundational work in this field is Erikson but further developments have been made by Loevinger, Chickering, Perry, Sheehy and Kohlberg. The still unfinished work of James Fowler attempts to correlate the life stages with faith development. This body of knowledge has immense practical implications for pastoral ministry. When the pastoral minister is aware that it is one thing to be ill at 25 and another at 53, or that it is one thing to rebel at 19 and quite another to rebel at 38, and that religious perceptions will be given a sympathetic hearing at one stage and a hostile hearing at another, his/her chances for doing ministerial theology effectively are greatly increased.

The development of systematic skills-training is only about a decade old. Foremost in this field is the work of Robert Carkhuff and associates (*Helping and Human Relations,* 2 vols. [Holt, Rinehart & Winston, 1969]) and N. Kagan (*Influencing Human Interaction* [Michigan State University CCTV, 1971]). For the purposes of doing ministerial theology the developmental model proposed by Gerard Egan (*Encounter* [Brooks-Cole, 1970], *The Skilled Helper* [Brooks-Cole, 1975], *Interpersonal Living* [Brooks-Cole, 1976]) has immense potential.

Egan's developmental model has three stages. In the first stage the helper responds to the helpee in such a way that he helps him explore his feelings, attitudes, behavior, etc. At this stage the helper needs the skills of accurate empathy (primary level), respect, genuineness and concreteness to be effective. The goal of stage two is to help the person see these unpacked feelings, attitudes and behaviors in a larger context. The skills necessary for this stage are accurate empathy (advanced level), self-disclosure, immediacy, confrontation, and alternative frames of reference. For doing ministerial theology the skills of advanced accurate empathy and providing alternate frames of reference are key. In advanced accurate empathy the helper must communicate to the person an understanding not only of what he has said but what was implied and hinted at. In presenting an alternative frame of reference the helper reconfigures the problem. This is where Christian perspectives and values are introduced into the helping process and the enterprise of ministerial theology engaged in.

Once the person's attitudes, feelings, behaviors have been accurately explored (stage one) and placed in a context that gives a direction for action (stage two), the third stage of facilitating the action is undertaken. The skills of this stage are the elaboration of action programs and support. Action programs may include problem-solving techniques, decision-making processes, behavior modification programs, etc. These three stages are organic or developmental, i.e., if the work of stage one is incomplete or unfinished, the further stages are ineffective.

In doing ministerial theology it must be remembered that there are no theological questions, only *people* with theological questions. Therefore although the content of a personal exchange or group exploration may be theological, the process that is going on is a helping one. If the minister can filter his/her theological insights through this developmental model, his/her chances for effective communication of faith perspectives and values are greatly increased.

CHANGE AGENT ABILITIES

The second locus of ministerial theology which can be distinguished but not separated from the first is the minister and people engaged in the process of change. The literature on the technology of change is extremely valuable for anyone involved in the process of making systems more responsive to human needs. Some of the most helpful literature is: Argyris, *Increasing Leadership Effectiveness* (Wiley, 1976); Argyris and Schön, *Theory in Practise* (Jossey-Bass, 1974); Tharp, "The Triadic Model of Consultation: Current Considerations," in *Psychological Consultation: Helping Teachers Meet Special Needs* (Leadership Training Institutes/Special Education, University of Minnesota, 1975); Tharp and Wetzel, *Behavior Modification and Natural Environment* (New York Academic Press, 1969); Egan, "Behavioral Clarity in Consultation: The Triadic Model as Instrument," in *Group Facilitators Handbook* (University Associates Press, 1978); Egan, *Change Agent Skills* (Brooks-Cole, 1978).

In general the change agent abilities (following the scheme of Egan) can be broken down into four stages and their corresponding sets of skills: a diagnostic stage which accurately analyzes the situations and surfaces the needs; a goal-setting stage which formulates concrete, behaviorally orientated goals; the program-development stage which designs programs that will effectively achieve the stated goals; an implementation stage which carries the programs out and evaluates their effectiveness. This systematic process, informed by behavioral laws, is extremely helpful for anyone engaged in formulating programs to bring about change.

THEOLOGICAL ABILITIES

Although the helping and change agent abilities are built on assumptions about human nature, systems, and the processes of change, there is a way in which they are neutral. They are methods which can be applied to any content. They become components of the skill of ministerial theology when they are linked to the theological ability and exercised in relation to the agenda which that ability carries. This ability and its agenda can be characterized in (at least) four ways.

1. Hearing the religious dimension when it is articulated in secular language and responding to it with Christian religious perception. On the pastoral scene religious reality is often expressed without using an explicit religious vocabulary (cf. John Cobb, *Theology and Pastoral Care* [Fortress, 1977]). People talk about ultimate meaning, identity, hope, their own distortedness, suffering and mystery without resorting to words like God, sin, grace, Christ, heaven and cross. Religious attitudes and convictions have not disappeared but they usually are not expressed in coded, traditional ways. The minister who is to facilitate the Church's faith exploration must be sensitive to these incognito forms and the corresponding Christian perspective.

2. Hearing the explicitly theological questions and responding to them with accurate theology. The Catholic peoples are in transition from one theological self-understanding to another. As such the pastoral minister, today more than ever, encounters explicit theological questions. These questions surface with teachers, liturgy teams, Bible groups, parish councils, as well as in individual situations. They concern anything from consciousness of Jesus to the behavioral implications of an image of God to the role of the Church in political life. Part of doing ministerial theology is to respond well to explicitly theological situations.

In both these situations of doing ministerial theology (nos. 1 and 2) the helping abilities are continually operative as the religious and theological dimensions are explored.

3. Hearing the assumptive world and responding by surfacing it. In any Church situation there are religious, theological and ecclesiological assumptions. Although these assumptions usually remain unnamed, they are operative and influential. To surface the assumptive world behind decisions and programs is a way of evaluation and direction (cf. McBrien, *The Remaking of the Church* [Harper & Row, 1973]). To spell out what ecclesiology or anthropology or concept of ministry is at work is to free the group to choose, to critically appropriate or reject. To surface the assumptive world is to allow the faith perspective to reflectively enter into decisions and programs.

4. Hearing the relationship between the Christian story and concrete activity and responding to it in the formulation of programs. The Christian story is the foundation and continual context of Church activity. As such, the telling of the story directs attention to certain areas and certain problems. It harnesses our energies to certain needs. The relationship between the story and the concrete activity must continuously be explored and reformulated. All Church activity must, on the one hand, be inspired by the Story and, on the other, illuminate the true meaning of the Story. For example, the aspect of the Story that says the followers of Jesus are distinguished by their care for each other directs our attention to the alienated and lonely in our midst. In turn, our people and program response to them reveals in concrete activity what the Christian mandate of care means. The theologically reflective minister is sensitive to this relationship and is continually bringing it to consciousness.

In both of these situations of doing ministerial theology (nos. 3 and 4) the change agent abilities are continually operative as the assumptive world is surfaced and the connections between faith and activity are drawn.

The major resource for the theological ability is the Christian tradition. If the minister is to relate the pastoral situation to the perspectives and values of that tradition, he/she must have access to it. Therefore central to the theological ability is knowledge of Christian Scripture and theology. This knowledge must not be self-contained, data with nowhere to go. It must be knowledge which understands its relation to ongoing life situations and its power to influence decision and action. This knowledge is not vaguely applied or overlaid on the pastoral situation but through the helping and change agent abilities integrated into the lives of people and the systems in which they live.

In summary, doing ministerial theology is both a specialist and generalist skill. It is specialist in that it involves three distinctive abilities with their own criteria and training procedures. It is generalist in that this skill is exercised in concrete human situations where these three abilities cannot be separated but intimately interact to constitute the ministerial moment. No one ability is exclusively engaged in, then abandoned, and another pursued. Helping, change agent, and theological abilities are simultaneously at work in the skill of doing ministerial theology.

William W. Bassett

Canon Law and Reform: An Agenda for a New Beginning

THE documents of the Second Vatican Council reveal a pervasive desire to bring the Church up to date and make it a more effective instrumentality of grace in the contemporary world. The post-conciliar decrees and instructions of the Roman congregations have reiterated this theme and interpreted it in a decade of intense ecclesiological reflection and development. To reform the Church by accommodating its laws and institutions to the culture and spirit of the present generation was a mandate of radical implications. It was, indeed, part of the hope of the new Pentecost, a revitalization of life and mission, the precondition of a new *oicumene* of the Christian churches.

This paper will consider the theme of church reform in its post-conciliar dress from a single, and admittedly narrow point of view. As far as the revision of the canon law is concerned, its basic thesis is that the post-conciliar interpretation given to the Council's mandate for reform by the Pontifical Commission for the Revision of the Code of Canon Law is not only a deradicalization of the hope of the Vatican Council; it is that the new code of canon law now nearing completion under the Commission's exclusive control domesticates, dilutes and, to this extent, betrays the expectation the Council gave to the Christian people. The revised code of canon law will not be a new law for the Church. It will be, rather, the end product of an era dominated by philosophical and canonical presuppositions that have effectively withstood the challenge to significant change. The new code of canon law in its present elaboration[1] will end the work of the Council by institutionalizing the most minimal interpretation of its principles. What is needed now is the agenda for a new beginning that will lead to real and significant change in the law of the Church.

NO PLAN FOR INSTITUTIONAL REFORM

The idea of reform in the Church is an ancient and regularly recurring theme in Western theological traditions.[2] It is interwoven with myriad historical movements and proposals whose implementation or condemnation mark the trajectory of church life through the centuries. Since the promulgation of the papal decretals in the early Middle Ages reform in the Catholic tradition has been closely aligned with law. Law has been used repeatedly to enshrine the practical dimension of progressively unfolding insights into human nature and the demands of the Gospel in the context of the various contemporary cultures in which the Christian faith is lived. The canon law reflected scholastic philosophical and theological methodologies in the Middle Ages, assimilated the organic harmony of the Roman law in the era of the Renaissance and adopted the presuppositions of the great codification movements in the nineteenth century. Yet, paradoxically, the call to reform the canon law issued by Pope John XXIII even before the Second Vatican Council[3] has had practical repercussions so disconcerting as to have thrust upon the Catholic Church an unprecedented confusion and disarray. For, in spite of a history of assimilation of new ideas into the canon law of the past, the Church in council was at a loss to propose a practical, legal paradigm of reform that could meet general assent and acceptance. Models of the Church as servant, people of God, communion, sacrament, herald or institution were singularly lacking in any agreed-upon human counterpart. The pastoral council ignited a spirit of reform, but could not give directions on *how* to reform, to adapt the Church to the spirit of the times.

The council fathers wished to bring the Church out of its ghetto[4] and, as the Constitution on the Church in the Modern World says, speak "to all men."[5] The pastoral concerns of the Church were to extend far beyond the confines of the Catholic Church to a universal, cosmic horizon.[6] The Council stressed a more profound willingness to probe the implications of the Church's presence in the world and act in accordance with the consequences of that awareness. Such an awareness called for an "accommodation to the times" as a fundamental axiom of renewal. The idea was accepted in a matrix of conflicting expectations and without a felt need to probe more deeply the implications of what a new relationship with the world might mean.

Vatican II, indeed, described the updating or *aggiornamento* as adjustment or accommodation. In his allocution opening the first session

of the Council, October 11, 1962, Pope John XXIII spoke of introducing "appropriate emendations" into the Church.[7] Perhaps this mentality is best expressed when, on the question of doctrine, the Pope spoke
of the permissibility, and even necessity, of dressing up the old truths in
new words.[8] The conservative intent of the pope's words is clearly
suggested by the fact that they seem to allude to the Dogmatic Constitution on the Catholic Faith of Vatican I.[9] The Council, indeed,
proposed a general program to "return to the sources" of the Christian
life.[10] The purpose of such a return was to derive assurance that in
making pastoral accommodations to the modern world, even to the
extent of introducing "new forms" and "innovations" and of making
generous allowance for variety, only that would be changed from the
past which was properly subject to change.[11] A decade of experience
and reflection following the Council shows that it is impossible to
contain the thrust of *aggiornamento* within the minimal limits imposed
by the past, for the stated goals and purposes of reform far outstrip
the conciliar limitations.

GROWTH, PROGRESS AND RENEWAL

The Constitution on the Church, though it never loses sight of the
transcendent aspect of the Church, insists that the Church truly enters
the history of men.[12] With Christ described as "the key, center, and
end of all human history," the Council considers religious truth in its
historical dimension with as much seriousness as had traditionally been
applied to its metaphysical dimension.[13]

While there is no doubt that Vatican II evidences a strong sense of
continuity with the past and a desire to remain true to it, it is also true
that the Council was acutely aware of change in the world, aware of
how the conditions of modern life differ from what went before. There
is in the Council a sense of change and a perspective on the temporal
order which expressed itself in the general term "progress." The
Council applied the same term to the Church, so that *growth, progress*
and *development* became major conciliar themes almost synonymous
with renewal itself. The continuity with the past of which Vatican II
was aware was in many instances a developmental continuity. Men
have learned to think in patterns of progress, evolution and development, as the Constitution on the Church in the Modern World itself
points out.[14] We should not be surprised, therefore, if such patterns are
applied to the Church itself to help explain the phenomenon of change
of which the Church has become increasingly aware.

This "progress of the People of God" is sometimes spoken of in
general terms.[15] At other times it is applied to something as specific as

liturgical changes or growth in devotion to Mary.[16] But the area to which it is most frequently applied is that of doctrine. Alongside Vatican II's repeated allusions to a progress, evolution, maturation, or growing understanding of doctrine, Vatican I's few lines on the subject seem scant indeed.[17]

Although "development of doctrine" is a recurring theme of Vatican II, the Council gives us very little help in understanding *how* "development" takes place.[18] The old conciliar figure of the Church as the Lord's field practically disappears from the pages of Vatican II, and it is replaced especially by "People of God" and "Mystical Body of Christ." In conjunction with this latter term, we often find the words "increase" and "augment" in the Council's documents, but it is not always easy to specify just what is increasing or augmenting.[19] In the context of the body metaphor, at any rate, the model of organic growth is suggested, and the Council occasionally refers explicitly to the organic nature of the Church's life and constitution.[20] However, the Council never explicitly associates doctrinal development with a model of organic growth.

Vatican II is just as vague concerning the process by which the general "progress" of the Church takes place as it is concerning the "development of doctrine." As a matter of fact, the term "progress" is less frequently used to describe what is happening in the Church than are the traditional descriptions of "renewal," "renovation" and "rejuvenation" *(renovare, instaurare, iuvenescere)*.[21] These terms in themselves suggest cyclic or repetitive patterns of history rather than linear progress. In the Decree on Religious Life we can find prescriptions for a critical revision *(recognoscere)* of rules and constitutions,[22] and in the Constitution on the Sacred Liturgy we find similar prescriptions for a revision of the liturgical books in the light of "accurate, historical, theological and pastoral" investigations.[23]

The Decree on Ecumenism, however, calls for more. It clearly mandates institutional reform in the Catholic Church. While speaking of faults committed against unity, it on two occasions admits in a generic way that Catholics have to bear their share of the blame.[24] And on two further occasions it calls for "reform." In the first instance "reform" is made synonymous with "renovation," and in context it seems to refer especially to the personal reform of the individual Christian.[25] The second instance, however, for the first time in a conciliar document since the Council of Basel, clearly speaks of "reform of the Church." It deserves quotation in full:

> Christ summons the Church, as she goes her pilgrim way, to that continual reformation of which she always has need, insofar as she is

an institution of men here on earth. Therefore, if the influence of events or of the times has led to deficiencies [*quae minus accurate servata fuerint*] in conduct, in Church discipline, or even in the formulation of doctrine (which must be carefully distinguished from the deposit of faith itself), these should be appropriately rectified at the proper moment.[26]

Several comments are in order concerning the above statement. It is the Church which is to be reformed, not the Christian people. It is a reforming which is ongoing, continual, so that we can infer that there will never be a time when "conduct, discipline, and doctrine" will arrive at a condition of perfection which will render them "irreformable." Although the phrase *quae minus accurate servata fuerint* is not an unmistakable admission of fault or defect, it does form a remarkable contrast with Trent's description of its doctrine of the Eucharist as *omni ex parte perfecta*. The very description of the Church as in pilgrimage suggests the lowly, precarious, and human character of its strivings and hence suggests its need for reform.

The description of the Church as in pilgrimage is closely related to the Council's description of the Church as the "People of God."[27] This is the favorite and characteristic description of the Church in the dogmatic Constitution on the Church, and it has been interpreted as signifying a breakdown of the old dichotomy between the Church and the Christian people, which allowed the Church to be without fault and untouched by history while the Christian people sin and are subject to the "injury of time."[28] Such an interpretation contains profound implications for the idea of a reform of laws and institutions in the Church. The Code Commission, however, in its current revision of canon law has clearly rejected the implication that the Council called for reform by any major structural changes in the institutions of the Church.

THE INTERPRETATION OF THE CODE COMMISSION

The Pontifical Commission for the Revision of the Code of Canon Law has submitted its policies and the progress of its work to each of the international meetings of the Synod of Bishops in Rome. These reports were accepted and approved by the synods, not only as a general encouragement of the immense work of canonical revision, but as a particular and specific approbation of each major part of this project.

To its consultors and the episcopal delegates attending the Synod of Bishops in Rome in 1967, the Commission offered a detailed position paper containing the principles it would follow in revising the code of canon law.[29] These principles were discussed in the synod at length.

The synodal bishops then approved ten general principles to guide the revision of the canon law. First, rather than radically alter the canon law, the Commission opted basically to follow the juridical format of the 1917 code. The new code is to be a modernization and adaptation of the Gasparri code, with special emphasis upon the definition and protection of rights and obligations of persons within the visible society of the Church. Secondly, the new code will attempt to eliminate conflicts between the internal and external forum. It will be basically concerned with the external social order of the Church, not matters of individual conscience. Thirdly, the new code will be more pastoral: minimalizing invalidating and incapacitating laws, emphasizing exhortation over strict duty, and providing greater freedom and flexibility in general norms. Fourthly, the office of bishop will be positively cast with detailed inclusion of the bishops' individual and collegial authority in the Church. This will entail a rethinking of the institute of faculties and powers of dispensation. The fifth principle is that of subsidiarity, with greater recognition in the revised law of the independence and competencies of rites, episcopal conferences, regional and local councils. The sixth principle affirms the fundamental equality of all persons in the Church and the protection of the rights of all the baptized by norms of accountability to curb arbitrary use of authority. The seventh principle elaborates a procedure for protecting subjective rights through judicial recourse and appeal and a new system of administrative tribunals. The eighth principle is that the new law maintain the basic territorial division of jurisdiction in the Church accepted by the 1917 code. Extraordinary provisions will be considered in jurisdictional units wherein strict territorial delimitation should not be solely determinative. The ninth principle concerns a reduction in the penal law and a desire that ecclesiastical penalties be imposed and remitted only in the external forum. Finally, the synod approved study of a new systematic ordering of the code to fit the spirit of the Vatican Council and the scientific requisites of canonical legislation.

The 1967 Synod of Bishops, in approving these general principles, thus sanctioned a very definite canonical interpretation of Vatican II and a clear goal to guide the Commission in revising canon law. In so doing, it urged that a new code be completed as soon as possible and that broad consultation take place in the Church prior to its final promulgation. We have every reason to believe that these principles continue to be operative today. Without doubt, their implementation will have a considerable effect in stabilizing the present organization and administration of the Church. The drafting of a new code according to the Commission's stated principles will involve a settling by law of many issues now clearly the subject of extensive theological debate.

The Canon Law Society of America responded to this position paper by a series of urgent suggestions.[30] To the membership of the Commission it spoke for the addition of noncanonists, e.g. theologians, sociologists, Scripture scholars, etc., lay persons, men and women, and more persons familiar with Anglo-American legal traditions and culture. To date the Commission remains exclusively one of canon lawyers, with no women, and only eleven of its members identifiable with a non-Roman-law legal and cultural tradition. The Society asked that the work of the Commission be made public; it remains largely unknown to this day. It further suggested that a canon-by-canon process of rethinking the old code was inadequate to meet the needs of the Church today. A definitive new code in the same mold as the old one is premature at a time when broader experimentation in structures is being called for. It asked for ecumenical consultation and subsidiary study groups to examine the principal issues of legal reform interdisciplinarily, suggesting a methodology of study in successive symposia of constitutionalism, human rights, co-responsibility and subsidiarity, and the role of women in the Church.

The proposals of the Canon Law Society of America were communicated directly to the Code Commission, but with no acknowledgment of receipt or consideration. The work of the Commission has not been influenced in any marked way by external criticism or suggestion. It is the work of "specialists," as Pope Paul VI remarked, "men learned in the science of canon law."[31] The narrowness of vision is clearly apparent in the product of its work.

As of the present writing the Code Commission has completed the initial work of revising the new law. A text of an entire new code has been prepared and transmitted to the pope for his judgment whether or not it is to be forwarded to others involved in the consultative process. Texts of various parts of the new code, as published in the Commission's newsletter, *Communicationes,* reveal the extent to which the Commission and its consultors have resisted change. There is a studied effort to draft a revised law that, in effect, will be no revision at all. It will be simply the old 1917 code gussied up in the makeup of new titles and footnotes.

The systematic order of the old code is preserved, with the simple addition of a provision for an administrative procedure to structure appeals against decisions of ecclesiastical authorities.[32] Beginning with a section on the interpretation of canon law, general norms, and going through persons, things and processes to end with the penal law, the revised code in format will exactly parallel the old code. Apparent changes in titles, rubrics, numeration of canons and extensive citation of conciliar sources are merely cosmetic.[33] The revised code, on the whole, merely reiterates the old law. To this extent it provides a legal bulwark against change, precluding further change in the Church as much as law and legal process can.

Paralleling the work of codification is the continuing canonical interpretation of the council documents by a committee composed of members of the Roman Curia, most of whom are also on the Code Commission. On April 14, 1969, the competency of the Commission for the Interpretation of the Decrees of the Second Vatican Council was broadened by Pope Paul VI to include also the canonical interpretation of all post-conciliar decrees.[34] What this means is that the same narrow group of curial canon lawyers is both making the new laws and officially empowered to interpret them. It is this committee and the Code Commission who alone give an official interpretation of the Council insofar as it affects the canon law.

NEW VALUES AND OLD THEORY

A general codification of laws must be guided by an identifiable legal theory. "In the course of the Church's history," Stephan Kuttner remarked of the 1917 code, "no legislation had ever been enacted which so completely absorbed all preceding discipline and formally abolished all earlier collections."[35] Cardinal Gasparri and his collaborators had espoused a method of conceptual juridical abstraction, the *Begriffsjurisprudenz* of German legal philosophy popular at the turn of the century. The code of church law was in form and theory an imitation of the popular civil law codifications of the day, the *Code Napoléon* of France and the *Burgerliches Gesetzbuch* of Germany. Laws were abstractly formulated in briefest statement and set out in the systemic order of the Justinian Code; persons, things and processes, preceded by norms of interpretation and concluding with penalties for infractions of the law. Regardless of how necessary law may be for the Church and regardless of how convenient it may be to collect all laws in one place, such a systematization lends a rigidity to law far beyond that merited only by reasoned decisions promulgated for the common good. Individual laws cease to convey their own reasonableness, unlike the carefully explained decretal law in force before 1918. Codification becomes confirmation of a descending theory of hierarchical authority enforcing all canons equally; interpretation of law depends on a technical "constructionism."

Since the juridical nature of the 1917 code is being followed in theory and form, the new code will be aimed at capping a period of structural legislation that will be completed with its promulgation. Such a code will enshrine stability and permanence in canon law. The value of a readily accessible collection of laws may be overshadowed by a new sacralization of juridical formularies. In the meanwhile, the reform of laws will leave relatively unaffected the more imperative reform in the Catholic Church, namely, *a reform of the decisional process itself.* The decisional system and its basic foundations will be beyond scrutiny, as legal experimentation beyond or contrary to codified law will be more and more exceptional, if not plainly impossible. In other words, the attempt itself to formulate a new code of laws at this time has important ecclesiological implications, not as a collection, but as a juridical codification in the proper acceptance of the term.

Since the conclusion of the Council a variety of entirely new agencies of participation have been chartered in the particular churches, such as national, diocesan and parochial pastoral councils, senates of priests and episcopal conferences. In addition to these canonical institutes numerous paracanonical structures are emerging, e.g., assemblies of religious men and women, associations of priests, local and national organizations of the laity, state Catholic conferences, etc. Functionally, these are now major participants in the ecclesiastical decisional process. Yet they are in a state of experimentation and development so extensive that their role will not admit of definitive legal description. On the level of international cooperation the Synod of Bishops continues in a primitive developmental stage. The role of the Patriarchs and the autonomy of the ritual churches, apparently assured in the Council document on the Eastern Catholic Churches, remain severely hampered to this day. The *Lex Ecclesiae Fundamentalis* almost completely overlooked the Oriental churches, and in stressing papal primacy left no room at all for a structurally viable *communio ecclesiarum.* This is an extremely serious omission but one which apparently reflects a deliberate choice. The major problems that beset the Church, however, are not only ones that admit of solution by organizational decision. Dialogue concerning the role of law itself in the Church reveals profound cultural and ideological divergences. A systematic codification of the common law may well inhibit freedom to explore new solutions to problems of church order. A period of learning, inter-church cooperation, and tentative exploration is necessary. A collection of easily understandable new laws would be helpful, but only if it is clear that many, if not most of the new laws, will be *ad experimentum.* More than this should not be attempted in a time of disquiet and major institutional crisis.

A CRISIS OF INSTITUTION

The Catholic Church today, like the major social institutions of Western civilization, is experiencing a historical moment of profound institutional crisis. More serious than the discontent of those abused by liturgical change; more serious than the violence of the social activists or those who react to them; more serious even than the confusion of endlessly repeated and contradictory allegations regarding the cause of the crisis, is a subtle but certain fact that is very difficult to express. This is that over the past decade there has been an almost totally unexpected, yet thoroughly pervasive change of mentality among Catholics. The lived experience of the Church is not the same as it was; more importantly, there is a great uneasiness in knowing that the secure ecclesiastical milieu of the past, such as that mirrored in the 1917 code, can never be recaptured.

A new understanding of the commitment and role of those who follow the Lord is settling upon the Church. This vision is more than a little disquieting for Catholics in general and most canon lawyers in particular; it has brought with it a very real anxiety for the preservation of the Latin Church or, perhaps, for one's personal relationship with the Church. The Synods of Bishops and, indeed, the Code Commission itself has failed to admit any change in the decisional process of the Church during a time when it is conceived that the Church may be about to lose many, if not most, of its cherished traditions. With this loss, it is feared, the Catholic Church may even lose its corporate identity. The debate on flexibility of ministries, a married clergy, the ordination of women, the election of bishops, administrative decentralization from Rome, the propriety of theological dissent, changing patterns in the life and work of members of religious communities, the role of women in the Church, etc., has become very strenuous, often bitter and almost always accompanied by a note of great personal anxiety. These issues are so interrelated that to change any one radically would not only affect all the others, but would lead to a certain social transformation of the entire institution itself. The Second Vatican Council, a pastoral council, provided for a change of the language of worship and gave to Christians generally an open forum of debate. This has profoundly shaken the security of Catholics. What has occurred in the decade has been a real revolution of institutional values, expectations and fears among Catholics. This revolution simply cannot be turned back, as many hope, by a new set of clear and certain laws.

A change of institutional values is changing the Church. Such a change of values does not depend on good will nor can it be controlled under the guise of a united front. It proceeds unevenly and usually with notable unease and tension. A new generation, and an old generation newly sighted, will change the Church. They cannot be stopped, nor do I believe they can even be led without the assumption of great risks. Risks must be taken. But it is in the area of risk that canon lawyers are most uncomfortable, for the law itself is generally conceived and used as a hedge against risk. This dynamic of cultural change, however, engenders its own environment and stirs deeply the aspirations of those it endlessly goads into hopes for a better tomorrow. This is true of all men, of all Catholics, as well as those caught up in social revolution everywhere.

CANON LAWYERS AND THE NEW VALUES

Among canon lawyers concerned with the reform of law in the Church today there seem to be three fairly clear responses to what is occurring and its effect upon canon law. Though this division is somewhat arbitrary and no one certainly is a pure type, a model of these different mentalities may be useful. These are types of consciousness of the Church that are significantly at variance and their clash underlies a great deal of the conflict of the present.

Consciousness, as I use the term here, is not merely a set of opinions, values and stores of information. It is a total configuration of personal experience making up in an individual a complete perception of the reality of the Church in human life. There was a consciousness that went with the culture of small town pre-industrial Western European life. This is recognizably different from that of the modern city-dweller or university student. So also are types of consciousness of the Church and its discipline formed during the fifties, in the time of the Council and the third which has begun to emerge perceptibly during the last couple of years.

In the first category are those who still remain comfortable with the Latin Church like it was, the steadfast but beleaguered Christendom, whose thinking is yet molded by canonical categories taken from the 1917 code, e.g., faculties, gravity of sins, validating factors in acts and events, etc. The Church and its law fulfilled a need for perennial stability, strength of character, defense against the uncertainties of life and kept intact the beauty of the Latin tradition. At its best it was a milieu of personal piety, asceticism and sanctification. It gave to individual lives a visible historical continuity, an association in the ark of the saved, a clear line between the friends and enemies of the faith, and thus, of God. A large number of Catholics are conscious of the Church in this way, a consciousness appropriate to pilgrimages, conclaves, novenas, monsignors and papal knights, building drives and the ordered life of unchanging rules.

Many of these saw no real need for the Council. Yet they accepted it because Pope John XXIII wanted it and the Holy Spirit directs such things. But for this category of persons now concerned with the revision of law in the Church the Vatican Council meant only *aggiornamento,* only updating. It meant merely streamlining, modernizing and making more efficient the traditional law and structures of the Church.

Many of these are now very resentful about what has happened in the Church since the closing of the Council. The theologians who have misled the faithful, rebellious young priests and nuns, secularization—all are blamed for what is going on. There is a real fear that the uniqueness and Lordship of Christ are being compromised and with this the unique and transcendant character of the Church; in brief, they fear that an exalted humanism is taking the place of the Christian Gospel among Catholics. To almost every urging for creative innovation, the answer is given that such an innovation was not called for by the Council. The first imperative is to implement the Council documents and these did not call explicitly for radical change in the Catholic Church.

Illustrative of this first canonical approach, I believe, are the principles accepted by the Code Commission and approved by the 1967 synod. These preclude a radical change both in structures and in the nature of canon law in the Church. They reflect the imperative of the continental legal tradition to systematically order and securely settle by law the complexity of human relationships. The *Lex Ecclesiae Fundamentalis,* the first product of the Commission's work, was basically an attempt to encompass juridically the constitutive and fundamental nucleus of the Church (the *status ecclesiae,* as the medieval canonists would say). This cannot adequately be formulated by means of the instruments of the legal sciences because these are by their very nature schematic, unidimensional, positive, systematic, and therefore useful in the Church only for the purpose of specific and concrete decrees *(statuta ecclesiae).* The *Lex* canonized a narrow ecclesiological interpretation of Vatican II, identifying the Church primarily as a juridically organized and self-sufficient society, rather than as a believing people with a mission to the world. In over-emphasizing papal and hierarchical authority and prerogatives it totally de-emphasized the role of the non-ordained faithful in the life of the Church. A clear insight into the mentality of the redactors might be gained by critical contextual comparison of the canons and their cited references to the conciliar documents. A uniformly restrictive interpretation has been used throughout.

The structural legislation of the postconciliar period reflects a similar approach restricting change to a very narrow degree of modernization. For example, in the prologue to the constitutions reforming the Roman Curia,[36] the papal representatives,[37] the process of selecting bishops,[38] the procedure for adjudicating marriage cases,[39] and renewing religious formation,[40] the Pope affirms emphatically that he is following the mind of the Vatican Council. Yet each of these enactments strongly confirms the status quo in the Church and precludes any perceptible change. Modernization means making more efficient traditional structures and procedures in the Catholic Church. The revision of cannon law officially until this time has been only an updating.

A second approach to the revision of canon law may be seen in those who read the Council documents as calling for a major reform in the life of the Church. The documents, it is thought, in their acceptance of the principles of collegiality, ecumenism, active co-responsibility of the faithful, liturgical reform, and a diaconal ministry of authority must lead to far more than merely a modernization. There must be a complete reformulation of law and structures in the life of the Catholic Church as a prelude to the reunion of the churches. Broad cultural diversities should be able to co-exist in the Catholic Church without subjugation to a Latin cultural and legal ascendancy. The Canon Law Society of America in its multiple and diverse activities since 1965 exemplifies this second approach to the reform of canon law.

The revisionist spirit has leaned heavily upon organization, cooperation and responsibility, reform through parish and diocesan councils, senates, consultative and elective processes, streamlined pastoral agencies, more and more participation. Noteworthy in this effort has been the securing of papal approbation for extensive procedures of arbitration and conciliation in the Church.

Behind a facade of optimism and intense activity, however, liberal canonists of Vatican II are becoming more and more disenchanted. They have had no official access to the Code Commission. Moreover, liturgical reform has been accompanied by very little experimentation and has scarcely progressed beyond the revision of the ritual books. Senates and associations of priests have not solved the problems of priestly identity and anxiety; indeed, they have been stymied by the restrictions of the unchanged canon law. Shared responsibility is often shared confusion; and due process is of limited utility as the more serious problems of authority go untouched. In the meanwhile the Catholic Church seems stalled in a posture of simply baffling introspection.

The reformist spirit of those in the second category puts great faith in institutions, laws, committees, and structures. They accepted debate as a way of attaining the greatest possible rationality and they supported pluralism in order as a way of attaining balance in the Church. But the emphasis was on the solving of problems, the "cure" of conflict. Is this "Church," however, the Church of historical reality? It is true? Francis Oakley, in arguing a new conciliarism, reveals medieval divergencies of belief on church government hardly realizable in the Catholic Church today.[41] The medieval world was one in which extreme contrasts, inconsistencies, and violent conflicts were not "settled," but lived side by side, lending a color to life that order cannot provide. The second mentality seeks the resolution of conflict by laws; its goal for the Church is an organization possessing an appropriate tribunal, agency, procedure or authority whereby problems can always be "solved." The liberal canonist wanted reform within the cultural tradition and through structures of conflict and problem resolution. Yet it becomes increasingly clear that even the best of laws have a very limited value, that the Church needs reform beyond traditional structures and beyond the assumptions of the present canonical tradition. The Catholic Church needs time to assimilate the cultural diversity of a multiplicity of human experiences of the life of faith. How much diversity in church order is compatible with unity? To what extent would a plurality of distinct organizational models of the Church be theologically sound in Christianity today?

Since the Council, ecumenically oriented theologians have tended to amplify the Council's concessions to non-substantialist positions rather than to insist on the substantialist elements that undoubtedly remain in the Council documents. Under the probing of scholarly research, Catholics are increasingly aware of the difficulty of clearly distinguishing between the substantials and the accidentals of the Church. They tend to subordinate the institutional features to the mission of the Church, and to hold that a heavy burden of proof rests upon anyone who wishes to show that a given structure is immutable. Accenting the common bonds between all committed believers, many younger Christians question the importance of the distinctive features of any particular denomination. All of this puts strong pressures on academic and official theology to insist less on confessional differences and to enlarge the area of common Christian sharing.[42]

What Avery Dulles says of "younger Christians" characterizes an increasing number of canonists in yet a third category of perception. These are not anti-institutional nor do they purport to downplay the necessity of laws for the Church. While valuing some institutions, they basically consider structures and institutions in the Church as entirely subsidiary to the real issues Christians must face. Rather than tidy up matrimonial law, for instance, or improve the efficiency of tribunals, they speak of the Church stepping out of a canonical approach to marriage entirely or at least re-examining its fundamental stand on indissolubility in the light of the different human experiences of marriage. Rather than improving procedures of dispensation, they ask for a simple, modern method of resignation from the ministry. Rather than a new institute of episcopal faculties, they may call for a radical strategy of grass-roots transformation of the Church. While valuing the past, many in this category are relatively free of the past, free of institutional intimidation, free to use or not use the agencies and offices of the Church. Canon law in this perspective tends to be considerably less absolute, more clearly functional and pragmatic.

This mentality was born in the Council of the promise of a new Pentecost, the reunion of Christianity, and the demystification of the Roman organizational imperatives in the compromise and acrimonies of conciliar debate and post-conciliar failure to effect significant change in a yet rigid and monolithic canonical system. The grave weakness of this mentality is in oversimplifying complex issues and too great a willingness to sacrifice confessional values that yet remain imperative in Catholic tradition and precious for the churches outside it. Impatience conveys the impression that others may be fostering irrelevancies; that is the ultimate scorn, the great Christian sin of our day. Yet in spite of weaknesses, there is strength in seeing what is relative and culturally conditioned in canon law and not confusing this with right reason or the Gospel itself.

The acceptance of a revised canon law in the Catholic Church will require a new synthesis of opinion, a new science of law in the Church. In the meanwhile the Code Commission is proceeding to completion of a new Code in a time of grave cultural and institutional crisis in the Church. It is directed by a restrictive legal methodology of questionable persuasiveness. The work of the Commission continues in the almost certain expectation that most canonists outside of Rome equally concerned about a new law will have grave reservations about its new code.

CONCLUSION: A NEW AGENDA

The revision of the code of canon law in the Roman Catholic Church is an extensive project that merits the closest scrutiny. The law must necessarily be reformed and reformulated. All agree to this. Canon lawyers are not agreed, however, upon the wisdom of promulgating a complete new code. Perhaps the deepest difference among them is ultimately cultural and ecclesiological. Should the Roman Catholic Church change from the great Latin legal orientation of its past or not? If so, to what extent? Without doubt, the interpretation of the documents of Vatican II by the Code Commission is so minimalistic that it will neither bring the Church out of its ghetto nor effect a significant accommodation of canon law to the culture and consciousness of these times. How far the forces of change now operating in and on the Catholic Church can overcome the forces operating against change, whether these latter are of mere inertia or conviction, is the question.

We need a new, practical agenda for the reform of canon law in the Church. Among the items to be included on that agenda to accomplish the conciliar goals of a revitalization of the life and mission of the Catholic Church and a preparation of the Church for the reunion of the churches are:

1. A removal of the canonical disabilities to the fullest participation of women in the life and ministries of the Church.

2. A full recognition of a communion of the Eastern and Western churches, with complete self-direction acknowledged in the great churches of the east.

3. A reform of the Roman Curia to become a center of international cooperation and assistance, instead of the present center of control and domination.

4. The development of a system of administrative law and agencies to secure the protection of law of the rights of the faithful.

5. A declericalization of the nonsacramental ministries of church order and service.

6. The implementation of procedures to restore the right of the ministry and laity of electing bishops and pastors.

7. The abolition of the Roman practice of translating bishops from see to see.

8. The rejection of an absolute law of celibacy for the priesthood and a discarding of the trappings, heraldry and symbolism of the ages of the Church's *imperium* that surround it.

9. The pastoral, nonjudicial care of persons in marriage cases.

10. The integration of the laity in pastoral councils and deliberative assemblies in the Church.

11. The development of standards of fiduciary responsibility and accountability for the open financial administration of the goods of the Church.

12. The accommodation of the institute of incardination to allow the fullest measure of freedom and self-responsibility compatible with human dignity to the clerical ministry.

13. Granting to the faithful of the right of free association and assembly in the Church.

14. Granting canonical exemption to the Catholic universities and theological faculties.

15. Discarding the vindictive penalties of the old code of canon law.

This agenda is one of accommodation of human laws and human structures to the felt needs of men and women in the Church after the Council. Its acceptance would lead to that radical step towards "progress" the Council hesitatingly promised. Implementation even *ad experimentum* would cast the canon law into an entirely new role in the Church in service to the People of God in a pilgrimage in time.

Notes

1. A 1974 progress report of the Pontifical Commission for the Revision of the Code of Canon Law indicates that a complete, revised text of a new code has been written. See *Communicationes* 6 (1974): 29–59, at p. 30. The president of the Commission, Cardinal Pericles Felici, seemed quite optimistic about the text and the possibility of its imminent promulgation in a personal report: "De opere iuris canonici recognoscendi," *Periodica* 64 (1975): 13–25.

2. An exceptionally good analysis of the literature and concept of reform in the Church is that of J. W. O'Malley, "Reform, Historical Consciousness and Vatican II's Aggiornamento," *Theological Studies* 32 (1971): 573–601.

3. Pope John XXIII called for the revision of canon law in his memorable address of January 25, 1959, announcing the forthcoming Second Council of the Vatican (*A.A.S.* 51 [1959]: 65–69). The Pontifical Commission for the Revision of the Code of Canon Law was established March 28, 1963 (*A.A.S.* 55 [1963]: 363).

4. See Pope Paul VI's allocution to the Council, September 29, 1963 (*A.A.S.* 55 [1963]: 847, 854–58).

5. *A.A.S.* 58 (1966): 1026.

6. *A.A.S.* 54 (1962): 794; 58 (1966): 947.

7. *A.A.S.* 54 (1962): 788.

8. Ibid. 792.

9. *Conciliorum Oecumenicorum Decreta,* eds. G. Alberigo et al. 2nd ed. (Rome, 1962), p. 785.

10. *A.A.S.* 58 (1966): 703.

11. *A.A.S.* 54 (1962): 9; 56 (1964): 97, 105–6, 110, 114; 58 (1966): 706, 713, 720, etc.

12. *A.A.S.* 57 (1965): 14.

13. *A.A.S.* 58 (1966): 1033, 1066.

14. *A.A.S.* 58 (1966): 1029, 1076.

15. *A.A.S.* 58 (1966): 731; see also ibid. 57 (1965): 65.

16. *A.A.S.* 56 (1964): 106; 57 (1965): 65.

17. See *A.A.S.* 57 (1965): 13, 16, 59, 107; 58 (1966): 738, 821, 862, 930, 935, 938–39, 1085.

18. See John C. Murray, "This Matter of Religious Freedom," *America* 112 (Jan. 9, 1965): 43.

19. See *A.A.S.*, e.g., 57 (1965): 11; 58 (1966): 690, 707.

20. See *A.A.S.* 57 (1965): 26–27; 58 (1966): 674, 684, 855.

21. See *A.A.S.* 56 (1964): 97, 104, 105; 57 (1965): 7, 14, 81, 95; 58 (1966): 703, 704, 713, 739, 1010, etc.

22. *A.A.S.* 58 (1966): 704, 705.

23. *A.A.S.* 56 (1964): 98, 107, 114, and esp. 106.

24. *A.A.S.* 57 (1965): 92–93, 97. See also ibid. p. 95, as well as 58 (1966): 938.

25. *A.A.S.* 57 (1965): 94.

26. *A.A.S.* 57 (1965): 96–97.

27. See, e.g., *A.A.S.* 57 (1965): 94; 58 (1966): 938, 1065.

28. See, e.g., M. Hoffman, "Church and History in Vatican II's Constitution on the Church: A Protestant Perspective," *Theological Studies* 29 (1968): 191–214, esp. 199–201.

29. *Communicationes* 1 (1969): 77–100.

30. "Resolutions of the Canon Law Society of America," *The Jurist* 29 (1969): 26–38.

31. In an allocution to the International Meeting of Canon Lawyers in Rome, May 25, 1968, marking the fiftieth anniversary of the promulgation of the Code of Canon Law, *Communicationes* 1 (1969): 65–70.

32. The last official report we have on the status of a new administrative law refers to a committee meeting called to discuss the responses of consultors to whom the project was sent. That was in February 1973 (*Communicationes* 5 [1973]: 235–253). After extensive public criticism, the project *Lex Ecclesiae Fundamentalis* has apparently been withdrawn from consideration as a part of a new code. It is still being worked on, however, although it is not certain for what purpose. See *Communicationes* 6 (1974): 199–200; 7 (1975): 25.

33. A shocking analysis of the texts of the new code, revealing the trivialization of the Commission's revisionary work, is found in a report of Thomas J. Green, "The Revision of the Code: The First Decade," *The Jurist* 36 (1976): 353–441.

34. *Communicationes* 1 (1969): 78.

35. "The Code of Canon Law in Historical Perspective," *The Jurist* 28 (1968): 139.

36. *Regimini Ecclesiae Universae* (Aug. 15, 1967) (*A.A.S.* 59 [1967]: 885–928).

37. *Sollicitudo omnium ecclesiarum* (June 24, 1969) (*A.A.S.* 61 [1969]: 473–84).

38. These norms are contained in a letter to the heads of the episcopal conferences sent by the Cardinal Secretary of State, September 1, 1970. An English translation may be found in W. W. Bassett, ed., *The Choosing of Bishops* (Hartford, Conn., 1971), pp. 103–107.

39. (*A.A.S.* 58 [1971] 441–46).

40. *Instruction on the Renewal of Religious Formation* (Rome, 1969).

41. "The 'New Conciliarism' and Its Implications: A Problem in History and Hermeneutics," *Journal of Ecumenical Studies* 8 (1971).

42. "The Church, the Churches and the Catholic Church," *Theological Studies* 33 (1972): 234.

Peter Huizing

Vatican III: A Constitution on Church Order

1. Vatican II neglected to translate its teachings into Church institutions. Doctrinal statements on collegiality of bishops, responsibility of laymen, the nature of Christian marriage, and so forth, do not work if they are not translated into Church institutions. This is the main reason for the failure of Vatican II. Vatican III should fill this gap. It should make a constitution on Church order.

2. This constitution should be prepared by an interdisciplinary group of scholars and practicioners from the whole Church, with a few young canonists.

II. ON DELIMITING THE FIELD OF CANON LAW

1. The purpose of canon law is to lay down interpersonal relationships of justice and the institutions to maintain and to protect them: in a word, to create and to maintain an order of justice. Canon law must be an efficient guarantee of equal justice in the Church community for all its members.

2. Personal religious actions such as "hearing mass," "praying the breviary," "fast and abstinence," "eucharistic fast," "periodic confession and communion," and the like, are not objects of law. The ridiculous results of laws on such matters and of the juridical interpretation of such laws can be found in pre-conciliar manuals of canon law and moral theology.

3. Ethical or moral behavior is not the object of juridical or quasi-juridical rules. Ethical and moral decisions can be influenced by counseling and guidance on human and Christian values, not by precepts.

4. Faith and the profession of faith are not the object of law. Nobody has the right to impose faith, the articles of faith or the profession of faith on anybody else. Faith and the profession of faith are by definition free human actions. This holds true even if the bishops, in communion with the bishop of Rome, can give authentic testimony on the faith of the Church.

5. The validity of canon law exists only for men who freely believe in its validity. Canon law cannot apply to non-Catholic baptized persons nor to ex-Catholics.

6. Ecumenical or inter-ecclesiastical law can only be based on the communion, though imperfect, of Christian churches, and on the consent of all churches concerned.

III. ON THE SACRAMENTAL BASIS OF CANON LAW

1. The unity of the Church community is fundamentally based on the faith in the active presence of Jesus among his people, radically celebrated in the Eucharist and the sacraments. The fundamental relations between the members of the Church are based on their sacramental missions, that is to say, on missions given and received in the name and on the authority of Jesus (missions of "divine law"). The Church community is built up by and in the sacraments.

2. The system of canon law must be built, like the Church community itself, on the sacraments. In the system of the code of canon law the Church community of clerics, religious and laymen exists before and without sacraments, and the sacraments are given or committed to this pre-existing community. On the contrary, this community exists in virtue of the missions received in the sacraments. It is composed of baptized, confirmed, penitent, Eucharist-celebrating, anointed, married and ordained members.

3. In the present state of the Church in the world, after a long tradition of a selfish and sterile understanding of the sacraments as redemption automats instead of commitments to the missions of Christians in the world, the pastoral opportunity of infant baptism, though of itself legitimate, must be seriously reconsidered. At least parents should not be burdened with the obligation to have their infants baptized.

4. For the same reason the practice of the "first communion" should be seriously reconsidered.

5. The way the Roman Curia is checking the urgent need for a more reasonable human and Christian treatment of broken marriages is unrealistic and un-Christian.

6. The way in which the mission to leadership in the Church community is linked up with a juridical obligation of celibacy is unrealistic and often hypocritical. The treatment of married priests is frankly un-Christian.

IV. SOME GENERAL STATEMENTS

1. The attitude of Jesus towards the Law still remains exemplary for the Christian attitude to canon law: "the whole Law of Moses and the teachings of the prophets depend on these two commandments," the commandments of the love of God and the love of neighbor (Matt 22:40); "the sabbath was made for man, not man for the sabbath" (Mark 2:27). The possibility of contravention of the law for the good of men is essential to canon law.

2. Certainly in canon law the principle that law, being for the common good, eventually may be against the good of individuals is not valid. The spiritual good of a man cannot be sacrificed for any superior good.

3. In principle, in canon law the opposition "Church of charity" and "Church of law" does not exist. As this is not automatically true in reality, it means that the Church community must continuously strive to overcome situations in which the law in fact is in opposition to charity.

4. For the real validity of law, acceptance of the law by the community is necessary. Mere formal validity of the law is useless. This should be constantly in the mind of canon-law legislators.

5. The formal legal procedures in marriage cases and in cases of dispensation of celibacy or solemn religious vows do not serve the purpose of canon law. These matters should be left to the local churches. The magical idea of a "vicarious power" should be dropped.

6. Penal law should not exist in the Church community, insofar as it supposes that the Church community is able to judge on a man's relationship to God; but it has a right to disciplinary law, that is, a system of measures to defend its own identity.

V. ON ROME

1. No normal pope or cardinal or other official of the Roman Curia lives under the impression that he personally or they all together are holy or holier than any other Christian may be; nevertheless they continue making the whole Church community ashamed and ridiculous by claiming such titles as "Holy See," "Holy Father," "Holy Congregation," "sacra potestas," etc. It is as stupid as if a president or prime

minister would claim titles like "most patriotic citizen" or "father of the nation" or contend to have a "patriotic power." Also, titles like "Vicar of Christ" run the risk of confusing the faith in Jesus by almost identifying the person of the popes with His unique personality. A realistic desacralization of the Roman Curia is a substantial condition for a reform of the Curia.

2. A serious reform of the Curia supposes a thorough inquiry into the real output of its various departments and its effects on the Church community and on the whole society—something like a Kinsey report.

PART 7

Church and Worship

Luis Maldonado

The Church's Liturgy: Present and Future

AS we face the task of drawing some suggestions for the liturgical life
of the future it seems sensible to look at the present with all its positive
accomplishments, its failures, deficiencies and problems.

The scope of these remarks are limited to the Catholic Church. Inevitably they will be limited by the author's southern European perspective. The intention is however to be as broad as possible. They are
addressed to those who have opened themselves to the norms and spirit
of Vatican Council II and have made the effort to implement them.
Quite other words would have to be directed to those who have hardly
noticed the theological mandates of the Council and have failed the
spirit of its liturgy as it has been moving the Church.

I

The liturgical reform as brought about three outstanding and clearly
positive accomplishments: the rediscovery of the Word, the adoption
of the vernacular, and the acceptance of a secular sense both in and of
the liturgy.

The positive nature of these accomplishments is evident and we will
not enter into it now. On the contrary, we must single out the problems
brought about by these positive acquisitions. The values contained in
these gains have been misunderstood as they have been integrated with
the other elements of the liturgy, The end result being that of exaggera-
tion, imbalance and an unwarranted swing of the pendulum.

The "greater use" of the Word which is called for by the constitution

Sacrosanctum Concilium (arts. 35.1, 51, 92.a) has been put into practice, not only bringing about numerous biblical readings but another type of reading, and also the commentary of both the minister and the faithful, e.g., conversation, the dialogue homily, spontaneous prayers.

This has produced an inflation of words, that is to say, a wordiness with great detriment to other means of expression (symbols, images, gestures, rites, music, etc.).

The introduction of native languages has facilitated communication and has strengthened the catechetical value of the liturgy, as called for in *Sacrosanctum Concilium*, art. 33; nevertheless there has been a very simplistic, one-dimensional understanding of the nature of what communication and catechesis are all about, for they have been identified with rational intelligibility. It is here that we find the reason for the strongly rationalistic, intellectualistic and didactic, or doctrinary, character of the new liturgy.

Finally, the sense of secularization within the liturgical ambience has been an added value. I shall explain.

In recent years there has been insistent talk about the Christian liturgy as secular, or secularized, liturgy. By so speaking, reference is made to an important reality within Christianity and also within contemporary culture: the secular nature of the faith. This discovery is a somewhat definitive fact that will remain.

The theses on the secular character of the Christian liturgy can be summed up as follows: the liturgical celebration must be situated in the secular context that is proper to man, not in "the other world," not constituting "the other world," a separate world, but in the only real world, in the *saeculum*, that is to say, in the midst of the material-temporal (history), which is at the same time the only "means" through which both the transtemporal and, if you want, the other-worldly approach us. This is the thesis of the nonduality, non-extraterritoriality of faith, of worship, etc.

The acceptance of such a thesis can be called secularization by way of *syn-tax* or *syn-thesis* (the way that brings together and arranges in pairs the material and the spiritual, the profane and the sacred, the worldly and the religious, the temporal and the faith, the history of man and the eternity of God).

On the other hand, we can speak of secularization, as in former times, by way of *diastasis*, i.e., in terms of an opposition that is neither mutually exclusive nor contradictory. This method continues to be legitimate and timely, i.e., the method which supports a separation of the ecclesial from the civil, that is to say, the emancipation and autonomy of the temporal with regard to any control on the part of the Church.

Four groups of biblical assertions (understood in the literal sense) can be posited. These assertions clearly express a secular tendency.

The first group of assertions, in the context of Romans 12:1–2, hardly reveals a "sacred" understanding of worship. Here worship is seen as the totality of Christian life, not just certain particular actions. Also evangelization is considered worship in the New Testament (Rom. 1:9; 15:16; Phil. 2:17; 2 Tim. 4:6); so is charity (Rom. 15:25–27; 2 Cor. 9:11–12; Phil. 4:18; Jas. 1:27; Heb. 13:15).

The second, third and fourth groups of biblical assertions center around the questioning which the New Testament makes of "sacred places" (Jn. 4:21–24; Acts 6:12–14; 7:44–50), "sacred times (Gal. 4:8–11; Rom. 14:5; Col. 2:16–17), "sacred things" and "sacred persons" (Mk. 7:1–23; Acts 10:1–16; Mt. 11:19; Lk. 7:34; 15:1–10; Mk. 2:16; 1 Pet. 2:5–9; Rev. 1:6; 5:9; 10; 20:6).

Certainly this questioning does not signify nullification, but de-absolutization, deidolization and "desacralization" (overcoming dualism).

Here we wish to bring out the fact that cultic acts, temples and liturgical feasts are not suppressed; rather they are relativized, situated in a fuller, more secular context. They are brought closer to other realities and circumstances in the life of man considered to be alien to worship in former sacral times. The liturgist makes his own the *nihil alienum a me puto* of Terence, that is to say, the struggle against all that is foreign or "alien." In so doing he avoids all dangers of alienation.

This does not presuppose bringing all things to the same level and converting life into a terrible monotony of uniform, one-dimensional egalitarianism. Once a thesis of secularization, which formerly was an antithesis to the sacralization of other times, is assimilated, the synthesis of a new liturgy—which, while being secular, is nonetheless liturgy and is not reduced to everyday prose—should be achieved dialectically. This is what is proposed by the so-called festive theology (ludic or dionysiac), which inevitably had to come because of the excesses perpetrated on the road toward secularization.

One practical consequence of this line of secularization has been the entrance into the liturgy of such things as information, the news and, in general, the most pressing of current issues, especially the problems posed by injustice, war and violence.

It is here that the liturgy has gained a strong prophetic character. This prophetic character implies three things: (1) an announcing of the presence of God and of Christ in current events; (2) a denouncing of the concrete situations of sin; (3) an exhortation directed toward the Christian and the community calling them to a commitment in the struggle to solve such problems.

This recovery of the prophetic sense of Christian worship is a positive fact; nevertheless, it has posed a number of problems which perhaps can be summed up in one. Let us enumerate them:

—A politicization of the liturgy (recall the book published by Dorothy Sölle, entitled *Liturgisches Nachtgebet*, and as well those edited in France by Jean Guichard: *Politique et vocabulaire liturgique* and *Liturgie et lutte de classes*).

—A loss of identity of the liturgical act (a moment comes in which a clear distinction is not seen between cultic assembly and party, union, neighborhood meetings, etc.).

—A concealment of the gratuitous nature of the liturgy. This signifies two things: (a) the liturgy is an end and not a means; it cannot be "instrumentalized" as a launching pad for action; (b) the liturgy is welcome, praise, thanksgiving, hope against all hope; that is to say, it is a recognition of the unmerited, of that which is given to us, of grace.

—An overemphasis and poor understanding of the sense of evangelization in the liturgy. Liturgy is certainly evangelization (1 Cor. 11:26); nevertheless, it is also predominantly another thing, as has just been stated. It is not primarily a means of conversion, and even less if conversion is understood in a moralistic sense as a springboard for any concrete action.

II

It is my belief that the three great trends that I have described both from a positive and negative point of view (word-verbalism; communication in its comprehension-intellectualism; and secular sense as moralizing or "zelot" secularism) can be brought together under a more general category, namely, the category of prophetism which I have mentioned above. The postconciliar liturgy has turned out to be predominantly prophetic and this because it has left free rein to the Word, to the comprehension of the same Word (through its outpouring into native tongues) and by the emphasis it gives to the *saeculum*, history.

This type of worship was already practiced, *secundum quid* and *mutatis mutandis*, in some Protestant denominations whose liturgies were centered on the sermon as the culmination of the entire service. At the opposite end of the spectrum we find the liturgy of the Orthodox churches as well as the preconciliar Catholic liturgy. In these latter it is not the Word which predominates but rather the symbol, the image, the gesture, the rite, the ceremonial. Yet it must be mentioned that among many Catholics there is a returning desire for this type of liturgy. For this reason I believe that it is here that we must situate the problem of liturgical pluralism.

Liturgical pluralism is not just a juridical or rubrical question. (Without a doubt, nevertheless, it is. The Holy See ought to cede its legislative monopoly in favor of the local churches in a more ample manner than it has done until now.) As well, it is neither a question exclusively of pluralism of liturgical structures nor of ethnic cultures (although, nevertheless, it is).

I believe that liturgical pluralism posits, as an antecedent, a recognition of the value of diverse attitudes toward the liturgy; that is to say, the positive appreciation of different environments, different styles and different spiritualities within the liturgy.

Certainly, in the Church there should be a place for both celebrations tailored specially to a prophetic character and those which are *liturgical*; that is to say, liturgies of a more prophetic type and, as well, others of a predominantly ludic-festive type should be admitted.

My thought at this time is of Christian laymen and priests who are in the vanguard of evangelization. They are working men and participate quite directly in the working man's struggle at the factory level, at the union level and at the neighborhood level. For them the sacramental liturgy is a liturgy which in a *quasi-manner* continues the line of evangelization. This liturgy is strongly prophetic and sober. My opinion is that their liturgy is legitimate if it avoids the pitfalls to which I alluded above when speaking of prophetism, that is to say, if in this "*quasi-manner* of continuing the line of evangelization" the *quasi-manner* has a minimum of entity.

However, I do not believe *that* liturgy is the *only* liturgy, nor do I believe that anyone has the right to impose it on everyone. There are communities and people who, because of their nature or the concrete situation in which they live, require a liturgy that is more festive, richer in the line of symbolic expression and giving more emphasis to praise, thanksgiving, etc. I dare say that those very persons who normally prefer the prophetic type of liturgy will at times demand this second type, or more symbolic liturgy, and vice versa. Certainly, I believe that to analyze the life of Jesus from an anticultic, prophetic perspective, as some do, and to affirm that Christ has suppressed all cult and replaced it with a monopoly of the Word or of faith, is a passé thesis although it might appear progressive. Moreover, this thesis is unjust both in its reference to Jesus and in its reference to prophetism in the Old Testament.

It is quite evident that here we must apply the criteria for all ecclesial pluralism, namely: pluralism has its limits and is never equivalent to relativism or arbitrariness. All prophetic liturgy must be *real* liturgy; that is to say, it must have a minimum of that festive, doxological, witnessing, free-giving character to which we have already alluded. Also all liturgy that is predominantly ludic-festive cannot be without a minimum of a prophetic character. It could never be alienating, legitimizing injustice (not even by its silence).

In this day and age it is very difficult to obtain a harmonious and well-balanced synthesis of this double typology. Only a few are equal to the task. Perhaps Taizé offers us an example of this synthesis in Europe; perhaps in Latin America the examples are more abundant.

For those, however, who have not been graced with this harmony, it would be well to grant them the right and possibility of participating in these diverse types of liturgy.

I concur with Nietsche in his advice to foster and strengthen differences (not divisions), variety. In our case the ideal would be to foster the diversity of liturgical models; first, in order that there might be a real confrontation and cross-fertilization among them producing a healthy competition; and second, in order that the richness of man and of the Body of Christ might be manifested, not only on the universal level but also on the local level.

Taking into account present-day tensions and the strong contrasts which have already developed in the liturgy (just as they have developed within ecumenism, not only at the intra-Christian level but also at the extra- or trans-Christian level, which is fast approaching), I call to mind an old distinction, perhaps of a philosophic-cultural or of a religious type, but which, like many things, is not to be suppressed by faith but rather assumed and integrated. Already the early Guardini incorporated it in his essay *The Spirit of the Liturgy*.

First of all, let us recall that human life, and Christian life as well, has a double dimension: the ethical and the esthetic. Although it is true that we should not have the esthetic without the ethical nor the ethical without the esthetic, nevertheless it is true that there are persons ethically inclined and others esthetically inclined.

Alongside this typological pairing we find another parallel which is similar in nature. There is a type of culture and people for whom the oral-aural communication predominates and another for whom the visual (the image, the figure, color, ritual representation) communication is more predominant. The first group prizes the temporal, the second the spatial.

To the first group belongs the Judaic and Arabic (Semitic) culture, with their religions "of the book." To the second group, by way of example, belongs the Greek culture and its mystery religions. In Christianity this double typology has been reproduced through the two branches which in past times formed a certain Catholicism (visual and image-filled) and a certain Protestantism (audio-verbal). Today frontiers have been eliminated and many Catholics find themselves attracted, at times without knowing it, to the Protestant attitude, and vice versa.

The Orthodox liturgy (Greek, Russian, etc.) continues to place high value on the force of the image and, in general, on all the human senses. For this reason, it exercises an influence outside of its confessional boundaries.

In other words, this is what is meant by the recovery of the esthetic sense, as we are reminded by Marcuse and the neo-Marxist humanists who understand the term "esthetic" in its etymological sense. Esthetic is the development of "feeling" *(aisthanomai)*. We can then say that to develop the esthetic dimension of the celebration is something very concrete. Truly it is to put into play, into action, all of the senses of the participant in the liturgy; therefore, not only his hearing and his sight, but also his smell, his taste and his touch.

III

The above can produce the impression of a false harmonious equilibrium. Looking toward the future this pluralism handed out in doses is not sufficient. This is a real norm, which is still very abstract or generic. Actually I believe that today there exists an imbalance at the level of theological-pastoral reflection with regard to elucidating the diverse questions presented by this pluralism.

In the recent past all that refers to Word, faith and prophetism in Christian life and liturgy has been sufficiently elaborated. On the contrary, other questions closely related to the liturgy—such as rite, expression, ritual communication, and festive experience in the actual historical situation—have been thoroughly neglected.

The very problem of pluralism, understood as creativity, in spite of being a common topic, continues to be treated in a way which is elementary, simplistic and superficial.

This perplexity of a theoretical order is linked to many experiences which are both negative and frustrating in the practical order. All of which increases the denigration of the liturgy and, as well, slovenly celebration.

We could synthesize this situation by saying that we find ourselves very perplexed and ignorant with regard to liturgical language in its most specific sense as distinct from language which is evangelizing, missionary, kerygmatic, catechumenal-catechetical or sermonizing.

The problem of liturgical language implies the issue of the subject who communicates in a specific way through that language; that is to say, the issue is one of subjectivity and of its usage for communication. It is quite evident that the theme of subjectivity is joined to that of religious experience, at least within the liturgical context. Also, it would include sentiment, mysticism and, as well, the phenomenology of all these realities. Here we have a series of issues which we liturgists, overly influenced by a radical theology (polarizing faith and religion) and a concurrent pastoral approach, had hastily overlooked or even eliminated. Also, we must admit that these issues had been neglected even in the conciliar reform. Now they recur.

Consequently, the countercultures of contemporary youth, the turnabout expressed in the cultural revolution by the new generation in recent years, the religious spring that flourishes among many young people who search sincerely for a rediscovery of monasticism, contemplative mysticism, experiential prayer and spirit-filled enthusiasm—all of this has come about to corroborate an already voiced protest, arising years ago among artists, intellectuals and writers, against the conciliar reform. The liturgists had not really paid attention to this protest due to the fact that they had precipitously identified it with integralist, that is, reactionary movements.

Today there are many young people who have become disenchanted with the liturgical changes brought about by the Council. They stay away, not for lack of the Church's adaptation to the secular world, but rather because they find the Church empty of her true profound and specific substance. The liturgical reform was brought about by criteria which are considerably out of line with the entire cultural and spiritual change of recent years. As an example of this, I point out the criterion which is repeated frequently and almost obsessively throughout *Sacrosanctum Concilium* indicating that rites should be simple, brief, facile and clear. They should be simplified as much as possible in order that they might be understood without difficulty. (See articles 21, 34, 35, 50.a, 50.b, 59, 62, 72.)

Today we find many who want exactly the opposite, who miss rites which are complex, polychromatic, abundant, lavish, rich, long, with elaborate ceremonial. Why must rites always be simple and brief when the object is to enter by their means into the extraordinary and festive world? Above all, whatever is meant by rites which are "clear"? What type of anthropology is presumed here? Do we not find ourselves confronted with an anthropology which is very rationalist, Westernizing, as we have indicated before?

The world of the new generation, as well as the world of contemporary culture and serious thought, is deeply antirationalist, or even suprarationalist. Thus, the clash. But there is more. Great sectors of the older generation of churchgoers are tuned to the same wave. As a result we see both groups presenting a common cause. Without a doubt it is Archbishop Lefèvre who has brought about a crystalized union of this heterogeneous conglomerate (in which, for added confusion, have been joined a good part of the reactionaries and even fascist "Catholics").

In the course of these recent years nostalgia has increased for a liturgy clothed in authentically expressive and beautiful forms. The artistic dimension of worship, so absent in postconciliar liturgies, is today truly missed. This tendency is not one of bourgeois or esthetic deformation. With poor means one can also obtain beauty and expressivity. There are liturgical celebrations in nonbourgeois, popular milieux with first-class artistic values. Here I refer to diverse achievements in the area of popular religiosity, of popular Catholicism (for example, Holy Week celebrations in Spain). Precisely, the crisis of the reformed liturgy is one of the causes of this surprising boom which all things connected with popular Catholicism are presently experiencing.

IV

At a higher level of abstraction, we can subsume the foregoing by saying that the liturgist *must* face again that important dimension of celebration which is personal experience. Many took religious sentiment for sentimentalism. This mistake was due to insufficient analysis by the authors (I think here of a classical one such as Schleiermacher) who, following the rationalist trend, had allowed this dimension of personal experience to fall in disgrace and, consequently, under repression.

Thanks to the diverse anthropological sciences, we know today that the sentiment stirred up by symbols (both artistic and religious-liturgical) is neither a peripheral reality nor something to be ashamed of but a profound reality, symptom of the most radical dynamism of the person. A symbol is not a mere *illustration* of a given idea (i.e., what gives color, clarity, force to an idea). This is the typical rationalistic conception by which the abstract idea is of primary importance while the image is really secondary.

I believe that the conception of symbol that both arises from and is disseminated by certain psychoanalytic anthropologies is richer and more profound. Here symbol is the expression, better, the crystalization of the deepest pulsations of the person. It is the end result of man's most powerful and concrete movements, of his most radical instincts (*eros, thanatos* . . . finally, of his desire).

It is in this sudden manner that symbol abandons the cognitive plane, the intellectual sphere in which it had been imprisoned, and enters the realm of the volitive, the passional, the affective. Symbol then turns into something much more dynamic, more "dramatic."

Symbol is not only the product of man's great instinctual movements. Through a retroactive effect of reciprocity, symbol is simultaneously what unleashes and catalyzes these passional dynamisms which constitute both the most decisive and the most specific elements of the person (person understood as concrete desire, as desire incarnate).

According to Ricoeur, symbolism communicates subterraneously with our libidinal sphere and, through it, with the "combat of giants" (Freud), that is to say, with the battle between the giants *Eros* and *Thanatos*.

As we come in contact with symbols, a general thawing of our personal reality takes place which mobilizes our innermost forces and, therefore, our innermost experiences. Without symbolism there is no interior dynamism, no force of passion, no emotion; there is neither energy nor desire, neither love for living nor for life. Thus symbolism's revulsive virtuality which is also cathartic. The images of our dreams either mobilize or pacify our vital springs.

It must be added now that ritual is none other than a version of symbol, an imitative bodily gesture, a *mimesis* of the symbol through the action of gesture. Better, ritual through gesture is a version of myth, inasmuch as myth is a kind of symbol which becomes distended in a narrative and articulated in a time and in a place. Ritual is the casting in body language of this diachrony by which the mythical word is distended. The mythical word, in turn, is symbolic reality shaped in narrative discourse. Thus, all that we predicate about symbol may be, and indeed should be, predicated of ritual.

We arrive here at one of the main tasks of today's liturgical movement, to wit, to demonstrate the importance of ritual and of ritualism in all liturgical celebration. How can we accomplish this task?

Above all, the distinction between symbol and word must be clarified. Many speak today of word as symbol. We are aware of this development. However, we can establish a distinction between the linguistic symbol, or sign, and symbol properly so-called. Let us turn now to this distinction.

Paul Ricoeur has been dealing with this distinction for many years now. He has recently published new analyses which are very illustrative of the distinction between symbol and other magnitudes, among them the word. He especially focuses on metaphors. (See his "Parole et symbole," *Revue des Sciences Religieuses* 49 [1975]:142–161.)

What is the main reason for this distinction? Ricoeur sees it in the nonlanguage dimension of symbol. To this I would add that symbol has a nonverbal, or supraverbal, dimension. There is something in symbol that does not carry over to metaphor, something that resists a linguistic, semantic or logical transcription. This dimension of symbol prevents it from being mistaken for a word (the metaphor included) as its logical-linguistic unfolding. This distinction excludes any attempt to interchange symbol and word, to substitute word for symbol or to take one for the other.

In fact, symbol finds its roots at diverse and dispersed planes, while the metaphoric word is limited to the already purified realm of the *logos*. Symbol oscillates, fluctuates, between *bios* and *logos*, it is witness to the primeval roots of human discourse within life itself. Symbol is born at the point of confluence between force and form.

The realm of symbolics possesses a character of power, of force; it is not inscribed in the categories of the *logos*; it can neither be transmitted nor interpreted through proclamation because symbol is not primarily speech or verbal. The power, force, the potency do not carry over to the articulation of sense, of the *verbum*, because efficacy par excellence is quite different from *word*. This efficacy manifests itself in stones, in trees . . . in nature, full of vitality.

Symbolism refers to that life which manifests itself in the cosmic rhythms, in the return of vegetation, in the alternation between births and deaths; its joints operate at the level of the "elements of nature"—sky, earth, air and water.

Herein is the whole difference between symbol and (metaphoric) word. The former is grounded in the configurations of the cosmos; the latter is discourse, a free invention of discourse. Certainly symbol asks to be cast into language, though it does not go entirely into language (according to Ricoeur, language only captures the foam at the surface of life). Thus there is really no dualism between symbol and word.

By way of conclusion we can say that if the liturgy is to produce a radical "impact," a profound experience, a quasi-mystical feeling, a joy and a fruition that will make it not only unforgettable but desired, it must be eminently symbolic and ritualized. Symbolism reaches inwardly and is in communion with what is our ground, with our very roots, and it stirs these roots. The liturgy should be incarnate in the corporeal, in matter, in the cosmos. Symbols are precisely the cosmic and material realities which include the human body (that is to say, the symbolic gesture, the body movements, etc.).

There are no other symbols and, in this sense, there is no possibility for change, for substitution or replacement. Outside symbolism there is only its liquidation and thus an iconoclasm, with its consequences for the person: it burns the person to ashes. This is happening today in our culture with its lack of symbolism (in the sense understood here), our people are being deflagrated. Our people have become pathological. Therefore we experience today the advent of the counterculture and the birth of ecology as a movement of recuperation, both physical and existential, and, even more, mystical.

Ricoeur corroborates this corollary. He says that symbolism, sinking its roots into the durable constellations of life, the cosmos and sentiment, has an incredible stability which leads us to think that symbols never die, they are only transformed.

We must add that art *re-creates* in a sense that previous reality of the primordial symbol which we have called cosmic-material or corporeal. In this sense the artistic symbol actualizes, in certain measure, the primordial symbol, or *sine adjecto*, and is as such an important mediator. Thus the unity that exists between the symbol properly so-called and the artistic symbol. Further, thus the legitimate and even necessary place of art in the liturgy. A third and less intense reflection of the primordial symbol is the iconic or "imaginary" word. As said above, it is here that we find the junction and confluence between symbolic reality and discourse.

These last statements seem to challenge important currents within contemporary fields of esthetics. I have made my formulation taking care not to give the impression that I am advocating an "imitative" conception of art or a naïve, passé realism.

In light of our previous observations, which come from an up-to-date anthropology, an anthropology least suspect of being conservative, how ridiculous are the postures of a certain clerical "progressivism" bent either on axing symbols or on creating new ones. Yet, not only the spontaneous and progressive liturgies, but the official one has incurred in a like defect, albeit in a more tenuous manner. That is to say, the reformed liturgy, as practiced by pastors, relegates ritual to a secondary plane.

V

There is yet another aspect of ritual that we liturgists have forgotten, I mean repetition, reiteration. We should look at this aspect of ritual because it better explains the present-day crisis.

Rite is by definition repetitive, reiterative, though, of course, admitting some variables. This aspect of ritual in fact appears in all its definitions (thirty such definitions were entered in the colloquium organized by the Royal Society of London in 1966).

Mircea Eliade, in his already classic work *The Myth of the Eternal Return or Cosmos and History* (Princeton University Press, 1954) says:

> Every ritual has a divine model, an archetype. . . . "We must do what the gods did in the beginning." "Thus the gods did; thus men do." This Indian adage summarizes all the theories underlying rituals in all countries. We find the theory among so-called primitive peoples no less than we do in developed cultures. . . . All religious acts are held to have been founded by gods, civilizing heroes, or mythical ancestors. It may be mentioned in passing that, among primitives, . . . the power of rite and word possessed by the priest was

due to imitation of the primordial gesture. . . . [R]eligious festivals were instituted to commemorate the stages of the cosmic Creation. . . . The sacred year ceaselessly repeats the Creation; man is contemporary with the cosmogony and the anthropogony because ritual projects him into the mythical epoch of the beginning. A bacchant, through his orgiastic rites, imitates the drama of the suffering Dionysos; an Orphic, through his initiation ceremonial, repeats the original gestures of Orpheus. . . . The Judeo-Christian Sabbath is also an *imitatio dei*. . . . Jesus said to them: "For I have given you an example, that ye should do as I have done to you" (Jn. 13:15). [pp. 21–23]

Eliade could have added that the more recent theology considers the sacraments as Christ's own actions. They are the prolongation of Christ's salvific deeds. It is therefore said that it is Christ who baptizes, confirms, anoints. It is Christ who in the Eucharist commands: "Do this in memory of me."

Another testimony to the same idea comes from J. Cazeneuve (*Les Rites et la condition humaine* [Paris, 1958], p. 2):

What is a rite? Rite is an action. This action may be performed by an individual or by a collectivity. Though it provides for a margin of improvisation, the rite remains faithful to certain rules which, precisely, constitute in it what there is of ritual in it. A gesture, a word, which does not repeat something of another gesture or of another word, or which does not have some element destined for repetition, . . . may be called a religious action but not a ritual.

Other more recent definitions speak of rite as a program. Here the understanding of program is that of a system of formal determinations with an identity which is both designable and repeatable (cf. J. Y. Hameline, "Aspects du rite," *Maison Dieu* 119 [1974]:101–11). Rite is a programmed activity, that is, an activity that includes a program and repetition (cf. R. Didier, *Les sacrements de la foi* [Paris, 1975], p. 22).

The present-day current *pro*-creativity has frequently forgotten this important chapter of the phenomenology of ritual. For ritual is not only "religious," it reappears in Christianity, as seen above.

Beyond these phenomenological reasons in favor of repetition in ritual (which we have only mentioned and not really examined in order to find their ultimate sense), there are other reasons, psycho-sociological reasons. We shall be more thorough with these because of the part they play in the present crisis of the liturgical reform.

Change finds its worth only within certain constants. These constants are not only structural. It is the only way to penetrate into the meaning of a gesture, of a text, or even in its subjective resonance, that is to say, in one's own personal experience. Only permanent repetition allows us to establish the link with past living experiences, to relive them and, in so doing, to forge an expanding identity. This identity can then mature both in individuals and in groups. Indeed the term *celebrare* etymologically means "to frequent," "to go over," "to visit many times," "to reiterate."

We now return to the issue of personal experience but under the aspect of collective personal memory. A ritual, repeated throughout a whole life, becomes the cord that threads together all past experiences, unifies them with both the present and the future of the person. Think of the yearly festivals attended by peoples of all ages. Through these celebrations infancy, the youthful years, the presence of already dead loved ones—all these experiences are relived. These celebrations penetrate the most inaccessible depths of the *psyche* with greater strength than any psychoanalysis. For this reason—though not explicitly aware of it—so many nonpracticing Christians, even unbelievers, flock to these masses. It is there they find a pleasant therapeutic, a unifying catharsis that purifies their inmost self.

When the rite changes or disappears that thread is broken, the person is lost, pruned from the trunk of its personality. Thus we see how throughout history ritual changes have produced schisms and insurrections.

VI

Some may object that all the aforesaid sidesteps the specificity of Christian worship because it moves on the phenomenological and anthropological planes. It may be argued that the Christian liturgy is a contestation, a negation, of all those things.

Yes, the theological fads until recently spoke of the opposition between faith and religion. These were the radical and/or dialectic theologies. According to them, the statements that have validity in the realm of religion lose this validity when moved into the context of faith.

Today we have abandoned this simplistic theological position. Again Ricoeur, a Calvinist, of the same confession as Karl Barth (the dialectic theologian who lead a furious attack on religion), helps us Catholics to find a new equilibrium so required by present-day circumstances. An irony, sign of these present times.

Following in the steps of Jean Ladriere (*L'Articulation du sans*, 1970), Ricoeur distinguishes between the hermeneutic of proclamation and the hermeneutic of manifestation. In substance he refers to Judeo-

Christian religiosity, founded upon the Word (that is, in proclamation) and, on the other hand, to other religiosities founded upon symbolic sacralities or in images (where the sacred is manifested and the transcendent finds its epiphany). (I refer here to Ricoeur's "Manifestation et proclamation," published in the volume *Le Sacré* [Paris, 1974], pp. 57–77.)

Ricoeur says that those who undertake the hermeneutic of proclamation in such manner as to mobilize themselves in war against the hermeneutic of manifestation, in order to destroy it, are the new iconoclasts. The iconoclast reasons thus: "We live in a desacralized world. Nature has ceased to be a quarry for signs. Man, in creating science and technology, has left behind the age of symbols and its correspondents. Man no longer partakes of the cosmos, he possesses a universe that he thinks and exploits. The only religious message that can be listened to today is a kerygmatic one (that is, the religion based on the kerygma of the Word). This message is antisacral, it is the Yahwist religion of the Jewish prophets."

What can we say in the face of such a posture? It is a posture that still enjoys a following. It still underlies the application of much liturgical reform.

First, we have to say that this faith placed on science and its empire, this scientism, is a new fraud; Marcuse, Habermas, Ellul—all have clearly shown it.

Both the scientist illusion and the placing aside of the sacred make us forget our own roots, and thus the desert that surrounds us becomes more and more extensive. Today we again discover that man cannot exist deprived of the sacred. "We look for our native land, the place of our first love, the scene of a historical event, because it is there that a different reality erupts, a reality quite different from everyday reality. Because of this we are not wandering beings, lost beings. The actions of building and inhabiting, being born and dying, cannot be desacralized. The symbols of the lintel, the door, the home, the ritual of entrance and greeting, initiation rites, rites of passage, cannot be abolished. Sexuality turns mad when the link to the great play of cosmic unions is broken."

In the Prologue to his gospel, St. John tells us that word and manifestation (symbol) can be reconciled (Jn. 1:14). This reconciliation has been the foundation for the concept of revelation which, from the Greek Fathers until Hegel, has been the key category for Christian thought.

It is frequent to say today that word is opposed to hierophany, history to nature. This is true, *but* a dialectical truth which in itself implies its contrary. Faith without sign is impossible. Exegesis shows that the cosmic sign has been reinterpreted, not abolished, according to the requirements of the proclamation. Thus Yahweh is proclaimed as Lord of the starry armies *(Sabaoth)*. His face appears bright as the sun; the cosmogonic myths are incorporated into a historical vision of the divine. The celebration of the great events incorporates the dramatic themes of mythology, especially the victory of the waters over chaos; the new Zion recalls the sacred city, and Golgotha is the *axis mundi*.

Let us remember with Kittel and Evdokimov (cf. the latter's book *L'Art de l'icone* [Paris, 1972]) that the famous *Shema Yisrael* is supplanted by "open your eyes and see" in the messianic texts. The aural gives way to the visual. The entire Old Testament shows a constant struggle against false images but, at the end, God shows his human face. "Blessed are those whose eyes see what your eyes see" (Lk. 10:23). "He who sees me sees the Father" (Jn. 14:9). "Christ is the visible image of the invisible God" (Col. 1:15).

From this point on, the image, the symbol, is as much a part of the essence of Christianity as the word.

The cosmic symbolism does not die, it is transformed when placed under the rule of proclamation. Without the support of the cosmic-vital sacred, the word becomes cerebral, abstract. The word's fate and its hearing depends upon a new birth of both the sacred and symbolism beyond its death.

Before closing I want to make a final observation. We have spoken of ritual in a positive way, yet we all know that ritual lends itself to gross tergiversations. Because everybody knows this I have avoided the issue until now. To go over this subject seems superfluous. The air of suspicion cunningly cast over this subject by Freud and Nietsche has been by now recognized and dissipated. The relationship that Freud established between rite and obsessive neurosis, between ritual repetition and regressive involution, nevertheless seems to me an important element in any analysis of the matter in question.

This neurotic aspect shows in the criticisms that are made of the liturgical reforms; it plays an important role because it acts as an echo chamber for all other difficulties. To take refuge in "the old rites" as a security shelter is evidently a means used by the integralists.

This is only one aspect of the issue. It is probably the best known aspect, maybe the only one. It is now time to break away from this reductionism that is, almost demagogically, threatening our ecclesial liturgical life with the eradication of any sense of ritual; especially at a time when, outside the Church, the artistic, theatrical and literary worlds are entering into a movement toward ritual.

Another topic that paralyzes many is the identification of ritual with magic. It is a pity to see the general ignorance that abounds regarding this topic, especially of how it has been treated in recent scholarship. Recent investigatons clearly show the distinction between rite and magic. The latter is a deformation of the former, thus it really does not in any way invalidate the importance of ritual.

Through the ignorance of the positive qualities of ritual, many are astonished to see the great following enjoyed by those who oppose or criticize the conciliar reform. Many thought that this opposition would only come from the quarter of fanatic conservatives. Through this ignorance they find themselves unable to understand that a similar (though not equal) opposition may be found both among integralists and normal Christians.

It is therefore urgent to undertake the task of showing the importance and positive value of ritual. The urgent need of its presence in the lives of both pagan and Christian human beings must be stressed. The lack of balance that its absence or eclipse obtains must be shown. This, then, is the task which in good measure should be undertaken by both the liturgists and those who preside over the liturgical assembly.

Translated by Guillermo P. Romagosa

Myles M. Bourke

The Future of the Liturgy: Some New Testament Guidelines

AS I understand it, the task which I have been assigned is to make some observations about what the acceptable Roman Catholic liturgy of the future might be. In the space of a short paper it is impossible to speak except in the broadest terms about an acceptable liturgy for a church which extends throughout the world and embraces many cultures. In a cautiously worded section of the Constitution on the Sacred Liturgy (nos. 37–40), Vatican II recognized the need of ordering divine worship according to the requirements of different cultures, and what was there advanced has often been urged since, frequently in terms as strong as those of the Council were reserved. We have been told that the liturgy of the new Roman Missal is unsuitable for blacks, and that claim was given sharp expression at the recent Eucharistic Congress in Philadelphia when one of the architects of the "black liturgy" of the congress proposed a celebration which the papal legate refused to attend. Yet anyone with more than a slight acquaintance with blacks knows that many of them would side more readily with the legate than with their supposed spokesman. It is illusory to think that all who belong to groups purportedly in need of a rather different liturgy than that now officially set forth by the Roman Church—blacks, the young, "intellectuals," etc.—would agree either on the need or on what form the suitable liturgy should have. Before one takes the easy way out of that fact, namely, writing off the dissenters as "medieval men" or by some equally pejorative designation, it would be well to recognize that diversity of needs and tastes cuts both ways, not only out of traditional molds but out of the most "meaningful" forms devised.

At the beginning of the recent liturgical reforms in the Roman Church, many who were dissatisfied with the initial projects criticized them as the work of liturgical scholars who were remote from the people, work devised without interdisciplinary consultation. Anthropology and sociology were the disciplines whose contributions were thought especially valuable. We hear less nowadays about the value of the anthropologists' insights; is that because such scholars as Mary Douglas and Victor Turner have found merit in the old rituals? Following the truth wherever it leads one can turn out to be boring if one finds that the supposed truth leads back to the house which one had thought should be abandoned for good.

All this is not to suggest that I think diversity in liturgy is not desirable or that it is incapable of satisfactory accomplishment but simply to recall the complexity of a problem which will be solved, if at all, only by years of patient and collaborative work. Yet while the task is enormous, it is possible to find standards which must be observed in all liturgical celebration, however diverse and varied according to the race, nation, age, or occupation of the participants. These can be drawn from some New Testament testimonies either directly or indirectly related to the eucharist.

The origin of the eucharist is a complicated problem, and I do not think that any purpose would be served by my attempting to review the various opinions which have been proposed on that subject. A surer point of departure is the fact that, whatever the origins, around 55 A.D. in the First Epistle to the Corinthians Paul gives it as a tradition which he had received that the eucharist is the meal whose reason for existence is the command of Jesus given at the Last Supper, "Do this in memory of me." Similarly, the eucharistic tradition of the Gospel of Mark, almost certainly the earliest of the canonical gospels, a tradition different in several ways from that found in 1 Corinthians but clearly a reflection of the eucharistic celebration of the church for which that gospel was written, grounds the sacrament in the Last Supper of Jesus. If, as Hans Lietzmann supposed, the eucharist of the primitive Jerusalem community had a different origin; if those early Christians of the holy city who gathered for the eucharistic meal had no thought of doing what Jesus had done at the Last Supper, it must be at least conceded that very soon the church as a whole had accepted the Last Supper-eucharist connection, as Mark and 1 Corinthians show. Rather than attempt to determine what the meals of the Jerusalem community meant, and use our hypothetical and largely imaginary reconstruction as a basis for a theory of how the eucharist ought to be celebrated today, it is from the Last Supper tradition that we ought to proceed if we wish to be on sure and certainly very ancient ground.

I should like to make a remark, however, about Lietzmann's theory, because it is sometimes used, quite wrongly, as furnishing justification for a type of eucharist which, so one is told, is the sort which the church must have if she is ever to attract modern man, and especially modern youth, to an appreciation of the Mass. Lietzmann believed that the most primitive Christian eucharist was simply a meal of the community which recalled the meals which Jesus had eaten during his mortal life, a meal marked by a joyous sense of the spiritual presence of the Lord and a keen expectation of his imminent return. For him, these meals were in no way connected with the Last Supper and the sombre memory of Jesus' death. But even if one were to accept that view, it would be quite impossible to deny the *sacred* character of the meal. The early Christians of Jerusalem were Jews who had come to faith in Jesus as Messiah, and for a Jew every meal was sacred; there was no such thing as a "profane" gathering together to eat. Nor was the sacred character of the meal simply given a perfunctory bow, so to speak, in a hastily spoken "grace before meals" and "thanksgiving after meals" such as one finds now in those Christian circles where that tradition survives.

In the tractate Berakoth of the Mishnah, the codification of Jewish oral law made around 200 A.D. but containing much material of an earlier period, we have many examples of the food blessings[1] which were said both at the beginning and during the course of the meal and, in the Jewish prayer book, an example of the "thanksgiving" at its end. I should like to quote from a portion of the latter in order to show how inaccurate is the notion that the Jewish "ordinary" meal could be considered in any way as a meal of good fellowship with little explicitly religious content.

> Blessed art thou, O Lord our God, eternal King, who feedest the whole world with thy goodness, with grace, with loving-kindness, and with tender mercy. Thou givest food to all flesh, for thy loving-kindness endureth forever. Through thy great goodness food hath never failed us; O may it not fail us forever, for thy great name's sake, since thou nourishest and sustainest all living things and doest good unto all, and providest food for all thy creatures whom thou hast made. We thank thee, O Lord our God, because thou didst give us an heritage unto our fathers, a desirable, good and ample land; as well as for thy covenant which thou hast sealed in our flesh; for thy Torah which thou hast taught us, thy statutes which thou hast made known to us; life, grace, and loving-kindness which thou hast bestowed upon us, and for the food with which thou dost constantly feed and sustain us. For all this, O Lord our God, we thank and bless thee.

This prayer, now much expanded, is a fair sample of the way in which the devout Jew blessed God for his "ordinary" meal. Even if the community meals of the primitive Jerusalem Christians were meals in which no connection was made with the Last Supper, we can see from this prayer of blessing how much "sacralized" those meals were—an impression which is only confirmed by the meal prayers in chapters 9 and 10 of an early Jewish-Christian work, the Didache.[2]

But if it is the Last Supper which was the model of the eucharists of the early church, as indeed seems to be the case, does that mean that those eucharistic celebrations were gloomy recollections of the death of Christ only? And that the authentic Christian eucharist is, then, primarily cross-centered, as was indeed quite commonly thought not so long ago? Hardly. The Passover setting of the Last Supper and the eschatological saying in Mark 14:25 ("Truly I say to you, I shall not drink again of the fruit of the vine until that day when I drink it new in the kingdom of God") show plainly that the motif of joy, deliverance, and of the anticipated blessedness of the coming kingdom are present in the Last Supper tradition. It is justifiable to speak of the "Passover setting" of the supper, whether in fact it was a Passover meal or not. The majority opinion among exegetes is that it was not, but that is a matter of no great consequence for the present purpose. The synoptics certainly make it a Passover meal, an interpretation of it which is of primary importance for their understanding of the eucharist. The ancient tradition cited in 1 Corinthians 11 does not explicitly connect the supper and the Passover, and Paul himself is silent on the matter. But in that same tradition there is an emphasis on the eucharist as the memorial of the Lord's death, and earlier in the epistle that death is interpreted by Paul as the Christian Passover (1 Cor 5:6–8).

The exodus theme was foremost in Israel's yearly Passover meal; the prayer of thanksgiving over the third (or fourth) cup of wine, the direct ancestor of our eucharistic prayer, was among other things a commemoration of that saving act of God on behalf of his people. That was all retained, but retained in a profoundly transformed manner, in the Christian eucharist. For the exodus which the church commemorated at the Eucharist was not primarily that of Israel from Egypt, but the deliverance of which that had been simply a foreshadowing: the exodus of Jesus, his passage from that existence marked by the evils which man's sin had brought into the glorious creation of God, a passage through death to the new life of the resurrection. As servant of the Lord, Jesus had taken upon himself the condition of his sinful brethren, the state of existence which was the consequence of man's sin, and which Saint Paul calls "the flesh." By his death and resurrection he passed into a new state of existence, that which Paul calls "the spirit";

by his resurrection, he became a "life-giving spirit" (1 Cor 15:45), capable of conferring the Holy Spirit upon those who believe in him. Here was the true exodus, the passage through death to everlasting life, brought about once for all by Jesus' death and resurrection. When the early church "did this in memory of him," it was that which she was recalling. Paul's description of the eucharist in 1 Cor. 11, which, in order to correct the cross-forgetting enthusiasm of the Corinthians at their celebration, emphasizes the death of the Lord, is no less resurrection-centered because of that; for Paul, the death and resurrection of the Lord are but two, equally indispensable aspects of the one act of redemption: "As often as you eat this bread and drink the cup, you proclaim the death of the Lord, until he come" (1 Cor. 11:26). But the life of the resurrection is entered into only through the cross, and that is no less true in our case than in that of Jesus. Jesus' exodus, which is what our eucharist celebrates, is the means whereby we are empowered to make our own exodus, with and after him, through suffering and death to life. If we lose sight of either aspect, we are in danger of misunderstanding, and of celebrating wrongly—a danger into which the church of Corinth had fallen, and from which Paul wished to rescue them by his recalling of the meaning of the Lord's supper. The eucharist is indeed a celebration of life, but of that life which was won for us by the cross and resurrection of Jesus Christ, that life which has been begun in us through baptism and which is deepened by every celebration of the eucharist, that life which will be ours in its fullness not when human effort and technological advances have reached their climax of perfection, but when the parousia of Jesus will perfect the work which he began in his cross and resurrection.

This is indeed a "sacred mystery," and, like all mystery, it envokes from those who have become truly aware of it reverence and awe.[3] If "modern man" cannot share that reverence, we should at least be prepared to entertain the possibility that there is something wrong with him, rather than with the liturgy which expresses it. By the paradox of the fact that the awesome God, the "wholly Other," has drawn near to us in the gracious person of his Son, our reverence must not be one which causes us to turn from him in terror, but to "approach with confidence to the throne of grace" (Heb. 4:16). But the elements of reverence and assurance must be held in proper balance, and a liturgy in which one or the other is sacrificed is not a truly Christian liturgy.

I should like now to call your attention to the Epistle to the Hebrews. It may seem strange, at first, that that epistle be taken as a New Testament book which can give us an understanding of the eucharist, for it probably does not speak of that sacrament at all, and, in any case, it does not do so in any clear and unmistakable way. But the way in which the epistle speaks of the redemptive work of Jesus, of his death and heavenly exaltation, gives the basis on which some conclusions may be drawn as to the meaning of the eucharist of the church on earth. Hebrews is the only New Testament writing which draws extensively on the language of Old Testament sacrifice to portray the Lord's death and resurrection. He is seen as the pre-existent Son who has entered into the full reality of man's existence by his incarnation, and who has offered himself in sacrifice, thus effecting that reunion between God and man which the Old Testament sacrifices sought to achieve but could not. His passage from death to new life is described as his entrance as high priest into the heavenly sanctuary, where his sacrifice is brought to completion, just as the Jewish high priest, on the Day of Atonement, brought the blood of the sacrificed victim into the holy of holies of the tabernacle, behind the veil, and sprinkled it on the mercy seat over the ark of the covenant. By that symbolic act, Israel's sins were forgiven, and the union between God and his people, broken by those sins, was restored—or so it was thought, but for the author of Hebrews that was not so. Only the sacrifice of Jesus could abolish sin and really restore that union. And that had taken place once-for-all, when Jesus entered into the new life of the resurrection, after having shown that perfect obedience which led him to the cross. His new situation vis-à-vis God is compared by the author of Hebrews to the situation of the high priest in the holy of holies: "We have a high priest who has passed through the heavens, Jesus the Son of God" (Heb 4:14); "Christ has entered, not into a sanctuary made with hands . . . but into heaven itself, to appear now in the presence of God on our behalf" (9:24); "he is able to save those who draw near to God through him, since he always lives to make intercession for them" (7:25).

The First Epistle of Clement to the Corinthians, traditionally assigned to the Clement who appears in early episcopal lists as a bishop of Rome towards the end of the first century, is the earliest document which makes a connection between the heavenly worship of Jesus the high priest, of which Hebrews speaks, and the eucharist of the church on earth. Clement calls Jesus "the high priest of our offerings."[4] The origin of this expression is probably the joining together of Hebrews 3:1 ("Jesus, the high priest of our confession") and Hebrews 13:13, where the "sacrifice of praise" which the Christians offer God through Jesus is defined as "the fruit of lips confessing his name." The relation of these two texts is much disputed, as well as the eucharistic meaning of the second, but Clement would hardly have been concerned with problems of scientific exegesis. For him, the offerings of which Jesus Christ is high priest are the offerings made by the Christian people in the sacrifice of praise, the eucharistic sacrifice: the body and blood of

Christ and the sacrifice of themselves which they offer to God in union with the all-sufficient and perfect sacrifice of Jesus.

What appears to be the case is that Clement, or the tradition on which he depends, found in Hebrews not only its unmistakably sacrificial interpretation of Jesus' death and heavenly exaltation, but a relationship between that once-for-all sacrifice and the eucharistic worship of the church, a relationship because of which the eucharist itself was seen to be sacrificial. Since the eucharistic worship is united to Jesus' ministry in the "heavenly sanctuary" (Heb. 8:2), he can be called "the high priest of our offerings."

This line of thought is reflected in the eucharistic theology of the later patristic writers: so much so that Gregory Dix could say: "There is no pre-Nicene author, Eastern or Western, whose eucharistic doctrine is at all fully stated, who does not regard the offering and consecration of the eucharist as the present action of our Lord himself . . . and in the overwhelming majority of writers, it is made clear that their whole conception revolves around the figure of the high priest at the altar in heaven."[5] Similarly, Alan Richardson: "The patristic writers stress in many different ways the truth that the reality of which the eucharist is the sacrament has its centre and meaning in heaven, and not upon earth. The oblation of the church on earth is made one with Christ's self-offering in heaven, and the worship of the church below is a participation in the worship of him who sits upon the throne in heaven . . . Already the church is eschatologically present in heaven, and her eucharistic worship is a participation even now in the worship of heaven."[6]

These ideas are distinctly out of favor with those who find the New Testament's "realized eschatology" hard to take, and it has even been argued in the interesting work of Gerd Theissen[7] that Hebrews, so far from being their source, was written precisely to oppose them. This is not the place to discuss Theissen's position, though I can only say that I think his arguments for it on balance unconvincing. As for the aversion to the images of the eucharistic theology based on the epistle, one must ask: Are they not intimately related to a current of New Testament thought which must not be taken in isolation, but equally must not be repudiated if one is to hear the full message of the New Testament? The full message speaks not only of a *theologia crucis* but of a *theologia gloriae*. And the images which express the latter should not be regarded as so much useless and misleading mythology but as pointers to a reality which can be expressed in no other way. A prejudice against the "heavenly" dimension of eucharistic worship can lead only to its impoverishment.

Finally, there are the hymns of the Book of Revelation. This book was the product of a church under severe persecution—probably that of Diocletian in the last decade of the first century of our era. The book is punctuated with "visions" of heaven intended for the strengthening of the author's fellow Christians who are being called to witness to Christ even at the cost of their lives. In these visions, a prominent element is the worship of heaven, depicted in a manner related to that of Hebrews, although without any express reference to the priesthood of Jesus. It is rather Jesus the triumphant Lamb, slain for mankind, now victor and reigning king, and God through whose power Christ triumphed, that are the major concern of the author. The scenes of heaven are frankly "triumphalist," and why not? Triumphalism is certainly out of place if its object is the exaltation of humans who are still on pilgrimage to their goal; it is not only justified but necessary if its object is the glorification of Jesus Christ.

It is particularly the hymns of the book which deserve attention, for while it would surely be too much to say that the visions of the heavenly worship are in every detail the projection upon the heavenly scene of the earthly worship which the author knew, it is most probable that that is precisely the origin of the hymns.[8]

"Worthy art thou to take the scroll and to open its seals, for thou wast slain and by thy blood didst ransom men for God from every tribe and tongue and people and nation, and hast made them a kingdom and priests to our God" (Rev 5:9). "To him who sits upon the throne and to the Lamb be blessing, and honor and glory and might forever and ever!" (5:13). If that was the way in which the persecuted church of the Book of Revelation worshipped, then we are given a most important insight into what our own worship is meant to be. It cannot be forgetful of human suffering any more than that early church was, but in the midst of that it cannot forget that its sufferings are a share in those of the now victorious Lamb, whose triumph it celebrates. There are few more eloquent testimonies to both the worldly realism and the other-worldly joy which ought to be the mark of the authentic Christian. And those who would forget the latter are in grave danger of making the former a short-sighted piety which will soon lose any element of Christian hope.

These New Testament indications provide material from which important conclusions can be drawn about the way in which the eucharist should be celebrated. Worship faithful to the New Testament traditions is possible only when the form of celebration is such that the gathered community realizes that it is responding to a mystery which can be approached only with utmost reverence based on a living faith,[9] and there is no doubt that much of the liturgical tradition of the later church has been faithful to the foundational standards. But as the later tradition itself abundantly indicates, there is no one way alone in which that fidelity must be maintained, and the principal liturgical task of the future will be to explore the ways in which cultures which have as yet not contributed to the rich variety of Christian worship may draw not only on their common Christian faith but upon their distinctive cultural heritages in doing so. I should think that in the process it will become evident that if much can be accepted, much also will have to be rejected, for there are cultural expressions which are radically different from the ethos of the eucharistic liturgy. But in any case the New Testament offers standards which cannot be disregarded if the worship is to be a Christian celebration.

Notes

1. Cf. *The Mishnah,* tr. H. Danby (Oxford, 1933), pp. 6–9.
2. Cf. K. Lake, ed., *The Apostolic Fathers,* I (New York, 1919), pp. 322–25.
3. Cf. C. F. D. Moule, *Worship in the New Testament* (Richmond, 1961), p. 79: "As a condition of worship there must be awe—a sense of the 'numinous,' of the mysterious—a feeling sometimes indicated in the New Testament by *thambos,* when the more than human majesty of Jesus is felt and recognized."
4. 1 Clement 36:1; cf. Lake, op. cit. pp. 70–71.
5. *The Shape of the Liturgy* (Westminster, 1945), p. 253.
6. *An Introduction to the Theology of the New Testament* (London, 1958), p. 383.
7. *Untersuchungen zum Hebräerbrief* (Gütersloh, 1969).
8. Cf. S. Läuchli, "Eine Gottesdienststruktur in der Johannesoffenbarung," *Theologische Zeitschrift* 16 (1960): 359–78.
9. In his remarkable essay "Neutestamentliche Marginalien zur Frage der Entsakralisierung," in *Ursprung und Gestalt* (Düsseldorf, 1970), pp. 299–325, Heinz Schürmann has rightly emphasized that a living faith is the principle by which all sacral forms are to be judged as suitable or unsuitable in Christian worship. The eucharist looks to the past, the death of Christ, and to the future coming of the kingdom, but it also celebrates the presence of the exalted Lord in the midst of his disciples. Because of that, the sacral has its legitimate place in the Christian eucharistic celebration. If I would distance myself somewhat from Schürmann, it is only in so far as he seems excessively cautious about the ability of "modern *homo faber*" to appreciate the sacral. I would also suggest that the power of artistic beauty to lead people to deeper faith should not be minimized. In the past beauty may have become an end in itself, so that worship was turned into aesthetic enjoyment. But at least in the Roman Catholic Church of the present, that danger is utterly remote; we suffer rather from a pervading ugliness and banality.

PART 8

Social Scientific Perspectives

James T. Barry

A Sociology of Belief and Disbelief: Notes toward a Perspective on Religious Faith and Community

THIS article concerns the connections between faith and community—that is, with the equation that exists between believing and belonging. To be more specific, the article argues that people believe in order to belong (and vice versa), and that this sharing of beliefs is constantly in flux, is multi-dimensional, and is resistant to standardization. This argument derives from sources within the social sciences rather than from theological observations. Obviously then, the paper has nothing to say about the dogmatic correctness of what people believe, except to suggest that central authorities (in this case, the episcopacy and theologians) do not exert the control over people's beliefs that they might wish. Actually, the "beliefs" under consideration really have little directly to do with dogma or sexual ethics or the Church's teaching on social issues. Rather, the article has in mind the symbolic musings of individuals and their groups on life and death. These are pre-conscious or pre-figurative perspectives that are related to social and political interests and sexual mores, but also distinguishable from them. This author believes that basic beliefs which have emerged from a confrontation with the inescapable mysteriousness of life and death are *the* irreducible religious experiences: all else is derivative religiously.

The article begins with a social-science perspective drawn from the sociology of knowledge. It then proceeds to apply some of these ideas to the twin issues of religious belief and disbelief. In a concluding section, these basic points are restated, and some suggestions for further research are made.

THE SOCIAL SCIENCE PERSPECTIVE: RELIGION AND THE SOCIOLOGY OF KNOWLEDGE

The sociology of knowledge begins with the observation that man is not biologically pre-determined, thereby producing the situation in which man must create his reality. Clifford Geertz has described the process this way:

> What happened to us in the Ice Age is that we were obliged to abandon the regularity and precision of detailed genetic control over our conduct for the flexibility and adaptability of a more generalized, though of course no less real, genetic control over it. To supply the additional information necessary to act, we were forced, in turn, to rely more and more heavily on cultural sources—the accumulated fund of significant symbols. Such symbols are thus not merely expressions, instrumentalities, or correlates of our biological, psychological, and social existence; they are prerequisites of it. Without men, no culture, certainly; but equally, and more significantly, without culture, no men.[1]

From this view, man necessarily is seen as a "creator," in that reality is completed through acts of his imagination, will and choice. The success of this venture rests heavily on the extent to which we are reciprocally conscious of—that is, have useful knowledge about—that which we are continually in the process of creating.

This set of arguments entails a redefinition of subjectivity versus objectivity. As we can see, reality is a socially (culturally) completed phenomenon which is enforced to the extent that it is shared. Truth—valid knowledge, supposedly—therefore becomes an event which has to do with attributes of the social bonds cementing that reality about which we desire to have truth.

The ancient disjunction between the subjective and objective (ditto for the supposed superiority of the latter) has rested upon a model which posits an order of reality existing totally independent of man and discoverable by treading what Michael Polanyi has called "the straight and narrow path of doubt." He elaborates this point as follows:

Descartes had declared that universal doubt should purge his mind of all opinions held merely on trust and open it to knowledge firmly grounded in reason. In its stricter formulations the principle of doubt forbids us altogether to indulge in *any desire to believe* and demands that we should keep our minds empty, rather than to allow any but irrefutable beliefs to take possession of them. . . . The method of doubt is a logical corollary of objectivism. It trusts that the uprooting of all voluntary components of belief will leave behind unassailed a residue of knowledge that is completely determined by the objective evidence. [emphasis added][2]

This ideology, which Polanyi considers a "massive modern absurdity," can be shown to be not at all the manner in which knowledge, even scientific knowledge, originates.

According to Polanyi, all knowledge is assertive, active and communal. This is as true of practical knowledge as it is of scientific knowledge. Without going into all of his detailed epistemology, Polanyi's view can be over-summarized by saying that he believes the possibility of "objective knowledge" depends upon an almost seamless web of commitments, traditions and personal judgments which link "knowers" into a community within which knowledge is produced and, in the case of scientific knowledge, verified. Thus, the subjectivity and objectivity of knowledge is not a simple attribute of an individual's relation to an object, but is instead a complex communal process.

For Berger and Luckman, culture-as-reality evolves outward from the individual in what could be considered concentric zones of influence. These authors maintain that it is "everyday life" which constitutes the "paramount reality" for each of us. The most important aspect of everyday life is that

the reality of everyday life further presents itself to me as an intersubjective world, a world that I share with others. This intersubjectivity *sharply differentiates* everyday life from other realities of which I am conscious.[3]

Thus, Berger and Luckman have described an "intersubjective community," a tribe within the boundaries between the objective and subjective, and which, by the quality of its sharedness, is effectively bounded.

The intersubjective community looms as a massive phenomenon. It is a highly rooting community, at the core of which there is a merger of belief and belonging. As Berger and Luckman put it:

Suspension of doubt is so firm that to abandon it, as I might want to do, say in theoretical or religious speculation, I have to make an extreme transition.[4]

The quality of intersubjectivity is the nucleus of contemporary tribalism. It is a catalytic experience through which knowledge becomes intentional, communal and accepted.

(These tribal-like ties have been identified empirically. For example, research on the opinion-forming power of the mass media consistently has found that people do not attend to these forums as disaffiliated individuals. What is transmitted across television as an example, and in what must be considered the prototypical exchange of mass society, in actuality is discussed, analyzed and interpreted among members of long-standing primary groups before anything approximating an opinion is formed. In other research, Edward O. Laumann and his colleagues have concluded that any reasonably accurate model of the underlying structure of urban life must include religious background and occupational location [as more generalized associations] and religio-ethnic identity [a far more localized set of ties].)[5]

One arrives, therefore, at the conclusion that consciousness and community are two sides of the same coin: one belongs by believing and believes so as to belong. The merger of the two is historical; that is, it is processual and interactive rather than static. For example, each individual is born into an intersubjective community and yet invariably is presented with the necessity of choosing for or against that inheritance. In doing so, an individual will be deciding about not only the set of beliefs that go with membership but also about the emotional satisfactions or dissatisfactions which have been his or her history of membership. Furthermore, the equation between belief and belonging can be both an evolutionary and a cyclical product. In certain areas, most especially technology and formal knowledge, man's consciousness has grown in a more or less linear fashion; new knowledge and technologies have been produced generally at the cost of earlier social forms. And yet, certain experiences—such as death—are recurrently baffling and apparently not amenable to any but the most primordial of responses.

To the extent that these aspects of reality and community are historical, therefore, the boundaries and modes of believing and belonging in all circumstances are processual and flexible. Attention is being given constantly to the task of maintaining or adjusting the intersubjective community, to creating a new one when necessary. How the community is maintained will vary from group to group, from time to time, from circumstance to circumstance. Definitions of orthodoxy and heresy, of membership and separation are interpreted rather than fixed. And the interplay between orthodoxy and heresy, depending upon how the community commits itself to handling these tensions, can be the foundation for the adaptability of the community.

IMPLICATIONS FOR THE STUDY OF RELIGIOUS BELONGING

These reflections lead to the following general and ancillary considerations about the structure of religious life. First, the quality of believing—of faith—must be considered processual. There are a number of contingencies which can affect the appreciation of religious symbols; among them are the fact that in contemporary society, the communities of everyday life—the intersubjective communities—seldom coincide with the expectations of the official Church (a problem also shared by the state); there is an almost invariable disjunction between the "symbol-making" of the official Church and the manner in which these symbols are vivified at the local or parish level; and the Church, as a consequence, must make itself visible in many guises, each of which accomplishes a tailoring of the symbol to the audience. Second, the boundaries of membership in the Church should be constructed broadly. For example, some beliefs derive from ascriptive membership in the Church while others are arrived at more voluntarily, and these two forms of belief should be distinguished. It can be argued that disbelief does not necessarily rupture all communal ties with the Church; often the choice of disbelief entails a rejection of the community rather than of the symbols and beliefs *in toto* and this situation can produce distortions in the belief process. Finally, empirical evidence would suggest that for the disbeliever primordial vestiges of the symbols or metaphors of one's ascriptive religion do persist.

THE SOCIOLOGY OF BELIEF AND COMMUNITY

The bonds of knowledge and value are strongest when nearest at hand, when they are shared as intersubjective. This level of shared consciousness is practical and intentional; it thrives when it can be considered as given. The paramount reality is that which is most intimate, peopled with family and friends going about the practical tasks of career and leisure. Universal values or reflective experiences are perceived either as remote or as something which transports us beyond this known nucleus. For this reason, communing with realities outside of the everyday is resisted. Therefore, if symbols of the sacredness of life are to be influential, they must persistently penetrate to the core of the everyday reality. This process does not occur without effort and will encounter the following specific problems.

The Tension between Everyday Life and Transcendent Experiences

Religious life is a system of symbols which actualize the presence of transcendent, awesome or baffling experiences. A symbol—religious or otherwise—has an attractiveness in and of itself. However, while a symbol can attract or even seduce, it cannot compel the community that will objectify it. Authentic religious symbols or experiences are manifestly beyond the pale of everyday life. When influential, they are, as Clifford Geertz puts it, "the pale, remembered reflection of an experience in the midst of everyday life."[6] In other words, the intersubjective community acts to either resist or modify these experiences or symbols, and yet they are also the only circumstances within which the symbol can be vivified. This tension can be seen to be operating in two circumstances.

1. The advances of man's power and knowledge have narrowed the ranges of baffling experiences, but it has not eliminated them. Two experiences of bafflement which immediately come to mind as readily available are the ineluctable "facticity" of life and the impenetrability of death. However, these experiences are by their very nature fleeting and unwilled, even if they can occur frequently. Believing, therefore, is not a constant ecstatic experience, an uninterrupted indwelling within the ultimate. It follows then that participation in systems of ultimate values is episodic, constantly subject to the impression that other realities are more pressing.

Of course, this denigration of religion is not altogether new. The earliest priestly roles involved specialized intercession with the gods on behalf of very, very practical concerns. Both then as now, few men have a fondness for religion for its own sake. The chief difference which distinguishes modern man is that we can evade or flee the unwelcome presence of the religious with far greater impunity.

2. The transcendent is resisted because it is unknown. Therefore, participation with such symbols is often experienced as transporting, as if some leap were required out from our primary reality. Such a leap, when made, is succeeded by a returning to the everyday reality. As Berger and Luckman point out, "consciousness always returns to the paramount reality as from an excursion."[7] Herein lies another source of resistance put up against the transcendent by the intersubjective community. The nature of the former often is distorted by the language of the latter.

As one passes back into the everyday reality, one moves further away from the revelatory experience and, relying ever more upon memory, one must communicate the experience by using the idiosyncratic language of one's group. Ultimately, Geertz's "pale, remembered reflection" is what remains of the original experience.

The Disjunction between Universal Symbols and the Intersubjective Community

In a Church, especially an international one with aspirations toward widespread ecumenical relations, and one which does not stress individual revelations, these issues take on a special importance. For example, universally available symbols become central. And yet, the evidence clearly shows that the elite (the producers and shapers of symbols) envision the truths of the Church in a different manner than the laity. The elite will see the symbols in more abstract terms, being moved by their interior logic, literary sophistication or simple poetry. For the laity, regardless of educational level, the appearance and influence of the symbol will be overlaid with particular communal eccentricities, perhaps even with outright misinformation.

Thus, the Church must face the question of how much control an episcopal structure exercises over either the origins of revelatory experiences or over the exchange of religious symbols. Are there within the Church parallel orders of reality—those official revelations of the total Church, co-existing with those which have arisen directly from within the midst of the Church on its various neighborhood levels? Ought not the Church begin to think in terms of a dialogue which must take place between the official symbols of the central authority and the concrete manifestations of these and other symbols in the folk-local milieus of the laity?

Tailoring the Church to the Neighborhood

What these thoughts lead to is the conclusion that belief and community are not to be considered a static phenomenon, capable of assuming one, and only one, appearance. The parish in America has taken on a variety of forms, none of which can be disparaged or even considered remnants of the past. For example, the parish has historically played a major role in the assimilation of Catholic immigrants. Over time, especially so in the large urban centers, parish boundaries were often coterminous with the boundaries of ethnic settlement. Immigrant life often was centered around the parish and these parishes passed into the political culture of the city as shorthand identifications of politically important realities. On the other hand, suburban parishes have presented their own unique challenges—as Greeley has reported, for example, the suburban parish often required a specially tailored ministry to the youth. Of course, the parish has also been the major provider of elementary and, often, secondary education.

All of these functions have accompanied the more formally religious or sacramental roles performed within the parish. And it is remarkable the extent to which the parish still is called upon to provide these "extra-religious" functions. The Church ignores these specifying contexts of everyday reality at the peril of losing its sacramental role. The Church must have many faces; it must be capable of tailoring itself to many circumstances.

These reflections certainly lead to an idealized definition of the role of the priest. He (or she!) is the visible manifestation of religion's claim to have real knowledge about the world, and will therefore be the person caught at the vortex of the dialectics just discussed. The priest must be able to penetrate the shell of the intersubjective community while simultaneously resisting the allurements of the believing-belonging nexus which defines that community. The priest must be a person able to recognize both authentic and inauthentic religious experiences.

If religion has to do with the charisma of sacred symbols, the priest becomes a specialized "man of knowledge." Obviously, no man or collection of men can perform all of these tasks without fail. However, the ideal typology is suggested by the theoretical evidence, and the imperfection or frailty of the priest is a part of the sociology of the Church.

THE SOCIOLOGY OF DISBELIEF AND COMMUNITY

Ties to a community are not the result of uni-dimensional beliefs. Because beliefs come in many forms and are held with many degrees of intensity, the equation between believing and belonging is not rigid. In particular, the distinction between beliefs held by virtue of ascriptive membership as opposed to those which are the result of conscious choice cause the differences between belief and disbelief, as that difference applies to membership, to become blurred; the evidence shows that for those who have chosen disbelief, there are discernible traces of inherited symbolic structures still inhabiting one's world-view; and disbelievers have often chosen against emotional histories with the community rather than against its values, a choice which can distort their conceptual life. In other words, membership can be considered malleable enough that, processually if not formally, disbelief seldom produces a total severing of ties.

Voluntary and Ascriptive Membership

There is every indication that intersubjective communities derive from ascriptive traditions rather than from pure individual choice. And yet one would at least hope, if not expect, that true religious commitments are voluntary. Thus, one must agree that the difference between ascriptive beliefs and voluntary beliefs produces some tensions with regard to gauging membership. Is there in the nature of human groups some need to enforce thresholds of belief which determine membership? Is belief simply substantive or doctrinal? Does voluntary disbelief eradicate all claims to membership based upon ascriptive inheritance? Conversely, does ascriptive belief produce authentic religious membership regardless of the quality of voluntary assent?

In other words, is believing simply a matter of having answers, or is there some quality of the act of questioning which implies attachment? Revelatory experiences do not automatically produce or reinforce faith—this is the crux of the matter. A direct experience of the impenetrability of death is capable of destroying a level of faith previously sustained in a particular community. The outcome of a revelatory experience will often depend upon the circumstances within which that experience was produced and understood. However, regardless of the outcome in terms of belief, are not these experiences to be considered authentically religious in nature, and does not the commonality of experience serve to mitigate some of the separativeness of contrary explanations?

It is important not to overstate this point, since belief and disbelief are different, and involve people in different sets of expectations and commitments. However, there are reasons to argue that the differences need not be considered absolute. It is important to realize that both belief and disbelief are fragile and potentially impermanent.

The Persistence of Inherited Symbolic Structures

Deciding against the communities of one's birth is always possible. And yet, the actual target of that act of rejection is not always clear-cut. Is it because of dissatisfactions with the community, regardless of its belief structure? Or, is it because one can no longer support belief in the values and knowledge of the community? Of course, most acts of rejection derive from a combination of both reasons, and yet one suspects that the act of rejection germinates first in dissatisfactions with the emotional quality of the community, and that these dissatisfactions ultimately turn against the beliefs and values.

And yet, even though the rupture with people, institutions and rituals may be quite complete, the community has not been left behind entirely. Empirical evidence has shown clearly that people seldom shed their symbolic inheritance in its entirety; those pre-rational, primordial metaphors which are instilled in the earliest stages of socialization persistently reappear in the adult consciousness of the disbeliever.

The most readily available evidence for this assertion can be found in literature, with those "agnostic" writers for whom the symbols of a cultural inheritance appear abundantly. For Catholics, one could immediately think of James Joyce. For Joyce, as well as for many others, the symbolic inheritance constituted a core of their literary talent. Even if their desire was to produce through writing a total exorcism of their past (which is not manifestly apparent), coming to grips with and expressing this inheritance undoubtedly contributed to their imaginative genius.

Two Possible Distortions of the Belief Process

It is possible that the act of rejection involves a choice against an ascriptive membership. However, this does not free one from the necessity of having community in order to sustain belief. This rejection of community can produce two different types of problems. One possible effect is that the sacral impulse remains as a characterological trait, and the disbeliever will persist in an attempt to recreate a community of messianic promise, but now on secular grounds. Rather than experiencing and attempting to placate some "transcendent other," the secular messianic community celebrates its own power. Usually this transmogrification of the ultimate is the result of what was an overblown religious impulse to begin with.

A second possible effect eschews messianism. It accepts, indeed insists upon, the reality of limitations upon human willfulness, and while not intrinsically hostile to the religious, is unable nonetheless to believe or belong. While intellectually more honest than its antireligious counterpart, this position runs the risk of lacking any vitalizing impulse. Vision and community, despite the problems that that merger can create, go hand-in-hand. The inability to join community vitiates the ability to internalize symbols.

CONCLUSION

This paper has attempted to demonstrate that all reality derives in some measure from human experience. Revelatory experiences themselves originate in some human embodiment—the teachings of the prophets, the person of Christ. The fate of these experiences become the responsibility of actual men and women; they are sustained solely by the qualities of the communities entrusted to their care. As the history of religion quite clearly reveals, the origin of revelation in no way guarantees the success of subsequent religious institutions. The ability of a community to resist untruth (in this case, idolatry?) is a continually unfolding process. As an example drawn from the success of the scientific community, Polanyi has shown that scientific knowledge is possible primarily because of the commitments and traditions which bind scientists to standards of evidence; equally important, new knowledge, or advances in knowledge, are also produced through the interactions of men with these same traditions and commitments. Religion is a similar human endeavor and, to be understood properly, the sociology of knowledge provides some useful perspectives.

What these perspectives show are that belief is not automatic or even infinitely renewable, that authentic religious symbols must traverse a labyrinthian path to daylight, and that disbelief is not a simple inversion of membership. The Church, when alive, is so at the parish level. Much to the chagrin perhaps of theologians (or other rationalists, such as political theorists), ultimate values or sacred symbols influence the lives of people to the extent that the intersubjective community permits it. The construction and maintenance of systems of belief proceeds outward from the individual rather than inward from central sources of authority. Furthermore, revelatory experiences of the modern kind are invariably personal and local in the first instance.

Therefore, the Church needs to spend considerably more time in an attempt to discover how religious values are transmitted, and to some considerable reorganization of both its self-image and its structure to accommodate itself to these highly affective, processual authority patterns. The Church should sponsor more of the type of research into ultimate value systems and mystical experiences such as Greeley and his colleagues are doing. They should also push this research forward, to see how (and whether) people restructure their lives because of these experiences, and how and with whom they share the experiences.

Furthermore, the sociology of knowledge would suggest that disbelief is as varied a condition as is belief, and that the former does not produce unilateral withdrawal. The boundaries of the religious community can be conceived broadly, and membership treated as processual rather than complete at any given moment. The defensiveness of the immigrant Church about doctrinal orthodoxy is not necessary. A theological view of membership in the Church could be similar to the emerging theology of marriage: both are processual or historical bonds. Thus, there would be many modes of affiliation, an approach which could lessen significantly the need to revolt in the face of doubt or dissatisfaction, and which could more openly allow people continually to draw upon the riches of their traditions.

In other words, theological speculation could benefit from research into the sociology of disbelief. How does one structure disbelief? What is the behavior of disbelief? Which behavior of the community does the disbeliever reject, and what does theology say about the importance of the rejected acts? If disbelief can be considered no more static than belief, then what reinforces and what mitigates disbelief?

Religion has not disappeared from contemporary Western civilization. Experiences with transcendence and/or bafflement persist, despite—or maybe even because of—what man has been able to do to increase his power over reality. They occur with far greater frequency and in the lives of far more people than one commonly assumes. Even when, or if, these experiences do not arrive at or support the presumption of the presence of a deity, they do keep alive the religious enterprise. Religious thinkers must view themselves as a part of the culture and as competitive with other world-views. Religion is not locked into a life-or-death struggle with the secular realms of culture, but each cultural sector does have its own styles, assumptions and prejudices which only uneasily accommodate the presence of the others. What religious thinkers need to reflect upon is the manner in which their domain—organizing around transcendent experiences—jibes with the rest of the ongoing human activity. This paper has been an attempt to point to some of the interactions which merit consideration.

Notes

1. Clifford Geertz, "Religion as a Cultural System," in Donald Cutler, ed., *The Religious Situation: 1968* (Boston: Beacon Press, 1968), p. 641.

2. Michael Polanyi, *Personal Knowledge Towards a Post-Critical Philosophy* (Chicago: University of Chicago Press, 1958), p. 73.

3. Peter L. Berger and Thomas Luckman, *The Social Construction of Reality: A Treatise in the Sociology of Knowledge* (Garden City, N.Y.: Doubleday, 1966), p. 60.

4. Ibid., p. 93.

5. Edward O. Laumann, *Prestige and Association in an Urban Community: An Analysis of an Urban Stratification System* (Indianapolis: Bobbs-Merrill, 1966).

6. Geertz, p. 677.

7. Berger and Luckman, p. 41.

John N. Kotre

Of Human Fertility

FOR all its faults, the encyclical *Humanae Vitae* expressed a truth with which we are losing touch: procreation is essential to sex. To render sex infertile, to deny Eros a future, is to render sex trivial and, ultimately, to enervate it. *Humanae Vitae* faltered, however, as do those who hope to excise procreation from sex, by defining procreation in its narrowest sense, as the physical begetting of offspring. It seems incredible that a church—its pope and his critics alike—concerned with the spiritual life of its members would fail to appreciate the phenomenon of spiritual procreation and so lose sight of religion's capacity to nourish that very phenomenon.

Several years ago I began to involve myself in the study of human fertility. By fertility I do not mean principally the bearing and nurturing of children—the passing on of physical life. Rather, my focus is on spiritual generation, that is, on certain qualities psychoanalyst Erik Erikson has labelled "generativity" and on others we ordinarily think of as creativity. Generativity refers to "a concern for establishing and guiding the next generation,"[1] a desire to pass on to children, students, or successors the skills, customs, and interpretations of life that define one's people. Creativity, on the other hand, refers to the ability to produce novel yet appropriate solutions to problems, to discover and express original yet insightful perspectives. In practice, the two concepts are not that distinct: though creative products appear to emerge *ex nihilo,* they contain far more of the work of previous generations than even their creators may realize.

My method is biographical. I approach individuals who appear to be fertile in either of the above senses and who are in the middle or near the end of their life's work. These are people working within a specific tradition or at the confluence of several traditions. I study their work, interview them intensively, and write a book about them. The poor devils don't realize that the book is only the beginning of it, for I will return every few years for more in-depth interviews. The decades of data I hope to gather in this fashion ought to provide material for decent "psychobiography," for placing a person's generative or creative activity in the context of an entire lifespan.

In this paper I will not discuss these individuals but will reflect on contemporary feelings toward human fertility. I will first describe the neglect and even disparagement of it by several influential strains of current psychology and then go on to suggest ways it may be sustained by resources within the Judaeo-Christian and American Catholic traditions.

I

Popular psychology has a curious hold on many affluent Americans. In its books and workshops and therapies it does more than enlighten or help with personal problems; it defines existence, as religion once did. The kind of psychology developed for and by the mobile, educated segment of our population is a reflection of the strains, ambiguities and aspirations it feels. To comment on this psychology, then, is to comment on the socio-economic niche in which it resides—a niche, by the way, into which increasing numbers of American Catholics are moving.

Historian Christopher Lasch writes that the dominant mood of the 1970s is therapeutic, not religious. "People today hunger not for personal salvation, let alone for the restoration of an earlier golden age, but for the feeling—even if it is only a momentary illusion—of personal well-being, health, and psychic security."[2] It is not the existence of therapy that alarms me, for competent therapy is a blessing, but the conception many therapists have of a "fully-functioning" or "self-actualized" human being. As a member of a psychology faculty, I see the influence of their thinking daily. (Because of the location of the university where I teach, I see its influence specifically on the children and grandchildren of immigrant Catholics.) In no case of which I am aware do popular models of psychic health have any interest in progeny. In sharp contrast to the people I study, the "healthy" individual cultivates, or at least acquiesces in, spiritual sterility.

Current psychotherapies—and the seminars and training sessions into which their view of life spills—dampen the instinct to beget in at least three ways. First, they encourage "open," transient relationships in place of bounded, durable ones. Second, they view the past as a prison and seek, with great success, to liberate individuals from it.

Third, they set as an ideal a limitless, fluid self with ever expanding consciousness. All three characteristics dovetail in an interpretation of life that rules out concern for posterity. Lasch writes, "To encourage the subject to subordinate his needs and interests to those of others, to someone or some cause or tradition outside himself . . . strike[s] the therapeutic sensibility as intolerably oppressive, offensive to common sense and injurious to personal health and well-being."[3]

The orientation of which Lasch speaks developed in the 1960s, a time when social commentators began to see and welcome the increasing transiency of human relationships. In *The Secular City* theologian Harvey Cox described the anonymity and mobility of the modern metropolis and insisted it was a blessing, for it delivered us from the Law and gave us choice in personal relationships, ideas and values.[4] Tradition was disintegrating, he said, long-term acquaintanceships declining, impersonality on the upswing; we were, as a result, freer, more tolerant, more open to change. Psychologists Warren Bennis and Philip Slater were less euphoric than Cox about the increase in "quick" relationships, but in *The Temporary Society* they made one thing clear: the tide would not turn, so we had better learn to move—to be flexible, to "get love, to love and to lose love."[5] As the divorce rate continued to climb, Nena and George O'Neill spoke of the benefits of "open marriage."[6] And Alvin Toffler predicted in *Future Shock* that "people of the future" would know how to plug only part of their personality into any new relationship and would become adept at breaking off old ones.[7]

In a different vein, Margaret Mead spoke of a cultural shift in the United States from "post-figuration" to "co-figuration."[8] She meant that influence no longer flowed from elders to the young, that the shape (the *figura*) of our culture was no longer set by the past. Instead, the young, cut off by a generation gap, modeled their behavior on that of their peers and were influenced by the present.

One need not be in total agreement with these analyses to recognize that the psychotherapies propagated in the 1960s and 1970s treat their clients on a temporary basis and focus on the present. They are "co-figurative." The years required for a psychoanalysis have become the weekend required for a marathon. From one-to-one contact with an "elder" interested in a patient's past, therapy has moved to groups of peers who refuse to consider anything but the present. The objective is no longer to alter durable and resistant inner structures but to modify a segment of outer behavior, to eliminate "games" the patient is playing.

The client-centered approach of Carl Rogers, conceived in the 1940s, was an important precursor of these co-figurative therapies. Rogers was the first to relinquish the role of elder in therapy, the first to be "non-directive." To Rogers' way of thinking, the therapist's only task is to empathize with his client and "reflect" his feelings in an atmosphere of caring and warmth. Reconstructions and interpretations of the past are studiously avoided; what matters is the feeling the client articulates and the therapist clarifies in the present moment. The client's inner self is thought of as fluid, constantly changing, constantly emerging. Though client-centered therapy is neither quick therapy nor group therapy, its philosophy and techniques—and, indeed, its originator—have been easily absorbed into the group movement.

Sensitivity training originated in the same decade as client-centered therapy and was based on Kurt Lewin's field theory, another psychology of the present. Sensitivity training, however, did not become a cultural force until the late sixties, some two decades after its official birthdate. According to Kurt Back, the growth of the movement was intertwined, both as cause and effect, with the social unrest of the sixties. It finally took hold in the United States, as it failed to in Europe, because of our postwar affluence (we had the time for T-groups and the money to pay for them), because of secularization (the decline of traditional religion created a void in people's lives), and especially because of mobility. Back notes that sensitivity and encounter group centers took hold in recipient areas of internal migration in the United States, particularly in suburbs and in California.[9] And what have they offered to people "on the move"? A new ritual expressed in the language of science that enables broken roots and severed connections to regenerate *quickly.* A chance to find identity, to become aware of how one "comes off," even with a group of strangers. An opportunity to develop one's ability to adapt to any new situation, to become intimate in a hurry. The group trainer, therefore, steers the participants to a consideration of their own transactions and construes as escapes references to pasts and futures outside the group. It is most significant that the catchword of the sensitivity/encounter movement is *here-and-now,* and that the title of the popular magazine reporting on its rapid mutations is *Psychology Today.*

One of those mutations was the Gestalt therapy of the late Fritz Perls. Perls was very much an elder—a tyrant, some say—in the groups he directed; yet his therapy is predominantly co-figurative. The person in a Gestalt group's "hot seat" is forbidden to bring up his personal history; others in the group join as therapists or become the target person's "alter ego." Direct, aggressive intervention is used to get to a person's problems as quickly as possible, to get him to act them out, to make him dramatically aware of the splits and the missing parts in his personality, and, hopefully, to enable him to construct a better whole (Gestalt) than he previously possessed. Responsibility for the future, for what happens to someone after therapy, is disclaimed. Perls wrote,

"Sir, if you wanted to go crazy, commit suicide, improve, get turned on, or get an experience that would change your life, that is up to you. You came here of your own free will."[10]

Behavior therapy, having different roots than either the client-centered, sensitivity, or Gestalt approaches, nevertheless shares their concentration on the present. Behaviorism, a distinctly American school of psychology, always has stressed that at birth man is a *tabula rasa,* a blank slate unmarked by the impress of past generations, capable of bearing whatever inscriptions the environment makes. But the behavior modification techniques that spread rapidly in the sixties and seventies carry Locke's dictum a step further: adults, thirty or forty years old, are now slates, if not blank, then at least erasable. The past has no holding power; it can be unlearned. A phobia, for example, does not lie in some durable internal structure; it is not symptomatic of a deeper disease. It is simply an overt behavior that can be disposed of.

An apparent exception to these therapies of the present is transactional analysis, originated by Erich Berne and popularized in *Games People Play, I'm OK–You're OK,* and *Born to Win.*[11] Indeed, when TA speaks of parent and child ego-states (roughly equivalent to Freud's *superego* and *id*), it recognizes the importance of "scripts" that a person carries from the past to the present. Yet in practice transactional analysis is a close cousin of encounter-group therapy, Gestalt therapy, and even behavior therapy; it draws little or nothing from its theoretical parent, classical psychoanalysis. Indeed, Berne's original intent was to shorten the process of psychotherapy, to eliminate harmful "games" rather than to rework an entire personality. The popularity of transactional analysis, I am suggesting, like the popularity of the other new therapies, is due to its compatibility with a configurative clientele, cut off from the past, centered on the present, more and more transient.

Carl Rogers often has preached the hope offered by these new therapeutic techniques to the affluent, politically leftish, well-educated middle class. He told a graduating class at Sonoma State College of a New Man emerging from "encounter groups, sensitivity training, so-called T-Groups." The New Man "recognizes that he will be living his transient life mostly in temporary relationships and that he must be able to establish closeness quickly. He must be able to leave these close relationships behind, without excessive conflict or mourning."[12] He has a distrust of marriage as an institution, religion as an institution, education as an institution. His culture is a "cocoon" from which he struggles to break free. "Liberated" from the past, he is "turned on" by interpersonal experience, by meditation, by drugs—by the present.

Not only is the New Man of popular psychology skilled at temporary relationships, not only is he "liberated" from the past, he also believes he carries unlimited human potential. All things seem possible now that he has left the "cocoon" of tradition, the confines of durable intimate relationships. Gurus from the East tell him that lines between himself and everything else are illusory, that his self is to become immersed in a cosmic consciousness. Gurus from the West insist on the opposite: his self is to be asserted, expanded, and fulfilled—in Fritz Perls' words, "You do your thing and I'll do my thing." But there is a curious similarity between the transpersonal humanistic psychology of the East and the assertive humanistic psychology of the West. The two agree that the self has no limits. Therefore, says one, let it passively flow into a cosmic consciousness. Therefore, says the other, let it actively taste of every experience, let it become now this impulse now that, let it "expand" and "raise" its consciousness. Consciousness, of course, is never expanded in the direction of recovering early experience, for the past must be fled at all costs. Nor is there recognition of the fact that expansion can only take place by way of self-imposed frontiers that both hold a person in and give him something to go beyond.

The boundless, infinitely changeable self of humanistic psychology is actually a relative of behaviorism's empty, unknowable self, even though humanistic psychology considers itself distinct from behaviorism. The self that is "into behavior mod" shops in the supermarket of human traits for whatever it needs (and is featured) this year: better sexual performance, less anxiety, less weight, more assertiveness, whatever. Such a self unknowingly assumes it has no permanence, no physiological substratum that affects its traits, no early experiences that stamp indelible marks. There is no identity, no internal structure around which it scribes an ego-boundary, saying I am this way, I am not that way, for life. Humanistic psychology talks incessantly about the self, telling us either to lose it or expand it. Behaviorism ignores the self. But both, explicity or not, preach the virtues of a fluid self, without limits, incapable of choice, incapable of loyalty to something outside itself.

Though Slater admits in *The Temporary Society* that it is difficult "to imagine ways of integrating the rearing of children with temporary systems,"[13] psychologists at large fail to notice that its New Man is a spiritual eunuch. He cannot be tied down long enough to a single place, be it spiritual or physical, to be a parent—again, spiritually or physically. Having lost a sense of historical continuity, he is incapable of identifying with predecessors or posterity and is left with the goal of psychic self-improvement. And though he speaks of mankind's unlimited potential, the truth is that his unbounded self is so dissipated, so blurred that it cannot harness the energy to create.

To its credit, psychology has devoted considerable energy to children and continually strives to identify the kinds of climate in which they flourish. It also has facilitated the escape of individuals from those pasts that deserve abandonment and helped them cope with the resultant fluidity. I would hope, however, that it will begin to teach other "skills"—permanence, loyalty, fidelity, and duty—and that it will begin to see that limited, contained, rooted selves are the only kind capable of creativity and generativity. Whether psychology will ever do so is another matter altogether.

II

According to anthropologist Clifford Geertz, religion is a set of symbols that creates long-lasting moods and motivations in men by providing interpretations of life that seem to them uniquely realistic. Religion generates convictions about such things as birth, death, intimacy and nature by saying that to believe in this, or to act in this way, is to live in harmony with a fundamental reality. Psychology grounds a particular attitude toward life by saying it is "healthy," religion by saying it accords with the way things "really" are. Having outlined some attitudes of recent psychology toward human fertility, I would now like to bring a specific question to religion. What resources does religion have—in particular, what resources does the Judaeo-Christian symbol system have—to generate those moods and motivations that nourish such fertility? What capacity does it have to underwrite convictions about human life that stand in contrast to those of psychology's New Man?

The human imagination has always closely associated divinity and fertility. All the earth's cosmogonies, all those mythical accounts that tell the nature of things by narrating their origins, are stories of the generation of life. Indians from the Pacific Northwest speak of a woman turning into the earth, her hair becoming the trees and grass, her flesh the clay, her bones the rocks, her blood the springs of water. Children spring from her, derive nourishment from her, and ultimately return to her. Polynesians describe the beginnings as Heaven and Earth in intercourse; children confined in the darkness between them push them apart and see the light of day for the first time. California Indians say the world was made by a turtle who dove to the bottom of the sea for a speck of dirt and by a dove who found a single grain of meal; the dirt and the meal are combined and grow into an earth covered with seeds and fruit. Jews and Christians tell of a God who fills an eternal void with the simple power of his word and commands his creatures to be fruitful, multiply, and fill his earth. To live in a world with plants and animals that reproduce themselves, and to be fertile oneself, these creation stories say, is to be favored by the forces of the universe.

Religion, too, has always incorporated in its ritual the experience of returning to "the beginnings," to the sacred time and place of creation. The experience of renewing contact with roots, of being cleansed by living in the idealized time of the ancestors, is indeed a fertile one. David Bakan has argued that the insights of psychoanalysis came to Sigmund Freud at a time in his life when he felt rejected by the Gentile world of science and so returned home, psychologically, to a Jewish mystical culture. That culture regarded human beings religiously the way Freud "discovered" them to be in a secular context.[14] Similarly, the people I continue to study, religious or not, are individuals who maintain a strong sense of connection with their origins and do not hesitate to draw on them.

Even though *Humanae Vitae's* understanding of fertility was constricted, there are symbols within its parent tradition that are capable of supporting fertility in the fullest sense of the word. May I suggest only a few?

1. *The Demanding Fidelity of Yahweh.* The relationship that Yahweh insists on between himself and his people is one of permanence, exclusivity, and loyalty. It is hardly "open." On Sinai, God tells the Hebrews, "I am Yahweh your God . . . you shall have no gods except me."[15] Demands and promises are made; a covenant is struck. In current psychological jargon, "boundaries" are firmly established. As the Old and New Testaments unfold, the promises are not always kept, the boundaries not always observed. Yet the covenant—the "frame" or "ground rules" of the relationship—is returned to and ratified again and again. In the Old Testament God is a king who punishes violations of the boundaries; in the New Testament He is a Father who mercifully welcomes prodigals who stray beyond them. In both, the frame of the relationship is indispensable; it creates the trust that allows love to develop.

To take the relationship between Yahweh and his people as the prototype of human relationships is to assert that what is essential to intimacy is the assurance of fidelity, the conviction that the other will always be there and on your side. This fidelity is not the "unconditional positive regard" of client-centered therapy, for it is a fidelity that sets conditions, makes demands, and insists on a certain closedness in relationships. I am suggesting that the security of such confines sets the stage for true intimacy and, later, for generativity.

2. *Humanity's Stewardship.* My colleague Patrick Dobel recently has taken issue with ecologists who claim that the command in Genesis to dominate nature has led to Western man's exploitation of the world's resources.[16] Dobel believes an exegesis of the Old Testament would show that man is not to be the absolute lord of nature but its trustee. The earth is owned by God. It is bestowed upon humanity "for all generations" and strict limits are placed upon its use. Judging from the parables of the Good Steward and the Talents in the New Testament, each generation is not merely to preserve God's estate but also to improve it. The world is not to be left in its natural state; it is to be acted upon and controlled for the betterment of mankind. Its resources are to be husbanded but not exhausted, passed on in better condition than they were received.

Human beings who regard themselves as stewards take a far different stance toward their own life than the New Man of recent psychology. They believe that their life is owned not by themselves but by God. If life is something received, it is something that ultimately has to be passed on. Consequently, rights to self-fulfillment are tempered by duties to predecessors and successors. In contrast to the position taken in *Humanae Vitae,* stewards regard their reproductive processes as part of a heritage that is to be acted upon and controlled for the well-being of posterity.

3. *Pruning.* The steward treats nature the way a farmer treats his orchard. Reverence does not demand that the trees be allowed to grow untrammeled. It requires instead that they be cut and limited, sometimes extensively, so that they bring forth an abundant harvest.

Metaphors of fruitfulness appear frequently in the Gospels and barrenness is treated with impatience. A tree that fails to produce good fruit will be put to the axe and thrown into the fire. The kingdom of God will be taken from the chief priests and the scribes and given to a people who will produce its fruit. Jesus curses a fig tree with nothing but leaves, even though it is not the season for figs, and the tree withers and dies. Later, he likens himself to a vine, his disciples to the branches, his Father to the vinedresser. "Every branch in me that bears no fruit he cuts away, and every branch that does bear fruit he prunes to make it bear even more. You are pruned already." The disciples are commissioned to "go out and bear fruit, fruit that will last."[17] To do so they must remain in contact with the vine and they must be cut back. To be fertile one cannot grow without limitation.

4. *Spiritual Parenthood.* The Catholic Church has long been the home of "fathers" and "mothers" who are celibate and childless. Such symbols of spiritual parenthood are of great importance during a time when it is imperative to restrict population growth while nourishing feelings

of fertility. What an example of generativity is offered by someone like Mother Teresa of India!

Though I have not observed firsthand the Church's examination of its tradition of celibacy, I wonder how much emphasis is being given to spiritual fatherhood and motherhood in emerging rationales. (Donald Goergen's *The Sexual Celibate* said next to nothing of these archetypal Catholic symbols.[18]) To choose celibacy is to place a limit on oneself so that one can care for more human beings. It is an act of pruning that remains an enigma to those expanding their consciousness in all directions.

5. *The Eucharist*. John's account of the Last Supper begins with Jesus' realization that his hour has come. The prospect of death, a death that will extend the fidelity of Yahweh, heightens his concern for posterity. In a simple gesture of sharing bread and wine, he passes his life on to others.

In the Eucharist Christ is symbolically transmitted from generation to generation, so that for millennia his followers have been able to return to the beginnings, participate in their own creation, and nourish themselves on the person of their founder. The core ritual of Christianity is a guarantee of continuity and generativity through time. It reaffirms that one is a steward, not an owner, of one's life.

American Catholicism consists not only of symbols like these but also of experiences that may appear merely incidental. For me, the experience was one of growing up in a family and an urban neighborhood where most everyone shared the same world-view. No one talked about religion but everyone did religion. It was part of the atmosphere. I lived in a "post-figurative" culture—rigid, to be sure, and incapable of change—but it was not (at least where I lived) oppressive. Everybody belonged. As a kid I was able to walk unannounced into half the houses or apartments on the street. A block in one direction was the blacktop behind the parochial school where we played basketball and Johnny-over. A block the other way was a Catholic high school and a great green lawn where we faithfully played baseball and the nuns faithfully kicked us out. It was a secure, limited, rooted environment. I knew my place. There were numerous people, numerous "fathers" and "mothers" and "sisters" whom I pleased and displeased, but on whose word I always counted.

Such a setting was neither uniquely Catholic nor uniquely American, but it happens to be the one that shaped the lives of many American Catholics of my generation. As I stepped from that environment to the one I now inhabit—the mobile, secular, co-figurative world of the psychologized affluent—I could not help but feel, somewhere in my bones, the loss of something of value. I argue now for bounded relationships, for connection with the past, for selves with limits, for fertility, because doing so, in a way, recaptures my own (admittedly idealized) beginnings.

So I hope the spiritual, intellectual, emotional and moral resources of American Catholicism will be mustered to support the god-like impulse of fertility that is today a source of so much ambivalence. The impulse will have to be nurtured, controlled, redirected, its proper place in sex asserted. To do so American Catholics have much to draw on: the riches of the Judaeo-Christian symbol system, their own experience growing up in the parishes of this land of immigrants.

Notes

1. Erik H. Erikson, *Identity, Youth and Crisis* (New York: Norton, 1968), p. 138.

2. Christopher Lasch, "The Narcissist Society," *New York Review of Books,* September 30, 1976, p. 5.

3. Ibid.

4. Harvey Cox, *The Secular City* (New York: Macmillan, 1965).

5. Warren Bennis and Philip Slater, *The Temporary Society* (New York: Harper and Row, 1968), p. 127.

6. Nena and George O'Neill, *Open Marriage* (New York: M. Evans, 1972).

7. Alvin Toffler, *Future Shock* (New York: Random House, 1970).

8. Margaret Mead, *Culture and Commitment* (Garden City, N.Y.: Natural History Press, 1970).

9. Kurt Back, *Beyond Words* (New York: Russell Sage, 1972).

10. Fritz Perls, *Gestalt Therapy Verbatim* (Lafayette, Calif.: Real People Press, 1969), p. 75.

11. Eric Berne, *Games People Play* (New York: Grove Press, 1964); Thomas Harris, *I'm OK–You're OK* (New York: Harper and Row, 1969); Muriel James and Dorothy Jongeward, *Born to Win* (Reading, Mass.: Addison-Wesley, 1971).

12. Carl Rogers, "The Person of Tomorrow," in Gwen B. Carr, ed., *Marriage and Family in a Decade of Change* (Reading, Mass.: Addison-Wesley, 1972), p. 6.

13. Warren Bennis and Philip Slater, *The Temporary Society* (New York: Harper and Row, 1968), p. 93.

14. David Bakan, *Sigmund Freud and the Jewish Mystical Tradition* (Princeton, N.J.: Van Nostrand, 1958).

15. Exodus 20:2–3, *The Jerusalem Bible.*

16. Patrick Dobel, "Resources and Stewardship: A Christian Response to Ecology," *The Christian Century,* October 12, 1977, pp. 906–9.

17. John 15:2–3 and 16, *The Jerusalem Bible.*

18. Donald Goergen, *The Sexual Celibate* (New York: Seabury, 1974).

William C. McCready

Religion and the Life Cycle

Oh, how I long to muse on the days of
my boyhood, though four-score and
three years have flitted since then; yet
they bring sweet reflections as every
young joy should, for the merry-hearted
boys make the best of old men.—*"The
Bard of Armagh"*

YOUNG men and women grow old, and although they may change in
many ways there remain important continuities through the cycles of
individual lives. It is not quite correct to speak of "cycles" since
humans do not repeat themselves. Perhaps it would be better to think in
terms of "life histories," those stages or phases or periods we move
through on our journey from birth to death. In this paper the focus will
be the way in which movement through the stages of life illuminates the
religious questions we ask. A growing body of social science data has
begun to describe the content of these stages, and these data generate
questions of a religious nature having to do with the way in which
individuals integrate their certain knowledge of self-mortality into systems of interpretive symbols. Such a network of symbols is more than a
superficial map for the individual; it serves as an immediate reality in
the stead of the ultimate reality which cannot be known. The anthropologist Clifford Geertz has said that man is suspended in symbolic
webs which are self-spun and those webs are modified throughout the
life cycle (Geertz, 1975). Symbolic webs are modeled on ultimate reality, but they do not replace it.

The adage about death and taxes being the only sure things in life
does not fully apply to those wealthy enough to afford loophole-
lawyers, but death alone is another matter. Humans are distinguished
from all other species by our foreknowledge of our own demise. Other
creatures go merrily through life surviving day to day, and one day
survival ends. There is no anxiety about it, however. Humans, on the
other hand, spend much of their time being preoccupied with the

272

knowledge that this life is very temporary even when it is by our current standards a long one. Rough calculation provides the following information: subtracting time for sleeping and eating, and assuming that independent activity begins in a technological society about the age of 25, the average person will have about 400 months to spend as he or she pleases! It seems a short time in which to become great and accomplish great things.

CHILDHOOD

Erikson (1950) extended Piaget's conceptions about how we learn and posited that childhood was a time when basic trust was or was not attained. Very young children do a great deal of exploring through such mechanisms as steady-staring and grasping, but we have little knowledge about what such activities mean to the children themselves (White, 1975). We also know from studies of very young children and their families that they recognize their mothers earlier than their fathers and that even when researchers try to fool them by matching a recording of the mother with a picture of the researcher, three-week-old babies can spot the deception (White, 1975).

Children engage in a variety of testing behaviors designed to discover how far trust extends. The testing may take the form of violating rules to see what punishment is in store or of deceiving the parents or other adults to see if they will catch on. To the extent that misbehavior is punished and adults are not able to be fooled boundaries are established.

Children who are not able to find such boundaries or those who find boundaries that are too harsh have their basic sense of trust severely altered. The tragic consequences for children caught in the Ulster violence have been documented by social scientists, and the overwhelming finding was that they had lost all sense of trust (Fields, 1972). Similar findings have been reported by those observing high crime urban areas. These children wake in the middle of the night fearful that someone will kill them or take them away. They no longer trust the ability of adults even to protect them from harm.

The trust which personality theorists say should be instilled in childhood bears a strong resemblance to that elemental faith in the graciousness of being which underpins religious belief. This is not to say that faith flowers in childhood, or that children who do not trust cannot believe, it is simply to point to a connection. The question for the child is whether survival from moment to moment will be assured enough for development to begin. After all when one is as powerless as a child survival for more than a few days is an open question. The faith question is the same: Is survival possible even though there are witnesses to death all around?

Bettleheim (1975) in his discussion of the value of fairy tales over modern childrens' books tells us that those stories which affirm the child's belief in the imaginary and fantastical are the most useful in terms of promoting sound development of trust in the future:

> The child feels that he is not alone in his fantasy life—that it is shared by the person he needs and loves most. Under such favorable conditions, fairy tales communicate to the child an intuitive, sub-conscious understanding of his own nature and of what his future may hold if he develops his potential. He senses that to be a human being means having to accept difficult challenges, but also means encountering the most wondrous adventures.

ADOLESCENCE

According to Erikson and others who have commented on the stages of living, adolescence is a continuation of the "faith" question posed during childhood. The child wonders what the world is like and what it will do to him; the adolescent wonders what he is like and what will happen to him. This is the time when the person asks, "Who am I?" Another way of thinking about it is that children wonder who God is and adolescents wonder who they are.

Adolescence is a by-product of industrialized society and is due to the fact that greater levels of skill are required in order to function in and contribute to such societies. Longer periods of schooling and enforced unemployment are essential, and these in turn promote age-grouping of people just after childhood. It is within these age groups that adolescent culture begins to form. Adolescents are most likely to deal with each other and tell each other their innermost thoughts and least likely to tell adults what is taking place in the group. However, this does not mean they pay no attention at all to adults.

Research on the mechanisms of religious socialization have focused on the adolescent, partially because they are old enough to answer questions. In a study of American Catholics the author found that fathers were more critical to the development of religiosity in their children than were mothers (McCready, 1972). Furthermore the relationship between the parents influenced the boys' religious development but not the girls'. Another study, using different techniques, found that father-symbols were more complex than mother-symbols and were therefore used by older children and adolescents more often as representations of God (Vergote and Aubert, 1972). Research into the way in which parents promote the sex-typing of their children has reinforced the importance of the father in that function as well (Block, 1971). Sex-typing is that process which leads the individual to assume certain characteristics are more masculine- or feminine-appropriate than others. A study of religious socialization among specific groups, rather than a national sample, found that the father's role was again unusually important (Weigert and Thomas, 1970). The subsequent analysis of these particular data led to the speculation that fathers who exerted a high degree of control over their children were more effective socializers, regardless of the level of emotional support offered.

For the adolescent person, socialization seems to be closely tied up with the father and with perception of the father. (A brief caveat: We have very little information from one-parent families although there are hints from research on functional black families that single parents can play dual roles for their children [Hill, 1975].) This is particularly true when we consider religious socialization. One way of reflecting upon this finding is to regard it as a continuation of the trust question posed in childhood. Faith is closely related to trust in the graciousness of being and the assurance of survival during childhood. During adolescence it is closely related to the definition of self that begins to emerge in the father-child relationship.

The reason that fathers appear more important than mothers at this time may well be because of the complexity of the father-image mentioned before. Mother is a simple, direct survival image linked to food and warmth. Father is linked to security and self-definition and is much more complicated for the child and the adolescent to understand. However, in understanding the role of father and in becoming distinct as a self opposed to that role, the adolescent person pushes trust, and implicitly faith, one step further and relates it not only to the world outside, but to the inner world of self. One way of answering the adolescent question of "Who am I? What will happen to me?" is "I am faithful and therefore saved."

YOUNG ADULTHOOD

Erikson says that the task of the young adult is to learn how to create intimacy between the self and other persons. Another way of thinking about this is that the young person is asking the question, "Who can I count on besides myself?" This is the time the peer culture begins to break up because the groups are too large for each member to feel that they can count on each other member in any important way. Whereas the religious issue in the previous stages was faith, in this stage it is love.

A psychoanalytic study of young adults has shed a great deal of light on the problems and struggles these people are having in trying to create intimate relationships, and the core of the problem seems to be their inability to feel they can count on any other person outside themselves not to hurt them (Hendin, 1975).

> Out of this disaffection has come a generation of young people who are trying to stop their own romantic impulses in the suspicion that intimacy may end in disaster. Where the parents of this generation may have expected too much from each other, young people today have gone the length toward becoming a generation of no expectations. This is a generation characterized by a belief that intimacy is dangerous, that the way to live safely is to reduce your vulnerability or combativeness to the low level survival requires. Expect nothing, they seem to suggest. You cannot get less.

Hendin's findings suggest that faith or trust problems, begun in an early phase of development, do not appear really serious until the inability to love is surfaced. Young people expect that they will find someone with whom they can share themselves and someone they can count on in all situations, only to discover that intimacy has turned into a battleground in which no one is to be trusted. The disappointment drives them back into the redoubt of self-indulgence and narcissism.

A concomitant question for the young adult is "What is it possible for me to do?" Both this question and the query of whom one can count on involve choices on the part of the self. Of all the people it is possible to know, and of all the tasks which one might possibly do, the individual person must begin to choose some and leave others. Love and intimacy involve choice simply because one cannot develop and nurture the required vulnerability with everyone. Career commitments and goal orientations require that some paths be selected and others ignored. Young adulthood is the time when individuals need to select from the alternatives before them, yet it appears as though it is increasingly a time when people feel most alone. Important choices cannot be successfully made in a vacuum. There are strengths and powers to be gained in the relationship of the young person to those who have had to make hard choices before, but if the present generation is denied those supports they will remain too tentative to choose. Another psychoanalyst (Coles, 1966) writing about his profession has said:

> Out of a bleak childhood almost fiercely met, and for a while relived, will come the willful perspective that the artist at work possesses. I suppose that is what psychoanalysis at its best can sometimes do,

help people live intimately enough with their past to learn how to use its power, not simply to know the details.

Learning how to use the power of a personal past is inextricably tied up with determining whether or not you can count on people close to you to be careful of your vulnerability. Whether one was loved or not in the past must be resolved before one can love in the present. Young adults frequently appear to be less than religious since they may be moving in opposite directions from religious institutions, but they need to answer some very elemental religious questions before they can become full adults.

ADULTHOOD

If the question of the young adult was "Who can I count on and what is it possible for me to do?" the question for the mature adult is "Who counts on me and what will I do?" Adults take care of the world. They make the decisions and generate the resources, raise the children and worry about the future. The religious correlate for this stage of life is compassion. Adults need to be aware of the needs of others and attend to them the best they can.

In a book about the crises of middle age the burden of caring for others and worrying about the well-being of one's family appeared as a major debilitating force in the lives of many people (Sheehy, 1976). Men who had been thought successful and who had thought of themselves as successful found that they could not cope with the burden over the long haul and abruptly changed their life styles, shedding responsibilities as they went, in order to relieve the pressure that had accumulated. The seemingly terrible weight of making decisions, both personal and professional, finally got to them and they opted for lives where decisions were thought to be unnecessary and where they could "just live day to day."

Other commentators have observed that there is not so much a mid-life crisis as a re-evaluation and review period (Clausen, 1972). This is a time for stock-taking and re-directing for the remaining years. However, to the extent that this period, be it defined as crisis or review, is preoccupied with the condition of the self, it is a regression to the earlier stage of adolescence. The adult has achieved selfhood and ought to be able to draw upon the resources of a personal past to go beyond self-concern to compassion or concern for others. There has only recently been any interest in researching the adult stage of life, probably because we have taken it for granted as the logical fruition of the previous stages. However, it is also the case that topics do not become the objects of research unless they pose some sort of problem; it is all too seldom that we study the nonpathological in life.

To the extent that we have information on functioning adults in our society we can point to two findings which support the contention that religiosity and adulthood are at least not inimical to each other. In a study of religious values the author and his colleague found that there was a very high correlation between psychological well-being or happiness and having had at least one mystical experience (Greeley and McCready, 1974). In another study researchers from NORC found that religious education was correlated with the kinds of social attitudes that could be called "compassionate" such as racial tolerance and support of social justice teachings (Greeley, McCready and McCourt, 1976). Therefore in the adult it appears that religious sensibilities are not only not bad but they can be very positive as reinforcements of the caretaking in which adults, by virtue of their very role, must engage.

OLD AGE

This has been a neglected stage of life until very recently, because it was considered to be the ending phase. For reasons that probably have to do with our own inability to face mortality, we as a society have not wanted to deal with the elderly and with the dying. However, modern therapists and researchers are increasingly telling us that old age is simply another stage of living and ought to be faced as such. The task which faces the older individual is to reflect on the past and to consider the imminence of death and what it means. Butler has noted that the life review is a universal phenomenon among older persons going back as far as the time of Aristotle (Butler, 1963). The stock-taking of the adult turns to a search for meaning in the older person. The process of reflecting on the past and searching for validation there, while at the same time preparing for the unknown future of death is an exercise in hope which is the religious correlate of old age.

Religious behavior among the old changes from a focus on ritualistic behavior outside the home to a concern for religious attitudes and feelings and the meaning of belief. Kuhlen has summarized the research in this area by saying that, except for church attendance, all other indicators of religious interest and activity increase with age even into extreme old age (Kuhlen, 1962). As the end of life approaches people sort themselves out according to those who do and do not feel as though they are ready to die (Kübler-Ross, 1969). Those who express less anxiety are also those who express most conviction about survival after death and most concern for those they are leaving behind.

Hopefulness is not looking through rose-tinted glasses, but rather it is the recognition of tragedy and the conviction that reality is gracious in spite of tragedy. In a study designed to measure hopefulness, among other dimensions of religiosity, the author found that old people tended to be less hopeful than those in their middle years, although those old people from religious families tended to be more hopeful than their age-group norm (McCready and Greeley, 1976). To be a sign of hope is not easy and many people cannot maintain their hopefulness as they grow old. Chronic illness and physical deterioration are severe obstacles to hopefulness in the elderly. However, it is also the most important contribution the old in society can make to the young. By reflecting their past as a hope-producing reservoir the old person communicates to the young that the questions of youth will be answered in a positive way and that the potential for adventure mentioned by Bettleheim can be a reality. What kind of men and women do we need to successfully traverse these life stages and still have enough strength to communicate a message of hope at the end of life? What kind of people can be sensitive to the religious dimensions of these stages and infuse them with meaning?

CONCLUSION

In a previous article the author has argued that the person best suited to raise children in the modern context is the person who is androgynous in the self-conception of sexuality (McCready and McCready, 1973). The masculine and feminine of every personality is needed to communicate the kind of support and rich encouragement which children need to thrive. Christianity has evidence of just this sort of reconciling of differences in human experience. St. Paul and the Gospel of John speak positively of androgyny as a characteristic of spiritual perfection. Jesus is described as saying that the kingdom will come when "two shall be one, the outside like the inside, the male with the female neither male nor female" (Doresse, 1958).

Men who can expose the tender and gentle facets of their personalities and women who can develop the assertive and self-directed facets of theirs will become people who traverse the life stages finding faith, love, compassion and hope along the way. The trust-identity crisis of childhood makes faith possible; the loyalty-intimacy crisis of young adulthood produces love; the caretaking-decision crisis of the adult leads to compassion; and the reflection on the past and anticipating-death crisis of old age leads to rebirth through hope.

People raised with androgynous role models will be able to bring more of their personality resources into play at each of these stages than those raised in stereotypical sex roles. The search for the transcendent, for that which cannot be explained by our experience—the search for God—is a search for unity, for a way to make sense out of all the fragments and apparent contradictions of our experiences. The androgynous self can come nearer the resemblance of that oneness, the imaginative and powerful wholeness which is beyond ourselves, and begin to be a witness to that reality.

The stanza of the Irish song quoted at the beginning of this article says that "merry-hearted boys make the best of old men." Being merry-hearted is not an easy thing for a boy to do if assertive self-direction is the only role open to him through his life stages. In order to produce the "best of old men" there must be tenderness and gentleness in fair measure all along the way. If there is then the life stages can be productive points for the reflection of religious symbols and sensibilities, and if there is not then the same stages become hurdles, each higher than the last until finally the person succumbs at the bottom of a hope-killing obstacle he cannot surmount.

References

Bruno Bettleheim. 1975. "The Uses of Enchantment." *New Yorker*, Dec. 8.

Jean Block. 1971. "Conceptions of Sex Role: some cross cultural and longitudinal perspectives." Paper presented at the Bernard Moses Lecture at the Institute of Human Development at Berkeley, University of California.

Robert Butler. 1963. "The Life Review: An Interpretation of Reminiscences in the Aged." *Psychiatry*, vol. 26, pp. 65–76.

John Clausen. 1972. "The Life Course of Individuals." In *Aging and Society*, ed. Matilda W. Riley. New York: Russell Sage.

Robert Coles. 1966. "Creativity, Leadership and Psychohistory." In *The Mind's Fate*. Boston: Little Brown.

J. Doresse. 1958. *Les Livres Secrets de Gnostiques d'Egypt*. Paris.

Erik Erikson. 1950. *Childhood and Society*. New York: Norton.

Rona Fields. 1972. "Prejudice, Hate and the Socialization Process—Children of Ireland." Paper presented to the American Psychological Association.

Clifford Geertz. 1975. *The Interpretation of Cultures*. New York: Basic.

Andrew Greeley and William McCready. 1974. "A Nation of Mystics?" *New York Times Magazine*, Jan. 28.

_____, Kathleen McCourt. 1976. *Catholic Schools in a Declining Church*. Mission, Kansas: Sheed & Ward.

Herbert Hendin. 1975. *The Age of Sensation*. New York: Norton.

Robert Hill. 1975. *The Strengths of Black Families*. Washington, D.C.: The Urban League.

Elizabeth Kübler-Ross. 1969. *On Death and Dying*. New York: Macmillan.

Raymond Kuhler. 1962. "Trends in Religious Behavior during the Adult Years." In *Wide Horizons in Christian Adult Education*, ed. L.C. Little. Pittsburgh: University of Pittsburgh Press.

William McCready. 1972. "Faith of Our Fathers." Ph.D. dissertation. University Microfilms.

_____, Nancy McCready. 1973. "Socialization and the Persistence of Religion." In *The Persistence of Religion, Concilium* 81, ed. Andrew Greeley and Gregory Baum, pp. 58–68. New York: Seabury Press, 1973.

_____, Andrew Greeley. 1976. *The Ultimate Values of the American Population.* Beverly Hills, Calif.: Sage Publications.

Gail Sheehy. 1976. *Passages.* New York: Dutton.

Antoine Vergote and Catherine Aubert. 1972. "Parental Images and Representations of God." *Social Compass,* vol. 19, pp. 431–44.

Andrew Weigert and Darwin Thomas. 1970. "Socialization and Religiosity: a Cross-National Study of Catholic Adolescents." *Sociometry,* vol. 33, pp. 305–26.

Burton White. 1975. *The First Three Years.* Cambridge, Mass.: MIT Press.

Teresa A. Sullivan

Numbering Our Days Aright: Human Longevity and the Problem of Intimacy[1]

WE are acutely conscious of our own lives, of the time allotted us from birth to death. We mark the milestones on our journey from birth to death by our significant human relationships. Parents, childhood peers, spouses, friends, and our own children mark our life stages. Most people experience most of these relationships. The "life cycle" is an abstract concept that tries to summarize the regularities in the pattern of relationships and responsibilities, through the life span of persons with average longevity. Length of life bounds the life cycle.

When relationships are difficult, when families squabble, when divorce rates climb, some of us recall the mythical "good old days" of family harmony and marital stability. But all life cycles have their characteristic troubles. Previous centuries probably were not Golden Ages of intimacy. Our current difficulties in human relationships may stand in sharper relief because today most people have the luxury of seeking intimate relations. The "luxury" of closer relations is available to us because of the quiet human revolution in the average time elapsed between birth and death—increased longevity.[2] Demographic studies of fertility and mortality—birth and death—offer insight about the quality of life between them. Demographic conditions affect how long one lives to participate in intimate associations and how many persons are available for close contact. Although the demographic perspective is not sufficient for understanding intimacy, its implications and application are useful.

The one-life perspective, because it concentrates on the uniqueness of our own lives and times, is distorted. It is often both egocentric and ethnocentric. In this paper, I will develop the demographic perspective and the insights it offers on relationships during the life cycles, and then argue that relationships themselves may be thought of as having life cycles.

THE DEMOGRAPHIC PERSPECTIVE

The practical limits of human life force us to rely on institutions, such as marriage, education, religion, government and the economy. Institutions endure, even though individuals come and go. Human values are learned, elaborated and passed on through institutions. Our deepest human relations are usually embedded in our institutional context; most of us are conscious of our institutional ties.

Both individual lives and institutions are embedded in a more remote collectivity, the human population. Like an institution, the population endures over generations, despite the coming and departure of its individual members. Unlike an institution, the structure of the population is determined by births and deaths—fertility and mortality.[3] The demographic structure underlies all social life, permitting and limiting activity. The schedule of births and deaths determines the number of children to be taught, the number of elderly to be supported, the number of women of marriageable age. These demographic structures set the scene for institutional activities—schools, hospitals, marriages. The institutions interact with the demographic structure by providing the setting for births and deaths.

Beginning in the late seventeenth century, a series of long-range population shifts began in Europe. Mortality rates began to decline. Individuals might not have noticed this—from the one-life perspective, it might merely have been good luck that more of one's children than one's sibs had survived to adulthood.

Nevertheless, the demographic substructure underlying institutional structures began to change, and the institutions responded—again, very slowly. In the course of time, conditions would change at three levels, but the *period* of change would differ at each level. Long-range population shifts occurred very slowly; institutional adjustments occurred later, in a somewhat shorter time frame. Human lives, although longer than before, were still so short by comparison that the major population shifts could go undetected. After World War II, when many developing nations began to capsulize the demographic changes into the space of a human life span, the lag in demographic and institutional adjustment was obvious and painful. In developed countries, where the adjustments had been more gradual, demographers and historians began to ask what life had been like before the mortality decline.

Short Lives and Social Control

What was family life like before the increase in the length of human life? Our direct evidence is fragmentary, but demographers have constructed a series of life tables for varying levels of mortality. By combining these life tables with simplifying assumptions about age at marriage and the proportion of people who married, a kind of synthetic history of family experience can be created. Although this technique does not describe any single family, it provides a general picture of the conditions of family life under the given mortality conditions.

Most of human existence has taken place under demographic conditions of high fertility and high mortality, with very little population growth. Crude birth and death rates were probably in the neighborhood of forty births and deaths per thousand population per year. (By comparison, the crude birth rate in the United States in 1974 was 14.9; the crude death rate was 9.2.) Because of the equilibrium of deaths and births, this is sometimes called the "high equilibrium" situation. However, death rates were not constant; they fluctuated with famines and epidemics.

Small settlements were always faced with the possibility of complete annihilation, for they had little economic surplus and were at the mercy of various natural disasters. Under these conditions, high fertility and large families helped assure community survival. A large family increased the chance that at least a few children would survive to adulthood. But communal and family interests often collided. High fertility can be achieved if most women marry and bear only a few children each, or if only a few women marry and bear many children. In the high equilibrium situation, the latter case was common because so many girls died before childbearing. It was necessary for the society's continuation that there be a large number of births, but it was often disastrous for the family that had to stretch its resources still further. Worse, the "investment" in children might be wasted if the children did not survive childhood. Hence, it is probably not surprising that abortion and infanticide were (and are) widespread in many high fertility societies.

Ryder (1973) models some consequences of the high equilibrium situation for hypothetical families. He uses a model life table (West-3; Coale and Demeny, 1966) in which the expectation of life at birth for females was 25. Under such a mortality regime, over half of the females would not survive to age 15. Of those who lived to age 15, their expectation of further life would be 34.2 years. The expectation of life at birth for males would be 22.9. Of every 100,000 male babies born alive, slightly over 46,000 would live to their fifteenth birthday, and at age fifteen their expectation of life would be 32.6 years. Ryder assumed a monogamous system in which women marry at the age of 20, and men marry at age 25. The mean duration of marriage would be only 12 years. After 25 years, of every 100,000 marriages contracted, only 21,832 couples would still survive. There would be 38,100 widows and 30,068 widowers. If the society did not forbid it, a high rate of remarriage would be likely.

The wastage of daughters who died in childhood, and the fairly short lives of persons who survived to become parents, meant that reproducing couples needed to have 6.48 children to ensure that one daughter would live to reproductive age. If you combine the model's predictions of life-years for parents and children, it is possible to compute the number of years that parents and children would live together in the parental home. By contemporary expectations, it was for a pitifully short time, ranging from 10.5 years for mothers-sons to 9.2 years for fathers-daughters.

What are the implications of such a family situation for child-rearing and for levels of intimacy in the home? It seems likely that children had, on the average, relatively little exposure to their parents. Most parental contact occurred while the children were very young. They had much less chance to develop a mature, adult relationship with a parent, or to observe parents handling complex human problems. Many children may have adopted their role models of adult behavior from outside their immediate family; they may also have retained an infantile image of the powerful parent figure. Socialization, crowded into short periods of time, must have stressed social sanctions and obligations. In some cases, socialization was probably left to parent surrogates, although there was little money or leisure for extended education. In such a circumstance, the commandment to "honor your father and your mother" was all too frequently a mandate to honor the memory of the dead.

From the parents' point of view, there may have been an attempt to limit the emotional investment in children, at least until the children were old enough to have survived the high infant mortality. This does not imply that parents were unfeeling or indifferent toward their children, although Shorter (1976) suggests the limited investment may have influenced higher infant mortality. Aries (1962) and other family historians have noted that the treatment of children in earlier centuries was more oriented to control and constraint than to sentiment. A large number of births may have aggravated this situation, or at least diluted the quality of the parent-child interaction.

While we cannot document it, one supposes that the high equilibrium situation was conducive to a general, harsh social control. The high-birth–high-death society, aggravated by limited economic resources and a hostile environment, encouraged what Durkheim called "mechanical solidarity." The conservative and cautious elements that we associate with traditional social orders may have originated in such demographic circumstances. Ironically, although in our own experience we may connect conservatism with advanced age, in earlier centuries it may have been the response to high infant death rates.

Disequilibrium: Rapid Population Growth

Disequilibrium occurs when mortality rates are falling rapidly, although fertility rates remain constant, or fall very slowly. When crude death rates and crude birth rates no longer balance each other, the difference between them is called natural increase (or decrease). A crude birth rate of 40 with a crude death rate of 10 would yield a growth of 3 per cent a year. Because population grows with a modified compound-interest formula, a sustained growth rate of 3 per cent would mean that the population would double in about 23 years. But this is called the "disequilibrium" situation precisely because demographers believe that this kind of growth cannot be sustained for very long. How long it can be sustained is a matter of dispute.

Mortality rates fall first among infants, and so the immediate effect of a fall in mortality is a younger population. As more of the surviving infants live to marry and reproduce, the youthfulness of the population is accentuated. Demographers generally concede that the decline in death rates occurred very slowly in Europe and was affected by modern sanitation, transportation, communication, nutrition and public health medicine. In developing countries, on the other hand, the decline in mortality came close on the heels of the large-scale import of public health and agricultural technology from the West. Much of Latin America, Africa and Asia could now be described in demographic disequilibrium. In some of these countries, growth rates approach 3 per cent per year. (Sustained rates higher than this are suspect; they are often an artifact of low-quality data.)

In the European experience, fertility rates fell after the mortality rates fell. Fertility did not decline uniformly among all segments of the population, nor did it decline at a uniform rate among countries. Eventually, a new "low equilibrium" was reached, with births and deaths again in near-equilibrium, but at a low level. The decline in fertility was influenced by a variety of factors: a higher age at marriage, a lower proportion of persons who married, a greater use of contraception. The *reasons* for higher marriage ages, lower nuptiality, and so on, are much more complex. Lower family sizes per couple did not result directly from the decline in mortality; but were filtered through a series of institutional changes. Some of these changes, in turn, reflected the demographic swings. Among them were the organization of land and inheritance rights; urbanization; the rise of new, industrial occupations; colonization of the new world, and so on.

What are the effects of the disequilibrium situation for family life? Ryder models these conditions with the same simplifying assumptions about marriage. With an expectation of life at birth for females of 60 (males = 56.5), 75,000 couples of every 100,000 married would survive for at least 25 years. Ryder assumes that fertility levels have not yet declined—this means that about two daughters per mother would survive to reproductive age. The joint-years of parent-child experience would rise dramatically: 20.5 years for mothers-sons, and 17.1 years for mothers-daughters; 19.8 years for fathers-sons, and 16.7 years for fathers-daughters. (Daughters spend less time at home because their marriage age is assumed to be younger than that of sons.)

This model suggests a different quality of family interaction, by virtue of its length and sibling rivalry. Many more of the sibs will live to compete for their parents' attention. It is interesting to compare the amount of time that siblings are likely to spend with each other in the parental home. In the disequilibrium situation, brothers would spend 17.3 years together, compared with 9.9 years in the high equilibrium situation. Older brothers and younger sisters would spend 17.7 years in the disequilibrium situation, but only 10.4 years in the high equilibrium situation. Too, because more children survive, the number of sibling combinations is greatly increased in the disequilibrium situation.

What are the consequences of demographic disequilibrium for the quality of human interactions? The time available for interaction and the variety of primary relationships that are possible in the home are increased by the greater longevity. On the other hand, a large number of dependent children strains the family resources; hard decisions may have to be made about which children will be endowed with limited resources. In Europe, economic strain led to child abandonment, infanticide, and early, cruel apprenticeships. Bands of hungry, unskilled children plagued European industrial cities. Similar problems are reported today in Latin American cities. For these children, the prospects of intimate relationship with an adult are very bleak. On the other hand, under conditions of rapid industrialization, urbanization and economic growth, it may be possible to "launch" the children in a variety of ventures. This can minimize the risk for every individual—he can call on the family if he fails—while maximizing the opportunities for the entire family. If one strikes it rich, he can bring the members of his family into the venture with him. Economic growth is a critical variable in assessing the implications of disequilibrium. One of the hottest controversies among demographers today is the extent to which rapid population growth itself accelerates or impedes economic expansion.

The Low Equilibrium Situation

In the low equilibrium situation, both death and birth rates are low. Birth rates may fluctuate with the business cycle, yet the completed family size remains well below the four or more in the disequilibrium situation. If we make the same assumptions about marriage, married couples will spend a greater proportion of their lives without any children at home. The number of person-years for parent-child interaction rises; the number of person-years for sibling interaction also rises. The number of possible combinations of siblings falls, of course, because there are fewer siblings per family.

TABLE 1*

Hypothetical Life Cycle Mean Age at Major Events of
Women in Mid-Nineteenth and Mid-Twentieth Centuries.

	BORN	
	1846–1855 (six children)	1946–1955 (two children)
First marriage	22.0	20.8
Birth of first child	23.5	22.3
Birth of last child	36.0	24.8
First marriage of last child	58.9	47.7
Death of spouse	56.4	67.7
Own death	60.7	77.1

* Source: Bane, 1976, p. 25.

Table 1 shows the difference that could be expected in time married couples spend together, using hypothetical data for the United States for 1846–1855 and 1946–1955. The data are hypothetical because they amalgamate the experience of a large number of women, and do not necessarily describe the experience of any particular woman. This table requires assumptions about child spacing and about the effect of incomplete data. Nevertheless, it is interesting for what it tells us about the "empty-nest" syndrome. Women born in the 1846–1855 period would have been widowed by the time their youngest child was married. They would have spent 1.5 years alone with their husbands. The woman born after World War II also spends 1.5 years with her husband before the birth of her first child. But she also spends another 20 years with him after the children leave home. Judging from these data, she could expect ten years of widowhood. More recent U. S. Census data shows the longevity gap between men and women has widened, and so an even longer widowhood may become common.

What are the consequences of the low equilibrium situation? Low fertility drastically changes the distribution of adult women's activities. They live much longer, and they bear and rear fewer children. These two facts alone may underlie much of the restiveness among women, their rising labor-force participation rates, and their growing dissatisfaction with rigid sex roles. Former role prescriptions of the husband-wife roles are likely to be inadequate, not only because the woman has more opportunities for working outside the home, but also because the length of time she spends with her husband is likely to be so much longer.

A longer individual life encourages us to shift our attention from the human life cycle to the marital life cycle. The stages in Table 1 may be considered a cycle in much the way that individual development constitutes a cycle. Does monogamous marriage experience an unusual strain when husbands and wives spend twenty or more years in two-person households? In the long sweep of history, the lengthy "empty-nest" period is a rarity; it would not be surprising if couples had trouble adjusting to it. Too, depending on decisions about child-spacing and number of children, couples may contract or eliminate altogether the period during which they have children in the home.

These changes in fertility and family composition apparently affect marital satisfaction. Just what the effects are is still somewhat in doubt. In 1972, the Gallup Poll asked a sample of Americans: "A typical married couple usually goes through a number of stages in the family cycle from marriage to when the last child leaves home. Which of the following stages do you think is the happiest?" Of the white males, 45 per cent of the Catholics and 41 per cent of the non-Catholics said it was while the babies were being born; 9 per cent and 11 per cent, respectively, said it was when all the children had left home. Among women, 52 per cent of the Catholics chose the birth period; only 9 per cent chose the empty-nest time. Among non-Catholic women, the percentages were 50 per cent and 5 per cent (Blake, 1974). Nor did increasing age seem to affect the answer. One might expect that as one approached the empty-nest syndrome, one would try to be optimistic about it. But there is only a very slight increase among older respondents who indicate that the empty nest is the happiest time.

In another series of studies, however, respondents were classified by their own stage in the marital life cycle and their own reported happiness—not by the happiness they imputed to a hypothetical family. In these studies, respondents were most likely to report their own marriages were very happy either before children were born or after they had left.[4] The differences in satisfaction over the marital life cycle are not very large, and these studies are cross-sectional, not longitudinal. (The respondents who said they were very happy before their children were born might report themselves even happier if they were re-interviewed after the children came.)

These conflicting results suggest that it is too soon to draw conclusions about marital satisfaction, but it does seem significant that the stage Americans *believe* to be happiest is the one that is shrinking most rapidly.

For children, the low equilibrium situation offers promise of a lengthy, highly individualized relationship that persists well into the child's adulthood. The smaller sibship makes it possible for parents to invest heavily in their children, not only in terms of money and material goods, but also in terms of time spent with the children. And this is probably true even if the mother of the children chooses to work while they are young. Although some of their physical care as infants may be taken over by other adults, the child will share, on the average, more time with the mother during later childhood and early adulthood.

Other effects of the low equilibrium situation include the rise in one-person households, either among young persons who have postponed marriage or among older persons who have been divorced or widowed (Kobrin, 1976). Over a period of time, this living situation may affect not only the number of intimate relationships one has, but also one's capacity for forming intimate relationships. In all of these areas, there is a lively research interest, but relatively few definitive results.

INTIMACY: BEYOND DEMOGRAPHIC DATA

The demographic structure permits or constrains certain types of household settings. I have used data about these structures to speculate on how the conditions and constraints of intimacy may have changed with demographic conditions. It can be reasonably argued that most persons have not lived under conditions that encourage numerous or long-lasting relationships. Exceptions to this, of course, would exist. Even so, today's "crisis of intimacy" may be perceived as a crisis simply because the "crisis of infant mortality" and the "crisis of epidemic" have receded.

In this section I would like to step even further from the conventional demographic data, but not from the topic of birth and death. The human life cycle has been used as the analogue for a number of fruitful concepts. The family life cycle represented in Table 1 is one example. This analogy implies that families—at least nuclear families—also die. In the model in Table 1, the family is dead when both spouses have died. But human relationships may die even when the persons continue to exist. For example, nuclear families "die" in some sense, or at least they are wounded, when a divorce or abandonment occurs. We have made great progress in "death control," lowering mortality. Can we lower the mortality rate for human relations? I propose several lines for reflection.

First, how do we deal with the problem of risk and intimacy? All human relations involve risk. One affirms the value of intimacy despite the fact that the intimacy must end—either through the death of the relationship, or through the death of the persons. We face the choice of maximizing opportunities for intimacy or minimizing the chances of being hurt. Some people seem to hold a general minimizing position: they are afraid to get married, afraid to have children, afraid to "commit themselves." They may make the death imagery explicit: "I don't want to see a beautiful relationship grow stale and die." A similar sentiment may have led parents to minimize their emotional involvement with their children when infant mortality was high.

For a healthy emotional life, we must take some risk of intimacy. Where the decision becomes more difficult is in high-risk relationships. Christ was well known in his own time for his "high-risk" relationships with uncertain friends like Judas and Peter, and with the socially disapproved: sinners, tax collectors and lepers. We are more likely to encourage our friends to minimize intimacy in high-risk relationships—for example, in interracial or interfaith marriages. The high-risk relationship may be defined as sinful. Institutions tend to reinforce the conventional advice with "I told you so" attitudes toward those who risked intimacy and lost. This sometimes includes sanctions on single parents and the divorced. More subtly, it may take the form of neglect of the widowed or bereaved.

Many of our ideas about marriage were elaborated in a day before mortality declined. The emphasis on procreation in marriage responded, at least in part, to the precarious community balance of births and deaths. High-risk marriages only complicated an already difficult situation; divorce, separation, and contraception, if practiced on a large scale, threatened community survival. That is no longer true. So it is not surprising that we can now re-evaluate our view of marriage and human sexuality. High-risk relations no longer threaten the community, so now the community can consider what risks in relationships it can support.

Second, one must consider how role-sets and role prescriptions, whether traditional or "modern," interfere with and possibly block intimate relations. Demographic conditions in the developed world permit and encourage men and women to undertake new roles. But a longer life may mean we "outgrow" roles. The longer we are expected to fill a role, especially one that has become inappropriate (e.g., the role of suburban housewife, or of absentee father), the more it may chafe and irritate. And to the extent that we relate to others only in our "roles," and not in any deeper sense, the more threatening any role change becomes. For married couples, the years after child-rearing offer new possibilities, but possibilities that may be neglected if role change is too threatening to be tried, or if the new role, when tried, causes serious disruption in the marriage.

"Pop psychology" has fostered awareness that individual lives have rhythms and stages. It would be helpful for us to understand that relationships also have stages, some caused by my growth, some caused by your growth, and some caused by our growth together. Not all these stages are pleasant, and strains in a relationship are inevitable. What is crucial is not mistaking a common cold for a terminal illness—not seeking to end a relationship just because a difficult period may have begun. These stages or levels of growth often follow or accompany role changes. For that reason, outsiders must be careful in projecting their expectations for others' relationships. I think this is especially true for those who would comment on the "vocation to the married life" in terms of the ideal wife, the ideal husband, and the ideal children.

Finally, one must consider the need for reconciliation and forgiveness within relations. If we are risk-averse to making commitments, perhaps it is because the consequences of failing in a relationship have been so severe. We are not always willing to forgive one another and try again; we would sometimes prefer to pronounce a relationship dead than to try to revive it. Worse, the community may confirm and condemn the failed relationship, heaping guilt and loneliness on top of the pain we already feel. There is a widespread perception of the death of relationships, but not of their resurrection.

One model of the Christian approach to intimacy is the relationship of the soul to God. How we approach God is certainly affected by our cultural apparatus—the concept of God as Father probably meant something quite different in the high equilibrium demographic situation, where many children had little experience of their biological fathers, than it does today. But regardless of the cultural baggage we carry in contemplating the Creator, that relationship also requires risk;

it requires growth and change, which are often painful; and it requires a constant assurance of forgiveness and reconciliation. But unlike many of our human relations, it carries the explicit promise of resurrection. The Church, in explaining the promise of resurrection, must challenge us to lose the fear of death—not only the death with which demographers are concerned, but also the risk of death implied in human intimacy.

Notes

1. Maria Luchesi Ring provided able research assistance for this paper. I am grateful for the suggestions and comments of both social scientists and theologians, especially Harley L. Browning, David Burrell, C.S.C., Anne Carr, B.V.M., Andrew Greeley, Philip M. Hauser, John and Ann-Marie Kotre, Michael McGarry, C.S.P., Jacques-Marie Pohier, O.P., Dudley L. Poston, and A. Van Eiff.

2. By "longevity" I mean what demographers call "expectation of life." The expectation of life at birth in the U.S. in 1974 was 76.6 years for women, 68.9 for men. This concept should be distinguished from the "life span," which is the maximum length of life recorded for a member of a species. Plainly, the life span is achieved by only a few individuals. In the psalms, the life span is conceptualized as seventy years, "eighty, with good health." Today, the life span is something over one hundred years, although the exact figure is in dispute.

3. For a subset of the human species, such as a nation, migration must be considered as well.

4. See Campbell, Converse, and Rogers, 1976; Bane, 1976; Spanier, Lewis and Cole, 1975.

References

Ariès, Phillipe. *Centuries of Childhood*. Translated by Robert Baldrik. New York: Knopf, 1962.

Bane, Mary Jo. *Here to Stay*. New York: Basic Books, 1976.

Blake, Judith. "Can We Believe Recent Data on Birth Expectations in the United States?" *Demography* 11 (February 1974): 25–44.

Campbell, Angus; Converse, Philip E.; and Rodgers, Willard L. *The Quality of American Life*. New York: Russell Sage, 1976.

Coale, Ansley, and Demeny, Paul. *Regional Model Life Tables and Stable Populations*. Princeton: Princeton University Press, 1966.

Kobrin, Frances E. "The Fall of Household Size and the Rise of the Primary Individual in the United States." *Demography* 13 (February 1976): 127–38.

Ryder, N. B. "Influence of Changes in the Family Cycle upon Family Life." United Nations Economic and Social Council, World Population Conference, 1974, Symposium on Population and the Family, Honolulu, August 6–15.

Shorter, Edward. *The Making of the Modern Family*. New York: Basic Books, 1975.

Spanier, Graham B.; Lewis, Robert A.; and Cole, Charles L. "Marital Adjustment Over the Family Life Cycle: The Issue of Curvilinearity." *Journal of Marriage and the Family* 37 (1975): 263–76.

Pastora San Juan Cafferty

The Church in Public Policy Making:
The Need for Professional Competence

THE causes and effects of social problems have always been the concern of organized society; thus, the concept of social planning is not new. However, specifically addressing social planning through organized institutions is a relatively modern concept. Contemporary definitions of social planning range from such sweeping definitions as "thinking about the problems of society" to activities "as specific as time-phased programming."[1] For the purpose of this discussion, one can define planning as "a method of determining policy under which developments may take place in a balanced orderly fashion in the best interests of the people in a given area."[2] This definition of the planning process makes it possible to argue that distinctions between social, economic and physical planning are mostly artificial since one cannot effectively take place without the other.

Public policies are defined as overt actions of government or agencies which operate in the public sector, and social policies are often defined as the body of public directly responsive to human needs.

However, I find these definitions to be increasingly artificial. Few—if any—public policies have no social consequences. It is the old "guns or butter" issue. The complexity and interdependence of public policy decisions is dramatized by fiscal accounting. A national treasury can only support so many endeavors. Choices are constantly being made simply by making budget allocations to government programs. These choices may be implicit or explicit. It matters not.

In contemporary society, scientism or the indiscriminate appreciation of technology has replaced value judgments in the making of public policy. Our technological society has abdicated the responsibility for determining the moral values underlying policy decisions to the scientists who measure the feasibility or efficiency of such decisions. The reason for this is clearly apparent: the ever-increasing complexity of society and the conflicting demands of public policy make it terribly difficult—if not impossible—to determine the absolute moral values of such policies. The complexity and conflict are a result of several factors. One is the fluctuation of class structures which make wealth the international measure of class; another, the impact technology has had on tradition and culture creating an international "pop" culture with no apparent historical roots; another is the ever-increasing factor of instant communication and its resultant influence on values. However, while it may be easier to have social scientists—as experts—make value decisions, it is a dangerous business for people to abdicate their right to make moral judgments.

I would further like to argue that the Church, because of its chosen mission as a guardian of faith and morals, has an obligation to participate in the making of public policies which radically affect human lives. I believe the Church—along with the rest of the world—has abdicated this duty. It was not always thus. At one time, the Church—not the social scientists—played a major role in the making of public policy. However, the Church is a reflection of its members, who—confused by the complexity of a modern world and awed by a simplistic interpretation of the separation of Church and state—have also abdicated participation in the creation and the implementation of public policies.

Most public policies include social components and produce social consequences in any society, regardless of its form of government. Therefore, public policies must be responsive to individual as well as to social needs.

Societies may differ in the delicate balance between individual and community rights; societies may differ in the relative purpose of the role to be played by government; and societies may differ in the allocation of individual and community resources. However, most societies agree that the aim of public policy is to define and to achieve a quality of life acceptable to its community. Quality of life may be defined by many or by an elite few but, generally, societies find it relatively easy to agree on the ends of public policies. The difficulty comes in defining the means to achieve these ends. In fact, a grave disparity between the stated ends of public policies and the achievement of these ends is often the traditional pattern.

The reasons for the disparity between the stated goals of a society as articulated in its political rhetoric and the preambles to its laws and the actual policies which implement these goals are many.

The creation and implementation of public policies are complex matters. Public policies are often reactions to problems rather than actions to implement ultimate goals. This is not only true in relatively democratic societies where a political process changing the markers of policy frequently prevents long-range planning, but also in more regulated societies. No society has yet implemented a five-year plan that has successfully achieved its stated goals. There is good reason for this. The creation of public policies affects the individual directly. At the same time the implementation of public policy is also affected directly by individuals acting alone or collectively in society.

The key to creating effective public policies is to reconcile three factors: social needs, political feasibility, and value preferences. Social needs can be determined in a variety of ways, since sociological and economic measures exist to measure change and variation from stated social norms. Political feasibility is most often tested early in the drafting of public policies since the makers of policies—whether chosen by many or by a few—most often refrain from implementing that which is politically unacceptable. Of the three factors, perhaps the most difficult to determine—and the most cursorily addressed—are value preferences. Yet all policy decisions are marked by value preferences.

It is in the area of value preferences where the Church *can*—and *should*—play an important role. In fact, the Church does play a role of relative importance in the making of public policy in most societies. By definition any large institution affects public policy either implicitly or explicitly. When the Church makes policy implicitly, it does so by taking actions without considering the implications these actions have on public policy. For example, in this country, the Catholic Church has repeatedly followed a policy of diminishing support for education. An explicit affect on public policy by the Catholic Church is a deliberate decision which takes into consideration the effect it is going to have on public policy. For example, the Church in its apostolic mission has deliberately decided to underwrite the cost of education in predominantly non-Christian countries. I believe that when the Church affects public policy implicitly it is playing a dangerous role, for the Church is acting without questioning the complexity of values which underlie all policy making—whether the Church's own or that of public and governmental institutions.

Indeed, the Church as an institution makes and implements policies which deeply affect the lives of its members and define its following. The carefully documented history of Church policy confirms this fact—but I will leave discussion of that to learned historians and theologians. Suffice it to say that the creation and implementation of policies within the Church and the consequences of those policies for members of the Church community closely mirrors the process of secular governments. I am going to address only the role where the Church, through internal decisions and external pronouncements, affects public policy. I am doing this to argue that the Church has a responsibility to participate in the creation and the implementation of the wide range of policies which shape society and affect the individual.

The complexity and interdependence of public policy decisions are dramatized by fiscal accounting. A national treasury can only support a limited number of endeavors. Choices are constantly being made simply by making budget allocations to government programs. These choices may be implicit or explicit. It does not matter. However, a *choice* must be made and acted upon in order to create a public policy. Inaction may indeed be "benign neglect" but it is exactly that—"neglect" not action. A society can only be held accountable to a body of public policies based on *action* rather than *non-action*. In reality, each policy decision has a ripple effect affecting many other decisions. And each policy decision affects the individual and society.

This is why the Church has a responsibility to participate actively in the wide range of activities associated with the creation and the implementation of public policy. The very size of the Church as an institution makes it a formidable force in the public and private decisions which shape public policy. Its longevity and continuity, as well as its financial resources, make it a giant among institutions. Furthermore, it is an institution which historically has assumed the responsibility for shaping moral values.

Yet, the contemporary Church has largely abdicated its responsibility to participate in the formulation and implementation of the wide range of public policy. In a way, this is understandable since most of the social issues addressed by public policies are desirable—yet most conflict. At the same time, absolute moral values are relatively easy to establish. Public policies should create a human community, and the establishment of policies which define dignity and freedom is a difficult task.

In a sense, the contemporary Church mirrors the abdication of modern man to search for moral values in the actions of government and public institutions. A society captivated by technology abdicates the determination of moral choice in the belief—or, perhaps, the vain hope—that social objectives lend themselves to technological solutions. The fact is that they do not. "Scientism" is a dangerous and pervasive influence in this age of technology. "Scientism" would argue that with rigorous tools of objective measure, we will avoid conflicting goals and conflicting means. The social scientist thus supplants the moral philosopher, with disastrous results. The determination of values has been supplanted by a blind faith, born of ignorance, in the social sciences. Yet social science does have a contribution to make: it can provide measures of needs. However, one must not overestimate the contribution the scientist can make. He can help measure the need and define the problem. He cannot define the moral and value choices that underlie policy decisions.

This is a role for those concerned with the study of philosophy, theology, and the shaping of values. The moral philosophers bring better tools than the social scientists to the measurement of values. It is these tools which the Church must apply to shaping the total range of public policies.

Martin Rein,[3] a noted American social policy analyst, identifies six strategies of intervention for social change. I shall basically use Rein's identifications and take the liberty of substituting the phrase "the individual" for his references to "the poor." I do this deliberately since the welfare of society is the legitimate goal of *all* public policies. I have chosen these strategies arbitrarily. The strategies listed by Rein apply particularly to a "free market" economy. Indeed, even in this "free market" context one could perhaps come up with a different list. However, these six strategies provide a basis for discussion of how strategies of intervention, while complex, are conflicting.

These six strategies provide potential alternatives in defining public policy involvement for the modern church.

1. *Amenities:* the provision of those services which enrich or strengthen the quality of life; the normal services man needs to survive in a changing society.

2. *Investment in Human Capacity:* the improvement of economic capabilities of the individual by providing schooling, job training, job opportunities, job information.

3. *Transfers:* the redistribution of income of one population to another (young to old, rich to poor); a guaranteed annual income.

4. *Rehabilitation:* the changing of people involving the use of psychological and socio-psychological approaches.

5. *Participation:* programs which promote social inclusion, providing the individual with a stake in society.

6. *Aggregative and Selective Economic Measures:* Aggregative measures are defined as those measures which dribble down to the individual, the benefits of economic growth resulting from tax cuts, capital depletion allowances, and other incentives to stimulate production. Selective measures are those which "bubble up" to the individual through the economic mainstream by creating jobs for the underskilled, establishing a minimum wage, etc.

This list is not exhaustive, and this learned assembly could come up with alternative interventions, each better suited to our native countries and their political systems. However, this list is adequate to establish two facts. The first fact is that the Church, if it is to intervene effectively in the public policy process, must develop its own effective strategies of intervention. And its strategies will be effective only if they are relevant to the political and economic realities of the particular society in which they are to be practiced. Perhaps more important, the second fact is that strategies of intervention are not good or evil *per se* but that to implement a strategy definite—and often times conflicting— moral choices *must* be made.

In order to illustrate conflicts in the strategies of intervention presented, we must realize that attitudes toward the individual are dependent on a value system. While all of us here believe in the dignity of the individual, and most of us would agree that man's ability to work fosters dignity, this does not facilitate the choice of a strategy. For example, an argument can be made that a society which is economically stable should foster individual dignity for its citizens. However, the Nobel-prize-winning economist Paul Samuelson tells us that goals of high-level employment and high stability conflict in a free market society.[4]

Again while all of us could agree on the importance of educating the individual and giving him the opportunity to better himself, it is not clear how this is to be done. Indeed, education for individual choice, which enables the individual to make a career choice disregarding society's needs, is often apparently contradictory to the equally worthy needs of his society. The conflict between individual and societal rights is ever present. Although "no man is an island," it is difficult to make him part of the mainstream with due deference to and respect for his individuality.

Perhaps it is this complexity that has led us to assign the right to examine and establish moral values to social scientists. However, the Church cannot morally abdicate that right and still fulfill its secular or its apostolic mission. If there is indeed a forfeit of the role of making moral judgments and establishing values in the making of public policy, the Church can easily step into that role. It will have to deal with few contenders for the duties of moral judge.

The Church must step into this role of moral judge without arbitrarily handing down dictums that lack the clarity of expression—or wisdom—of the Ten Commandments. Therefore, the Church must develop a methodology (in conjunction with policy-makers) to define values and examine the morality of public policies. And the Church could be more competent in doing this than the social scientists. After all, the Church has had more years of experience in this area.

In addition to the Ten Commandments—which are a good beginning—there are a series of basic standards which the Church can develop to measure the morality of public policies. Standards which offer a beginning include: (a) a maximization of individual freedom and dignity; (b) the maximization of the greatest good for the greatest number; (c) the least harm to the individual. Exactly what these standards mean when we begin to address such issues as unemployment compensation, international migration, economic stability and childhood education is at least as complex as the Thomistic argument of how many angels danced on the head of a pin. But it may be more relevant—and crucial—to the survival of humanity, and to the role of the Church in an individual's life.

The combination of Rein's methodology of strategies of interventions in conjunction with the application of these standards could suggest an approach to a methodology to be developed by the Catholic Church to affect public policy.

While I have argued that the Church has a responsibility to make value judgments in the creation and the implementation of public policies, it is difficult if not impossible to do so in certainty. The reason that we as individuals have abandoned the moral values and political choices to be made and have overestimated the contributions of the social scientists is precisely because of the ambiguity which characterizes the making of value judgments.

Perhaps some examples will illustrate this point. We can all argue that a maximization of individual freedom and dignity is fostered by strong family and community ties. A viable community gives the individual a sense of belonging and protection from the lonely anonymity of a faceless society. It is therefore logical to conclude that the preservation of a community should be an important goal for the makers of public policy. However, it is possible to argue that the ability to work also fosters individual freedom and dignity. Public-works projects, which inevitably disrupt and often destroy community, generate quickly and with predictable certainty both numbers of jobs and economic growth opportunities not only for the immediate community but for the surrounding area. The simple—and dangerously simplistic— solution to this dilemma could be to apply the standard of "the maximization of the greatest good for the greatest number" so that if one hundred families were to be displaced by the construction of an expressway which would generate several hundred needed jobs, the project would be acceptable. Obviously, both the goals of stability and increased job opportunity for the community are highly desirable. The determination of which action will do most harm to the individual is equally difficult.

Rather than construct a series of hypothetical labyrinths of the intricacies of public policy decisions, I would suggest that the question of public works—complex as it seems—is among the simplest. It is offered only to illustrate a point. Most often the choices open to policy makers are choices among relative goals. Accordingly, reasonable men with good intentions may intelligently disagree on what is best for the individual and society. The choices are seldom between good and evil but rather among a series limited benefits—all of which have related disbenefits.

If we accept the argument I have made that the Church has a responsibility to be involved in the formulation and the implementation of public policy, then we must also accept that the Church has a responsibility to develop its own strategies of intervention. These strategies will differ according to the social and economic systems in which they are developed. However, they will each offer a way of analyzing the moral values underlying policy issues and provide guidelines for effective involvement in the area of public policy.

If the Church is to participate effectively in public policy decisions, it must fully appreciate the ambiguity of the process and become an intelligent participant, not an arbitrary judge, in the determination of moral values.

Notes

1. Alfred J. Kahn, *Theory and Practice of Social Planning* (New York: Russell Sage, 1969), p. 1.

2. Joseph Bunzel, "Planning for the Aging," *Journal of the American Geriatrics Society* 9 (January 1961).

3. Martin Rein, *Social Policy: Issues of Choice and Change* (New York: Random House, 1970).

4. Paul Samuelson, *Economics,* 9th ed. (New York: McGraw-Hill, 1973).

John E. Coons

Choice and the Church

IN the structure of its laws Western society has long emphasized individual choice, especially through freedom of contract. In a generally thriving economic order this has permitted the citizen of average wealth to enjoy a substantial range of practical freedom through the market. Today America is preparing to underwrite increased market participation by lower-income individuals; the national government plans to replace in-kind public aid with cash and other devices that increase consumer options. One purpose is efficiency, but such measures also embody a particular and important view of human nature. If the Church hopes to speak effectively within the order of economic and political justice, it is important that she perceive the issues of principle involved and evaluate them from her own perspective.

Policies emphasizing choice are emerging by stages in several areas of basic importance, including housing, food and medicine. Public intervention in housing had begun in the eighteenth and nineteenth centuries with government provision of communal poorhouses for the destitute; it was followed in this century by other forms of take-it-or-leave-it housing, especially the multi-unit public housing structure familiar to our central cities. The 1960s, however, saw the advent of such new forms of public intervention as fiscal incentives which were offered to apartment owners and builders to induce them to cater to the individual housing tastes of low-income families. This was soon followed by the provision of rent supplements directly to the family or individual for approved housing, and, finally, by the provision of actual cash calculated as a housing grant but available for whatever other goods or services might be preferred.

Health policy appears to be following a similar course of development. Medicare and its state equivalents have begun to reduce the dependence of the poor upon either the odious public hospital or the charity of individual doctors. Though the delivery of medicine is still afflicted by private monopoly practices, most persons now are in a position to pick out a doctor for themselves and pay for his services with government aid. The same appears to be happening with nutrition. We have moved from government soup kitchens to in-kind distributions of surplus food, and now to food stamps. Now President Carter is considering the abolition of food stamps in favor of cash grants, and has made it plain that we are about to grapple with the question whether a full range of individual choice ought to be subsidized in the most direct manner—that is, by a guaranteed annual income disposable in whatever manner is preferred by the recipient.

Let us suppose that this tendency will continue, gradually moving us to a social order characterized by two levels of government aid. At the first level government would provide every adult an income based upon the political consensus as to what is needed for an individual to feed, clothe and house himself (plus a family where relevant) but with no strings attached except, perhaps, for compulsory health insurance. Imagine, for example, that an ordinary family of four would receive a monthly income of $600, tax-free, to spend as it chooses. Those with special objective needs and handicaps would receive additional cash support, but, again, without strings. If the individual or family nevertheless became destitute, the second and lower level of governmental support would provide temporary relief, not through cash, but by in-kind services publicly provided at a minimum level of sustenance and without choice.

Children and incompetents pose special problems that I will deal with later. For the moment let us assume that basic responsibility for such dependent persons would continue, as now, with the family. Education would remain compulsory, but the state would provide the family a separate subsidy for tuition in a school of the family's choice. Children and incompetents could be removed from their natural families (or their care compulsorily directed) but only where the family accepted such intervention or in cases where the dependent was manifestly in physical danger from assault or neglect.

The tendency toward subsidized private autonomy is an important and desirable development for two reasons. The first is the observable reality that society often cannot specify what is good for an individual, the real question being who will be empowered to specify it. The second is a preference for personal liberty over equality both in the order of value and as the efficent means to community.

I. INDETERMINACY AND CHOICE

For the professional interested in social justice the most arresting feature of the present intellectual landscape is the new humility among those who would reform and perfect the distribution of human services. The experience of the last decade in education, welfare, nutrition, medicine and day care has produced a painful awareness of the grave difficulties of making domestic policy a rational, orderly and democratic process. Not only has the hyperbolic optimism of the 1960s evaporated; the threats to progress now seem to transcend politics and economics and to involve limitations upon human knowledge itself. The problem is not technological stagnation; science remains clever, and the physical barriers to man's betterment seem passable. The difficulty rather is the poverty of our social knowledge. Society does not know how to engineer man to suit its purposes; indeed, it can rarely predict what he will do next.

Criminal recidivism is a prototypical case of indeterminacy. Its causes and cures have resisted the solutions of hard- and soft-liners alike. The professionals are in faction over the question of how to "treat" prisoners and offer only the most tenuous predictions of who will repeat. Often there seem to be no real experts; experiment suggests that professional parole boards are no better than laymen at identifying the likely repeater. And, as with crime, so with racial tolerance; even though a strongly committed social science has done everything in its power to specify the positive impacts of school integration, there is precious little that we understand about the process. The same appears true for the internalization of political values; though our public schools represent a colossal investment in the dissemination of middle-class attitudes, no one can say whether the effort has had the outcome intended or quite the opposite. Nor do we know the social means to a higher rate of class mobility, to the acquisition of "proper" attitudes toward work, or to an acceptance of the basic values imbedded in the Bill of Rights. How people acquire their attitudes in such fundamental matters and how the pattern may be altered by collective intervention remain essentially mysterious.

Even in rather mechanical affairs such as the acquisition of skills there is often basic professional doubt and conflict. The incapacity to raise reading and mathematics scores continues despite the many educational enthusiasms and experiments; it has done its part in giving Americans a new sense of intellectual and social limits. Most no longer expect that education will defeat poverty, just as they have abandoned hope that psychiatry will cure delinquency. We are in danger (or hope) of becoming a people deeply skeptical of the capacity of collectively imposed techniques to solve problems that prior generations had expected to wither before the assault of the learned professions in league with bureaucracy.

Yet this perception of epistemological barriers to social goals is but one aspect of the new humility. The other is the growing awareness that often the goals themselves elude collective definition. We differ in our views of the good life with a new self-confidence and an intensity that challenge political solutions long accepted as legitimate. Pluralism has been a fact of American life for 150 years but until yesterday had remained essentially problematic. Only in our time has serious criticism of the "melting pot" been removed from the index of political heresies. And, of course, the acceptance of life styles hitherto unthinkable have made value pluralism much broader than ethnicity or religion. As a consequence we are hard put to define the deviant behavior that might justify denial of parole; is homosexuality relevant? We cannot describe the model for racial relationships; is black cultural survival to be encouraged? And we are even in doubt as to the work ethic; our president now must assure us that work is a good thing.

In designing human services and making decisions that affect individual lives what is the relevance of this frequent indeterminacy of ends or means? First of all, by definition, where it occurs such indeterminacy shifts the social question away from collective goals and their achievement. The issue instead becomes which individuals or subgroups shall be commissioned by government to define the good life for whom. For example, if society is unable to specify how the poor should best spend their allotment of public resources, shall the individual welfare caseworker be given power to specify a code of behavior for them? Or, to the contrary, shall life style be left utterly to individual selection? Or shall we devise an intermediate system with alternate choices and vetoes? Put another way, when we do not agree as a people on what is best or how to get it, the question becomes: Who does decide? Nor can the issue be avoided by ignoring it; government inaction is simply a way of relegating the particular decision to private determination in one form or another.

What is not always understood is that government intervention itself can leave social goals to private determination. In the field of human services the welfare worker is a historical example. During most of this century he enjoyed the broadest discretion over the payment of benefits, effectively imposing behavioral conditions upon his "clients." Where society could not specify a clear legal standard, the professional with a captive clientele necessarily applied his own; the welfare "system" to that extent came to be a set of private dominions or micropaternalisms endowed by government. For those unable to afford private tuition the public-school bureaucracy today plays a similar dominating role.

The new perception of value pluralism and of the limits of professional knowledge helps considerably in reaching a different answer to the "who decides for the poor" question, at least in the case of adults. I can assume that for this audience the promotion of human freedom is at least one important value in judging public policy. What I would argue is that the advancement of freedom is curiously linked to indeterminacy; in a sense it is our very social ignorance that should make us free. For, insofar as society is unable to specify the optimal course, the case for official prescription of individual behavior becomes vacuous, and the argument for autonomy correspondingly becomes convincing. Why should we structure public assistance so as to put one man in subordination of another where we can demonstrate no benefit from the subordination either for the subject or society?

This is the argument of a minimalist. It holds only that, absent a public consensus to the contrary, personal choice is the only sensible regime. Certainly, the claims of liberty could be pressed far beyond this—beyond the mere right of the individual to choose where society cannot; I would myself defend the right to flout good sense and the public alike where one's own interest is the only matter at stake. But we need not go so far; given our present epistemological funk, the minimalist position based upon indeterminacy seems adequate to work basic change in the direction of personal liberty. It focuses our ready attention upon the reality that those programs which offer the poor nothing but in-kind government services could in many cases be converted into systems of choice in which poor people were permitted to make the same mistakes as the rest of us; it could help to solidify an incipient trend toward bureaucratic humility.

II. LIBERTY, EQUALITY AND THE MINIMUM

The current proposals for a guaranteed income are designed to secure the "minimum"; they increase liberty by providing—in unfettered form—a merely "adequate" income. They do not address the problem of wealth differences. Is this a fundamental flaw? By what standard are such proposals to be judged? Is liberty the only consideration?

The tendency in modern discourse about social justice has been to ground the claims of the disadvantaged less upon liberty than upon some variation of the principle of equality. All men are brothers; brothers should share. Ideally they should share equally. Equality has informed much of recent Christian criticism of an America in which large differences in wealth persist. Prima facie it is a powerful argument, and, extended logically, it would imply an unfavorable interpretation of policies supporting minimums. Even the most generous proposals for a guaranteed income fall far short of suggesting a uniform distribution of wealth. Are they yet tolerable, and, if so, is this only because they are the best that the politics of original sin can manage?

In my judgment the present trend is solidly based in fundamental and enduring values. Such non-egalitarian guarantees are superior in the order of justice to any version of "equality" with which I am familiar. Whatever difficulty there is in seeing this lies in a confusion about the nature of equality and in the failure to give to liberty the primacy it deserves. I will first try to make clear my own view of equality and then suggest its relation to liberty and to the proposals for minimum support programs.

Obviously all of us are similar in certain respects, and it is in virtue of these attributes that we are entitled to apply the generic "human." But it is also important—and obvious—that we are different in ways that are germane to social policy. We have distinct inequalities of function that can be relevant to legitimate public purposes. John and Mary can be equally intelligent but unequal in athletic ability. Likewise they may be equals in size but unequal in eyesight, singing, speaking French, or even in desert: Mary, after all, may be bad and John good. Any one of these differences could justify a difference in treatment of the individual by society, and for the moment that is all I mean by inequalities. In truth, for any two humans the last thing one expects to discover is sameness in needs, abilities and circumstances. Whatever might be meant by equality it fails as a description of our experience of one another.

Equality can, of course, exist as aspiration; indeed, this has clearly been its social and intellectual role since 1789. From a certain point of view it is this quality that makes it an ideal social principle. Being contrary to empirical fact and wholly incapable of satisfaction it provides an enduring basis for prophesy, envy, and social ferment. Equality is in this respect a form of eschatology; humans can only be equal outside of time. The concept verges, indeed, upon theology or at least mystery.

There is another description of equality which is intelligible and would help to clarify its relation to liberty. It is a view less dependent upon, though consistent with, a theological premise. It is simply that equality is the *effective moral parity* of all persons. I do not mean that persons are equally "good"—hence the qualifier "effective." I do mean that the public order is not well equipped to distinguish persons by their character. In private life, under some circumstances of intimacy, it is possible to evaluate character (roughly and mostly negatively). But this is a function for which political processes are incompetent. Moral worth of persons is inscrutable to government.

If one accepts this premise, there are two possible views of the relation of moral worth to social policy. One is that it is a fiction, hence irrelevant; the other is that moral worth is real and that its effective parity could provide a stable keystone for the fashioning of a just order. If we take the latter view, that all men are assumed to be deserving— but if the degree of individual worth is opaque—society has a reason to accord them equal dignity. We would have an important respect in which humans can be said to be alike.

The element of inscrutability is crucial. If moral differences were as plain as our other distinctions, relative moral worth, far from being egalitarian, would become a powerful rationale for discrimination. Historically it has been so used in societies that supposed it to be a discoverable fact; for them it was right that pains and privileges should match one's moral desert. Only when desert is recognized as both *real* and *inscrutable* does it cease to justify discrimination and, paradoxically, become a rationale for a civil order purged of arbitrary distinctions.

Yet this version of equality—useful to establish a ground for justice—is not very useful in judging any particular state of the polity. It produces no rationale for uniform treatment; it functions as a presumption against arbitrary distinctions, but it does not deny that humans are in countless ways objectively different and that government is entitled—even bound in justice—to consider these differences. Indeed it seems to me that making the right distinctions among us is most of what good government necessarily is about. What is needed is a principle (not equality) to suggest precisely which of mankind's differences should count in the making of the laws.

Such a principle, however, is already implied in the definition of equality; the larger importance of moral worth is not that it is inevitable (it is only inscrutable), but precisely that it is moral and thus free. Implicit in the concept of effective moral parity is a voluntaristic view of man. Just as there is no point in talking about equality without moral parity, there is no point in talking about moral parity unless there is a possibility of human freedom. We seek a social order addressed to what is unique in man; and, if man's nature were determined, there would be no objection to treating humans like other objects. It is the commitment to *moral* parity that makes it sensible to speak of an individual's responsibilities to self, other humans, and nature—in short to speak of liberty. And it is in the capacity for liberty that our status as humans principally resides.

Furthermore, while equality can tell us virtually nothing about which distinctions are just, liberty is a concept with analytical power and a capacity to distinguish among the forms of public policy. It is an intelligible proposition when we argue that government should not limit human options without substantial justification; conversely a presumption that government should enlarge the capacity and opportunity for free moral choice for the greatest number would be an effective rule of policy. While not free of ambiguity, it is a manageable premise for political inquiry.

The essence of my position, then, is that equality and freedom are inseparable and interdependent; there is no equality other than morality and no morality other than a free one. But there is an important distinction between equality and freedom. Equality is a fixed and unchanging moral datum, a merely descriptive term; freedom waxes and wanes in rhythm with the legislated structure of rights and duties. Freedom is society's major dependent variable. It is that which we can do something about through careful reform of law; and its promotion should be the primary business of society. Sometimes the increase of freedom will require wider dispersion of power or wealth; freedom, for example, is threatened by private and public monopolies either of the productive or consumptive variety. But anti-monopolistic policies which tend to level the distribution of goods are not to be understood as egalitarian in purpose; their object is to increase liberty. Uniformity of distribution would be a desired outcome only where it promoted that end. We should be indifferent to uniformity in itself, and, contrariwise, disuniformity is innocent unless it deprives someone of a liberty that would be available under another dispensation. Envy is not a sufficient basis for seeking uniformity, and politicians and philosophers who encourage it by insisting upon an unfathomable equality are irresponsible.

If this point is clear I may pause parenthetically for one important concession. Equality is more than descriptive and becomes a principle of policy to this extent: where there is *no rational basis* for a distinction among persons, equality stands as a presumption opposing the imposition of a disuniformity. In a world of widespread indeterminacy this can become an important commitment. For example, since race is in general an irrational basis for distinction, the presumption supports a general rule of racial neutrality. *Serrano v. Priest*, the California school-finance decision, presents another example; it imposes a presumption against discrimination by wealth in the special field of public education.

Removing arbitrary distinctions is important, but the promotion of freedom is the active principle of policy and vastly more important. Nor does the increase of liberty for all individuals forbid official recognition of differences among them. In fact, if one assumes that there are different capacities for freedom, some policy of discrimination is optimal. It would be fatuous to talk on abstractly in this manner, as if it were easy to specify practical policies with a positive outcome for liberty; nonetheless, it is wise to set a course in that general direction. In any case this is how proposals such as an "adequate" guaranteed income should be evaluated. The question is whether, on balance, the state's augmentation of the practical liberties of the poor is purchased at too great an injury to the liberty of us all.

In application the principle is complicated by the vagueness of the concept of a "minimum" in its relation to the overall increase of liberty. American philosophers, including Rawls and Nozick, have recently given considerable attention to these difficulties and deserve our serious study. Here I will simply assert that, if liberty is primary, no one ought to be permitted to fall below its minimum conditions; indeed, discourse concerning an annual income ought to begin with the defining of the practical essentials of moral liberty. But we must concede that minimum and overall liberty not only are interdependent but ordinarily are culturally and economically relative; they even differ from person to person. It is possible, for example, to imagine a society so impoverished that the absolute minimum conditions of liberty (bare survival) would require a distribution of all resources in amounts varying by the difference in corporeal needs of individuals. Conversely, a society with greater wealth must make a complex judgment as to how much is to be guaranteed above the minimum to achieve the greatest net enjoyment of liberty. This principle should inform the calculation of our national economic policy, and to a certain extent it does so even today. Note that the theory does not, for a wealthy society, exclude the adoption of a uniform distribution where that is done for the purpose of achieving maximum liberty. In practice, however, the vast differences in human need and aspiration would always make such a policy suboptimal for liberty, or so I believe.

III. LIBERTY AND THE PROFESSIONS

An important question is the impact of subsidized choice, including an incomes policy, upon the correlative roles of professional and client. "Professionalism" has been one of the enduring and successful ideologies of this century; it is familiar in both its benign and monopolistic aspects. Policies such as a guaranteed income, vouchers for education, and full medical insurance could provide low-income families and individuals broad choice among existing providers. Coupled with effective anti-trust policies and judicious retrenchment of licensing a genuine reform of the professions is quite imaginable.

The advent of choice for the poor would be both painful and salutary for professions now enjoying a captive low-income clientele. This is attested, for example, by the political resistance of teachers unions to vouchers. Choice would require public-school teachers for the first time to adopt the traditional client/professional relation common to lawyers, engineers and architects; it is a relation of liberty in which, if the professional does not satisfy the client, the alliance ceases. The opportunity to coerce and subordinate the client does not induce the professional's most efficient service; for that end the best incentive is an alternative provider. Americans like to call this competition; it has sometimes worked to the advantage of those who can pay.

This is not because clients know more than professionals; at best they know different things (though this may be crucial when the important information is subjective). But final judgment should be the client's simply on grounds of human dignity. This conclusion is, of course, reinforced whenever the "best" solution is indeterminate. The ideal is a judgment informed by the professional but made by the client. It is the essence of *advice* that it be subject to rejection or modification. A compulsory judgment imposed by a professional upon a client is in truth a contradiction. It is a sin against liberty and a corruption of the profession. A general preference for liberty would have reforming applications to public bureaucracies and private monopolies wherever choice has been frustrated unnecessarily by licensing, credentialing, compulsory attendance or other devices which empower and protect a professional class. Expertise in itself is never a justification for subordination of the individual.

Many who support professional hegemony discredit the capacity of low-income persons to make decisions in their self-interest. Since the poor have had so little opportunity to make decisions this criticism can only be viewed as prejudice. Even if true, the problem is no more than inexperience with choice; no one is willing to argue that those with low incomes are inherently incompetent. But if it is through exercise of liberty that we gain responsibility and competence, when do the poor get to start? There is no risk-free approach, but is not the phasing in of choice for all the optimal strategy to achieve a society of free humanity?

IV. LIBERTY AND COMMUNITY

Uncritical sympathy for economic leveling has Christian roots distinct from and more substantial than the bias for equality. There is a historic suspicion that a broad freedom to choose one's satisfactions

and associations tends to be antithetic to community; liberty is important, but too much of it can be a fragmenting and factional influence in
human affairs. This kind of criticism is based ultimately upon a concern
for charity. Community is the organic union of persons linked in social
cooperation by genuine mutual benevolence; community is charity incorporated. Since charity is our worthiest individual aspiration, its
expression in community is a high object of social policy. Liberty by
contrast is essentially instrumental. Where it is a barrier to community
it must yield.

To speak intelligently of this issue we must identify the relevant
"community." The relation of liberty to group life could be treated in
an enormous variety of contexts real and imagined. We could, for
example, ask whether a guaranteed income would conduce to an
earthly communion of saints; criticism sometimes seems informed by
such a Teilhardian vision of the future. When I speak of community,
however, I will assume a more modest time frame, one in which persons now living might expect to have significant participation; I speak
of communities that we might experience ourselves. I do this in part
because earthly perfectibility and "Omega points"—though exciting as
science fiction—strike me as unintentionally anti-human and a defamation of the dead; by exalting the future they cheapen our own lives.
More relevantly, in the space allotted I can scarcely scratch the surface
of this issue.

My own observation is that, aside from the child-parent relation,
which is *sui generis,* communities formed by legal compulsion are seldom the architects of love. I would even suggest as a loose principle
that, to the extent that social aggregation is imposed upon the individual, to that extent its effect is antithetic to the goal of community, for it
is the nature of charity to be given freely or not at all. Of course charity
can coexist with and transcend coercive relationships, but coercion
never makes love easier and often makes it harder. Perhaps for certain
heroic spirits this burden may in a mysterious way make love greater,
but the public order should not be designed for heroes.

Consider the example of the movement for "community control" of
schools. This was largely an ethnic and racial phenomenon in the large
cities of America; blacks, in particular, wished to fragment the
monolithic urban school districts like New York City into neighborhood districts which would be run by the neighborhood itself. This
movement was often informed by an authentic charity among neighborhood residents. And, when such control was in fact achieved, that
charity sometimes managed to express itself within the newly formed

unit in ways that had been quite impossible under the faceless and bureaucratic regime that had preceded it. The smaller unit had to this extent tapped a genuine affective resource.

However, if the new mechanism tapped the resource, it did not create it. In fact to some extent the locally elected regime actually frustrated the expression of community and became an occasion for new hostilities. The resentment came, of course, from the losers in the politics of the local unit. There were those who did not share the educational views of the local majority. They would have preferred schools of a different sort; some even liked the schools as they had been before the reform. Forcing these individuals and their children into an aggregation that they rejected was not productive of love.

It will be seen what such an example implies. Freely chosen relationships tend to provide for the average person the natural occasion for charity, hence for community. Sound policy does not ordinarily force clustering but augments the capacity of humans to link freely with others in mutual pursuit of significant ends. The application of this rule to the educational problem is obvious. Government should seek to insure that all persons can form educational communities of choice. This can be accomplished by providing the public subsidy directly to the individuals who consume education rather than to the providers— public or private, secular or religious.

In a society still bearing the marks of racism such systems of educational choice would need substantial public regulation to become truly voluntary. America's experience of the 1950s with "freedom of choice" plans in the South demonstrates the need for a well-designed apparatus of controls over admissions, transport, information, tuition and students' rights, if liberty of the child and his family is the object. Such systems have been designed and await their political moment. By the way, they well illustrate freedom's constant dependence upon political intervention. There is no paradox in designing "compulsions" that "liberate"; or, if there is, nature is the author. The only question, in any historical situation, is what policy structure will maximize liberty. One always concedes the possibility that the ideal dispensation already obtains; every argument for a best system is contingent.

Variations of family choice in education have operated in several European countries including Denmark, Holland, Northern Ireland and—in part—England. One of the fascinating empirical issues is the role such institutions have played in producing contemporary society. American defenders of our present dispensation point to the Ulster example; here, they say, is the fruit of free choice in education, a people riven by religious intolerance. Libertarians prefer to cite the other examples. No serious comparative work traces the impact of family freedom upon community; such work is badly needed. In its absence I will state my own view based upon informal observation in several of these nations. This is that the social effect of educational clustering by family choice varies with the justness of the general social order. In a just society the bestowal of choice begets further trust and mutual charity among its ideological minorities. Holland is no longer the religious bear-pit it once was and manifests instead a growing ecumenism and mutual respect.

By contrast, in an unjust society where separation by family choice often is accompanied by discrimination against minorities, the separation is not likely to be perceived as truly voluntary; it may even exacerbate the sense of injustice and hostility. I fear this shoe fits the Ulster scene. What shoe fits the rest of us? I can only give my own view that, in a nation sincerely struggling to end historic discrimination, a new commitment to educational liberty may itself tip the scale toward a just order, hence toward a richer communal life both within and among minority groups. If this be correct, the principle has applications that are as various as the ideologies and cultures that move our hearts. Society should not discourage these chosen affinities as sources of division; it should encourage them as necessary steps to a broader community.

V. FREEDOM AND DEPENDENCY

For a social order based in freedom the most difficult problems arise in relation to dependencies. These are of two kinds. One involves dependent persons—the senile, the insane, the children of tender years; the other involves the multitude of functions which individuals who are otherwise adult and autonomous cannot perform without some form of subordination to a collective—defense against foreign invasion is perhaps the most extreme example; collective bargaining is another. Again I can do no more here than outline the issue and my own position. I will confine my illustrations narrowly to the class of personal dependencies and to the sub-class of children; young persons represent the most difficult of the dependent groups to analyze because of their constantly growing competence and because of the tension in adult thinking between the child present and the child future.

The initial and fundamental problem is that children (like adult incompetents) are radically incapable of autonomy in the adult sense. To bestow such general "liberty" upon the child—at least the younger child—is simply to deliver him to another dominion of man or nature. Children are small, weak, and inexperienced in a world of actors who are large, strong and sophisticated. Children will be dominated; even their "liberties" will be determined for them. This domination will, however, decrease steadily with age.

Now I will make two simplifying assumptions. First, I will assume that society has a benign attitude toward children; it wishes to protect them from injury and to advance their individual interests. Second, I will assume that society wishes as much liberty for each child as he can accommodate; this means maximizing his future capacity to exercise autonomy as an adult while providing as much of genuine liberty here and now as is compatible with such a future.

The foremost difficulty in pursuing this end—even if it be accepted as the appropriate objective—is that society cannot agree how it is best achieved. Beyond the rather primitive minimums of food, clothing, shelter and the three R's, the child-rearing practices said to produce autonomous adults are in sharp conflict. There is a classic indeterminacy, and the policy maker again must concern himself not with what is best but with who should get to decide what is best for the individual child. Here, however, our previous argument for individual self-determination based upon indeterminacy is inapplicable; by definition our subject person is incapable of autonomous direction. If liberty is to remain the central value, it must be a form of liberty somehow compatible with subordination; the question becomes which form of micropaternalism is optimal for the child's autonomy. We need, in short, a theory for choosing choosers, one that will help us maximize liberty even for the individual who necessarily is under the dominion of another. I will here ignore a good deal of relevant intellectual history and drive to what I assume will be a familiar ground—the concept of subsidiarity. This broad doctrine not only addresses the problem of dependency but, I will argue, is libertarian to the core.

It is the essence of subsidiarity that, where personal autonomy is unattainable, decisional authority affecting the individual should be located in that collective nearest him in knowledge, sympathy and responsibility. Functionally viewed such a rule has two objectives, and the first is libertarian. Often this fact has been obscured by the form of argument commonly employed by the Church to support the family. The doctrine has been promoted principally as a prop to family authority and integrity; the Church has emphasized the right of the collective rather than that of the individual. In my judgment an individualistic interpretation would be far more intelligible and serve the same purposes. There is no evidence that any collective can serve the development of autonomy better than the child's own family or some surrogate relationship with similar characteristics. Small, intimate groups are best for autonomy, because it is only in such a collective that the voice of the weak cannot be submerged; the child is inescapably present, and even his silence speaks. Unlike a protected bureaucrat in a Kafka story, the parent or parent surrogate who ignores the child pays a dear price; and it is a price the child controls. Ultimately the parent suffers if the child suffers. This is as near as society can come to providing liberty for the child; subsidiarity is, indeed, best regarded as proxy for the libertarian ideal. It imitates the functions of personal liberty as nearly as collective decision and paternalism will allow. The parallel could be drawn for other classes of dependent persons and, generally, for institutions in government and the economy. First and foremost the doctrine functions to preserve as much of individual choice as can be managed in discharging a collective function.

Communality is a related function of subsidiarity. The image of the guild, the family and the religious (and even military) orders as loving brotherhoods which institutionalize Christian charity has a historic basis and plenty of modern applications that need not be enumerated. What I would again urge is that any group's success in maintaining internal and external brotherhood is linked to the degree to which individual members are entitled to a voice in the association. Community is to a great extent nothing more than individualism respected.

CONCLUSION: THE CHURCH AND LIBERTY

The Church has been unable to establish an intelligible position from which to judge capitalist society. It saw early that it opposed unrestrained laissez-faire, but it has never understood just why. Its historic reaction to bourgeois libertarian rhetoric was understandable, but there is no longer any excuse for Christian intellectuals to undervalue freedom in the political and economic order. At least this is so if they can offer no more than a vapid equality as the foundation of justice and community; equality has proved largely impotent except to oppose injustices which were already manifest on grounds of rationality. Worse, it has impeded our capacity to judge policy changes which would increase liberty without closing the gap in income between economic classes.

Many policy issues in the next generation are likely to involve human services such as infant day care, youth employment, and paramedical licensing in which a proposed extension of individual choice will be opposed by well-organized bureaucratic and professional interests. These latter will purport to speak for the best interest of the individual and in particular the poor. They will ask in all good faith for an extension of their professional hegemony, the better to achieve the benign end in view. Such conflicts cannot be decided in terms of equality. They represent crucial confrontations of liberty and micro-paternalism. The Church should be prepared wholeheartedly to enter the lists on the side of free choice. In doing so it will commit itself to the most distinctly human of our political values; at the same time it will be laying the groundwork for authentic community.

Bruno V. Manno

Subsidiarity and Pluralism: A Social Philosophical Perspective

AFTER accepting the invitation to write this paper I was overcome by what can only be described as a profound case of the "shakes," better known in some circles as the lay person's form of what Søren Kierkegaard calls fear and trembling. What helped me overcome this feeling was a piece of folk wisdom spoken by an Italian grandfather to a young Italian grandson many years ago, the wisdom of which continues to overwhelm that same grandson.

In listening to this wisdom of the ages one must keep in mind it was uttered by a staunch, card-carrying Democrat after said Democrat found himself caught in a situation which demanded a quick but thoughtful reversal of what hitherto was an unchanging position. The statement is this: There is nothing more durable than the provisional.

I use this interesting piece of folk wisdom for two reasons. First, in the invitation I received to write this paper I was told the convenors expected "not so much a piece of original research as speculation and reflection." What follows, then, is primarily speculation and reflection. In that sense, it is provisional and merely a starting point to be used for discussing an involved and complex topic—subsidiarity and pluralism.

Second, to talk about subsidiarity and pluralism is to talk about the provisional and the many guises under which it goes—the flexible, the malleable, the changeable, the negotiable, and, perish the thought, compromise, consensus, and what in America sometimes goes under the name "big-city machine politics."[1]

As I begin with fear and trembling armed with the comforting thought there is nothing more durable than the provisional, in this paper

I propose to do the following: (a) offer a working definition of the term subsidiarity and the major conceptual components necessary to support this definition; (b) list and briefly discuss the major organizing values of any community which claims to be pluralistic; (c) show the importance of subsidiarity and pluralism in both the American social structure and Catholic social theory and praxis; (d) state some of the major presuppositions inherent in a pluralistic perspective.

I. SUBSIDIARITY: A WORKING DEFINITION

Subsidiarity refers to a way of organizing and ordering groups to pursue common purposes and objectives. The etymology of the word includes notions of support, aid and help in standing up. The term, then, points to a particular manner of organizing communities to assist each other in the task of standing up and pursuing common goals. To accept this principle is to imply something inherently good about groups organizing around interests and helping each other seek common ends, the ultimate end being to put things right and help everyone stand on their feet.

More specifically, subsidiarity is a principle of justice. It is the name given to the way organizations relate to one another in the structure of the common good. It names groups or communities of interests and purposes that function from top to bottom through various levels of the common good. It is a way of formulating and pursuing true social order. Even though groups have varying interests, subsidiarity implies that common ends are not antithetical to the pursuit of particular interests. In fact, the common good is defined through the interaction of these varying interests conducting themselves with an eye to social charity.

There are two principal parts to the general theory of subsidiarity. First, it is against social justice for a higher organization in the structure of the common good to claim for itself functions which a lower organization can perform adequately. Second, it is against social justice for a lower organization to try to capture and claim for its own goals any organization that is higher than it in the care of the common good.[2]

The doctrine of subsidiarity values both individual liberty and community. It is sceptical about the ability of large bureaucracies and corporate structures to centrally plan solutions to social ills.[3] It believes the growth and development of human identity and community is best fostered when groups are free of incessant invasion, domination, compulsion and intrusion by large outside forces.

Maximizing individual participation in decision making is the aim of the doctrine of subsidiarity, because when people have a say in what happens they tend to be more committed to acting on the outcome.

When a decision is made by an outside person, it is arrived at by someone nearest in the accountability structure of the larger common good. This person possesses knowledge of the circumstances surrounding the case and empathy and compassion for the person affected.

In summary, the constant question before one who is committed to the doctrine of subsidiarity is this: ever acting out of *social charity,* how can one structure interlocking groups so as to maximize liberty and still pursue a *common good* ordered toward the achievement of *social justice?*

II. THE MAJOR ORGANIZING VALUES OF A PLURAL COMMUNITY

A community organized along the lines of the doctrine of subsidiarity is, in reality, a plurality of communities, a community of communities. This plural community possesses five major organizing principles or values.

The arrangement into a higher and lower stratification of communities reflecting common values and goals is a prized and cherished dimension of the plural community. This *hierarchy* or stratification of function, authority and responsibility is good in itself, something which is fostered and encouraged. Its elimination produces the mass leveled society.

Hierarchy of function and authority demands the dispersion, distribution or *decentralization* of function and authority to smaller groups. Each of these groups possess a measure of authority based on its unique function in the hierarchy. This de-centering or delegation of authority guards individual freedom against the incursions of the large corporate society.

Both the stratification of groups and the delegation of authority encourage and promote the exercise of *autonomy.* This exercise of free choice is carried on without excessive outside intervention. Each group is endowed with the greatest possible autonomy consistent with its function in the hierarchy. Diminishing the exercise of autonomy and free will leads to the loss of a sense of participation and control over corporate and individual destiny.

As discussed above, autonomy and decentralization are both consonant with function in the hierarchy. These functions are embedded in *tradition.* The Latin *traditio* can be translated "giving over by means of words." Tradition, then, involves personal communication. It emerges from community discussion and consensus, encourages social interaction, and leads to coalitions of like-minded persons. An emphasis on handing over tradition by means of story-telling and other forms of personal communication guards against the impersonal and abstract aspects associated with the formal prescriptive law of massive bureaucracies.

Finally, the "giving over by means of words" takes place in small, local units of association. This *localism* emphasizes family and neighborhood as primary and important forms of association. This sense of place, of having somewhere to anchor oneself, insulates the person and the community against various forms of estrangement and alienation. It offers a sense of roots.

Though this list is by no means exhaustive, it contains the primary organizing values of the plural community. To recapitulate, they are: hierarchy, decentralization, autonomy, tradition and localism. Subsidiarity as a principle of social organization calls for the decentralization of function and authority throughout the hierarchy so that, supported by tradition, autonomy and localism are encouraged. Guided by social charity this community of communities pursues a common good aimed at achieving social justice. Underlying the plural community is the presupposition that the nature of human personhood and human community demand a social multiplicity of expressions. Diversity of belief, idea and life-style is therefore good.

III. OUTLINES OF AN AMERICAN AND CATHOLIC PERSPECTIVE ON SUBSIDIARITY AND PLURALISM

The doctrine of subsidiarity is central to both the American social and political fabric and Catholic social theory. What follows is a brief illustration of this claim.

The American Political Structure

Colonial America confronted two fundamental political problems.[4] The first, a predominantly seventeenth-century question, asked how it was possible to legitimate political power and still preserve freedom. The solution to this dilemma was accomplished by naming "we the people" the touchstone of legitimacy and power. What resulted was a notion of *limited sovereignty* whereby governments possessed only those powers delegated to them by "the great body of the people."[5]

The second question, confronted in the eighteenth century, concerned what James Madison called the "violence of faction."[6] Madison wondered whether it would be possible to validate the extensive social pluralism that was part of the new American situation and still guarantee freedom and justice. Would the tremendous diversity of colonial life lead to anarchy, chaos and disorder, or could this diversity serve to protect liberty and promote justice? Madison answered the latter question affirmatively and his argumentation illustrates the genius of the American political system.[7]

In brief, he suggests the anarchy associated with "the violence of faction" is broken when rival groups are prevented from getting enough power to impose their will on the rest of society. This is accomplished not by eliminating diversity and faction but by playing off various interests one against another. In Madison's words, "ambition must be made to counteract ambition."[8]

This clash of interests creates a situation where no one group ever controls an excess of power, because power is dispersed throughout the system. By breaking the system into many parts, interests and classes, all the people are protected against the oppression of rulers and the injustices of other citizens. According to Madison, "an unjust combination of a majority of the whole [is] very improbable, if not impracticable."[9] In order for any one group to accomplish an end, a coalition of interests must be built around principles of justice and the general good. In this way liberty is preserved and maximized.

The principle underlying this dispersal of power throughout a multitude of communities participating in the governmental process is the *federal principle*. This tenet, along with the precept of limited sovereignty, guards against the centralization of power and the growth of tyranny. In looking with hindsight on Madison's vision one may conclude he did engage in some wishful thinking when claiming an unjust combination "improbable, if not impracticable." Nevertheless, the system has proved to be workable.

Many of the groups constituting the large network of rival and related communities that are part of the whole system are founded on the *voluntary principle*.[10] Membership in them is by free choice and easy to terminate. Some of these organizations are political, others intellectual and still others cultural or social.

Voluntary associations vigorously pursue the self-interests of their constituencies. Their proper functioning depends upon the establishment of a firm consensus. It is often these associations which foster localism, depend upon tradition and promote the exercise of free will and autonomy so essential to maintaining the social bond.

While not exhausting the principles undergirding the American political structure, limited sovereignty, federalism and voluntaryism are certainly pivotal. Without them there would be no American political structure. These principles work to oppose centralization, maximize liberty and force the creation of autonomous, subsidiary, freely chosen associations which guard against feelings of atomization and alienation.

Groups can accomplish goals and power can be put together only by the skillful molding of diverse interests into broad coalitions. Politics in the American context is the art of making subsidiarity work.

Emerging out of this discussion are questions that theologians along with historians, political scientists and other theorists must begin to discuss. The most basic one is whether there are any distinct contributions which the American notions of limited sovereignty, federalism and voluntaryism have to make to understanding what the Church is.[11] There are many which derive from this fundamental question.

What does it mean from an ecclesiological perspective to govern with and by the consent of the governed? In what ways is the Church similar to and different from the American political structure understood as a community of communities? What are the implications of the voluntary principle for the possibility of dissent in Church life and for the formation and revival of voluntary groupings in the Church? How is the shaping of the sense of the faithful different from and related to coalition building? In what ways are Church leaders coalition builders? What are the implications these principles have for the way in which infallibility is discussed and exercised? These questions only scratch the surface. Much work needs to be done.

Catholic Social Theory

Modern Catholic social theory and its resulting ethic function on two levels. One is represented by the papal social encyclicals, the writings of Catholic social philosophers and the numerous social-action statements of the American Catholic hierarchy. A more grass-roots tradition is portrayed in those aspects of Catholicism which give it its special American hue—neighborhoods, wards, precincts, unions, national parishes, parochial schools and so forth.

The Theoretical Tradition

The philosophical assumptions of the theoretical perspective are rooted in Thomistic philosophy and reflection on the function and nature of medieval guilds. This tradition had its first official papal pronouncement in 1891 when *Rerum Novarum* was published by Leo XIII. Pius XI's *Quadragesimo Anno* in 1931 and sections of his *Divini Redemptoris* in 1937 enlarged upon and grounded the message of Leo. In more recent years a number of pronouncements have added to this tradition.[12]

These writings outline a theory of social justice, social charity and the common good based upon the principle of subsidiary function. All of what was said in parts I and II of this paper can be viewed as a summary of this theory. What follows is a brief recapitulation of its major concepts.

Social justice demands something specifically social—the reorganization of unjust systems to better serve the common good. Social charity and respect for equal dignity are the principles upon which reorganization is to take place. These reorganized systems are managed so as to offer the greatest possible number the opportunity of obtaining a suitable means of livelihood. No institution in the vast hierarchy making up the common good can usurp the particular actions of an institution or person below it.[13]

The roots of the American Catholic social tradition go back beyond *Rerum Novarum* to at least 1887, when Cardinal James Gibbons defended the Knights of Labor.[14] Perhaps its most famous statements are the 1919 document of the American bishops on the problem of postwar reconstruction and the 1939 document *The Church and the Social Order*. These writings, primarily the inspiration of John A. Ryan, form the core of a tradition fueled by a passion to relate the Catholic Christian symbol system to human history and civil society.

Research by John A. Coleman, David Hollenbach and others suggests there are parts of this social philosophical tradition which need to be outgrown.[15] There are also parts which form a stable legacy. Coleman concludes a reflection on the thought of John Courtney Murray by saying:

The thought of . . . Murray puts us in contact with what seems to me to be the permanent legacy of social Catholicism: the theory of societal pluralism in authority and a doctrine of social and civil rights of the human person within society.[16]

Much research needs to be done on the historical development and present status of the legacy Coleman and others outline. What specific contributions have been made by Orestes Brownson, John A. Ryan, Isaac Hecker, William Onahan, Terence Powderly, Patrick Conway, John Courtney Murray and others to the development of American Catholic social thought? Do these contributions offer insights into ways of approaching the major social questions of today?

Moving in another but related direction, the implicit question at the base of this legacy concerns the relationship between the social, the moral and the religious, between grace and nature. Does recent research in the social sciences on the structure of cognition, the life cycle, value development, moral development and faith development offer new insights into these questions? Are there any threads of connection between Catholic social theory and the insights of modern social science? Only after much research and patient dialogue between social scientists, social theorists, theologians and all aspects of the Catholic population will anyone really be able to offer an intelligent answer.

The Grass-Roots Tradition

A discussion of Catholic social theory commits a grave injustice when it talks only about the perspective elaborated in the preceding discussion. It was the ethnic Catholic immigrants who made subsidiarity work while they pursued their great dream of freedom, often without knowing anything about subsidiarity, encyclicals or bishops' statements.

They made it work by creating what is perhaps the most unique product of American urban Catholicism—the ethnic neighborhood and its conglomerate of human services. They made it work by organizing great numbers of themselves into voluntary associations dedicated to pursuing the basic requisites necessary for a suitable means of human livelihood. They made it work in a very short period of time in spite of pervasive and often overpowering anti-Catholic bigotry.

Unfortunately, this miracle has yet to be noticed, and very little research has been done on the phenomenon.[17] Rather than engage in a speculative discussion of what those few researchers are saying on the various dimensions of this miracle, permit me to reflect on my own experience of what it means to be a committed Roman Catholic of Italian descent who grew up in an urban neighborhood environment.

At the center of the recollections I have of growing up in Cleveland, Ohio, is a very positive remembrance of my neighborhood—Collinwood—and the families who lived there with me. As soon as I use the word "neighborhood," though, I find myself caught in a dilemma. The more I try to define precisely what the word means, the more I become convinced it means many things to many people.

Collinwood as a neighborhood means Holy Redeemer if you're Italian, St. Joseph's if you're Irish, St. Mary's if you're Slovenian, or maybe even St. Jerome's, an unusual mixture of all three. It means the piece of land bounded by Euclid Avenue, East 140th Street and London Road. At the center of this tract of land was the meeting of five streets creatively nicknamed Five Points and pronounced by those in the know "Fi Points." Outsiders were easily known because of their inability to pronounce the phrase correctly.

On another level, if you went to Catholic school in my section of Collinwood, you went to Holy Redeemer for grade school and either St. Joseph or Cathedral Latin for high school. If you were one of "them publics"—an "affectionate" term for those who went to public school—you attended William H. Brett Grade School and Collinwood High School.

What these reflections have recently led me to discover about how one actually defines a neighborhood is simply that there is no one way of doing it. The word is transparent.[18] It functions as a symbol through which a multiplicity and complex of social meanings are revealed.[19]

What I remember most about my neighborhood is that it was mine. I belonged to it, and it belonged to me. It wasn't mine, though, in an exclusive sense. It also belonged to others, and they belonged to it. Together, we cared for it, and it cared for us whenever we needed to be cared for—and there were times when all of us needed care and received it.

The word I find most descriptive in communicating what this "mineness" means is neighborliness. The Old English form of the word means "near dweller." Neighborliness means dwelling near or close to each other not only in the physical sense of houses, alleys, porches and other buildings being close, but also in the sense of a real care and concern for, a loyalty to, a trust of the other. Neighborliness always consisted in organizing the neighborhood and the dwellers in it to take care of each other.

At the center of our neighborhood life were families, lots of them. I can remember how difficult it was at first to know where one started and another ended. I soon discovered the advantages of this situation. There was always someone to play with at any time of the day. There was always somewhere to run when I pushed someone at home a bit too far. There was always someone eating and drinking who didn't mind another mouth to be fed or thirst to be quenched. If you brought a friend, that didn't matter either. When a road was blocked at home, I could look for greener fields down the corner.

This ability to roam freely weaving in and out of boundaries, looking for other roads to travel when my first choice seemed closed, taught me that boundaries are flexible and there is, as my grandfather often said, nothing more durable than the provisional. In a way that is difficult to explain, the flexible boundaries of the family mirrored the larger but still flexible reality of the world I inhabited. Just as my smaller world could be trusted and worked with, so also that larger reality could be trusted and worked with because it too seemed friendly and flexible.

In my neighborhood, there was room for every character imaginable—and it seems we had them all. Mrs. DeFranco was the crazy lady who would appear on her back porch swinging her bull whip as we taunted her by throwing rocks at her cats or running through her back yard. Nicky was both physically and mentally handicapped with no living blood relations. He was never hungry, never looked upon as worthless and was involved in all neighborhood activities. Angelo was the character who lived with us. His eccentricities included shaving his head of all its hair—"It was easier to wash and comb," he said—and purchasing size thirteen shoes to fit his size ten feet—"You pay the same money, so why not get more?". Angelo compensated for the three-size difference by stuffing his shoes with crumpled paper bags changed as often as he went to the grocery store—"I like to keep clean," he would say.

The neighborhood was also an inexhaustible center of every human service imaginable. There was, first, Holy Redeemer parish with connecting grade school, large physical plant and staff of priests, nuns and lay people. There was also the fire station, police station, grocery store, bar, restaurant, barber shop, pool hall, undertaker, politician, doctor, etc. The boundaries between them were often not very distinct. The best source for used tires was not the local mechanic, Mr. Campy, but our assistant pastor.

Besides being an embodiment of virtue and goodness, the neighborhood was fairly good at embodying vice and evil. Any outsider who tried to become an unwanted insider experienced an earlier and more aggressive form of affirmative action. Things could be rigid, narrow, parochial and inflexible, but as we all know, these characteristics are not connected exclusively with ethnic neighborhoods, least of all Collinwood. To be human has always meant to be wrapped up in both good and evil, ambiguities and contradictions. In this sense, more than anything else, Collinwood was a good human place to live and spend the first eighteen years of my life.

I could go on for quite some time describing my neighborhood experience, but let me stop here. The neighborhood I describe with all its diversity and differentiation, its numerous voluntary associations and decentralization of power, its storytellers and storymakers, its inclinations toward both good and evil, is a paradigm for viewing subsidiarity and pluralism in action. Sadly, little research has been done to try to more fully understand what Gerald D. Suttles calls this "creative imposition on the city,"[20] this model of subsidiarity in action. Though some research is beginning to emerge, there is a desperate need to reflect on the sociology, history, psychology and theology of urban Catholic neighborhoods. This is a vast challenge which confronts the American Church and, I might add, American Catholic universities.

There are many more specific questions which need to be addressed. Is there a specific Catholic view of human nature, society and political organization? In what way is it similar to and different from the perspective presented by James Madison? What is the Catholic contribution to the formulation of social policy?[21]

What are the different structural characteristics of the extended ethnic family? Do their patterns of caring and concern for the elderly offer insights into how elders can be a vital and integrated part of American life? In what sense can the extended family serve as a model for Church life and as an example of the life cycle paradigm of human growth?

What does neighborhood life tell us about community building? What contributions can a study of neighborhood life make to the discussion among philosophers and developmental psychologists studying the structure and characteristics of moral communities and moral growth? Can modern health delivery systems learn anything from the service structure of ethnic neighborhoods?

How are values transmitted in the informal context of neighborhood life? What does the Catholic neighborhood ethic of smallness and diversity have to say about revitalizing decaying cities? What is the style or what are the characteristics of the way neighborhood leaders acted in building coalitions? What does this say about how Church leaders need to act in discerning and helping to mold the "sense of the faithful"?

The questions are endless. They are only now being discussed and mostly in a manner far from adequate and far from sensitive to the many complexities of the issues involved.

An observation made at the beginning of this discussion of the grassroots tradition offers an opportunity to present one last comment. Most Catholics living in neighborhoods know very little about the philosophical and social theory underlying the way neighborhoods are structured. This raises an interesting question. Why were they inclined to organize themselves the way they did? Certainly, part of the answer is found in the background they brought with them from the old country. But might there not be more at work here? Could it be their tremendous desire for freedom naturally issued in diversity and pluralism? Might it be that freedom evokes its own response, and a genuine contact with this unfolding reality can only issue in diversity of thought, life-style, attitudes, etc.? It seems, then, that true freedom requires diversity and pluralism.

IV. SOME PRESUPPOSITIONS

Thus far this paper has outlined the major conceptual components and organizing values of any community structured in accordance with the doctrine of subsidiarity and demonstrated the primacy of this doc-

trine in both Catholic social theory and praxis. What follows are statements summarizing *some* of the presuppositions underlying this
perspective.

1. Reality is mediated through multiple forms. No one form or model
exhausts the totality of reality. In this sense reality is best understood
analogically.

2. These forms or models are symbolic generalizations. They possess a multivalent or transparent character.

3. Reality can never be exhaustively grasped by any one model. It is
fundamentally mystery.

4. Pluralism of expression is essential to the pursuit of truth. It is
good and ought to be encouraged, valued and affirmed on all levels of
human thought, feeling and action.

5. Pluralism protects and fosters human freedom. It maximizes liberty. Compulsion as a principle of social change is detrimental to the
functioning of individuals and groups.

6. Pluralism is not separatism. It is the right to have one's particular
perspective respected as part of the larger common good.

7. The acceptance of a plural approach to understanding reality does
not necessarily imply that all models are of equal validity or possess the
same truth value. Two principles which are helpful in assessing the
validity and truth value of a particular model are adequacy to human
experience and fidelity to tradition.

8. The personal aspect of human freedom—the liberty to assert
oneself—is always held in tension with its social aspect—the liberty to
surrender to the service of the common good.

9. The common good is defined through the interaction of varying
interests conducting themselves with an eye to social charity. Consensus and coalition building are crucial to this process.

10. Humans exist primarily as members of small, local communities.
Through the interaction of these communities patterns of social structure emerge. The key to changing the social order lies in beginning with
small, local patterns of relationship.

11. The doctrine of subsidiarity best governs how patterns of relationship are changed. In short, they are changed without the intervention of higher organizations.

12. Since consensus forming, coalition building, voluntaryism and
subsidiary function are essential aspects of the Catholic social ethic,
gradualism and cooperation are two key elements of all attempts at
social change.

13. The desire to differentiate is a constitutive aspect of human personality. With proper discernment and guidance, this differentiation can

be integrated into a more comprehensive vision of reality and become socially constructive.

CONCLUSION

The legacy of Catholicism's concept of subsidiarity is a loud cry for primacy of liberty, freedom of choice, voluntary association, local community and pluralism of custom and manner. From this perspective, immunity from coercion is an indispensible human right. It forms the basis for achieving true humanity and human community.

The task of any organization which promotes the development of people is to foster and facilitate the creation of contexts which maximize liberty and encourage voluntary diversity. The challenge which the Church faces as it continues to travel through the recurring cycle of death and birth is to promote and encourage these contexts.

Notes

1. A standard line going around the urban neighborhood circles I was part of in the 1960s was how ironic it was that compromise and consensus could be used at the proper moment by husband and wife to keep a marriage healthy. When these same techniques were used at the proper moment to try to keep a neighborhood healthy the person using them was a dirty politician who had no sense of principles, no sense of right and wrong. Well, more about neighborhoods later.

2. For a similar formulation see: William Ferree, *Administration and Social Ethics* (Dayton, Ohio: Marianist Publications, 1967), p. 47; William Ferree and Colin Brisbane, *An Introduction to Economic and Social Development* (Dayton, Ohio: Marianist Publications, 1966), pp. 62–74, entitled "The Theory of Administration as Social Ethics."

3. On the inadequacies of central planning see: Michael Polanyi, *The Logic of Liberty* (Chicago: University of Chicago Press, 1951), especially pp. 111–200; Michael Polanyi, *Science, Faith and Society* (Chicago: University of Chicago Press, 1946).

4. This presentation relies on the following discussions: Erik Erikson, *Dimensions of a New Identity* (New York: W. W. Norton and Co., 1974); Michael Kammen, *People of Paradox* (New York: Alfred A. Knopf, 1973); Gordon S. Wood, *The Creation of the American Republic* (New York: W. W. Norton and Co., 1972).

5. Alexander Hamilton, James Madison and John Jay, *The Federalist Papers* (New York: New American Library, 1961), p. 241.

6. Ibid., p. 77.

7. In particular, see *Federalist Papers* nos. 10 and 51. An interesting question which arises out of Madison's discussion in No. 51 concerns the paradigm he uses to solve the problem of political pluralism. It seems he uses religious pluralism as a model for political pluralism. For a presentation which suggests how the Great Awakening helped solve the problems associated with religious pluralism, see Winthrop S. Hudson, *Religion in America* (New York: Charles Scribner's Sons, 1973), pp. 59–82.

8. Hamilton and others, p. 322.

9. *Ibid.*, 324.

10. On this principle see James Luther Adams, "The Voluntary Principle in the Forming of American Religion," in *The Religion of the Republic*, ed. Elwyn A. Smith (Philadelphia: Fortress Press, 1971), pp. 217–46; Andrew Greeley, "Some Questions for Theologians," *The Critic*, Spring 1977, pp. 14–21.

11. For discussions along this line see: Greeley, pp. 14–25; Richard McBrien, "Is There a Distinct American Contribution to the Notion of Church?" in *Dimensions in Religious Education*, ed. John R. McCall (Havertown, Pa.: CIM Books, 1973), pp. 113–24.

12. For an overview of Catholic social teaching since Pope John see Joseph Gremillion, *The Gospel of Peace and Justice* (Maryknoll, New York: Orbis Books, 1976). This book presents both the primary documents and a prospectus on them.

13. See paragraph nos. 71, 74, 80 and 88 of *Quadragesimo Anno* for specific references here. These full paragraphs can be found in William Ferree, *Introduction to Social Justice* (Dayton, Ohio: Marianist Publications, 1948), pp. 13–19, 37. For a more comprehensive attempt to determine the precise nature of the act of social justice, see William Ferree, *The Act of Social Justice* (Dayton, Ohio: Marianist Publications, 1943).

14. For an interpretation of the history of American Catholicism see: Andrew Greeley, *The Catholic Experience* (New York: Doubleday and Co., 1967); Andrew Greeley, "Catholicism in America," *The Critic*, Summer 1976, pp. 14–47, 54–70.

15. John A. Coleman, "Vision and Praxis in American Theology," *Theological Studies* 37 (March 1976): 3–40; David Hollenbach, "Public Theology in America," *Theological Studies* 37 (June 1976): 290–303; Donald Pelotte, *John Courtney Murray* (New York: Paulist Press, 1975).

16. Coleman, pp. 38–39.

17. See the following for initial attempts at understanding the general phenomenon: Andrew Greeley, *The American Catholic* (New York: Basic Books, 1977); Andrew Greeley, *Ethnicity in the United States* (New York: John Wiley and Sons, 1974). See the following for two studies directed at an analysis of particular aspects of this phenomenon: Silvano Tomasi, *Piety and Power* (New York: Center for Migration Studies, 1975); Jay P. Dolan, *The Immigrant Church* (Baltimore: Johns Hopkins University Press, 1975).

18. The transparency of all language is discussed by Michael Polanyi, *Knowing and Being* (Chicago: University of Chicago Press, 1964), p. 184.

19. For a similar understanding of neighborhood as symbol see Andrew Greeley, *The Communal Catholic* (New York: Seabury Press, 1976), p. 112.

20. George Suttles, *The Social Construction of Communities* (Chicago: University of Chicago Press, 1972), p. 28.

21. For some proposals in this regard see Greeley, *The Communal Catholic*, pp. 93–110.